The British Communist Party and the Trade Unions

1933–45

The British Communist Party and the Trade Unions

1933–45

Nina Fishman

SCOLAR PRESS

Published by
SCOLAR PRESS
Gower House
Croft Road
Aldershot
Hants GU11 3HR
England

Ashgate Publishing Company
Old Post Road
Brookfield
Vermont 05036
USA

British Library Cataloguing in Publication Data
Fishman, Nina
    British Communist Party and the Trade
    Unions, 1933–45
    I. Title
    331.880941

    ISBN 1–85928–116–8

Library of Congress Cataloging-in-Publication Data
Fishman, Nina.
    The British Communish Party and the trade unions, 1933–45 / Nina
    Fishman.
        p.   cm.
    Includes index.
    ISBN 1–85928–118–8
    1. Communist Party of Great Britain.   2. Trade-unions and
    communism—Great Britain.   3. Great Britain—Politics and
    government—1986–1945.   I. Title
    JN1128. C82F57   1994
    224.241'0976—cc20   94–5837
                                        CIP

Typeset in Sabon by Raven Typesetters, Chester, and printed in Great Britain at the University Press, Cambridge

To my father and mother and the men and women who fought the economic struggle, who were generous with their time and memories, from whom I have learned and come to admire greatly.

Contents

List of Abbreviations

ACM	Amalgamation Committee Movement
AEU	Amalgamated Engineering Union
ASE	Amalgamated Society of Engineers
ASLEF	Associated Society of Locomotive Engineers and Firemen
ASSNC	Aircraft Shop Stewards' National Council
AST	Amalgamated Society of Toolmakers
ASW	Amalgamated Society of Woodworkers
AScW	Association of Scientific Workers
ATTI	Association of Teachers in Technical Institutions
AUBTW	Amalgamated Union of Building Trade Workers
BDC	Biennial Delegate Conference
B&MM	National Society of Brass and Metal Mechanics
BSP	British Socialist Party
CAWU	Clerical and Administrative Workers' Union
CBC	Central Bus Committee of the Transport and General Workers' Union
CGT	Confederation Generale du Travail
Confed.	Confederation of Shipbuilding and Engineering Trade Unions
Comintern	Communist International
CPGB ⎫ CP ⎭	Communist Party of Great Britain
CWC	Clyde Workers' Committee
DMA	Durham Miners' Association
DPC	District Party Committee of the CPGB
EATSSNC	Engineering and Allied Trades Shop Stewards National Council
EEF	Engineering Employers' Federation
ESC	English Steel Corporation
ETU	Electrical Trades Union
FKCMA	Fife, Kinross and Clackmannan Mineworkers' Association
the Fed	South Wales Miners' Federation (also described as the Federation and the SWMF)
F&GP	Finance & General Purposes Committee
GEC	General Executive Council
ILO	International Labour Organisation

ILP	Independent Labour Party
Inprecorr	International Press Correspondence
IWW	Industrial Workers of the World
JPC	Joint Production Committee
KPD	Kommunistische Partei Deutschlands (German Communist Party)
LCC	London County Council
LGOC	London General Omnibus Company
LMU	Lanarkshire Miners' Union
LPC	Local Party Committee of the CPGB
LPTB	London Passenger Transport Board
LRD	Labour Research Department
MFGB	Miners' Federation of Great Britain
MMM	Metalworkers' Minority Movement
NAUL	National Amalgamated Union of Labour
NMA	Nottinghamshire Miners' Association
NMIU	Nottinghamshire and District Miners' Industrial Union
NMM	National Minority Movement
'non'	non-trade unionist
'non-pol'	non-political trade union
NPWU	National Passenger Workers' Union
NUDAW	National Union of Distributive and Allied Workers
NUGMW	National Union of General and Municipal Workers
NUM	National Union of Mineworkers
NUR	National Union of Railwaymen
NUT	National Union of Teachers
NUTGW	National Union of Tailors and Garment Workers
NUSMW	National Union of Scottish Mineworkers
NUVB	National Union of Vehicle Builders
NUWM	National Unemployed Workers Movement
ODD	Organising Divisional Delegate of the AEU
PCF	Parti Communiste Francais (French Communist Party)
PCI	Partito Communista Italiano (Italian Communist Party)
PEP	Political and Economic Planning
Politburo	Political Bureau of the CPGB ('inner cabinet')
RILU	Red International of Labour Unions
RIRO	Regional Industrial Relations Officer (title given to the Ministry of Labour chief regional Conciliation Officers during the 1939–45 war)
RTUO	Revolutionary Trade Union Opposition
SDF	Social Democratic Federation
SDP	(British) Social Democratic Party
SLP	Socialist Labour Party

SMW	National Union of Sheet Metal Workers and Braziers
SPGB	Socialist Party of Great Britain
STC	Standard Telephone Company
SWMF	South Wales Miners' Federation (also referred to as 'the Fed' and the Federation)
SWMIU	South Wales Miners' Industrial Union
SWML	South Wales Miners' Library
TGWU T&G	Transport and General Workers' Union
TMM	Transport Minority Movement
TUC	Trades Union Congress
UMS	United Mineworkers of Scotland
UMWA	United Machine Workers' Association
USSR Soviet Union	Union of Soviet Socialist Republics
UVW	United Vehicle Builders
VIAS	Voluntary Industrial Aid for Spain
WU	Workers' Union
WIL	Workers' International League
YCL	Young Communist League
YMA	Yorkshire Miners' Association

Acknowledgements

I have incurred many debts in this book's gestation. Regan Scott provided an introduction to Edmund and Ruth Frow at the outset of my PhD research. Their warm hospitality and continuing interest, combined with Eddie's wonderful contacts inside the AEU, were of incalculable assistance. I first met Hywel Francis during the 1972 miners' strike when he worked at the TUC and I was a secretary in the NUM research department. We renewed our acquaintance at the South Wales Miners' Library in 1976. He has been generous both with fascinating insights and encouragement. When I wrote to Communist veterans who were not part of the networks which I had tapped, my supervisor, Professor Eric Hobsbawm, generously allowed me to use his name and this secured me a warm welcome.

Eric Hobsbawm's support throughout the vicissitudes of my research has been invaluable. On his retirement, Jonathan Zeitlin took over the unenviable task of supervising me with admirable detachment and commitment. I am sincerely grateful to both of them and appreciative of their staying power in seeing me through a protracted re-write. Professor Richard Hyman and Professor Hugh Clegg read the PhD in both drafts and offered most pertinent comments. My examiners, Pat Thane and James Hinton, were helpful and immensely patient critics. When I embarked on turning my PhD thesis into this book, James Hinton generously allowed me to read his own book on Joint Production Committees, *Shopfloor Citizens: Planning and Democracy in the British Engineering Industry, 1941–7*, in manuscript.

The archive which I used frequently and most intensively was the Marx Memorial Library. I spent many happy and productive days and evenings there. The librarians, Margaret Kentfield and Nick Wettin, were hospitable and liberal in their provision of afternoon tea. They were also tactfully tolerant of my habitual catnaps in the afternoon. I usually put my head down beside the lectern which held the large bound copies of the *Daily Worker*, specially commissioned by Margaret from a library volunteer who was a joiner. I am still using 'my lectern' now that I have progressed to reading the *Daily Worker* for the post-war years.

I am grateful to Professor David Howell for finding the time to read this book in its first draft. His comments were invariably to the point and

I found them a sound foundation from which to undertake the final revision. David Howell also introduced me to Kevin Morgan, whose knowledge of CPGB history and continuing commitment to it has enabled me to spend many happy hours talking about Harry Pollitt and Johnny Campbell and other interesting things. Alec McAulay has been a wonderful editor, because he cared about the Communist Party and trade unions.

Last but not least there are the friends who patiently understood and ministered the requisite succour and sympathy: Terry and Phyllis Harrison; Paul and Jan OMahony; Ros Mitchell; Christopher and Francis Brumfit; Anne Showstack Sassoon; Dick Pountain, Marion Hills and Jack Hills; Martin Vogel and Carolyn Bonnyman; Tim and Vicky Johnson; Winston Moore and Isobel Bastos, Ulrich and Brigitte Pothast; Sybil Crouch and David Phillips; Donald Sassoon; and, of course, Phil McManus and Billie Todd. Their forbearance and unfailing good humour restored my equanimity and ensured that I did not miss the wood for the trees.

CHAPTER ONE

Introduction

This book is based on my PhD research, which began in 1976. Initially, I wanted to investigate the Joint Production Committees (JPCs), which were established in British engineering factories during 1941–2 as part of the war effort in which Communists were reputed to have played a leading role. I knew about Coventry JPCs from a friend whose father, an enterprising local journalist, had worked in a war factory and become friendly with the Transport and General Workers' Union (TGWU) District Officer, Jack Jones. My friend retold his dad's stories in the reverent tone normally reserved for wartime exploits of relatives who had been fighter pilots.

As a product of the post-war baby boom, I was intensely curious about wartime events. Within my own time horizon, the 1939–45 war formed an absolute watershed. I was interested in industrial democracy and assumed that JPCs had produced qualitative, if temporary, changes in workplace relations during their heroic wartime existence. I was keen to find out what Communist activists had been doing on them and how they had affected the balance of power on the factory floor.

Professor Eric Hobsbawm agreed to supervise my research but suggested that I should begin looking at Communists, factories and trade unions six years earlier, in 1933. He pointed to the revival in trade union membership in that year and observed that Communist activists' role should be viewed from this longer perspective. I set out accordingly to discover what and why Party members had been doing in British trade unions between 1933 and 1945. I was greatly assisted by making early contact with Communist veterans of the 'economic struggle' who gave generously of their time, hospitality and memories. The networks of Party activists which had been forged in the 1930s were still functioning well in the 1970s and I found that one interview soon led to another.

Given the vicissitudes of research, I found myself immersed in this fascinating past for nearly a generation. This has included reliving events over and over as the men and women who had made them happen recalled them. It is not surprising that I have assimilated much of their idiom. I am well aware that my prose may seem anachronistic to many readers. I have tried to compensate, for example by adding inverted commas to the 'economic struggle' and 'rank-and-file' when I remember. I was somewhat reassured by Lord Taylor of Mansfield's unselfconscious use of 'economic struggle' and 'revolt' to describe the same economic conflicts.[1] The pervasive martial terminology of British trade union culture coincides with the era of militarism and total war in Europe and would repay a more scholarly examination by a semiologist.

I have used 'the Party' throughout to denote the Communist Party. This idiomatic contraction gained wide currency in the 1930s and 1940s among people who were interested in politics and participated in the culture of the 'working class movement'. For these labour/trade union activists, the CPGB was '*the* Party' because it extracted and expected rigorous and almost secret things from its members. As the General Secretary Harry Pollitt ruefully remarked in 1935: 'We still believe it is better to have "a small party of the elect" of those "we can rely on in a crisis" than to have a mass party of the workers.'[2]

It seems not only convenient but also meet to continue using this idiom with all its Calvinist connotations. This aspect of Party membership is one of the unusual sides of British Communism which we shall explore in Chapter 8. I have usually used the contemporary term used by Party members to describe their Party leadership, the Anglicized bolshevik terminology Party Centre. (I have sometimes adopted the contemporary idiom of King Street, the place in Covent Garden, London, where the Communist Party's national headquarters were located throughout 1933–45.)

My research fell somewhat awkwardly between two historiographical specialisms, labour and political history. Moreover, while there is an ample literature on inter-war and wartime economic history, there was a comparative paucity of research on interwar collective bargaining and trade unions on which to draw. I found myself involved in making some provisional judgements about engineering collective bargaining in particular which I am aware need more rigorous examination.

In the arena of political history, the Communist Party has been particularly ill served. British political history is almost exclusively Westminster-centred, and the British Communist Party has only had two MPs during its entire span. Henry Pelling's standard account of the Party was written in 1958, when the Cold War was still frozen and before any research into the Comintern and other Communist Parties afforded standards for comparison.[3] The excellent histories by L.J. Macfarlane and Roderick Martin do not go beyond 1929 and 1933 respectively.[4] I was forced to rely almost exclusively on primary sources for the political aspect of my research.

Perusal of the meagre store of secondary sources soon revealed two opposing mythologies which effectively obstructed my attempts at accurate historical vision. Communist mythology placed the Party and its doughty Communist/trade union heroes 'behind' every serious trade union struggle during the 1930s and the war. It pervaded the official histories and many Party veterans' autobiographies. Labour mythology offered a ritual denunciation of the Party's inflated claims and then descended into demonology within which Party activists appeared as the unscrupulous perpetrators of notorious strikes.[5] They were a duplicitous and tiny minority of highly motivated men and women who unaccountably contrived to disrupt trade union affairs.

The Labour mythology is found in standard histories of the inter-war and war periods, and autobiographies and biographies of trade union leaders. Communist Party activists are usually conspicuous by their absence from day-to-day life, the basic rhythms of existence and the varied vicissitudes of British trade unions. When Lord Taylor of Mansfield wrote his autobiography, he gave the official strike of the Nottinghamshire Miners' Association (NMA) at Harworth in the Nottinghamshire coalfield in 1937 pride of place. The strike was formally a conflict with the pit's owners, Barber-Walker. In fact it was also a pitched battle again the 'breakaway' union formed by Labour MP George Spencer in the wake of the General Strike. In retrospect, the strike seemed to Taylor to be perhaps the most portentous event in which he had participated. He told its story without mentioning the Communist Party. He wrote about Mick Kane, the President of the Harworth NMA lodge without informing the reader that he was a Party member. Nor did he offer any mature reflections about the important role which the Party's support networks, publications and other activists played in sustaining the dispute.

Similarly, Kenneth O. Morgan in an essay on the Labour leader Jim Griffiths, discusses his prominent part in the 1934–45 strikes in South Wales without once mentioning the other prominent roles played by Communist Party activists. This notable omission may be a reaction against the recent official history of the South Wales Miners' Federation by Hywel Francis and David Smith which reproduces much Communist mythology and devotes little space to Griffiths. Nevertheless, the reader of both books is left in some confusion about whether they are really addressing the same sequence of events.[6]

The difficulty for the scholar is that Communist and Labour mythologies are each accurate in some respects. They would not have survived otherwise. Party activists did play a unique and significant role in economic conflict between 1933–45 although, as we shall see, it was not always the part which Communist mythology and official histories assigned them. If Party activists are excised from accounts of inter-war collective bargaining and trade union organization, that history becomes distorted.

Party activists remained a small minority of trade union members. They nevertheless came to hold a substantial proportion of lay union positions and won increasing numbers of full-time positions up to 1945.

They were often the most skilled and capable leaders available on the ground. One of the carefully camouflaged parts of Party history is the rigorous self-selection which marked recruiting to the Communist Party. Despite the Party Centre's continued dedication to the goal of making the CPGB a mass Party, veteran Party activists discouraged indiscriminate recruiting. They felt that the hardships imposed by Communists' 'daily mass work' required people who were like themselves, who had emerged from the trials of life and learned the art of discernment in their judgements.

The most prominent union leader in the 1930s, TGWU General Secretary Ernest Bevin, publicly fulminated against the subversive activities of the Communist Party. But Bevin also worked with Party members daily and relied on their efforts on the shopfloor to recruit more union members.[7] Pragmatic union officials' behaviour was marked by tolerance and trust towards Communists. They recognized well enough the veracity of Harry Pollitt's New Year statement in 1937. He appealed to 'the tens of thousands of militants' who were in 'complete agreement' with the Communist programme but were not joining the Party: 'If they would only realise that joining the Communist Party does not mean *weakening* the Labour Party, the trade union or co-operative organisation in which they are already working, but will actually *strengthen* it.'[8]

Pollitt's *cri de coeur* was accurate. From 1931, he and his close colleague at the Party Centre, Johnny Campbell, had moulded the Party's attitude towards the 'economic struggle' to ensure that its members were trade union loyalists and activists. Moreover, Pollitt and Campbell were willing positively to enforce their injunction to union loyalty on members who proved sometimes reluctant to accept its strictures. As we shall see, however, they took care to hide this aspect of their approach.

*   *   *

The opening chapters describe the evolution of the British Communist Party's approach to trade unions and the 'economic struggle'. In 1930, faced with the Party's increasing isolation from the organized working class, Harry Pollitt and Johnny Campbell began a determined effort to guide Party members into undertaking their prescribed daily Communist duties of 'mass work' inside trade unions, as lay officials and activists. Their vision of Communist trade union activists was highly contentious inside the Party leadership. They had the firm backing of a group of contemporaries who like themselves had risen to prominence in the foundation years of the Party, the pragmatic proletarian cohort, including Willie Gallacher, Arthur Horner, Wally Hannington and Bob Lovell.

This cohort keenly supported Pollitt's and Campbell's arguments about the need for Communists to become shop stewards and lead mundane factory 'economic struggle'. Their support at the Party Centre was reinforced by other members who were working on the ground, such as Joe Scott, Claude Berridge and George Crane, who had similar political and trade union backgrounds and whom we will frequently encounter leading industrial conflict. These activists also were tireless in organizing trade union branch and district activity. They moved steadily up the hierarchy of trade union office. They were responsible for the successful implementation of Pollitt's and Campbell's injunctions.

I have focused on Harry Pollitt and Johnny Campbell when examining the development of the Communist Party leadership's attitude to trade unions and 'the economic struggle'. The evidence shows that by 1930 Pollitt and Campbell had become the key figures in formulating and overseeing Party policy towards trade unions. They proved particularly apt and increasingly adept. They shared a common socialization in socialist and trade union culture with the founding cohort of Party working-class activists in the 'economic struggle'. Their reflexes and impulses were usually representative of a critical mass inside the Party who came to accord these two men an increasingly strong loyalty.

Throughout his tenure at the Party Centre, Harry Pollitt laboured under a keen sense of his own intellectual inferiority. He was unfailing in acknowledging a personal debt to Palme Dutt for keeping him from straying from the Marxist straight and narrow. But Pollitt actually had no need to become fluent in Marxism. Indeed, by remaining regretfully inured to theory, his excellent political pragmatic reflexes could operate unimpeded. His supposed mental block clearly had great practical utility. One wonders when he recognized that he was often the one who discovered the 'correct' answer to a difficult problem, and that solutions rarely originated from the Party intellectuals who were adept at manipulating the Marxist–Leninist canon.

Johnny Campbell found the ideological cement with which to bind members to Party policy. This was a particularly difficult job as collective bargaining in Britain appeared to be taking a most 'reformist' course. He combined a command of Marxist dialectic with an unrelenting will to achieve practical results. His fluent Marxist defences of apparently common sense policies which were not 'revolutionary' ensured his indispensability. His writing illuminated a bolshevik approach in contradistinction to earlier left-sectarianism.

Pollitt contributed to the developing partnership exceptional personal charisma, Utopian socialist oratory, and a shrewd grasp of the realities of trade union organization and the 'economic struggle'. Campbell became habituated to translating Pollitt's emotional and subjective reactions, rendering them into effective policy and propaganda. He developed great skill in giving Pollitt's pragmatic, often reflexive, responses to the British 'economic struggle' an ideological shape which conformed to Comintern strictures while retaining and communicating their crucial practical content.[9]

Pollitt learned to trust Campbell's judgements about how to manœuvre Party policy between often conflicting views coming from Party activists about how to wage the 'economic struggle': more or less militantly, in expeditious retreat or epic struggle. Despite the evidence, however, received Party mythology does not view Pollitt and Campbell as a duo. This may explain why non-Party historians, with the exception of Macfarlane, failed to discern the partnership.

Macfarlane observed Pollitt's and Campbell's growing combined effectiveness and concerted efforts to keep the CPGB from left extremes in 1926–8. He concluded that the firm alliance between the two had developed during this time.[10] The strength of the bond between them is reflected in Pollitt's decision to purchase a house in the same road as the Campbell family when they moved to Lodore Gardens in Colindale, north-west London, in the late 1920s. The two men would often spend their evenings in the local pub, deep in discussion. Douglas Hyde confirmed that their working relationship had continued to be habitually close and mutually reliant.[11]

Pollitt and Campbell worked with a strong sense of urgency. They possessed the advantages of youth: abundant reserves of energy, ambition and optimism. They had both become committed to socialist revolution and belief in its inevitability through their pre-war membership of the British Socialist Party (BSP). Their experiences in the industrial conflict which accompanied the 1914–18 war and its aftermath and the inspiration provided by the Russian revolution and the bolshevik seizure of power served to deepen their commitment to revolution and cement the new bond to Lenin's Third Communist International.

The task which Pollitt and Campbell set themselves was to make the Communist Party a major force inside trade unions and in the leadership of the 'economic struggle'. Following bolshevik doctrine and their own perception of the balance of class forces in Britain, they were certain that the terrain on which the fight for state power would take place was the factory floor and pit bottom. They were also convinced that trade unions provided the sturdy foundation of the proletarian new model army.

Communists needed to be in a pivotal position throughout the trade union movement. They had to transform their workplaces into 'factory fortresses' of class power from which they would be called on to lead the masses of organized workers in executing the difficult manœuvre which the bolsheviks had shown was eminently feasible. They would move from fighting partial 'economic struggle' to demanding the seizure of state power and a socialist State. The trade unions would become a vehicle for revolution.

In 1930, when Pollitt and Campbell began to articulate and form this vision, their belief in the efficacy of trade unions as serviceable vessels for Communist activity was coming back into favour at the centre of the Communist International (Comintern). The Comintern was interested in results. Its officials wanted Communist Parties with increasing membership and influence and a strong track record of leading the class struggle. Pollitt's and Campbell's extreme leftwing rivals at the British Party centre, whom I have described as Young Turks, failed dismally to deliver these goods. Accordingly, the Comintern switched horses and backed Pollitt's and Campbell's more pragmatic approach. The results were notably better and the two men used the Comintern's approval to consolidate their hold on the Party leadership.

Contrary to conventional assumptions, the British Communist Party leadership had already moved leftwards in late 1926, *before* the Comintern had enunciated Class Against Class. Concern over the growing gulf between the Party and trade union activists impelled the leadership to begin a centrewards turn during 1928. Their attempt to position the Party at the heart of the organized working class was temporarily overwhelmed in the spring of 1929 by the Comintern's support for the Young Turks who argued that CPGB's problems stemmed from not operating Independent Leadership rigorously enough.

We shall examine how Pollitt and Campbell integrated their new approach to the 'economic struggle' into Party members' practice. The slow but steady recovery of the British economy during 1933–34 from the 1931 financial crisis assisted their aim of anchoring the Party inside the organized working class. Party activists who agitated inside factories and pits found workers who listened to their message. They were also willing to 'have a go' in gaining redress for long-standing grievances or to fight employers' attempts to introduce new working practices which involved speed-up and more intensive exploitation.

We shall observe that Party activists often tried to escalate each dispute to the maximum possible extent and to fight each skirmish as if it were all-out war. The unspoken assumption was that revolution was imminent on the British horizon and that every outbreak of class struggle would bring it palpably nearer; the fiercer the fight at each factory, the sooner the revolution would arrive. However, during 1933 Pollitt and Campbell revised their own views about the proximity of the revolutionary crisis in the light of evidence that it was certainly not just over the horizon. Consequently, they began the arduous process of formally moving the Party's position and adjusting the membership's expectations to take account of this reality.

A powerful motivation for this awkward and potentially divisive rejigging was that the Party was suffering serious losses in the number of its members available for active industrial service. Too many able activists were being victimized and martyred in the course of leading intense economic struggle. How could Party members win leading positions inside the trade union movement if they were constantly being sacked and out of work?

The British Party leadership were assisted in their revisionism by parallel developments in the French Communist Party and also by some favourable currents and eddies swirling around the Comintern sea. Pollitt and Campbell charted their own course firmly towards the indefinite postponement of revolution. They returned to their own pre-war socialist culture with its emphasis on the Utopian aspects of revolution. It might have receded into the distance, but its presence was no less real for being far away. The inevitable certainty of revolution was a beacon, lighting the way for Communists toiling away at their unremitting daily mass work. Pollitt and Campbell revived this aspect of British socialism, and skilfully incorporated utopian idealism as part of the Communist Party of Great Britain's (CPGB) canon. I have described this part of their approach as Life Itself, drawing on their own perception of how the revolutionary crisis would eventually occur.[12]

By the time the Seventh World Congress of the Comintern finally convened in August 1935, the British Communist Party had already made most of the essential adjustments to enable its membership to cope with the non-   appearance of revolution. The new policy enunciated at the Congress, of a cross-class political alliance to fight fascism and secure democracy, made no discernible difference either to the CPGB's policy towards the trade union movement or to its industrial members' practical activity. Pollitt and Campbell had long relied on the continuing appearance of the 'united front from below' in the Comintern's *dicta* to justify their injunctions to British Party members to work inside 'reformist' trade unions.

In Chapter 3 we shall observe how they stretched and trimmed the 'united front from below' when the occasion demanded. Its various denominations moved from 'fighting united front' through 'united front of the rank and file' and finally to the 'real united front' which sealed the formal re-dedication of the Party to 'united frontism' after the Seventh World Congress. For Pollitt and Campbell, however, the united front's content continued substantially unchanged through its many nominal permutations.

The united front lay at the heart of their approach to the economic struggle because they conceived it to be the ultimate and lethal weapon which the working class possessed against the employing class. They had opposed the Young Turks' plans for revolutionary red unions in 1928–29 because they would fracture the united front. They opposed the London busmen's breakaway union in 1938 for the same reason. As Pollitt responded to Citrine when the TUC General Secretary had summarily refused to consider a formal alliance with the Party:

'The Communist Party fights for real trade unionism, the trade unionism which organises the working class for struggle against the exploiting class . . . The Communist party does all in its power to strengthen the trade union branches, to recruit the unorganised and to develop powerful movements of the rank and file, which are able to conduct the fight against the employers and their allies . . . Because of the consistent policy of the Communist Party in the interests of the whole working class . . . the united front of the rank and file against the employing class is becoming stronger day by day.'[13]

*   *   *

The economic recovery in Britain continued to gather momentum. After the 1935 general election, the Conservative Government intensified its rearmament programme and concentrated increasingly on aircraft production. We shall see in Chapters 4 and 5 that Party engineering activists were in a particularly good position to take advantage of the opportunities which government orders with guaranteed profits offered for economic struggle. Nevertheless, there were no notable pitched battles or all-out wars.

Most Party activists were content to extend trade union organization gradually, almost by stealth. They did not hesitate to embark on small engagements which did not involve a large commitment of force and thus did not carry the risk of wiping out their new union recruits and neophyte shop stewards. Moreover, they continued to record tangible, if mundane, concessions from employers from such skirmishing activity. It is no wonder that full-time union officials were content to cooperate with Party members.

The successes chalked up by Communist shop stewards in the economic struggle were not due to their following prescriptive formulae laid down by King Street, nor could they be ascribed to their earnest emulation of Marxist– Leninist methods of dialectical materialism. Most Party activists learned to wage the economic struggle through trial and error, watching their elders and peers and generally assimilating the trade union culture of which the Party Centre insisted they must become an integral part. This culture contained two generalized guides to action which transcended local differences and economic vicissitudes. I have described them in this book as 'trade union loyalism' and 'rank-and-filism'. While these denominations are not arbitrary, the same elements could as easily be described as the principles of 'solidarity' and 'militancy' or 'unity' and 'agitation', invoking the union ASE credo, 'Educate, Agitate and Organize'.

It has seemed appropriate to adopt 'trade union loyalism' and 'rank-and-filism' because Party members in this period viewed their own situation in these terms. The 'trade union movement' had gained in prestige and power as a result of the 1914–18 war, and that position was reinforced by the events of 1926–28, the General Strike and the subsequent Mond–Turner talks between prominent employers and union leaders. Trade union activists in the 1930s felt that they were part of an important civil institution, and their conduct of union branch business and relations with employers on the factory floor reflected their sense of worth and self-respect.

Trade union loyalism was not viewed as a stricture, but rather an acknowledgement of one's place in the order of things, a voluntary act of allegiance to one's primary social institution. Communists had imbibed trade union loyalism with their first experiences of work and economic conflict, along with every other working-class activist of their generation. They acquired the reflex developed by British trade union activists since the 1860s, that a 'good' trade union member was unflinchingly and unquestioningly loyal to the 'movement'.

When Pollitt pulled the British Party back from the brink of repudiating trade unions, he did so out of gut instinct. His initiation into trade union culture, before the war, at Gorton Tank in the Boilermakers' Amalgamation had bitten deeply. Johnny Campbell's analytic abilities arrived at the same conclusion as Pollitt's visceral emotions. They both recognized that if the Communist Party was to be at the centre of the proletariat, as Lenin and the Comintern decreed, then it must be in the very heart of the trade union movement. In practice, this meant accepting its culture – and solidarity or trade union loyalism was its first commandment.

Nevertheless, Pollitt's and Campbell's stance can be quite clearly distinguished from those 'reformist' leaders to whom they enjoined their members to pledge allegiance. They seized on the rich vein of rank-and-filism in British trade union culture and audaciously appropriated it for the Communist Party. We shall observe in Chapters 8 and 9 that it is hardly an exaggeration to observe that by 1938 any young man or woman whose shopfloor experience impelled them towards militancy was attracted to the Communist Party. They might not actually join the Party or they might belong to the Party only briefly. But as long as they remained militant trade union activists it was Party members with whom they had to work and come to terms. Other militants measured themselves against the standards set by the Communists around them.

The recent academic dispute about the importance of 'rank-and-filism' for British trade union culture has been curiously unproductive, perhaps because of the tendencies of some of the participants to impute thoroughly partisan and dogmatic positions to their 'opponents'. In the 1930s, lay activists were essential to sustaining trade unions. Despite the growth in numbers and arguably status of the full-time officialdom, unions still relied on lay activists to lavish large amounts of their voluntary labour. Richard Hyman has drawn attention to the tendency of this cadre of union activists to view themselves as the 'rank and file' from the 1890s.[14] He observed that the appropriation of the military terminology by trade unionists was unexceptional in view of the growing importance of militarism in European nation–states, a development in which Britain was an integral part.

The experiences of the 1914–18 war reinforced the tendency of union activists to view the 'rank-and-file' as the vital centre of trade unions. The people on the ground, the ones who were doing the actual fighting, were after all the foundation of the unions' power, without whom there could be no advance. Moreover, observant and able full-time union officials certainly recognized the importance of their foot-soldiers and of maintaining their troops' morale. Lay officials viewed themselves as being the 'NCOs of the movement', (the Webbs' phrase, coined in the period when militarism was becoming part of British popular parlance). It never occurred to them that because they were part of the 'rank-and-file', they were automatically opposed and in principled disagreement with their full-time officials. When activists defined themselves as rank-and-file, they were often only observing their place inside the movement The description was often an expression of self-confidence and pride in their own place rather than signifying their own unimportance.

When Pollitt and Campbell asserted the Party's primacy in the economic struggle, they did so on behalf of the rank and file. They unhesitatingly assumed its practical existence and told Party activists that if they did their daily mass work properly, they would be able to mobilize the 'rank-and-file' in militant economic struggle. As we shall see in Chapter 6, King Street knew as well as Ernest Bevin that 'the rank and file' did not always fight to the last ditch. They continued to purvey the myth that it was invariably the reformist leaders who halted the workers' forward march and prevented full victory being attained.

The evident potential for conflict between trade union loyalism and rank-and-filism did not deter Pollitt and Campbell from espousing both. Their insistence that Party members must act according to both principles was not disingenuous. They were convinced that Communists could not be effective leaders in the economic struggle without sincerely adhering to the two, and energetically denied that their contradictory nature might produce problems for Party activists.

*   *   *

I have described the four components of Pollitt's and Campbell's guide to action, trade union loyalism, rank-and-filism, the united front, and Life Itself, as revolutionary pragmatism. This paradoxical epithet seems apt to describe an approach to the world which succeeded precisely because it was contradictory. It provided Party members with a flexible guide to action and definite boundaries within which different activists made many different, sometimes opposing, decisions about how to conduct the 'economic struggle'.

Revolutionary pragmatism was hardly a hermetically sealed view of the world: its success depended on Party members possessing sound practical reflexes and a discerning judgement. They were required to choose the appropriate blend of its conflicting tenets to apply in their particular circumstances. Its conventions reflected the culture within which trade union militants had functioned in Britain since the 1890s. Pollitt and Campbell took the raw material from their own experience and adapted it to suit the changed circumstances of inter-war economic conflict.

Although rank-and-filism remained an important part of daily culture for shopfloor activists, they usually proved quite capable of striking bargains with the governor and not reflecting too deeply on their departure from its strictures. Concluded swiftly and cleanly in hot blood, compromise settlements appeared the only thing to do. They were entered into on the spur of the moment, under pressure from fellow workmates or under threat from an employer. Stewards might differ about whether the time had come to compromise and organize a united retreat. But the need to face up to this eventuality was habitually accepted by Party activists who were building factory organization and advancing working class strength on the shopfloor.

Party activists whose inexperience and/or idealism combined to create a belief in the infallible efficacy of rank-and-filism were disabused of this notion sooner or later through applying pragmatic common sense to their own observations and experiences and/or being trained up by a seasoned veteran. As a young Birmingham Communist and novice shop steward, Les Ambrose learned to emulate Teddy Ager, the full-time Birmingham District Secretary of the Algamated Engineering Union (AEU). Ager was not a Party member, but Ambrose found his judgement and opinions to be more reliable than AEU Party veterans, George Crane and Jim Crump. At the West London aero-engine factory, Napier's, Ralph Fuller and the other young AEU stewards learned the art of leading the economic struggle from the old Party hands, Fred Arter and Fred Elms. Party activists who failed to discover or were oblivious to the pragmatic, cautious techniques of waging economic war inside engineering collective bargaining conventions were routinely martyred.[15]

As the 1930s progressed, the balance maintained by Pollitt and Campbell within revolutionary pragmatism between rank-and-filism and union loyalty swung away from rank-and-filism. Some national union leaders had reacted to the setbacks and defeats of the early 1920s by rejecting all-out industrial conflict as a reliable instrument of collective bargaining. Instead of routine, endemic trials of strength, they wanted to adapt the comprehensive national negotiations of the war economy for peacetime use.

In the wake of the embarrassing débâcle of 1926, Walter Citrine, the resourceful General Secretary of the Trades Union Congress (TUC), steered the General Council towards a new understanding with employers embodying this approach. His efforts culminated in the Mond–Turner talks in 1928.[16] They anticipated the dominant trend in collective bargaining in the inter-war period towards centralization and control over 'custom and practice' by management. Trade union leaders, including the AEU Executive, who were imbued with the culture of British trade union activism, denounced the talks as 'collaborationist'. A new term of abuse, 'Mondism' appeared to describe the increasing tendency of union leaders to compromise in negotiations. Hugh Clegg concludes:

> It does not seem likely that rank and file trade union members had been converted to Citrine's new philosophy, which was elitist. Nineteenth century trade unionism had relied on the solidarity of the members to regulate industrial relations. Citrine, by contrast, emphasised negotiations and the skills of the negotiatior. Converts were therefore to be found primarily among full-time officers and executive members. Consequently support for Mond–Turner was probably assisted by the additional authority conferred on trade union leaders by national collective bargaining, the centralisation of power in the unions, and the advance of bureaucratisation.[17]

The new norm was a more incorporated collective bargaining with more elaborate and rationalized agreements. Full-time officials were under pressure to deliver a *more* disciplined, ordered and dispute-free shopfloor. Nevertheless, certainly the more flexible and opportunist union leaders, like Ernest Bevin and Arthur Horner, leading Communist activist who became President of the South Wales Miners' Federation (the Fed) in 1936, exploited this trend to great advantage in gaining concessions from employers, but also to concentrate more power in central union institutions. The union leaders often were forced to come to terms with the stubborn persistence of local exceptions to the rules which they had negotiated centrally with the employers. Both Horner and Bevin encountered difficulties in fulfilling their side of the comprehensive collective agreements which they had signed on behalf of their members.

In 1937, Horner signed away significant areas of union control over custom and practice, and agreed to a conciliation scheme which pre-empted the ability of pit militants to resist changes by industrial action. An important part of the friction inside the London Busmen's Rank-and-File Movement was the need to operate under the agreement which Bevin had made with London Transport: it required a surrender of lightning strikes, walk-outs and go-slows. The militant lay officials and activists concluded that their own ability to fight and win battles on the shopfloor had been seriously impaired by the new arrangements.

Full-time officials' justification for these new ways was twofold: they gained material results when no other way would have succeeded; and they permitted unions to keep their precious human and financial capital intact when strikes would only bring suffering and not gain their desired objective. Nevertheless a generation of union loyalists and activists was still operating at factory and pit level who had been socialized into the earlier, less structured *modus operandi*. They had reason to feel that things had changed and reacted accordingly.

It was clear by 1934 that the CPGB was reaping substantial gains from its membership's adopting Pollitt's and Campbell's approach towards the economic struggle. Communist Party membership had begun to expand, albeit not to the extent that King Street hoped. But a very high proportion of the new recruits were industrial workers who became active trade unionists and shop stewards. Pollitt in particular was proud of the place which Communists had earned inside the trade union move-ment by dint of dedicated daily mass work and exhibiting leadership qualities. The assumption was that whenever Life Itself produced the rev-olutionary crisis, these industrial activists would be in a strategic posi-tion: they would form the vanguard to lead the organized working class to take power.

Though the Party Centre had adjusted to the failure of revolution to appear on the scene, the widespread expectation persisted that a militant upsurge of the whole working class would occur if Party members were correctly organized in their unions to promote 'national wages move-ments'. Unlike a revolutionary situation, which remained hypothetical for British Communists, dramatic militant national industrial conflicts had occurred in the years before the 1914–18 war.

Then there had been the surprisingly volatile and spirited strikes of the wartime period, and then the protracted set-piece battles of the 1920s. A leading activist of the pre-war new unionism, Tom Mann was a founda-tion member of the CPGB. His continuing activity on behalf of the Party represented an important link with the militant upsurges and revolts of the past. He was a potent symbol of trade union militancy, and his unswerving optimism and faith in socialism was often invoked by King Street.

The Party Centre had enjoined members to promote 'national wages movements' inside trade unions from 1932, without result. The pattern of national collective bargaining became distinctly stable, and union leaders showed no inclination to embark on national confrontations. Though local militancy was increasing, there were few opportunities for transforming such sparks into prairie fires. And as most Party members became accustomed to the new terrain upon which the economic struggle was being waged in the 1930s, they made no attempt to do so.

We shall see in Chapter 5 that the wave of strikes and militant revolts in France after the Popular Front Government took office in 1936 revived expectations of a popular upsurge here. French Communists had assumed a leading role in their events; many British Communists, evidently including King Street, became convinced that their activists would lead 'national wages movements' which would decisively alter the balance of class forces. Their conviction led in the spring of 1937 to a renewed emphasis on rank-and-filism in Party propaganda and in the behaviour of many Party activists.

As we shall observe in Chapters 6 and 7, the result of the Party's subsequent *démarche* was not what activists had anticipated. In each of the much-vaunted confrontations between unions and employers, trade union leaders negotiated compromise agreements which were accepted by their members, though many of the returns to work were accompanied by great bitterness and resentment. Nevertheless, in each instance, Communists, including the Party Centre, invoked trade union loyalism. They not only acquiesced in these settlements but promoted 'unity' in the ranks behind them. Union leaders, like Bevin, might have betrayed the strikers, but their treachery could only be fought inside the unions.

Between 1935 and 1937, the problems encountered in operating rank-and-file movements presented an increasingly serious threat to the CPGB's growing industrial membership and influence inside trade unions. When rank-and-file movements were led by activists who took rank-and-filism seriously, their encounter with the fundamental contradiction between union loyalism and rank-and-filism was inescapable. Chapter 6 follows the fortunes of the the two most successful rank-and-file movements, the London Busmen's Rank and File Movement and the Aircraft Shop Stewards National Council (ASSNC). We analyse how Party activists reacted in the extreme situations where they were forced to choose between rank-and-filism and trade union loyalism. We also observe Pollitt's and Campbell's moves to ensure that union loyalism won out when the between-the-two imperatives reached crisis point.

Chapter 7 chronicles the official strike by miners at Harworth in 1936–37. During this strike, Party members also had to choose between rank-and-filism and union loyalism. Pollitt and Campbell had to deal with the reality of Arthur Horner promoting a compromise solution to the strike which violated rank-and-filism. We shall observe that the Harworth strike shows that the CPGB and its activists became a vital part of trade union and labour history because they chose to remain a loyal and integral part of the movement's united front.

Pollitt and Campbell tried to ensure that the Party abstained from any involvement in the conflicts which ensued between full-time officials and their 'rank-and-file'. This did not mean that their members or groups of their members did not take up their own positions against full-time officials, but rather that they did so on their own initiative, without instructions from the Party Centre. However, as their members were also increasingly elected to full-time positions inside unions, it meant that Party members were regularly called on to enforce collective agreements on an unenthusiastic or even rebellious 'rank-and-file' of lay activists, usually including other Communists.

*   *   *

King Street extricated the Party from a complex and difficult situation by invoking the potent ideological balm of Life Itself in large amounts. Even though the strikes of May 1937 had not produced the militant upsurge, it was still certain that Life Itself would eventually bring the revolution. In addition to this ritual repetition of the Communist catechism, the frightening conflicts on the Continent intervened to divert members' attention from any debilitating feelings of domestic disillusion. We shall observe in Chapter 9 that Party trade union activists were increasingly pre-occupied in discussing and thinking about fighting Franco and fascism, and comparatively successful in organizing activities to involve their workmates in support of the democratic side.

Pollitt and Campbell were also increasingly preoccupied by the European crisis. They continued to emphasize the importance of party members' mass work, but they did so within the context of the trade unions taking a political stand against fascism and Chamberlain's Government. They did not apply their minds to reflecting about some notable setbacks suffered by Party activists in the economic struggle. The four components of revolutionary pragmatism remained solidly in place and there was apparently no pressure on King Street from its own membership to revise its approach. Nor did the 1939–45 war throw up any situations with which the British Communist world view on the economic struggle was unable to cope.

We shall examine the Party's attitude to the war and the gains made by Party activists within the war economy in Chapters 10 and 11. The war economy machine which Ernest Bevin designed and presided over presented many favourable opportunities for Party trade union activists not only to lead successful skirmishes in the economic struggle but also to build up shopfloor union organization. Chapter 11 on the wartime economy looks in some detail at how Party activists responded to the circumstances of wartime engineering factories and charts the varied and sometimes conflicting initiatives to take advantage of extraordinary opportunities.

Most Party activists did not try to exploit the dislocation and flux of the war production drive to promote radical changes in trade unions and collective bargaining. They were content to operate within the strictures of Pollitt's and Campbell's injunctions to maximize production to save the Soviet Socialist Fatherland while not neglecting their duties as lay union officials to maintain the balance of class forces on the shopfloor. The different uses which Party members found for Joint Production Committees are surveyed and the question is considered whether JPCs were seen as potential vehicles of socialism or of radical structural reform.

The Party Centre made intermittent gestures towards implementing the Leninist model of tightly disciplined democratic centralist factory cells. We shall see in Chapter 8 that these 'factory groups', as they were renamed, became informal kitchen cabinets within which Party shop stewards could meet and discuss strategy without reference to King Street or the Comintern line. The reality of industrial activity within this notably uncentralized Party was that Party activists conducted the economic struggle within their own parochial parameters.

Communist engineering shop stewards in Glasgow behaved differently towards the union and employers than their counterparts in Barrow or Sheffield. Their trade union culture had evolved on a district basis. Despite attempts to centralize some engineering unions, their district committees had been the channel for relations with employers until the 1914–18 war, and many of them still functioned engergetically in the inter-war period and continued to exhibit wide variations in their conduct. For example, the AEU District Committees in Coventry and Birmingham took diametrically opposed attitudes towards the admission of semi-skilled workers.

Such parochial differences were not confined to engineering. As President of the Fed, Arthur Horner had to take account of widely differing customs and practice which had evolved in the different coalfields in South Wales, and even between different lodges in the same valley. These differences persisted despite serious attempts by employers and union officials to impose greater uniformity. The lay officials who were the pillars of trade union organization, without whom membership would fall away and recruitment cease, retained sufficient authority to respond to

'Mondist' attempts to rationalize production methods and energetically led their members to claim redress of traditional grievances, even if only in 'unofficial' strikes.

Despite these notable differences in the conduct of Party activists, rigidly monolithic stereotypes of Communist activists continue to permeate British historiography. Elsewhere, notably the USA, France and Italy, a 'revisionist' school of historians has begun to examine events and their respective Communist Parties' part in them with greater distance and objectivity. These scholars have decided that it is not conceding an ideological point to recognize that Party members were important participants in political and economic conflict in the inter-war and war periods. Freed from the need to see robotic uniformity in Party members' behaviour, they have been able to recognize great variation in their responses to events and difficult problems.[18]

My approach to writing Party history became revisionist because I soon found that Party members did not conform to the stereotypes of either official Communist heroics or ritual Labour witch-hunts. I have had the audacity to transcend the conventional polarities of British historiography in the hope of contributing to a revisionist approach to British Communism. Since British trade unions and the CPGB have now lost their important social and public roles as pillar of society and bogeymen/bolshevik heroes respectively it should now be possible to reveal their secrets. Kevin Morgan's account of Party members' attitudes to fascism and the 1939–45 war published in 1989 marked an important beginning.[19]

Remarkably few of the Party activists whom I interviewed were interested in repeating the myths of Party heroism and self-sacrifice. The few self-proclaimed heroes who proudly paraded their own and the Party's importance used knowing winks to gloss over silently the gaps in their story. Their true stories consisted of predictable Party clichés, interspersed with morsels of fact, anecdote and allusion. The paradoxical Achilles heel of the Labour myth is that Party union activists remained, for the most part, staunchly loyal to their respective trade unions and rarely indulged in back-stabbing 'reformist' Labour colleagues on the shopfloor.

On the whole, Party activists were outstandingly candid and open in their dealings with the full-time union officials for whom Labour mythology decreed they should feel profound distrust. There was, of course, regular Party caucusing about 'internal' union affairs, and concerted démarches organized by Party activists to influence union policy. But these 'conspiratorial' activities were conducted on the terrain of culture of trade union activism which they shared with their Labour colleagues/opponents.

Communist mythology has continued to conceal the Party Centre's consistent espousal of trade union loyalism as an absolute imperative in extreme situations. Equally Labour mythology certainly has had no interest in revealing that Party leaders promoted adherence to official union rules and decisions. It is not surprising that a distorted stereotype of Party activists has emerged from these polarities. I hope that this book will assist readers in judging for themselves whether there is not some point in between the two which accurately reflects the reality of Communists' contribution to British trade unions.

Notes

1. Lord Taylor of Mansfield, 1972; *Uphill All the Way*, Sidgwick & Jackson,19 and 64. For Taylor's involvement in the 'Battle of Harworth', see Chapter 7. Taylor's autobiography has a Foreword by Harold Wilson and an Afterword by Jim Griffiths. It is typical of the Labour hagiography which is interesting, but remains an account of events which is as partial as the Communist Party's crop of published memoirs.
2. *Daily Worker*, 16 January 1935.
3. Pelling, H., 1958, *The British Communist Party, A Historical Profile*, A. & C. Black.
4. Macfarlane, L. J., 1966, *The British Communist Party, Its Origin and Development until 1929*, Macgibbon and Kee. Martin R., 1969, *Communism and the British Trade Unions, 1924-1933, A Study of the National Minority Movement*, Oxford.
5. See for example, Bullock, A., 1960, *The Life and Times of Ernest Bevin*, vol. I, 1881–1940, Heinemann, 217–8 and 606–14.
6. Morgan, K. O., 1987, *Labour People*, Oxford University Press:198–9. Smith, D. and Francis, H., 1980, *The Fed, A History of the South Wales Miners in the Twentieth Century*, Lawrence & Wishart.
7. Party members were important recruiting agents for the TGWU in the early 1930s in Birmingham, in Pressed Steel, Oxford from 1934, in most engineering factories from 1939, and, of course, on the buses. See pp. 59, 67–8, 125–9 and 332.
8. *Daily Worker*, 2 January 1937.
9. There are two biographies of Pollitt. The first by John A. Mahon is a voluminous hagiography, while containing an enormous amount of interesting detail. Kevin Morgan's biography, published in 1993, marked an important first step in assessing Pollitt's career objectively. However, Morgan was constrained by space and does not deal with Pollitt's relation to the 'economic struggle' and trade unions in any depth. Johnny Campbell has not even inspired a Party hagiography.
10. Macfarlane, op. cit., 218–9. See also Martin, op.cit., 153–4.
11. Information from conversations with William Campbell and Douglas Hyde. The Campbells moved a mile away to Temple Fortune shortly before 1939; William Campbell felt the move had been precipitated by his mother's increasing resentment of the intimate bond between her husband and Pollitt.

12. See Chapter 4, note 19. Life Itself continued to play an important part in the world view of muscular pragmatic Communists. In 1990, Timothy Garton Ash observed Mikhail Gorbachev's regular invocations of 'life itself' to account for twists and turns of fate which did not accord with the Marxist view of the world, but which nevertheless had to be accommodated. ('Germany Unbound', 1990, *New York Review of Books*, Vol. XXXVII No. 18, 22 November:11.)

13. *Daily Worker*, 7 March 1934.

14. See Hyman, R., 1987, 'Rank and File Movements and Workplace Organisation 1914–39', Wrigley, C.J. (ed.), *A History of British Industrial Relations*, Vol. II, 1914–39, Harvester:129–31,139–42. See also *Bulletin of the Society for the Study of Labour History*, 1983, No. 46, Spring. 'Officialdom and Opposition: Leadership and Rank and File in Trade Unions', Report of Society Conference paper: 4. The 'rank-and-file' issue is debated by the main protagonists, Jonathan Zeitlin, Richard Price and James E. Cronin in the *International Review of Social History*, Vol. XXIV–1989–1: 42–102, and their debate is commented on by Hyman. R., 1989, in Vol. XXIV–1989–2, 'The Sound of One Hand Clapping': 136–49.

15. Les Ambrose described the Birmingham Party engineering activist Jim Crump as 'wanting to wear the martyr's crown' (interview with Les Ambrose by N. Fishman). For Ambrose and Fuller, see Chapter 8.

16. Clegg, H. A., 1985, *A History of British Trade Unions Since 1889*, Vol. II, 1911–1933, Clarendon Press, Oxford: 461–71.

17. Ibid: 471.

18. For the USA, see the review article by Brinkley, A., 1990, 'The Best Years of Their Lives', *The New York Review of Books,* 28 June. Brinkley welcomes the 'new' labour historians who have 'challenged the view (expressed most strongly by Theodore Draper and Harvey Klehr) that American communism had little significant life apart from its subservience to Moscow.' 'However obedient Communists may have been to national and international leaders in other ways, Nelson sees no evidence that they behaved as a disciplined, centrally directed cadre in their union activities.' (p. 18). (Brinkley is reviewing Bruce Nelson, 1990, *Workers on the Waterfront: Seamen, Longshoremen, and Unionism in the 1930s*, University of Illinois Press.)

    For France, see Stavall, T., 1989, 'French Communism and Suburban Development: The Rise of the Paris Red Belt', *Journal of Contemporary History*, Vol. 24: 437–60. For Italy, see Urban, J. B., 1986, *Moscow and the Italian Communist Party*, Tauris & Co., London. 'Revisionist' history probably started with Western European and US historians' investigations of the Soviet Communist Party and the USSR. Merle Fainsod (*How Russia is Ruled, 1963*), Jerry Hough (with Merle Fainsod, *How the Soviet Union is Governed*, Cambridge Mass., 1979) and Sheila Fitzpatrick (*The Russian Revolution, 1917–1932*, Oxford University Press, 1984; *Cultural Revolution in Russia, 1928–1931*, (Ed.), Bloomington, Ind., 1978.) are acknowledged 'revisionists'.

19. Morgan, K., 1989, *Against Fascism and War, Ruptures and continuities in British Communist politics, 1935–41*, Manchester University Press.

CHAPTER TWO

The Origins of Revolutionary Pragmatism

In 1933, the British Communist Party was 13 years old. For most of this time its members had expected the imminent arrival in Britain of the worldwide wave of proletarian revolution. The majority of foundation members were already Marxist socialists, who believed that the working class must emancipate itself through revolution. A desire to emulate the bolsheviks' success had stimulated them to join the British affiliate of the Third Communist International (Comintern) and accept the theses imposed by Lenin at its second congress in 1920 as a condition for membership. They now asserted that, for the British working class to fulfil its destiny and join in the worldwide proletarian revolution, the leadership of a vanguard Communist Party was required.

The process of bolshevization imposed by the Comintern on all affiliated parties in 1922–23 was comparatively painless and straightforward inside the British Communist Party. The veteran officials of the British Socialist Party (BSP) who had assumed comparable posts in the Communist party were swept aside by others who had discovered how to lead men and women during the wartime economic conflict. They emerged in 1918 with their youthful self-confidence not just intact, but reinforced by their experiences. Their experience of leading economic struggle combined with their idealistic commitment to socialism to produce an overweening desire to preside over revolutionary change in Britain.

The exception to this common background among the bolshevizers was Ranjani Palme Dutt, a highly proficient intellectual from a middle-class family. Dutt had recognized the Manchester boilermaker, Harry Pollitt, as a valuable and charismatic ally, and commended him to the Comintern's notice. Mainly because of this patronage, Pollitt soon became the *primus inter pares* of the working-class militants on the Central Committee – Johnny Campbell, Arthur Horner, Willie Gallacher and Wally Hannington.[1]

Harry Pollitt, born in 1890, followed in his mother's footsteps and joined the Openshaw Socialist Society in Manchester, his neighbourhood BSP branch, at the age of nineteen. He also became an active member of his craft union, the Boilermakers' Society. In 1915 he found work in the Southampton shipyards. He soon became a shop steward and from this cockpit experienced the extraordinary flux of wartime production conditions and the turbulent mood of fellow workers. At the outbreak of war, Johnny Campbell was a BSP member in Paisley (in the West of Scotland industrial belt). He was a clerk at the local Co-op, and immediately volunteered for the army. After early 'conspicuous valour' he was decorated and invalided out. He become a gifted propagandist for the shop stewards' Clyde Workers' Committee. Like Campbell, Willie Gallacher came from Paisley and was a keen BSP member. He was active in the skilled Brassmoulders' Union, and in 1914 arrived in Glasgow to take a prominent part in the Clyde Workers' Committee.[2]

Arthur Horner was a flamboyant miner from Maerdy who had given up a promising future as a Baptist preacher because he had become increasingly drawn to socialist faith through activities in the 'rank-and-file' South Wales Miners Unofficial Reform Movement and the Rhondda Socialist Society. After being blacklisted in the coalfield for unremitting militancy, he escaped from military service by arranging a covert passage to Dublin where in 1917 he joined the Citizen's Army. Arrested in Holyhead when he arrived home on leave with anti-war leaflets, he was imprisoned until April 1919. In his absence, he was elected a lay official at his local pit.[3]

Wally Hannington was one of many engineering shop stewards in West London who became Communists. He was active in the BSP, in his union, the Amalgamated Society of Toolmakers (AST) which became part of the Amalgamated Engineers Union (AEU) on amalgamation in 1920, and the unofficial Amalgamation Committee Movement (ACM), a 'rank-and-file' pressure group campaigning for an industrial union in engineering. He met another AST and BSP member, Bob Lovell, in the Amalgamation Committee Movement, and they soon became good friends. During the war they joined forces with militants from the main constituent union of the AEU, the Amalgamated Society of Engineers (ASE), notably George Crane, Joe Scott, Claude Berridge and Jack Tanner. Their loose network apparently was an important part of the West London shop stewards movement.

There were notable outbreaks of militant industrial conflict during the war and the early 1920s on the purpose-built industrial estate Park Royal and in the new factories along the Great West Road. But the strikes and agitation of which these men were leaders have been comparatively neglected by historians. Nevertheless their experiences were formative. They all featured prominently in the AEU's fortunes until the late 1950s. With the exception of Tanner, they all joined the infant Communist Party.[4]

Johnny Campbell and Palme Dutt soon proved to be the most astute and acute Party ideologues, possessing that scarce commodity, reliable political judgement, in ample supply. There were other equally qualified auto-didacts besides Campbell, notably Tommy Jackson, J.T. Murphy, and Tom Bell, who were often more prolific in the production of classical Marxist sermonizing.[5] But they were incapable of providing useful guides to action. Campbell's uniquely practical intellectual abilities were early acknowledged by the Party. Palme Dutt specialized in the production of Comintern orthodoxy and assumed the role of respected Party theoretician.

Before 1914 the BSP, of which Pollitt, Campbell, Gallacher and Hannington had all been members, was a Marxist sect which propagated its own version of socialism zealously enough. It had not aspired to influence events in the 'economic struggle' nor to monitor its members' conduct within it. The BSP leadership was positively hostile towards trade unions because they were 'reformist' organizations which fragmented the working class and diverted workers away from the fight for socialism. BSP working-class members were typically members of skilled trade unions, and indeed provided a vital militant element in trade union institutions. The young bolshevizers were no exception, having been shop stewards, branch officers, and involved in the 'rank-and-file' movements connected with their unions.

The pre-war 'rank-and-file' movements functioned alongside the official union structure. They were not viewed by their members as an alternative to their unions, but rather as a complement. Thus the Amalgamation Committee Movement and the South Wales Miners Unofficial Reform Movement both attempted to influence unions' political direction and elections for full-time and lay officials. Many ACM members became enthusiastic participants in the wartime shop stewards' movement, and the continuity between the outlooks of the two 'rank-and-file' movements has probably been underestimated by historians anxious to find a dramatic break in British working-class consciousness induced by the war and the bolshevik revolution.[6]

The experiences of the 1914–18 war reinforced the tendency of union activists to view the 'rank-and-file' as the vital centre of trade unions. The people on the ground, the ones who were doing the actual fighting, were after all the foundation of the unions' power, without whom there could be no advance. Moreover, observant and able full-time union officials certainly recognized the importance of their 'troops' and of maintaining their morale. The consciousness of lay officials of their position as the NCOs of the movement, as being part of the 'rank-and-file', did not imply their automatic opposition and *a priori* disagreement with full-time officials. It was often only an observation of their differing places inside the institution, and actually implied a recognition of the importance of both positions inside the movement.

BSP trade union activists were drawn towards Lenin's new Communist International. Their post-war outlook was marked by an important change of emphasis influenced by their wartime experiences. The October revolution was based on workplace soviets in Petrograd and Moscow, and this model now became a talisman for the youthful British Communists who had been shop stewards in Park Royal, the Clyde and Sheffield. They had come to the same conclusion as the Comintern: factory organization had a strategic political role in addition to its economic functions. Communists' immediate political task was to make every factory a fortress.

> No communist party will be in a position to lead the decisive masses of the proletariat to struggle and to defeat the bourgeoisie until it has this solid foundation in the factories, until every large factory has become a citadel of the communist party.[7]

It followed that their urgent priority was developing the Communist Party's ability to influence industrial conflict. For these men, it was axiomatic and uncontentious that as Party members became shopfloor leaders they would also be involved in trade unions. The unions might be 'reformist', but there was no doubt in their minds that they would be transformed into revolutionary institutions by pressure from below when the time was ripe.

> To become the Party of the masses the Party cannot ignore the unions. The character of the struggle they are compelled to wage becomes increasingly revolutionary, in spite of all the desire of the trade union bureaucracy to prevent it.
>   They [Communist shop stewards] will use that position for carrying out Communist work. Even though some of the duties may be distasteful to them, yet by accepting such positions and by fighting loyally on behalf of their workmates on every question affecting their interests, they will not only get the backing of their fellow workers, but may occupy an important place for Communist activity during the period of crisis.[8]

This first cohort of Communist trade union activists had all won their laurels in economic battles, and seen that their common political social-ization consisted of trade union, 'rank-and-file' movement and socialist sect. While displaying little active prejudice against the Labour Party, it evidently never occurred to them to concentrate their own or the Communist Party's energy exclusively in the political arena, which to them meant Westminster and the Westminster-oriented non-Marxist Independent Labour Party (ILP) and Fabians. Lenin's warnings to British Communists against left-wing sectarianism applied to Communist participation in both the unions and the Labour Party. While accepting the need to include Westminster Labour politics within their ambit, they nevertheless believed that the crucial battleground for British Communists would be the workplace.[9] It is worth noting that Ernest Bevin, whose political socialization was almost identical to theirs, also placed traditional politics firmly beneath the 'economic struggle' in his priorities and strategy at this time. It was only after the disasters of the 1931 Labour Government that he decided to apply his own mind and his union's forces systematically inside the Labour Party.[10]

This order of priorities is reflected in Harry Pollitt's own progress in the Party. Following on his rise to prominence during bolshevization, he was given the urgent task of developing the National Minority Movement (NMM), the militant 'rank-and-file movement' for trade unionists intended to operate as the 'transmission belt' conveying British workers from reformism to revolution. Pollitt proved a notable success as Hon. Secretary of the NMM. Horner and Hannington enthusiastically and ably assisted him in leading the miners' and metalworkers' sections. He finally joined the Party Centre, and became General Secretary in May 1929.

*   *   *

The 1922 Engineering Lock-Out presented the CPGB with an ideal opportunity to exercise its influence among engineering workers, which the Party Centre and engineering activists were not slow to exploit.[11] AEU District Committees were persuaded to form all-in Lock-Out Committees including representatives from the National Unemployed Workers Movement (NUWM), the CPGB and any other local rank-and-file organizations. The Party Centre criticized the AEU Executive for its failure to deploy all its forces to fight the employers. Nevertheless, after the unions' defeat, the Party Centre was swift to encourage activists to staunch the flow of disillusioned members from the AEU.

> the Communist Party launched a 'Back to the Unions' campaign. Conferences were held by the RILU [Red International] in the autumn in London, Glasgow, Newcastle, Birmingham, Sheffield and Cardiff . . . These conferences called for united resistance to attacks on wages and hours, trade union affiliation to the Red International and the reorganization of trade unions along industrial lines.[12]

After 1923, the bolshevized British Communist Party made rapid strides in its chosen fields of action. Its increasing influence inside the Miners' Federation of Great Britain (MFGB) can be gauged from the victory of Arthur Cook, the South Walian candidate endorsed by the Miners' Minority Movement, as MFGB Secretary during 1924. The MFGB was the largest and probably the most prestigious union in Britain at this time; its affiliates varied in size from the small county unions in the Midlands, Somerset and the Forest of Dean to the large and militant South Wales Miners Federation,(the Fed), the expanding and volatile Yorkshire Miners Association (YMA) and the well-established, populous Durham Miners' Association (DMA). Coalmining had been an expanding and profitable industry before the war. Two national mining conflicts in 1893 and 1912 had precipitated government legislation forcing the coal-owners to make significant wages and hours concessions.

The Miners Minority Movement had been established by appropriating the loose organization of the pre-war South Wales Unofficial Reform Movement, along with its considerable national reputation and connections derived from widespread evangelizing for militant trade unionism which had begun during the 1910 Cambrian Combine Strike.[13] The MFGB President, Herbert Smith, had been influenced by their uncompromising zeal for reforming the established coalfield unions when collectors for the Cambrian Combine strike had visited the South Yorkshire coalfield where he was a union activist.[14] Smith's legendary refusal to concede ground in negotiations coincided with the Miners' Minority Movement's insistence on the importance of no surrender in fighting economic battles.

In 1925 Cook and Smith, stiffened and encouraged by the Miners Minority Movement, convinced the MFGB to try the pre-war militant strategy of massed class force once more. The MFGB had endured a humiliating defeat on 'Black Friday' in 1921 when the Triple Alliance, an offensive 'treaty' concluded in 1919 between the most militant unions for mutual assistance in big strikes, had failed to support the MFGB in a national dispute with the coal-owners. This débâcle had caused many to doubt whether large-scale national battles could still be won. This time, the MFGB Executive used the newly established General Council of the TUC to mobilize all-union support for their set-piece battle with the Government and the coal-owners.

Hugh Clegg has pointed to Ernest Bevin's key role in propelling the infant General Council into action over the MFGB request. Bevin recognized that if the General Council had declined to take the lead in this first important trial it would never be able to gain credibility. The General Council had to assume and be seen to be playing its self-appointed role as the 'general staff' of the movement.[15] Bevin's calculated risk succeeded. The Government and the coal-owners believed in the General Council's threats of industrial action to support the miners. Sufficient concessions were forthcoming from the Government to enable the TUC and the MFGB to claim a victory on 'Red Friday'. The standing of the General Council and the strategy of total class confrontation were powerfully reinforced.

Nevertheless, the government concessions had been strictly limited. The state subsidy to the coal-owners, enabling them to maintain wage rates, expired after nine months. During that time no MFGB leader made any attempt to move towards serious negotiations with the coal-owners. Having staked their reputation on supporting the miners, the General Council could do little more than watch the clock count the time down to a real set-piece battle over pay and conditions in coalmining directed by the TUC. Despite some Council leaders' efforts to exert effective control over the situation, the MFGB continued to edge the movement towards this Armageddon, reinforced by the enthusiastic expectations of the growing number of activists in the Miners' Minority Movement, the National Minority Movement and the Communist Party.

The Party leadership agreed with militant union leaders, notably Bevin, that the General Council should lead a general strike. They both wanted the General Council to organize a vigorous, effective fight. But the Party Centre differed from the militants on the General Council in their expectation that the general strike would produce a revolutionary situation. British Communists knew that Russian factory soviets had been dominated by the 'reformist' mensheviks throughout 1917, often up to the last moment in October when the bolsheviks had swept into the lead. They anticipated that the same logic of history would prevail in Britain, and that during the general strike they would find the opportunity to transform the unions from 'reformism' to revolution.

In the first stages of this trajectory, the Party Centre concentrated on preparing the forces of the 'rank-and-file'. This meant building trade union loyalism and fuelling militant expectations to ensure that the General Council actually joined the movement in conflict. Party leaders also assumed that an active 'rank-and-file' would create unstoppable pressure from below to sweep away the 'reformist' leaders when they sounded the retreat. The Party's bolshevik sounding slogans, rallying cries for the National Minority Movement and the MFGB, reflected their optimism. 'All Power to the General Council' addressed the need to make the union side into a real fighting force. 'Resignation of the Forger's Government; Formation of a Labour Government' was an exemplary 'partial' demand. The Party Centre felt that, like Kerensky's socialists, Labour would try but then fail to govern, leaving the Communist Party to step into their putative role as the centre of revolutionary state power.

James Klugmann's official history and other accounts whose authors have a vested interest in conspiracy theories highlight the imprisonment of the Party leadership from November 1925 to September 1926, the 'crucial period' before and during the General Strike.[16] They are keen to use the Government's fears of Communists as proof that the Party could actually have made a revolution but was cheated of the chance to do so.

But although Baldwin's Government secured their conviction for sedition, Pollitt *et al.* had certainly not formulated any plans to take state power.

The imprisonment of the Party leadership made little difference to the Party's ability to respond to the general strike because their strategy assigned the pivotal role to the 'rank-and-file' in the opening stages, with the Communist Party intervening only once the rest of the stage had been cleared of reformist trade union leaders, Baldwin's Government and a hypothetical stopgap Labour Government. When the strike was called on 3 May all available Party members were despatched to the coalfields to strengthen the rank-and-file's will to fight, and the Government made no attempt to stop them. They undertook their task of mobilizing the rank-and-file and pressurizing the trade union leadership to lead from the front with conspicuous zeal, efficiency and enthusiasm. (Robin Page Arnot's part in organizing the General Strike in the Northumberland and Durham coalfields is well known. Pollitt went to Durham after his release from prison in September and made a substantial contribution to keeping Durham miners solid at the end of the Lock-Out.)[17]

The TUC General Council ended the General Strike after ten days when it was evident that no further concessions from either Government or coal-owners would be forthcoming because it had never intended to challenge the established order. However, the MFGB leadership were unable to accept the General Council's judgement that the dispute was over with so little gained. They continued their dispute with the coal-owners in a lock-out which lasted from May until December 1926. The official MFGB retreat began only after the growing tide of miners returning in defiance of their union had swelled to include the previously solid Durham and South Wales miners.

Post Second World War accounts of the General Strike have often reflected the politically polarized tendencies in cold war historiography. To prove that a revolutionary situation existed in which the rank-and-file were keen to fight, examples are cited where the strike escalated into a challenge to law and order, notably the workers' defence corps in the Fife coalfield. In contrast, when the writer's aim is to emphasize the British spirit of fair play and the pacific intentions with which trade unionists approached the strike, the football matches between police and strikers are invoked. These analyses by anecdote have neglected the evidently conflicting meanings of the strike for those involved on both sides. The trade union officials and their members prosecuted the General Strike in good faith as a national industrial dispute, the logical next step in the tendency of pre-war collective bargaining to become both nationalized and politicized in scope, which had been powerfully reinforced by wartime developments. Employers and the whole of the political establishment (including most Labour politicians who took Westminster politics seriously) viewed the General Strike as an unwonted and unwarranted threat to the established order.

Macfarlane is the only post-war historian who has investigated the Communist Party's role in these events. He concluded that the infant Communist Party, despite its small numbers, had actually played an important role on the working class side. Its policy and its activists had significantly contributed to the momentum propelling the MFGB and the TUC towards the General Strike in May 1926, and also in ensuring that miners resisted the Lock-Out which lasted seven months until the broken MFGB leaders finally accepted that their forces were exhausted and demoralized. His evidence is convincing, and coincides with contemporary perceptions.[18]

When the General Council called off the strike on 11 May, the Communist Party confidently called on trade unionists to repudiate them and remain loyal to the miners. Nevertheless, there was a general, if confused, return to work over the following two days. At this decisive moment no breach opened between union members and union leaders into which Communists could step and push the rank-and-file towards independent action. Comintern expectations that Communists would utilize their factory and pit cells to intervene decisively proved wholly misplaced. The British Party Centre did not possess the numbers, the means or the will to operate democratic centralist discipline over a strategic range of workplaces. When the General Council ordered the return to work, there was no semblance of an alternative leadership in place inside factories, depots and railway sheds which could challenge its writ.[19]

By 15 May, it was clear that the General Strike had failed to produce a revolutionary situation. The working class had not immediately flocked to the bolshevik side in an accession of revolutionary consciousness acquired from their experience of bitter defeat. Despite this disappointment the British Communist leadership still expected the moment of revolutionary crisis to arrive, and merely adjusted the anticipated date of its appearance to some point during the miners' lock-out when the trade union 'rank-and-file' would rally to the miners' side. The Party and the Minority Movement called on miners to stand firm and escalate their fight. This adapted, partial demand coincided with the militant reflexes of left-wing union activists and the inflexible elements in the MFGB leadership who could conceive of no other strategy. They called on their faith in the power of a determined rank-and-file to produce portents that the union would ultimately triumph over the coal-owners. From this vantage point, to suggest an ordered, expeditious retreat as a pragmatic means of salvaging the unions' forces and maintaining morale amounted to treason against the union. Compromise became abject surrender.

The Party's impassioned support for militancy gained many recruits in all coalfields; but many of them disappeared after the miners had returned to work in demoralized disarray. Throughout Britain, Party membership and support for the National Minority Movement and its industrial sections steadily declined. The MFGB's approach of total war had yielded profoundly negative results, and as a result disillusioned miners also left the coalfield unions in enormous numbers. The long-established Durham Miners' Association with its stern tradition of unquestioning loyalty was the coalfield union which suffered least from this haemorrhage.[20] The Party Centre's sanguine perspective of revolutionary optimism seemed sadly misplaced.

*   *   *

In the aftermath of the General Strike, the General Council's sensibilities were awakened to the Party's 'sinister' influence. The reaction against the Communist Party from the trade union establishment gained momentum during the Lock-Out. Many full-time officials and lay activists decided that the Communist Party was responsible for all the the movement's misfortunes. Clegg noted:

> Few wanted to argue that the general strike should not have been called . . . However both sides [the General Council and the MFGB] agreed on the choice of a scapegoat. Cramp [of the National Union of Railwaymen] told the conference [of trade union executives] that he did not blame the General Council for calling off the strike but 'our people who for years made it impossible for the General Council to resist the general strike'. His audience knew whom he had in mind: the Minority Movement and the Communist Party. At the Railwaymen's conference in July 1926, Thomas had replied to attacks on his part in the strike by producing a Communist document instructing delegates how to vote on the resolution on the agenda. Similar instructions were exposed at Congress that year, and at the Miners' annual conference in 1927.[21]

It is hardly surprising that a scapegoat should be discovered, nor that the *diabolus ex machina* should be the Communist Party. Union leaders who were reflective and learned from experience recognized that they shared responsibility for events with Communist Party activists. The Party and the Minority Movement had merely been the extreme end of the spectrum to which all trade-unionists adhered. The assumptions and perspective of the new, militant trade-unionism were held in common. The 'machinations' of Party and Minority Movement members consisted of little more than their enthusiastic dissemination of the 'rank-and-filist' rhetoric current before the war and which continued to provide a reference point for all trade union activists into the 1920s.

In the immediate aftermath of the General Strike, the Party Centre had responded with surprising élan and continuing revolutionary optimism to the disappointing and unexpected turn of events.[22] As the Lock-Out stretched from weeks into months with bleak prospects of other unions moving to the miners' side, most Communist leaders and members reacted by moving leftwards. Their response was no different in substance to the thousands of miners who felt betrayed by the TUC and believed that a harder fight should have been waged and could have been won by the trade union side. Pollitt blamed the union leaders for the situation, and called on the working class to reject their 'reformism'. Horner and Hannington made similar denunciations. Campbell evidently never lost sight of the continuing institutional dominance of 'social democratic' bodies. His prescriptions for the movement's recovery veered away from confrontation with 'reformist' leadership because he doubted that such methods would produce the desired results.

Even without the pressure from the Comintern, the CPGB would have undergone a period of internal conflict while digesting the 1926 events. With hindsight, many Party activists, including Pollitt, J.T. Murphy and Palme Dutt, began to question the strategy of waiting for the 'reformist' trade union leadership to betray the strikers before challenging their role at the centre. They argued that it was the Party's partial demands and slogans which were at fault, and that the working class would have responded in kind if the Party had proclaimed more militant, even revolutionary, slogans from the outset.

About the same time, the conflict in the Soviet Party over how the USSR should build socialism took a deadly serious turn. What had been an apparently interminable ideological dispute suddenly became a series of duels inside the Politburo from which losers emerged bowed and broken. Campbell swiftly trimmed his own moderation to suit the new winds. The British Party leadership regrouped around the triumvirate of Dutt/Pollitt/Campbell, and then closed ranks to pre-empt more extreme left moves. They manœuvred the Party leftwards, taking care to keep more moderate options open. However, their surprisingly adept execution was disrupted by the intervention of circumstances beyond their control.

Inside the Soviet Party and the Comintern, an apparently unending round of bolshevik self-criticism finally produced a painful catharsis. A new phase in the worldwide proletarian revolution was proclaimed, and a new line was enunciated, Class Against Class, which decisively affirmed the urgent necessity for Communists to lead revolutionary struggle. Pardoxically, as the Soviet Party and the Comintern continued to lurch further leftwards, domestic events were driving the British Party leadership back towards the centre.

During 1928, the Party's new policy had not yielded the expected results of more members and a comparable leftwards turn in the working class. The continuing failure of the trade union movement in Britain to succumb to revolutionary assault and the Party's increasingly parlous state induced Pollitt, Hannington and Horner to question their previous leftwards turn. The Party was becoming increasingly isolated from what they viewed as its natural constituency, the activists inside the trade union movement. To pre-empt the possibility of becoming a sect on the sidelines, they took the Party more towards the centre again, particularly in regard to trade union work, and despite the rigours of the new Class Against Class line they were not seriously hindered by the Comintern.[23]

Their calculation that to make the revolution Party members had to remain inside trade unions compelled the other three back towards Campbell and 'moderation' to varying degrees. In the process, their convictions of the importance of trade unions deepened, despite pressure from the Comintern to move the other way. Their conviction that the Party had to be anchored firmly inside the trade union movement had been reflexive. They had imbibed trade union loyalism with their first experiences of work and economic conflict, along with every other working class activist of their generation. They were socialized into the article of faith developed by British trade union activists since the 1860s, that a 'good' trade union member was unflinchingly and unquestioningly loyal to the 'movement'.

After 1926 they had condemned the trade union leadership and railed against their treacherous 'reformism'. Consequently they had worked and organized in order to encourage the spirit of revolt in 'rank-and-file'. However, after deploying their best efforts, they recognized that there was no likelihood of achieving a mobilization of the 'rank-and-file' to cleanse and re-dedicate the trade union movement to its 'true' ends. It was clear that the principal effect of their activities was to further weaken and divide an already demoralized membership.

They each arrived at this potentially rebellious conclusion in different ways, having to work through their differing experiences and intellectual formations. Wally Hannington's revolutionary inclinations had been reinforced by the TUC leadership's 'reformism'. However, he found no contradiction between his muscular revolutionary principles and his equally strong certainty that the Party had to operate inside the 'trade union movement'. Arthur Horner, on the other hand, was moved by vicissitudes in South Wales to abandon the orthodox Marxism he had learned from Noah Ablett. He soon benefited from his enforced leisure as a political prisoner to read, reflect and evolve his own personal approach to the class struggle.[24]

Having countenanced this partial *volte-face* towards 'reformism' from the CPGB, the Comintern was then swept even further towards uncompromising bolshevism by developments in the USSR. There, the potent optimism of the faithful had been miraculously renewed. The revolutionary promises contained in Class Against Class were being apparently more than fulfilled by the socialist achievements of the first Five-year Plan. Inside the Comintern, veterans who had once counselled caution and pragmatism now indulged in pious self-flagellation and self-doubt. A strong head of steam built up behind the ideological offensive of revolutionary voluntarism. Only find the revolutionary will, and there would be a way forward.

Under pressure of this momentum, prevailing orthodoxy was pushed to new extremes. It was confidently asserted that not merely the leadership but the actual institutions of social democracy, including trade unions, could be successfully challenged by Communist Parties and decisively defeated. The clearing away of this 'social fascist detritus' would enable Communists to lead the proletariat into new revolutionary organizations with Independent Leadership. This shift in the ideological balance had a de-stabilizing effect throughout Europe, as inexperienced activists imbued with copious amounts of revolutionary will and great expectations were propelled into party leaderships through Comintern pressure and patronage.[25]

In Italy, this left opposition were actually called 'the youth' because they were for the most part activists in the FGCI (Italian Communist Youth Federation). I have called the British Young Communist League activists promoted by the Comintern, the 'Young Turks'. They were led by the YCL leader Bill Rust, enthusiastically assisted by Johnnie Mahon. Most Young Turks were YCL activists, like Ernie Woolley, Wally Tapsell and Peter Zinkin, and possessed no leavening of experience of 'the economic struggle' or trade unions. Nevertheless, they seized their moment to take power at the Party Centre with a brief to finally enforce Class Against Class in Britain.[26]

In the spring of 1929 the Comintern backed the 'Young Turks' who were adamant that the CPGB make an immediate break with the 'social fascist' trade unions. Rust, Mahon and Tapsell were swiftly promoted by Moscow's influence, and in turn supported older foundation members who agreed with them. They were consumed with excitement at the renewed worldwide revolutionary expectations. They were certain that revolution would follow in Britain when the Comintern line was rigorously applied. They exhorted Party members to lead mass revolts of workers against the capitalists and in the process of struggle to forge new, red trade unions. Thus equipped with Independent Leadership, the lethal weapon of class struggle, the working class would go on to make the revolution.

Not surprisingly, Pollitt, Campbell, Hannington and Horner reacted

strongly against the Young Turks/Comintern's injunctions to lead workers out of trade unions. They also experienced a strong emotional shock
at being attacked by bolshevik comrades-in-arms for an allegiance to
trade unionism, which it had never occurred to them to question. As a
result, Hannington and Horner temporarily withdrew from the fray at
King Street, personally revolted and profoundly angry at the Young
Turks' tactics and misplaced zeal. Pollitt and Campbell stayed at the
Party Centre to fight. Pollitt's commitment to revolution remained as
strong as Hannington's. He had been increasingly drawn towards
Campbell's prudent counsels by his own observation of the baleful
results of attempting to lead the 'rank-and-file' leftwards. Pollitt sought
Campbell's advice more and more frequently, and came to rely on his
more reasoned, intellectual defences to justify his own emotional trade
union loyalism.

The intensifying leftwards pressure from the Comintern forced Pollitt
and Campbell to yield some ground. However, they organized their
retreat in exceptionally good order.[27] As a result of their expeditious
trimming, they retained the Comintern's support, evidently in the expectation that the two would be able to make Class Against Class yield better results. Campbell remained on the Party Secretariat and was joined
there in May 1929 by Pollitt who became General Secretary with a brief
to make this office more politically effective.[28]

While the two loyally implemented the new line, they did so resolutely
according to their own fashion. Their presence at the Centre constituted
a significant political counterweight to the Young Turks and enabled
Party members who agreed with them to ignore Class Against Class and
continue to function as loyal trade union activists.[29] The pragmatic proletarian cohort functioning at one remove from the Party Centre, including AEU activists Joe Scott, Claude Berridge, Bob Lovell, Trevor
Robinson, Herbert Howarth and young South Walian miners around
Arthur Horner, loyally supported Pollitt and Campbell, to whose side
Gallacher, Hannington and Horner had also publicly adhered in the face
of the Young Turks' intensifying initiative for breakaway red unions.

The cohort remained loyal trade union activists despite the Young
Turks' injunctions. Their passive resistance to the Independent
Leadership exhortations from King Street substantially minimized the
damage done to the Party's position inside trade unions. They were as
determined as Pollitt and Campbell to resist the Party being marginalized
into a sectlet. Like them, they 'felt in their bones' that a breach between
the Party and the trade union movement would have disastrous results.

Hence the Young Turks were unable to find many Party members on
the ground inside trade unions who would discredit their 'social fascist'
union leaders and lead colleagues into new red ones, realizing the goal of

Independent Leadership. There were a mere handful of attempts to form red unions and only one survived, the United Mineworkers of Scotland (UMS). Even the UMS was the result of earlier 'rank-and-filist' divisions and other exceptional circumstances. Militant socialist miners in Scotland had formed a breakaway 'Reform Union' in 1923 as the embodiment of the 'rank-and-file' tradition which had been taken to Scotland by the Unofficial Reform Movement. Its main support had been in Fife, though there were members throughout the coalfield.

Communist Party and Minority Movement leaders, notably Pollitt, had spent a great deal of time and energy trying to effect a reconciliation between the 'Reform' and Scottish county unions. The General Strike and the Lock-Out finally provided the practical occasion for unity, achieved when the Reform Union merged into the Fife county union in March 1927. In circumstances of growing demoralization in the coalfield, the old conflict precipitated a fresh split and the UMS emerged in 1929. Not surprisingly, support for the UMS was soon mainly confined to Fife, even though the political support for Independent Leadership had been strongest amongst Lanarkshire Communist activists.[30]

In the spring of 1930, the Comintern began a tactical withdrawal from the extremes to which Class Against Class had been taken by many of its affiliated Communist Parties. The twin 'left sectarian' and 'right legalist' errors had become part of the Communist canon in the early days of the Comintern. During Class Against Class the 'right' error had been increasingly stressed, almost to the exclusion of the 'left'.[31] The recall of the 'left' error to take its place along with the 'right' was an attempt by the Comintern to prevent zealous Communists committing *hara kiri* in the more violent and unpredictable class battles proceeding elsewhere in Europe. It was a timely reappearance for Pollitt and Campbell. They used the British Party's dismal record of achievements under the Young Turks' ascendancy to attack their ideological bona fides.

The Comintern's early move away from the extreme interpretation of Class Against Class has been highlighted by recent research on the Comintern and Western European Communist Parties. As a result, historians of non-British Communist history have revised many of their inherited cold-war historiographic conventions. The veterans in the Kremlin who intoned *Mea culpa* at the appropriate moments also took care to leave themselves and the International Communist Movement expeditious means of retreat. It may indeed be more appropriate to describe the Third Period Line as a Curve or Bend which veered between the centre and extreme left according to varying circumstances. It is also clear that leaders of Western European Parties possessed and exercised considerable latitude both in arriving at domestic political policies and in manœuvring their Parties inside their particular national circumstances.[32]

In Britain, when the Young Turks signally failed to deliver either the destruction of the 'social fascist' unions or proletarian armies in new red unions, the Comintern was prepared to question their interpretation of Class Against Class. In August 1930 the 5th Congress of RILU passed a resolution which cited the intertwined double dangers of 'right legalism' *and* 'left sectarianism' in relation to the British Party and its conduct of the NMM.[33] The RILU *apparat* had been the Young Turks' keenest supporters in Moscow. Moreover, since Pollitt's translation to the Party Secretariat, the Young Turks had transformed the NMM into a citadel of revolutionary voluntarism and red unions. RILU's expeditious retreat and implied criticism of the NMM occurred just months after the Comintern had pulled back from the extreme limits of the Third Period. It was tangible evidence that Pollitt and Campbell had succeeded in retaking the initiative.

British historians have failed to revise their standard accounts to take account of recent research which shows the Comintern's flexible interpretation of its own line. Not only have they ignored evidence of the Comintern's pragmatism, they have also not considered the published accounts of the CPGB's own particular political trajectory. Macfarlane's findings of the CPGB's post-1926 leftwards reaction against 'reformism' and its early return towards pragmatism have been apparently disregarded. Martin's conclusions of the short predominance of Third Period orthodoxy in Britain are also avoided. Both works are routinely cited, but their detailed evidence has not been adequately sifted. The standard portrait still paints the CPGB leadership as bending the knee completely to the Comintern's diktat. The a priori supposition is that the CPGB's policy only moved to the extreme left in 1927–28 to follow the Comintern's enunciation of the Third Period and remained there until August 1935, when the 7th World Congress adopted the Popular Front.[34] Historians of industrial relations and trade unions accept Pelling's assumptions, whilst citing Macfarlane and Martin on specific points. Their evidence thus becomes the exception which proves Pelling's rule! For example, 'the Communists completed the rout of their own movement by following Moscow into a 'class against class' policy . . . The most experienced trade unionists in the party . . . were reluctant to apply the policy, but the Communist International saw that it was forced through a conference of the British party at the end of 1929. . .'[35]

The 18 months during which the Young Turks tried to apply Independent Leadership were short and remarkably unproductive. Compared with the rest of Europe, where activities aimed at splitting working-class institutions and escalating the class war found fertile ground in the intensifying social disintegration and disorder, there were few raw materials to hand in the relatively stable British society to assist

Communists' putative role of increasing the social flux from which the desired revolutionary situation could emerge.

With hindsight, many revisionist historians have argued that the policy of splitting trade unions and socialist political parties was misplaced wherever it was pursued, since no socialist revolution emerged from the breaches which Communists encouraged and helped to widen in the social and political fabric. At the time, it was far from clear that Independent Leadership would be counter-productive. In Britain, the Young Turks' crusades were few on the ground, and short-lived when they occurred, yielding meagre and often negative results. But many Communist Parties, including the French and the German, actually increased their influence and membership through vigorously fighting 'social fascist' socialist and union leaders.

The precipitate decline in CPGB membership had continued despite the Young Turks' insistence that red revolutionary unions would spring up and flourish if daily mass work concentrated on repudiating existing trade unions. Pollitt and Campbell argued that the Party's failures were due to the Young Turks being guilty of the 'left sectarian error', first declared a sin by Lenin. The initial attack was aimed at their most vulnerable point: Party members were isolated because they had followed the Young Turks' splitting injunctions in their daily mass work inside factories and pits.

Under the Young Turks, Party members had led few strikes of any sort, or even isolated skirmishes or militant incidents in the economic struggle. Pollitt and Campbell explained this failure by the Young Turks' having committed the 'left sectarian' error, thereby fatally isolating the Party from the working class. They asserted that the return to trade union activity would actually enable the Party to realize the goals of Class Against Class by effectively mobilizing the 'rank-and-file' inside the unions against their 'reformist' leaders.

Pollitt and Campbell stressed the importance of Communists performing daily mass work inside factories and pits without any preconceptions of where it might lead. If Party members happened to encounter workers who were trade union members and even activists, they should work alongside them within trade union institutions, and not endeavour to expose their 'reformist' essence immediately. It was only through participating in 'economic struggle' led by Communists that workers would take the revolutionary road. 'Life Itself' would present the opportunity for workers to learn the limitations of 'reformist' trade unions.

In Moscow the ideological gymnastics involved in the reinstatement of the 'left sectarian error' were performed deftly within the formal confines of Class Against Class. The British Party membership, who had been bombarded with the Young Turks' enthusiasm and fervour for red unions and Independent Leadership, did not fall in behind this manœuvre as easily as the theological specialists in the Comintern. They were puzzled by the reappearance of the old policies of the 1920s which they thought had been condemned.

During 1930–32, Pollitt and Campbell moved the boundaries of permissible daily mass work inside the unions beyond opportunist intervention and towards outright trade union loyalism. They moved cautiously, and took good care to cover their flanks. Nevertheless, the conflict within the British Party over trade union activity remained unresolved. The Young Turks and their allies on the ground also had ample ideological space within which to mount a counterattack. Moscow had only approved of Pollitt's and Campbell's course of working inside unions so that Party activists could undermine union leaders more effectively. The Communist canon still contained not only the 'left sectarian' but also the 'right legalist' error. The conflict between the Young Turks and Pollitt and Campbell over working inside trade unions was finally decided by empirical results, and the success or failure of their respective policies in gaining members and influence.

The Young Turks' last serious attempt to regain power at the Party Centre was their denunciation of Arthur Horner as being guilty not only of the 'right legalist' error, but also of consciously leading a new and serious deviation from the Comintern line, 'Hornerism'. At the beginning of 1931 Horner had used his considerable prestige and influence inside the Fed and the South Wales Party to prevent the Party proclaiming an unofficial continuation of the coalfield strike which the Fed Executive had settled from a position of weakness.[36] The Young Turks in London and their allies in South Wales, who included many Fed activists, attacked Horner for his failure to provide Independent Leadership at a crucial moment. They argued that he had thrown away an opportunity to finally break the Fed and defeat the employers with a united rank-and-file under Communist leadership.

The substance of Horner's actions differed little from the official rhetoric being assiduously disseminated by the Party Centre about trade union work. But Pollitt and Campbell fashioned their propaganda in a circumspect, even coded, style. Their behaviour was guarded and cautious in its handling of the trade union question. Horner's conduct, by contrast, was highly visible and the union loyalist thrust of his arguments against the unofficial strike intention unmistakable. He had clearly committed the 'right legalist' error by arguing and acting against other Party members' attempts to outflank Fed officials and install an Independent Leadership.

Horner compounded his 'guilt' by refusing to recant under pressure. He continued to justify his actions by stressing the importance of working inside official trade unions. This produced an escalation of hostilities. Had he nominally repented, Pollitt and Campbell might well have been able to retrieve the situation. In the face of Horner's intransigent conscience, the Young Turks pressed their attack home without mercy, resisting Pollitt's and Campbell's desire to preserve Party unity by muddying the ideological dispute at the edges and allowing high feelings in South Wales to subside.

After months in which the internecine warfare raged without issue, Horner agreed to undertake the trip to Moscow so that his case might be judged in the highest quarters. His removal from the scene finally allowed tempers to cool. The Comintern's deliberations were protracted. Pollitt and Campbell stood their ground in this interval, and continued to dispense their diplomatic tracts about daily mass work inside trade unions unchallenged by the Young Turks who were still unable to produce any positive results from their uncompromising revolutionary approach.

Nearly a year after he had allegedly caused the unofficial strike to miscarry, Horner returned from Moscow convicted of a venal error of judgement, a tactical mistake committed in good faith. He was found *not guilty* of the cardinal sin of transgressing against the Third International line. The Comintern pronounced that there was no Hornerist deviation. Horner briskly undertook the prescribed repentance, and publicly apologized for having made the wrong calculations. Having admitted his tactical mistake, he immediately resumed his previous concentration on mass work *inside* the Fed and encouraging other Party activists back into union work.

Apparently against all the odds, Horner emerged from his ideological trial unscathed, with his bona fides intact. By this time, the Comintern was preoccupied with combatting the 'left sectarian' error in European Communist Parties and had no interest in making an example of Horner. The Young Turks received the nominal pound of flesh due to them under the formal terms of Class Against Class, but the ECCI's Leninist *realpolitik* ensured that they were unable to extract any red blood along with it.[37] In the event, Pollitt and Campbell were able to use the incident to their advantage. They became expert in dispensing token formal rhetorical obeisance to Independent Leadership and then directing members' attention to the mundane practical issues of the economic struggle as loyal leaders of the trade union 'rank-and-file'.

Hard on the heels of Horner's rehabilitation, the Comintern appointed a Commission to investigate the reasons for the CPGB's continuing meagre results. Pollitt painted a bleak but accurate picture of the Party's diminishing influence. In December 1931 he told the Commission in Moscow that the Minority Movement (under the Young Turks' direction) had become 'boxed up in itself'. He then executed a brilliant tactical sleight-of-hand by pointing out that other 'independent organizations' existed alongside trade unions, within which Party members were actually working successfully to achieve the goals of Class Aginst Class. He cited the resurrected London Busmen's Rank-and-File Movement and the AEU Members' Rights Movement as examples.[38] He declared that these 'rank-and-file movements' were the embodiment of Independent Leadership, which could become the revolutionary trade union opposition.

The Comintern Commission's report faithfully reflected Pollitt's submission including his tactical trick. Rank-and-file movements were presented as authentic models of Independent Leadership for Party activists to emulate and multiply in order to fulfil the injunctions of Independent Leadership. The CPGB Central Committee endorsed its report in an Open Letter to Party members in January 1932. It was a faithful rendering of Pollitt's and Campbell's arguments. There was a frank admission that the Party had taken a wrong turning on the road to revolution and a determination to find the true path by avoiding the twin errors of left-sectarianism and right-legalism.

> The whole basis of this work within the reformist trade unions . . . must serve as a basis for drawing the most active workers in these [rank-and-file] movements into the ranks of the revolutionary trade union opposition.
> The best preparation for strike action is above all stubborn daily work to rally the workers in small partial actions in the factories and trade unions. . . . [39]

Pollitt's willingness to abandon the NMM showed great realism. As Hon. Secretary of the Minority Movement in its most exciting and influential days, he had been responsible for its success and identified both politically and personally with its fortunes. Nevertheless, he had no compunction in trying to extricate the Communist Party from its present wreckage. Since 1926, the NMM had experienced diminishing membership and union affiliations, and a conspicuous decline in activity. But the NMM was also the stronghold of the Young Turks' activity. The lack of participation by trade union activists assisted them in maintaining a façade of pristine revolutionary sloganizing. The Young Turks now clung to their earlier status and reputation as a revolutionary transmission belt to maintain the momentum of their drive for Independent Leadership.

In practice, it was the pragmatic proletarian cohort who had provided the leadership for the most vigorous Minority Movements. Like Pollitt, they had recognized that these movements had become discredited by the Young Turks' national activities and had already begun to wind them down. Horner had dissociated the Miners' Minority Movement (MMM) from the injunctions to fight official unions which came from the Young Turks at NMM headquarters. The Young Turks removed him from MMM work at the end of 1929. But his withdrawal only compounded its atrophy in the face of general demoralization among mining activists.[40] Though the Young Turks tried to revive the MMM in a wave of revolutionary optimism, it remained a hollow shell. There were few Party mining activists left who shared the sanguine hopes of militant upsurges and all-out conflicts.

The 'rank-and-file movements' which Pollitt had cited in Moscow all derived their inspiration from pre-war and wartime militant trade union culture. In the next chapter we will examine the direct and continuous links between the London Busmen's Rank and File Movement with this vigorous past. Pollitt's citation of the Members' Rights Movement was disingenuous in the extreme. Party activists had founded it not to lead members out of the AEU, but rather to campaign for expelled members' reinstatement into the union.

Throughout the Third Period, the Party engineering activists had remained notably immune from the Young Turks' intense pressure to promote Independent Leadership. Jack Tanner's continuing commitment to the engineering Minority Movement helped to stiffen the Party AEU activists' resistance to sectarian pressures. For example, in January 1928, the Metalworkers' MM produced a measured pamphlet, 'The AEU. A Review and Policy', arguing the case for making partial limited immediate demands buttressed with a strong rank-and-filist determination to fight.[41]

Nevertheless the Metalworkers' Minority Movement could not escape from being tarred with the NMM's increasing extremism, and there were local examples where enthusiastic revolutionaries had attacked the union in the Minority Movement's name, notably Coventry and Manchester. The AEU Executive invoked the NMM as a scapegoat for the General Strike and disillusioned left-wing activists proposed motions to outlaw it from the union in 1928 and 1929.[42] Leading AEU Party activists responded by cutting their losses and allowing the Metalworkers' MM to atrophy. Since their militant activities relied on informal national networks inherited from the ACM and wartime shop stewards' movement, they could well afford to lose the Metalworkers' MM.

In the summer of 1931 these informal national networks operated to oppose an agreement for substantial wage reductions which the AEU Executive concluded with the Engineering Employers' Federation (EEF). Virtually unanimous anger was felt by AEU activists over the deal, whatever their politics. The Executive had gone against well-established precedent by not holding a ballot of the membership to approve it.

Nevertheless, the possibility of organizing unofficial action was clearly never considered by the Party activists and their allies. Strong protests were recorded by AEU district committees and district membership meetings in London, Sheffield, Glasgow, Birmingham, Manchester and Newcastle.[43] Jack Tanner and five leading Party AEU activists issued a carefully worded statement in the *Daily Worker*, which omitted all mention of the Minority Movement and unofficial action.

> Particularly do we appeal to all those Trade Union branches and District Committees which have already passed resolutions to at once convene conferences of all workers in their areas, in order to organise the resistance of the rank and file.[44]

The AEU Executive concluded that their authority had been undermined and expelled all six signatories from the union. Jack Tanner swiftly negotiated his own separate reinstatement with the Executive, with the tacit agreement of Party activists, in order to safeguard his position as a newly elected full-time official, (Organizing Divisional Delegate) of the union.[45]

The other five expelled men won immediate sympathy from non-Party activists, who felt that the Executive had clearly overstepped the mark. The men's action had amounted to nothing more than making public their legitimate 'rank-and-file' concerns. The Members' Rights Movement was established in emulation of pre-war movements like the Amalgamation Committee Movement, which aimed to influence their union executives' policies. These pressure groups had cultivated a robust distrust of full-time officers and union executives in the name of the more directly democratic district committees and 'the rank-and-file'.[46]

Though they had felt unable (or been unwilling) to embark on concerted action against the Executive agreement, AEU activists were keen to stand up against the Executive to defend the 'liberty of the member' inside the union. The Members' Rights Movement quickly gathered strong support for the expelled men inside the union's official institutions. It was almost a foregone conclusion that the expelled men were all reinstated by the AEU Final Appeals Court in July 1932. They reversed the Executive's verdict that the men had injured the union or acted contrary to its interests. The men had acted ill-advisedly, but in good faith as AEU members, and their conduct had not been inconsistent with the duties of an AEU member.[47]

For all its obsession with doctrinal rectitude, the Comintern never lost its Leninist inheritance which emphasized results. When the Young Turks failed to deliver their pledges of imminent revolution, Pollitt and Campbell benefited from the winds of adaptation blowing through the Kremlin. Having regained the advantage, Pollitt and Campbell continued to push the extreme Class Against Class line further back to the periphery of policy making. At first they confined their attack to one point: the need for Party members to go back to daily mass work inside trade unions, and once inside them not to proceed by frontal attack on union officials. In the face of a rapidly declining Party membership and the non-appearance of revolutionary upsurges or even militant strikes, there was no adequate reply to their accusation that the Young Turks had failed.

Notes

1. Macfarlane, 1966, *The British Communist Party*; 73–7 and 81–4; and Klugmann, J., 1969, *History of the CPGB*, Vol. I, 1919–1924, Lawrence & Wishart, 212. Pollitt and Gallacher were elected on to the Party Executive in 1922. In June 1923, as a result of Comintern pressure, Horner and Hannington were brought on to the Politburo as part-time members and J.R. Campbell was made a substitute member (Macfarlane, op.cit. 83–4).

2. See Pollitt, H., 1940, *Serving My Time*, Lawrence & Wishart 17–35; Gallacher, W., 1942, *Revolt on the Clyde*, Lawrence & Wishart:18–49 and 77–114.

3. Horner, A., 1960, *Incorrigible Rebel*, Macgibbon & Kee: 14–34. Macfarlane describes the Rhondda Socialist Society as being an extension of the Miners Reform Movement. 'It seems to have had about fifty members and to have confined itself mainly to holding Sunday evening discussion meetings at the Miners' Club in Tonypandy. Its mouthpiece was *The Rhondda Socialist*, known locally as the 'Workers' Bomb'. The agents, who distributed the 'Bomb' were regarded as the local representatives of the Rhondda Socialist Society, and in some areas like Abertillery and Swansea, they were successful in establishing local 'branches', i.e. groups of supporters (Macfarlane: 83).

4. See Gallacher, op. cit.; Hannington,W., 1967, *Never on Our Knees*, Lawrence & Wishart: 34–6 and 63–5.

5. For Tommy Jackson, see Ree,J., 1984, *Proletarian Philosophers*, Clarendon Press. J.T. Murphy and Tom Bell were both self-taught Marxists who were active in the wartime shop stewards movement.

6. See pp. 133–4 and p. 42. For the South Wales Unofficial Reform Movement, see Macfarlane: 45.

7. 'Theses and Tactics Adopted by the Fifth Comintern Congress', July 1924, *The Communist International*, Vol. II, 1923–28 (Ed.) Jane Degras, 1960, Oxford: 149. See also 'Theses on Bourgeois Democracy and Proletarian Dictatorship' adopted by the first Comintern Congress, March 1919, in *The Communist International*, 1956, Vol. I, 1919–22: 16.

8. 'Communist Industrial Policy: New Tasks for New Times', CPGB, 1923.

9. Lenin addressed ' "Left-Wing" Communism – An Infantile Disorder' to the sectarian elements in the British and Dutch Communist Parties in 1919–20. Selected Works, Vol. III, 1971, Progress Publishers, Moscow: 370–95. Lenin read this lesson in person to the impressionable Willie Gallacher at the Second Congress of the Comintern in 1920, making an indelible impression. Gallacher's subsequent determination to gain a seat in Parliament to fulfil Lenin's injunction was finally realised in November 1935.

10. Bullock, A., 1960, *The Life and Times of Ernest Bevin*, Vol. I, 1881–1940, Heinemann: 255–7.

11. Macfarlane, 1966: 119–21. For the Lock-Out see Hugh Clegg, 1985, *A History of British Trade Unions since 1889*, Vol. II 1911–1933, Oxford: 336–45.

12. Macfarlane, 1966: 121. Communist engineers in Coventry were so determined to transform the Lock-Out into a full-blown revolutionary struggle that they became isolated from other union members.

13. Horner,1960, *Incorrigible Rebel*: 43–4 and Macfarlane, 1966: 131. Arthur Cook had been, like Horner, a protege of Noah Ablett and the Unofficial Reform Committee. He was in the Party for a while, and then drifted out. This episode made no difference to his cordial relationship with South Walian Communists. Macfarlane observes that it is doubtful whether South Wales 'contributed more than a few dozen members to the Communist Party on its foundation. The importance of South Wales to the Communist Party lay in the fact that for thousands of miners the Communist Party was the natural heir to the tradition of militant rank-and-file struggle against the coal owners, weak Federation leadership and capitalism.' (Macfarlane, op.cit. 46).

14. Davis, P., 1977, 'Syndicalism and the Yorkshire Miners, 1910–1914', MSc, University of Leeds: 147. For Herbert Smith see Jack Lawson's biography, 1941, *Man in the Cap*, London.

15. Clegg, 1985, op. cit.: 387–92.

16. A succinct account of the Communist Party's political positions on the General Strike appears in Bell, T., 1937, *The British Communist Party*, Lawrence & Wishart: 108–16; James Klugmann's second volume (1969) is devoted to a hagiography of the strike and the Party's heroism (*History of the CPGB*, Vol. II, 1925–6, Lawrence & Wishart: 91–200). Branson deals with the post General Strike post-mortem (Branson, N., 1985, *History of the Communist Party of Britain, 1927–1941*, Lawrence & Wishart: 18–27.

17. Mason, A., 1967, 'The Miners' Unions of Northumberland and Durham, 1918–31, with special reference to the General Strike of 1926', University of Hull PhD: 217 and 288, and Klugmann, 1969: 162–3.

18. Macfarlane, 1966, 171–2. For an accurate analysis of the General Strike and Lock-Out, see Clegg, 1985, ch. 10: 383–426.

19. Reports of the Party's failure to build factory cells are found in Roebuck C. M. (Andrew Rothstein), 'Open Letter to a Party Comrade on Factory Groups'; *Communist Review*, June 1924 and 'Communist Work in the Factories. The Work of a Factory Group', CPGB pamphlet, September 1925.

20. For the increase in Party membership see Appendix 1. The most spectacular increase was in Northumberland and Durham. Before the General Strike, the Party district had been the smallest; afterwards it became the largest with 1900 members. Membership in South Wales doubled. For the decline in coalfield union membership see Appendix 2.

21. Clegg, 1985, 419–20.

22. See 'Communism is Commonsense, A Statement of Aims and Policy', July 1926, CPGB pamphlet, particularly pp.15–16.

23. Martin, 1969, *Communism and the British Trade Unions 1924–33*: 110–117.

24. See Macfarlane, 1966: 235 and 238.

25. See Urban, 1986, *Moscow and the Italian Communist Party*, op. cit.: 38. See also: 28, 37, 39–41, 43, 50–1.

26. Johnnie Mahon was the son of John Lincoln Mahon, a socialist ASE/ACM activist. Young Turks who had taken part in political and economic struggle included R.W. Robson, London District Secretary, George Renshaw, a London activist in the shopworkers' union USDAW, Willie Allan, a Lanarkshire miner and George Allison, a Fife miner, who had all worked at NMM Headquarters in London.

27. Macfarlane, 1966: 218–9 and ch. X: 221–42; and Martin, 1969, op.cit., 115–21 and 150–6.

28. See Branson, 1985, op. cit.: 43–4. Mahon reports that the CPGB Executive Committee formally appointed Pollitt General Secretary in August 1929. (Pollitt, 1940, op. cit.: 160–1.) Kevin Morgan concurs with Mahon in that Pollitt formally assumed his position in August, though he does not elucidate the reason for this late date. He states that Pollitt's appointment was 'the fulfilment of Pollitt's most cherished ambition', and that he and Dutt had anticipated his assumption of this office from the bolshevization period in 1923. (Morgan, K., 1993, *Harry Pollitt*, Manchester University Press, 1993, 59).

29. Ibid.: 67.

30. There is no adequate published account of its interesting but complicated history. Interested readers should consult Chapter 7, 'Party Coalmining Strongholds: South Wales and Scotland' in Fishman, N., 1991, 'The British Communist Party and the Trade Unions, 1933–45: the Dilemmas of Revolutionary Pragmatism', University of London PhD, January, (hereafter N. Fishman, PhD).

31. The first evidence that the link between the two errors had been reinstated was their linked inclusion in the analysis of the failings of the international Communist Movement accepted by the 16th Congress of the Russian Communist Party in June 1930. Carr, E.H., 1982, *The Twilight of the Comintern 1930–1935*, Macmillan: 18–23.

32. Ibid., Parts 1 and 2 deal with the highly elastic nature of the Third Period and the transition to the united front made before the 7th World Congress. An important examination of the PCI in this period is made by Urban, 1986, *Moscow and the Italian Communist Party*: 39–79 and 87–120. For the PCF see Adereth, M., 1984, *The French Communist Party a critical history (1920–1984)*, Manchester University Press: 35–80.

33. See Martin, 1969, op. cit.: 153–4, and 115 and 150–6.

34. The standard non-Party account of the CPGB remains Pelling, H., 1958, *The British Communist Party*, op. cit. Its assumption of Third Period rigidity inside the CPGB can be observed on pages 84, 86–7 and 105. It was republished in 1975 with a summary of recent developments in the CPGB, but took no account of Macfarlane's and Martin's evidence. Kevin Morgan chronicles the early leftwards turn of Pollitt, but he explains it merely as an early example of Class Against Class and omits all reference to British events in influencing Pollitt, 1993 (op.cit., pp.62–4.)

35. Clegg, 1985, op.cit.: 452–5 and 536–7. Another example is Chris Wrigley, 'The Trade Unions Between the Wars', Wrigley, C.J., ed., 1987, *A History of British Industrial Relations*, Vol. II, 1914–39, Harvester, p. 103 and p.120. Wrigley confines his observations to the CPGB's 'deviation' from Class Against Class to the opposition to independent trade unions.

36. For these events, see Francis, 1980, *The Fed.*, op. cit.: 175–9.

37.   Branson's account of Hornerism can be found in Branson, 1985, op. cit.: 85–8. Whilst accurate, it fails to capture the ebb and flow of the inter-Party and inter-personal conflict. For this dimension, see the *Daily Worker*, 17 January; 21,23,25,28 February; 3,5,7,10 March 1931.

38.   Branson, 1985, op.cit.: 88–9. The phrase 'boxed up in itself' reappeared in the Open Letter from the CPGB Central Committee, issued after the Comintern Commission had reported. It was repeated in the Secretariat's statement in the *Daily Worker* of 19 January 1932. In July 1931, Pollitt had told the Eleventh Plenum of the Comintern that there were only 32 factory cells with 843 members in the whole of the Party. He explained that part of the problem was that 53 per cent of all Party members were unemployed. (*Inprecorr*, Vol. 11, No. 36, 6 July 1931: 672). It is likely that much of this unemployment was due to victimization through trying to wage the economic struggle in a revolutionary manner.

39.   Open Letter quoted in 'The Road to Victory', Report of 12th Congress of the CPGB: 9–10.

40.   For Horner and the Miners' Minority Movement, see Martin, 1969, op.cit.: 120–1. Martin recites an interesting anecdote from George Renshaw: 'Hannington made his sympathy for Horner clear in the Party discussion over Horner's expulsion': 49.

41.   See also AEU National Committee Reports, 1928 and 1929. For a detailed discussion of Party AEU activists and evidence of their continuing union loyalism, see Fishman, N., 'The British Communist Party and the Trade Unions, 1933–45', unpublished typescript, University of Warwick Modern Records Centre (MRC) (hereafter N. Fishman, MRC) Chapter 3, 'Engineering and the CP': 218–237.

42.   For the vicissitudes of the Minority Movement inside the AEU, see Martin, 1969, op.cit.,: 62, 86–7 and 134. He makes the mistaken assumption that the Metalworkers MM behaved like its transport and mining counterparts between 1926 and 1928: 127.

43.   For the agreement see Jefferys, J., 1946, *The Story of the Engineers*, Lawrence & Wishart: 240–1. For the Party activists' campaign see the *Daily Worker*, 23, 24, 26 June 1931; 1, 3, 4 July 1931 and Frow, E. and Frow, R., 1982, *Engineering Struggles*, Manchester: 91–3.

44.   The *Daily Worker* 20 June 1931. The Party signatories were Joe Scott and Percy Glading, both members of the AEU London District Committee; Tommy Sillars, a member of the AEU Glasgow District Committee; Billy Stokes, who had been a Coventry District Committeeman until local sectarian Metalworkers' Minority Movement activity had isolated him, and Steve Nuttall, a Manchester district committeeman. (Claude Berridge was almost certainly in Moscow attending the Lenin School at this time. Wally Hannington and Bob Lovell had temporarily suspended union activity in order to devote themselves full time to other party work.)

45.   There were also 11 AEU members expelled in Manchester for signing a local Metalworkers' Minority Movement statement calling for a Manchester AEU conference and the formation of a Council of Action. See Frow and Frow, 1982, op. cit.: 91–3.

46.   The Amalgamation Committee Movement awaits a complete scholarly examination. However, Burdick, E., 1950, 'Syndicalism and Industrial Unionism in Engineering until 1918', M.Phil, Magdalen College, Oxford, is an interesting preliminary examination. Weekes, B.M., 1970, 'The ASE,

1880–1914' University of Warwick PhD, is also useful. For militants' congenital distrust of the ASE Executive, See Zeitlin, J., 1981, 'The Labour Strategies of British Engineering Employers, 1890–1914', Paper for SSRC Conference on Business and Labour History, LSE, 23 March 1981: 8–13 and 32–4. Zeitlin makes the important point that inside the ASE, district committees' opposition to Executive 'arbitrariness' was deployed in defence of craft regulation.

47. N. Fishman, MRC, loc. cit.: 233.

CHAPTER THREE

The British Road to the United Front

Having gained the Comintern imprimatur, Pollitt and Campbell worked to revive Party members' morale and self-confidence through propagating their new approach to the 'economic struggle'. Despite strong support from Moscow, they faced a formidable task. They had to convince doubters and sceptics to redirect their activity away from the Minority Movement back into trade union work. They needed to show that trade union work was *not* a retreat to the old line of the early 1920s, which had culminated in the failure of revolution to appear in the wake of the General Strike, but actually the only true way to fulfil the *new* line of Class Against Class. They also had to inspire demoralized Party activists to re-enter the 'economic struggle' and undertake daily mass work in the factories and pits. As a result of the unbroken string of almost unmitigated defeats and set-backs, many activists had lost heart and dropped out altogether.

The Comintern Commission had remained diplomatically silent about the future role of the Minority Movement. They acted with impressive diplomacy and tactical dexterity in relation to this contentious issue. Precisely because the NMM was the Young Turks' stronghold, Pollitt and Campbell chose not to attack it frontally and expose the Party to a full-scale political battle which might tire out and demoralize the membership even further. Instead, they bided their time and moved against the Minority Movement when favourable opportunities presented themselves.

Meanwhile the pragmatic proletarian cohort had already withdrawn from Minority Movement activity and were taking fresh initiatives to minimize the damage inflicted by the Young Turks' anti trade union propaganda. Pollitt and Campbell and their supporters were certain that a return to trade union activity was the only way to make the revolution in Britain. They made the restoration of the Party's fortunes inside union institutions their main priority.

Many Party activists had been sacked or removed from lay positions of influence in the aftermath of the General Strike. Others had reacted to the events of 1926 with implacable hostility towards all union leaders. They rejected the notion that revolution could develop out of existing union institutions and welcomed their own unemployment brought about either through victimization or the 1929–31 slump. They were convinced that unemployed agitation offered far greater revolutionary potential than trade union or shopfloor mass work. These former 'rank-and-file' militants lacked motivation for resuming trade union work and turned their attention to organizing the National Unemployed Workers Union with the aim of instilling revolutionary consciousness amongst its 'rank-and-file'.[1]

Pollitt and Campbell were fighting for their places as putative leaders of the emancipated British proletariat, and they responded creatively. They mounted a high-profile campaign to induce members to make a fresh start. Most Party members were relieved perhaps to be guided back into 'daily mass work' which aimed for tangible and feasible results, rather than the creation of revolutionary trade unions. They were probably also soothed by the copious amounts of Life Itself which Pollitt and Campbell applied to rebuild faith in the revolution to come.

A new monthly periodical, *Party Organiser*, was launched as an outlet for their enthusiastic outpourings: the *Daily Worker* under Bill Rust's editorship could not be relied upon to support them. *Party Organiser*'s pages magnified the small incidents of economic conflict which activists were again precipitating as the economic slump abated. They were cited as proof that their approach was effective: given the correct 'rank-and-file' leadership, workers in trade unions were striking:

> It is unfortunately a fact that so many of our members have had close contact with the workers, but after joining the Communist party they begin to use a jargon that is foreign to the everyday language and understanding of the masses they have to move amongst.[2]

> There has been a strong tendency to believe that the new [Third Period] line . . . meant there was no further need to work inside the trade unions. This is the exact opposite as the successful carrying through of the new line demands increased activity inside the trade unions and factories.[3]

> This sectarianism is not a new thing with the revolutionary movement . . .
> It is much easier to cry 'Traitor' or shout 'Let's form a Red Union' than it is to fight persistently and grimly inside the trade union branches in order to win the masses inside them for the policy of class struggle and unity as against the policy of class collaboration and Mondism of the reformist leaders . . .
> The whole national apparatus of the trade unions cannot be won by us, but the lower organs of the trade unions – the branches and the District Committees – can be won for the policy of class struggle and fight if we make a determined effort to do this on the basis of the concrete issues that arise both in the factories and inside the trade unions themselves.[4]

In South Wales, Party members continued to ask the obvious question: if working inside trade unions had been rejected in 1929 as being incompatible with Independent Leadership, what had changed in 1932? They could not forget that the features of Pollitt's and Campbell's fresh start mirrored the tactical error of which Arthur Horner had recently recanted. The Party Centre responded with good-quality flannel. The disgruntled revolutionaries in South Wales kept their own counsels. They acquiesced in the drift back into union-based activity when it achieved results, but continued to argue the case for more rigorous prosecution of Independent Leadership.[5]

By June 1932 Pollitt and Campbell felt confident enough to counsel members to contest union elections:

> The old line in the unions was for the purpose of winning the union apparatus in order to make the leaders fight. What is the line in new conditions of independent struggle? To win every position we possibly can in the union branches, every contact we can, and to take into the union branches not merely ourselves, but masses of workers that we have influenced, in order that these union branches can become powerful allies in the independent struggle of the working class, in the conduct of the fight . . .
>
> We are not merely to go into the branches on our own so that it becomes a dog fight, but must take every worker who wants to fight against the line of the bureaucracy and for struggle.[6]

Nevertheless, Pollitt and Campbell took care not to flout the anti-union position of Class Against Class. In January 1932 Party activists' daily mass work at the main Lucas factory in Birmingham bore fruit when a revolt occurred among the unorganized women workers. The women reacted determinedly against the introduction of the Bedaux bonus system, an American form of payment by results which had become fashionable with modernizing British factory managers, particularly for semi-skilled work. The Birmingham Party activists were Young Turks and recruited the women directly into the Minority Movement. The Party Centre directed them to organize an independent rank-and-file factory committee. Pollitt and Campbell did not care to risk being accused of the 'right legalist' error by urging that Communists should actually recruit unorganized workers into 'reformist' trade unions. The Birmingham comrades reluctantly stopped Minority Movement recruitment, but the rank-and-file factory committee proved short lived. Management speedily conceded the withdrawal of Bedaux and the spirit of revolt was dissipated. Having regained their nerve, management sacked the Party activists, notably Lily Ferguson, and the rank-and-file factory committee disappeared without trace.[7]

Later in the year, Pollitt and Campbell exploited a more favourable opportunity to attack Minority Movement sectarianism. Since 1929 the Transport Minority Movement (TMM) in London had waged unrelenting 'class war' against non-Party left-wingers on the London buses who were grouped in a Rank-and-File Committee, for their continuing support of the 'social fascist' TGWU.[8] Pollitt and Campbell strongly backed the Rank-and-File Committee in its victorious campaign against an agreement which Bevin had concluded with the London General Omnibus Company (LGOC).

The serious business of stopping a 'sell-out' by the union was left to the Rank and File Committee. Its most charismatic leader, Bert Papworth, Secretary of the Chelverton Road garage branch, wrote to all London bus lay officials in August 1932, convening a meeting to discuss the unacceptable compromise which Bevin had negotiated. Other leaders included veterans of the United Vehicle Workers (UVW) like Bill Payne from Dalston Garage, Frank Snelling, a strong SPGB Marxist from Merton garage, and Bill Jones, an ILP member from Dalston.[9] At this point Pollitt and Campbell lent the full weight of their public support to the Rank and File. The *Daily Worker* published Papworth's letter in full, and exhorted:

> This meeting of rank and file busmen can roll back the employers' attack by giving the lead for the development of a united front of the Tram, Omnibus, Tube workers. A series of mass meetings can be quickly organised in various districts, organising and preparing the rank and file ... A *united fighting front* of the London passenger transport workers will smash the cuts as will nothing else.[10]

London bus activists had first formed a rank and file committee in 1919 to oppose the establishment of a Whitley Council by their newly merged union, the UVW. The Committee attacked the officials for being a 'professional leadership' even after they had withdrawn support for 'Whitleyism'. Its vigorous 'rank-and-filism' reflected the direct participation in union affairs practised by the UVW's predecessor in London, the 'Red Button Union'. (A strike sparked off by the suspension of 12 conductors for wearing the union's red badge was the origin of its diminutive.)[11]

Activists in the Red Button Union were caught up in the wave of enthusiasm for revolutionary syndicalism after 1915, along with their union colleagues in London engineering and aircraft. A busmen's Vigilance Committee was formed and union officials enthusiastically co-operated with it. A syndicalist busman, George Sanders edited the union's journal, *The Record*, from 1915. After the war he published articles by Party members about the Soviet Union and the Communist Party. Sanders became a member of the London Executive of the Red International of Labour Unions (RILU) and helped to organize a London Conference of RILU's new British Bureau at which 15 UVW branches were represented. He was elected Busmen's Organizing Secretary of the UVW.[12]

Given the strength of rank-and-filism, it is not surprising that when Bevin proposed to amalgamate the UVW into the TGWU in 1921, three of the most militant London bus garages refused to forward their members' subscriptions to the new union. Two of them had previously announced their intention of leading a breakaway union. Bevin met London bus delegates at the Anderton Hotel and guaranteed a virtual return to their previous autonomy inside the Red Button Union in return for their support.[13]

Under the Anderton Hotel Agreement, the Red Button council of busmen's lay delegates was revived as the Central Bus Committee (CBC). All other parts of the TGWU were strictly subordinated to the General Executive Council (GEC) through two equally elaborate parallel structures: the trade groups and the region, to which power was devolved. (Bevin evidently designed the TGWU to maintain distances between its constituent parts and the centre.) The CBC was now given the unique right of direct access to the GEC without having to seek approval through either regional or trade-group channels to obtain a hearing. This fast track ensured that the GEC considered London bus disputes without delay, which facilitated the maintenance of the conflict's momentum and increased the probability of escalation by lay officials.[14]

The CBC duly presided over a rash of unofficial strikes[15] which were evidently operated satisfactorily for the militants. When an apolitical breakaway union was formed in 1929, the wartime Rank and File Committee was revived to fight it. The renegade organization was soon quelled by a *de facto* alliance of the Rank and File Committee, CBC, Bevin and the connivance of the LGOC. (The LGOC had acquiesced in a *de facto* closed shop in 1927.)[16] The Rank and File leaders followed up their success by maintaining their organization to fight for a Seven Hour Day, more wages in return for speed-up and protection against rationalization.

The Committee made a determined bid for unity by seeking the support of Communist busmen for its campaign, despite the TMM's unsavoury record of attacking the Committee for its alleged lack of militancy, in trying to start a Red Union in 1927 and then approaching the 1929 breakaway with offers of assistance which were refused presumably because of the TMM activists' strident political approach and opaque jargon.[17] Evidence of the Committee's good faith had been provided when TMM busmen led an unofficial strike at Cricklewood at Easter. Sympathy strikes had swiftly followed at Battersea, Willesden, Putney, Chelverton Road and Middle Row garages. The TMM was influential at Willesden and Battersea; Putney and Chelverton Road were Rank and File strongholds.[18]

The Rank and File Committee's campaign petered out. Communist busmen evidently remained hostile, and the TMM remained resolutely red revolutionary. Though the Committee hibernated, the loose network of militants across London bus garages remained, and the Committee was revived quickly enough at the end of 1931 when the LGOC gave the required three months notice to terminate the existing wages agreement, and stated that 300 busmen would be sacked because of the serious decline in passenger traffic. Party busmen, probably including Bernard Sharkey and Bill Ware, tried to organize a 'united front from below' to oppose the cuts based on the TGWU workplace garage branches. They were opposed by the Party activists in the TMM who argued that rank-and-file committees must be 'independent' and actively hostile to the TGWU.[19]

After this Party initiative failed, we have seen that Pollitt and Campbell lent all their weight to Papworth's moves to resuscitate the Rank and File Committee. The meeting Papworth convened of garage delegates in August 1932 was attended by 21 bus delegates. It condemned Bevin and the CBC for negotiating a compromise and then concealing it from the busmen's delegate conference. A Provisional Committee was formed to fight the settlement, with Bert Papworth, Bill Payne and Frank Snelling, along with Bill Ware and Bernard Sharkey. Armed with this example of the 'united front from below', Pollitt and Campbell applied further pressure on the remaining TMM activists.[20] The ballot organized by the CBC produced a 4–1 majority against Bevin's deal. The *Daily Worker*'s report of the result concluded: 'All busmen must insist that their branch is represented on this rank and file committee.'[21]

Faced with this overwhelming rejection, the TGWU Executive was forced to reconvene the London busmen's delegate conference. The *Daily Worker* and the London District Party both lined up behind the rank-and-file fight against Bevin. A Party busmen's paper, *Busman's Punch*, was converted from being a potential rival to the Rank and File leaders' paper, *The Bus Wheel*, into a vehicle for supporting the Provisional Committee's campaign.[22] The *Daily Worker* greeted the Provisional Committee's activities with the headline: 'Rank and File Movement Grows', and made no further references to the TMM.[23]

The reconvened delegate conference duly rejected the settlement by a vote of 51–7 and endorsed strike action. This victory was followed by a new issue of *Busman's Punch* and a pamphlet, *The Busmen's Case*, written by Emile Burns at the Labour Research Department. By the third week in September 30,000 copies had been sold by London District Communists and busmen and the *Daily Worker* was enjoining Party members to redouble their efforts.[24] Bevin had clearly miscalculated the strong response which the Provisional Committee were able to organize in garages where they were lay officials against the actions of their higher officials, including the CBC. Under such overwhelming pressure he promptly gave ground and returned to the negotiating table. The LGOC conceded that there would be no wage cuts and no enforced redundancies. In return, Bevin agreed a speeding-up of bus schedules and the reduction of the guaranteed week for 'spares' from 40 to 32 hours for eight months.[25]

The Provisional Committee remained true to its cultural roots and opposed the revised deal. Nevertheless its terms were so much improved that the delegate conference accepted by 33–25. After delegates had been officially mandated by branch meetings, there was an increased majority for the agreement, 39–21.[26] The Provisional Committee accepted the conference's verdict, but took steps to make its own existence permanent. The London Busmen's Rank and File Movement was established at a conference on 5 October 1932 with enthusiastic support from the Party Centre. Its structure ran parallel to the garage union branches in emulation of its rank-and-file predecessors, the wartime Vigilance Committee, the Rank and File Committee and the recent Provisional Committee. Garage branches formally affiliated and sent six representatives to the Rank and File Movement Organizing Committee, a number which enabled every shift and the inside staff to be directly represented. The *Daily Worker* reported:

> The rank and file movement is not a new union, nor does it stand for any breakaway from the TGWU. On the contrary the rank and file movement aims to strengthen the branches and to make it possible for them to become the medium through which the feelings and desires of the men can be expressed and given effect to.[27]

The formation of the Busmen's Rank and File Movement in October 1932 was the culmination of a most successful year for Pollitt's and Campbell's new approach. We have seen that the AEU Final Appeals Court had reinstated the expelled Party engineering activists in July. Events apparently vindicated Pollitt's declaration to the Comintern Commission in December 1931 that Party activists could successfully operate rank-and-file movements in tandem with trade union organization. Moreover, these activities were producing positive results for the Party itself. Branson records that 'By the end of 1932, Communist Party membership in the [London bus] fleet had risen from 12 to 40'.[28]

Despite these advances, however, the conflict between Pollitt and Campbell and the Young Turks over the correct interpretation of Class Against Class had continued. The 12th Party Congress was scheduled for November. Throughout the autumn, a conflict raged in the *Daily Worker* over the Party's attitude to trade unions. For the first time, Palme Dutt entered the lists and he supported Johnny Mahon against Pollitt.

The conflict was promoted by Bill Rust in the *Daily Worker* in the wide-ranging pre-Congress discussion. Dutt attacked with his usual formidable rigour and finesse, while Pollitt and Campbell stood their ground, assisted by Willie Gallacher and Jimmy Shields.[29]

The fact remained that Pollitt's and Campbell's reliance on the organized working class to make the revolution was certainly questionable from a Leninist perspective. In 1932, most British workers did not belong to trade unions. Pollitt's and Campbell's insistence that Party activity should be channelled inside trade unions assumed that the majority, the unorganized working class, could not be attracted to new revolutionary trade unions, and that the 'reformist' organized working class constituted the only potential fighting force. In a period when the Comintern had decreed the time was ripe for revolution, Pollitt and Campbell remained highly vulnerable to attack at the ideological level, even though they had empirical results on their side.[30]

In the event, Pollitt and Campbell scored an easy victory at the Party Congress. They surrendered a small amount of ideological ground to the Young Turks without the slightest intention of allowing them to roll back the practical advances made by Party activists on the ground. Pollitt cheerfully applied ideological balm to Dutt's and the Young Turks' wounded egos without the slightest intention of altering his approach to the 'economic struggle' in future.[31]

The Congress resolution on the 'economic struggle' confirmed the Central Committee's position in the Open Letter of January 1932, repeating the injunction against the twin errors of right-wing legalism and left-wing sectarianism. The embodiment of Independent Leadership was officially declared to be rank-and-file movements which were invested with the impressive sounding title, the Revolutionary Trade Union Opposition, imported from the German Communist Party (KPD).[32] At the Congress, discussion on the 'economic struggle' was dominated by Pollitt. He emphasized the 'left error': members had failed to work inside trade unions, and they had not concentrated on daily mass work in the factories and pits.

> There is not a Party member in this country who, if he works in the correct way, cannot become a shop steward officially endorsed by his trade union branch . . . We are working inside the unions as the logical, vital, integral part of our mass work in the factories and the object is the winning of the trade unionists and lower organs for the line of independent leadership and struggle.[33]

Pollitt assigned Party members two new tasks. First, he urged members to go out and build the Revolutionary Trade Union Opposition by multiplying rank-and-file movements alongside and in parallel to trade unions. The Minority Movement remained conspicuously absent from his prescriptions for the rosy future. He looked forward to:

> In six months from now of mobilising the resources of our Party for a series of well-prepared district conferences, initiating unofficial movements of this broad character [the London Busmen's Rank and File Movement], and at the end of this six months, the perspective of a National Conference at which, as a result of our revolutionary work inside the broad movements in which we have already gained the conviction and adherence of the masses, that they shall be unified under such a name as the Trade Union militant league, which would be for Britain the Revolutionary Trade Union Opposition.[34]

Second, there was

> the question and urgency of the development on the broadest possible scale of the fighting united front of the working class [and] throughout this work as the red stream, the ceaseless and persistent recruiting into the ranks of the Party of all the workers we are able to establish contact with and win for revolutionary struggle.[35]

Building the united front from below had been official Comintern policy since 1924. Like the right legalist error, it had been prudently retained throughout the Third Period, and even confirmed by the Ninth Plenum on the Trade Union Question in February 1928 to justify working in 'reformist' unions alongside lower union officials. The 'fighting united front' was a new permutation on this theme.

Pollitt and Campbell were magnanimous in victory, their overriding concern being to preserve a sense of unity and loyalty to Congress decisions. They refrained from inflicting serious loss of face on the Young Turks, and took care to conceal the substantial kink which they had successfully bent into the the the Comintern's line. At the time, the only people who noticed the CPGB's great 'deviation' were the 'Balham Group', ex-Party members and assorted revolutionaries who had become interested in Trotsky's writings and made contact with Trotskyist organizations abroad. They stood outside Battersea Baths, where the 12th Congress was meeting, and gave leaflets out to rally delegates against the descent into reformism which they had observed taking place over the past year.[36]

Dutt and the Young Turks were apparently eager to dissociate themselves from the 'Trotskyist' menace. Their desire to prove their loyalty may have influenced their decision to remain silent despite the dominance of Pollitt's and Campbell's trimming inside the hall. Nevertheless, Dutt knew well enough that he had been pushed back. After the 12th Congress he withdrew from routine participation in the direction of Party policy towards unions and the 'economic struggle'. It was invariably Johnny Campbell who provided the bread-and-butter explanations of what was going on in the British class war and why.

As the New Year approached, Pollitt and Campbell had every reason for self-congratulation. They had brought the British Party back to pragmatism, without ever exposing their own left flank, thereby executing a virtual volte-face with their revolutionary credentials still intact, a feat which was probably impossible anywhere else in the international Communist movement. The two men were in the prime of their active political lives. They possessed an abundance of energy and commitment and were rapidly acquiring the tactical skills essential to dominating any political party.

As the extreme interpretation of Class Against Class continued to wane in Moscow, Pollitt and Campbell pushed their advantage home against the Young Turks who continued to provide encouragement and ideological justification for Party activists who believed in the Revolutionary Trade Union Opposition (RTUO) and Independent Leadership. Bill Rust was replaced as editor of the *Daily Worker*, by Jimmy Shields, a young Scottish brassmoulder who had spent the previous year as British representative at the Comintern and also supported Pollitt and Campbell in the pre-Congress conflict.[37] We have seen that the Party's influence and members in union office had continued comparatively undiminished in the places where the pragmatic proletarian cohort had ignored the imperatives of Independent Leadership. It was now vital for Pollitt and Campbell that the rest of the membership be schooled to emulate their good examples.

The Trade Union Militant League which Pollitt had conjured up at the 12th Congress as the authentic embodiment of the RTUO was duly conceived and then buried stillborn without ceremony during the course of 1933.[38] The Party Centre was evidently unwilling to embark on any new venture outside official union institutions. Party AEU activists allowed the Members' Rights Movement to quietly expire. The activists who had resurrected the London Busmen's Rank-and-File Movement loyally settled down to work inside the TGWU. They sought and won official positions as lay officers so as to be better able to 'ginger up' the union.

Though many Party activists remained unconvinced by the new approach, they felt unable to overtly oppose it after the 12th Congress's endorsement. They simply passively refrained from doing their daily mass work inside trade unions. A substantial number of Party engineers in Glasgow withdrew from activity in 'reformist' unions. The minority of Party activists still at work in Glasgow routinely abstained from either union or shopfloor involvement from which they anticipated only partial, non-revolutionary results.[39]

In Coventry, the Communist Party had inherited the wartime shop stewards' movement's mantle. Party activists continued the vigorous fight against 'reformist' and conservative craft unionism. Their enthusiasm produced a strong counter-offensive from inside the AEU. By 1932, there was no trace of the left's earlier influence inside the union, and employers were reaping the benefits of the rump District Committee's pre-occupation with craft issues. In Manchester, the picture was more mixed. Party engineers worked within the resilient and pragmatic AEU District Committee, but were unable to manœuvre it towards the Metalworkers' Minority Movement. When the new Party District Secretary, Trevor Robinson, arrived in early 1933 fresh from the Lenin School, he despaired of Party engineers' 'sectarian' behaviour. The younger comrades, such as Edmund Frow, had turned to 'revolutionary' unemployed activity in preference to continuing their AEU mass work.[40]

Despite these pockets of 'left sectarianism', Johnny Campbell disseminated revolutionary optimism for the New Year in the *Daily Worker*. He repeated the prediction made at the 12th Congress that Party members could create a national 'wages movement' if they did their daily mass work correctly, i.e. inside trade unions.[41] Then Life Itself provided powerful reinforcement for his sanguine view. At the end of March there was a three-day strike at Fords Dagenham, in which Party members were prominently involved. The *Daily Worker* exulted:

> The great strike at Fords, in which Communists, ILPers [Independent Labour Party], Labour men, workers without any close political attachments, unionists and non-unionists participated, is an example of the *united front in action*. It showed that in spite of all difficulties the forces of the workers can be unified in effective struggle.[42]

> In the tool-room at Fords was the band of trade union members who were supporters of the revolutionary movement. They launched the strike . . . such is the spirit of revolt among engineering workers, which given revolutionary leadership will spread throughout the country.[43]

Party toolroom activists at Ford's had ensured that union recognition had been a central demand of the strike, which had been led by the AEU Organizing Divisional Delegate (ODD), Jack Tanner, the Party's London District Secretary, Ted Bramley (himself an AEU member), and Jack Longworth, Party AEU toolroom activist. The attempts made by enthusiastic Young Turks, notably Ernie Woolley, to preach Independent Leadership during the three days were rendered irrelevant by the American management's implacable hostility to 'reformist' unions. Everyone involved became a union loyalist in solidarity with the hundreds of men victimized by the Americans imported from Detroit to root out this contagion.[44]

Also in March, Party activists used the introduction of the Bedaux work study system at Hope's metal window-frame factory in Smethwick, West Midlands, to precipitate a strike. Three weeks into the strike, the *Daily Worker* reported that the Hopes' workers had joined the TGWU, 'with a view to building up a branch for the purpose of assisting in strengthening the factory organisation and being of some use to the working class in general.'[45]

After six weeks, management conceded union recognition, joint committees to investigate complaints about Bedaux and a halt to its extension inside the factory. The Party chairman of the strike committee, Sam Shelton, explained how he had conducted it according to the line of Independent Leadership *inside* the 'reformist' union structure. First, he ensured that there was a rank-and-file strike committee which would not tolerate any dictation from full-time union officials. Then the committee cooperated with the energetic TGWU officials, and duly accepted the settlement which they negotiated.

> The revolutionary workers in the strike at Hope's pursued the policy of recruiting to the unions; there were no hesitations on this score. But this was done only for the purpose of strengthening the struggle and for knitting the men together for work behind the factory leadership . . .
> In the [1932] Lucas strike, we, the revolutionary workers, while winning the dispute, failed to recruit to the Unions so that what we gained we have lost since.[46]

In July, Party activists led by Abe Lazarus helped to fight a bitter and hard-fought strike at Firestone's tyre factory on the Great West Road in west London. They recruited the men into the TGWU; but American management were immovable to good purpose, and the strike collapsed after six weeks. Even though there had been a strong rank-and-file, the *Daily Worker* blamed the union officials for ignoring their determination to fight on. Nevertheless, the *Daily Worker* found no reason to change its attitude towards the necessity to work inside trade unions:

> All these factors, and they could be multiplied with other instances, demonstrate the beginning of a new wave of class struggle which is assuming very significant proportions. It shows that the working class is fighting back against the capitalists ever more strongly, despite the sabotaging and disrupting activities being carried on by reformist Labour leaders . . .
> . . . the firm basis . . . exists for the developing and building up of the *united fighting front* of the working class on a broad mass scale. The heavy class battles which lie in front make this question of the organisation of the united front very pressing, and stress the need for the devoting of the utmost energy to the task of rapidly developing *the rank and file movements in the factories and trade unions*, and the mass movement of the unemployed.[47]

The empirical evidence from these strikes showed that Party activists had to be prepared to compromise in the heat of struggle when adverse conditions threatened. Indeed, the capability of leading some tactical retreats in economic struggle was reflexive to most seasoned party union activists, though there were bound to be disagreements among strike leaders about when and how far the retreat should proceed. However, the Young Turks and many of their supporters pursued daily mass work inside trade unions with a view to realizing the goals of Independent Leadership immediately and without any kind of compromise with 'reformism'. Their sincere and best efforts succeeded only in alienating local union officials and leaving many workers bemused and demoralized.

During 1934 these pure revolutionaries in south west London precipitated revolts against the Bedaux system among the young women workers at Mullard's radio valve factories in Balham and Mitcham and recruited them into the TGWU. The Party activists adopted an 'independent' attitude towards the TGWU officials whom they had invited to assist, and encouraged the workers to do the same. When militant walkouts ended in disarray, the TGWU officials denounced the Party and refused to have anything more to do either with Mullard's workers or the Party. The Party activists were apparently powerless to foment further conflict inside the factories without the union's support.[48]

Soon after his return from the Soviet Union in July 1932, the indefatigable Young Turk Peter Zinkin became Industrial Organizer for the London District. From this position, he led and directed other young Party activists in trying to multiply inside trade unions rank-and-file movements which would fully embody the goals of Independent Leadership. His autobiography describes his own hard work among civil servants, Post Office workers and nurses. But though his clandestine agitation among the nurses netted him a loyal, loving and supportive wife he could not make any of these rank-and-file movements survive.[49]

The failure of the Young Turks and their supporters to make the extreme left version of Independent Leadership yield positive results was reassuring to the Party Centre, which declined to promote the Revolutionary Trade Union Opposition. Pollitt and Campbell stressed the need for rank-and-file activities *inside* trade unions and omitted reference to either the RTUO or Independent Leadership. Using creative fudge, the Party Centre assumed that the 12th Party Congress resolution to multiply 'unofficial broad movements' was being fulfilled by every strike in which Party members were active. To cover their exposed left flank, Pollitt and Campbell expanded and elided the meaning of 'rank-and-file movement' and 'rank-and-file' to describe any organized militant occurrence. When Party members formed a strike committee, it became a 'rank-and-file strike committee' or even a 'rank-and-file movement'. In addition, members were directed to forge the 'fighting united front' in action.

The rash of inspiring and exciting strikes in 1933 convinced most Party activists that Pollitt's and Campbell's approach was right. The *Daily Worker* observed somewhat smugly that Life Itself was also playing its part:

> Every day brings the report of another strike . . . Despite the sabotage of most of the union officials . . . the strike movement is growing and extending . . . Never since 1924–5 has there been such a feeling in the country that workers of all industries should get together and go forward together. The union leaders work to prevent this, but the *rank and file movements* in the main industries continue to develop this *united front* movement.[50]

Notes

1. Interview with Will Paynter by N. Fishman; interview with Phil Abrahams by H. Francis, 14 January 1974, transcript in South Wales Miner's Library (SWML), p. 1; interview with Phil Abrahams by M. Jones, n.d., transcript in SWML, p.46; interview with Len Jefferys by H. Francis and D. Egan, 11 October 1972, transcript in SWML, pp. 25–6.
2. *Party Organiser*, No. 1, March 1932 p.22.
3. Ibid., p. 29.
4. Ibid., pp. 30–1.
5. See *Daily Worker*, 15, 18, 23 February; 21 March; 27 April 1932. See also interview with Frank Williams by H. Francis and D. Smith, 15 May 1973, transcript in SWML, p. 11. See N. Fishman (1991), PhD, Ch. 7.
6. Harry Pollitt's report to the June meeting of the Central Committee, *Party Organiser*, No. 4, June 1932, pp. 7–8.
7. See *Daily Worker*, 13, 19, 22, 29, 30 January; 1, 2 ,6, 12 February 1932. For the Bedaux bonus system, see Clegg, 1985, *History of British Trade Unions*, op. cit.: 532–4.
8. See p. 53.
9. *Daily Worker*, 11 August 1932. Bert Papworth had joined the Workers Union at Morgan Crucibles when he was 16. At 18, he was chairman of a shop committee at Woolwich Arsenal and participated in the 1917–18 strikes there. He started as a conductor on the LGOC in 1927 and had been active in the TGWU and the busmen's friendly society (Barrett, 1985, op.cit.: 147.) For Frank Snelling, see Corfield, February 1964, p. 44.
10. *Daily Worker*, 11 August 1932. My emphasis. Tram and tube workers faced similar cuts. The London District leadership issued a Special Statement instructing members to assist in 'every possible way the struggle of bus, tram and underground workers' (*Daily Worker*, 10 August 1932). Earlier in the year, the *Daily Worker* had supported the Party busmen who wanted to organize outside the TGWU. The shift in its views reflects Pollitt's and Campbell's growing influence over the paper compared with the waning influence of its editor, Bill Rust. See pp. 56–7.

11.   For the Rank and File Committee see Barrett, J., 1974, *Busman's Punch*, Rank and File Organisation and Unofficial Industrial Action among London Busmen 1913–37, University of Warwick MA: 25–9 and 36–7. For the 'Red Button Union' see Clegg, H.A., Fox, A., and Thompson, A.F., 1964, *A History of British Trade Unions since 1889* Vol. I, 1889–1910, Clarendon Press, Oxford. p. 78. It was founded in 1913, in the prevailing heady atmosphere of the nationwide militant upsurge. Its organizer, Ben Smith, was a cabman who had become prominent when acting as a collector for the miners' strike in 1912. For its reputation for 'militancy and readiness to strike' see Clegg, H.A., 1950, *Labour Relations in London Transport*, Blackwell: 14. For its culture of direct democracy see also Tony Corfield's series of articles on the London Busmen's Rank and File Movement in *The Record*, 1963–4, July 1963: 37–8 and Barrett, 1974, op.cit.: 25–9.

12.   Corfield, 1963, op.cit.: 37–8.

13.   See Corfield, T., 1963, *The Record*, October: 52–3. The garages were Merton, Old Kent Road and Nunhead.

14.   See Clegg, 1950, op.cit.: 15. The CBC was elected by the London Busmen's delegate conference which usually consisted of the chairman and secretary from each garage TGWU branch, with additional representatives for the 'inside staff'.

15.   Ibid.: 28–9.

16.   Barrett, 1974, 51, 66–7.

17.   Ibid.: 41–3 and 56–60. Bill Payne had attacked the TMM at the 1927 TGWU Biennial Delegate Conference (BDC) for splitting the movement and trying to organize a breakaway union after the General Strike.

18.   Ibid.: 57, and *The Worker*, 3, 10, 17 May 1929. (*The Worker* was the *Daily Worker*'s weekly predecessor.)

19.   See *Daily Worker*, 5, 8, 19, 23 and 26 February 1932, and Barrett, 1974: 73. Two of the garages where the Party had influence, Holloway and Cricklewood had been early supporters of the Red Button Union. Bernard Sharkey had become branch chairman of Willesden garage in 1926. He had gone into the police force in 1919 after being demobbed and had been active in the policemen's union. Bill Ware was a branch official at Enfield garage. Party members at Holloway garage were keen supporters of the TMM.

20.   *Daily Worker*, 16 August 1932 and Barrett, 1974, op.cit.: 78.

21.   *Daily Worker*, 22 February 1932. The *Daily Worker*'s first report of the Provisional Committee's formation had not mentioned that its members were all official TGWU delegates. By 1934, if any activist was a lay official, their status was always noted in the *Daily Worker*, since it carried the prestige of loyally serving in 'the trade union movement'.

22.   *Busman's Punch* had been launched in July 1931, probably as part of the attempt to move away from the TMM. TMM supporters favouring Independent Leadership published the *Holloway Bus Worker*. *The Bus Wheel*, had appeared in the Spring of 1931 and was attacked by the *Holloway Bus Worker* for giving a falsely militant impression.

23.   *Daily Worker*, 26 August 1932.

24.   *Daily Worker*, 1 September 1932 and 21 September 1932.

25.   Clegg, 1950, op.cit.: 16–17. Clegg observed that 'The Agreement eased the conditions of drivers and conductors to some extent in order to counteract the effects of strain due to speeded schedules'.

26. Ibid. p. 30 and *Daily Worker*, 24 September 1932.
27. *Daily Worker*, 6 October 1932.
28. Branson, 1985, *History of the CPGB*: 94.
29. See articles in the *Daily Worker*: Pollitt, 20 August 1932; letter from Dutt, 14 September 1932; Campbell, 15 September 1932; Willie Allan, 19 September 1932; Dutt against Pollitt, 19 September 1932; Gallacher, 21 September 1932; Rust, 24 September 1932. The Tyneside Party District leadership supported Dutt, whilst the Scottish leadership supported Pollitt. Willie Allan, the General Secretary of the UMS supported Pollitt. (Branson,1985, op.cit.: 90–2.)
30. Kevin Morgan describes Pollitt's position somewhat incredulously, since he is well aware of how far they had actually moved from Class Against Class (Morgan, 1989, op.cit.: 78–80). He concludes that 'Dutt can hardly be blamed if he saw in this a "tendency to revise our whole trade union line" '. (p. 79).
31. Morgan quotes Pollitt at a Politburo meeting in October: 'It was "not from the point of view of microscropes or letters from afar" that they had to decide these questions . . . but from the point of view of . . . what we would do if we were our lads.' (ibid., p. 80) .
32. Morgan agrees with the verdict that Pollitt gave ideological ground only, without conceding any ground in the policy-making arena. (Morgan, 1993: 80). The appropriation of the RTUO by two British Party 'centrists' was a fine irony. The German organization, *Revolutionare Gewerkschafts-opposition*, (RGO) was founded by the *left* faction of the KPD at the end of 1929 in emulation of the National Minority Movement. The translation of this imitation Minority Movement, Revolutionary Trade Union Opposition (RTUO), was then imported by Pollitt and Campbell as a sub-stitute for the MM! The Comintern subsequently restrained the RGO from sectarian behaviour. (See Carr, 1982: 7–9, 21–2 and 56–7.) Mahon states that Pollitt first used RTUO 'without capital letters' in early 1931 (Mahon J., 1976, *Harry Pollitt*, Lawrence & Wishart, London: 173) probably when making his submission to the Comintern Committee in January. Its capital-izing evidently was part of the ideological fudge which Pollitt and Campbell used to outflank the Minority Movement. Mahon's uncharacter-istic candour about the RTUO's appearance bristles with recollections of frustration at being worsted by Pollitt's manoeuvres in 1932 despite his later idolization of the man.
33. Harry Pollitt's speech to the 12th British Party Congress, 'Road to Victory', 1932, Congress Report, CPGB: 42. Pollitt lamented that there were only 80 factory cells with 550 members in the country, and that 60 per cent of Party members were unemployed. For an earlier estimate of unemployed Party members, see Chapter 2, note 38.
34. Pollitt, 1932, 'Road to Victory', loc.cit.: 48.
35. Ibid.: 5. For other permutations, see notes 42, 47, and 50 below.
36. For the Balham Group, see Bell, 1937, *British Communist Party*: 150, and Groves, R., 1974, *The Balham Group*, Pluto Press: 54–73. Groves implies that the Balhamites met Young Turks after the Congress who agreed with their denunciation of the Party's change of direction.
37. Branson, 1985, op. cit.: 92.
38. Tom Mann apparently invested considerable personal energy and emo-tional capital in the gestation of the Trade Union Militant League. A news-

paper, *The Trade Union Militant* appeared in May 1933 as its organ. The paper ceased publication after approximately three issues. The official explanation was its lack of 'rank-and-file' financial support. Denied access to the Party archives, the most recent biographers of Mann have been unable to satisfactorily explain this episode, which does indeed seem puzzling (Tsuzuki, C., 1991, *Tom Mann, 1856–1941: The Challenge of Labour* Clarendon, Oxford: 245–6. White, J., 1991, *Tom Mann*, Manchester Univesity Press: 203 and 214–15). I think that the League was conceived by Pollitt and Campbell primarily as an indulgence to Mann. It enabled him to keep busy and feel he was doing something for the Party without incurring any undue risks that he would launch the Party back into left-sectarian errors.

39.   See Kibblewhite, E., 1979, 'The Impact of Unemployment on the Development of Trade Unions in Scotland, 1918–39: Some Aspects', University of Aberdeen PhD: 203–4, 240; *Party Organiser*, Vol. I No. 8, Special Congress Number, December 1932: 24; *Daily Worker*, 4 February 1932, letter from Secretary of Glasgow Federation of Shipbuilding and Engineering Trades complaining about negative attitude of Party members towards the Federation's efforts on behalf of workers at Clydebank yard where a ship for the USSR was being constructed. As late as December 1935 the *Daily Worker* found it a notable fact worth reporting that there were Party members from Glasgow actually working and active in their unions, including an engineering leader of a factory group in an important shop. (18 December 1935). See also *Daily Worker*, 5 December 1934, article by Finlay Hart.

40.   For Coventry, see Carr, 1982: 142–3, 287–9, 291–3. For Manchester, see Frow, E. and R., 1982, 'The Communist Party in Manchester 1920–26', Working Class Movement Library, biographies of Party engineers, 1982, *Engineering Struggles*, op. cit.: 92–3, and Interviews with Edmund Frow and Trevor Robinson by N. Fishman.

41.   *Daily Worker*, 4 January 1933.

42.   *Daily Worker*, 31 March 1933 (my emphasis).

43.   *Daily Worker*, 5 April 1933.

44.   See Fishman, N., unpublished paper on Ford's Dagenham.

45.   *Daily Worker*, 15 April 1933.

46.   *Labour Monthly*, February 1934: 113. For the strike, see Clegg, 1985, *History of British Trade Unions*, op. cit.: 533.

47.   *Daily Worker*, 4 August 1933 (my emphasis). The 'factors' included the Firestone's strike and four other more minor incidents of economic conflict.

48.   See *Daily Worker*, 16, 23 and 24 May 1934; 25, 27 and 31 July 1934; 1, 6, 9, 11, 13, 14, 16, 21, 23 August 1934. A strike at Balham occurred at the end of July just before the Olympia radio show. The company made concessions, but refused union recognition. Busmen from the nearby Merton garage where the Busmen's Rank-and-File Movement was strong and had Marxist roots led a deputation of Mullard's girls to the TGWU Clapham office to demand help.

49.   Zinkin, P., 1985, *A Man To Be Watched Carefully*, People's Publications: 94–5 and 99–112. Zinkin had joined the CPGB in late 1923 at the age of nineteen. He had grown up in St Pancras and trained as a furrier. However, soon after joining the Party he became a permanent revolutionary.

50.   *Daily Worker*, 25 May 1934 (emphasis mine). The strikes cited were all

isolated episodes: at 'a large Yorkshire pit', the Wembley Exhibition building site, Mullard's wireless factory in Mitcham, and Maple's in west London. None of them were associated with a discrete rank-and-file movement.

CHAPTER FOUR

In Pursuit of the Real United Front

The new emphasis on trade union centred activity for Party members was reflected in the way in which the 1934 National Hunger March of unemployed workers was conceived by the Party Centre. Party members sought receptive constituency Labour Parties, trades councils and trade union branches along the routes with whom they could cooperate in establishing Hunger March Solidarity Committees. The Committees' purpose was to provide accommodation, succour, publicity and moral support for the hunger marchers. They embodied the united front in action.

A Congress of Action was held at Bermondsey Town Hall in February 1934 to mark the end of the march. Pollitt's speech to the delegates stressed both the united front and trade union activism:

> But we believe that most essential to the development of the most powerful forms of united struggle is for every worker not at present a member of a trade union to join one, and immediately for those who are in the factories to help in the formation of factory committees . . . to win the trade union branches and district committees for active participation in this great struggle and . . . to strengthen the factory committees as the chief means through which the fighting power of the whole working class may be strengthened.
>
> We can do nothing effective outside the trade unions, and our power becomes a thousand times stronger . . . when it is allied with fighting trade unionism on the basis, not of Mondism, but of class struggle.[1]

It was evident that Pollitt and Campbell were now leading a Party which believed in itself and the mission they had set it. This new self-confidence was reflected in a manifesto issued by the Central Committee in May 1934, headlined, 'Not For a Third Labour Government But Workers Power Through Soviet Rule'. It combined ritual obeisance to Class Against Class with barely concealed excitement over the upsurge in the 'economic struggle'.

> A mighty movement of working class struggle is rapidly developing, against the National Government and the employers' attacks on workers' conditions and against the growing menace of fascism and war. Strike after strike is taking place on the initiative of the rank and file, in defiance of the trade union bureaucrats. In every industry militants are being elected to branch and district positions. Unorganised workers, including women, are joining in great strikes

against Bedaux and cut wages. The resistance to capitalist rationali-
sation and lower earnings is bringing millions of workers into the
open class struggle. The working masses of Britain have come to
understand from their own experience, that the working class is at
the crossroads.[2]

In the Midlands, the impact of the victorious Hope's strike reverberated
throughout the surrounding industrial hinterland. In April 1934, there
was a strike at Withers Safemakers in West Bromwich when management introduced the Bedaux systems. The strikers turned to Sam Shelton
and other Party activists as advisers. Again a rank-and-file strike committee was elected, workers were recruited into the TGWU, mass picketing
was organized, grievances were tabulated and a negotiating committee
was elected to treat with management.[3]

At Lucas, management introduced a 'points system' which the young
women workers judged to be the Bedaux in another guise. Party activists
drew on the legacy of the 1932 revolt to organize opposition. Two years
after that first revolt had petered out, Party activists ensured that the
TGWU had a prominent place in the fight. The *Daily Worker* observed:
'The lessons of the Lucas strike have not been lost on the Withers strikers
. . . The wave of militancy which is rapidly rising in the Black Country
can only be led by the rank and file themselves with Communist guidance.'[4]

In view of their recent winning record, it is not surprising that local
workers went to Communist activists for advice and help when their
grievances escalated unredressed. Strikes of unorganized workers which
gained union recognition continued to occur sporadically in Birmingham
and the Black Country over the next three years. The Party activists
promoted membership of the TGWU and continued to work in evident
harmony with the local full-time officials. The three officials who were
most heavily involved were George Geobey, Julia Varley and Fred
Packwood. They had all been officials of the Workers' Union (WU) in
Birmingham, Geobey since 1911, Varley since 1912 and Packwood since
1920. Before becoming an official, Geobey had been a WU lay activist.
He worked at the Birmingham Small Arms factory, which had a large
number of semi-skilled workers and where the Workers' Union had
established an impressive membership base in 1911. As WU officials, he
and Varley played a part in the Black Country strikes of semi-skilled men
and women metalworkers in 1913.[5]

In Oxford, the Hunger March Solidarity Committee had turned its
attention to the large, new Pressed Steel body plant in Cowley. During
July 1934 a flare-up on the night shift over piece-rates was transformed
with Solidarity Committee/Communist encouragement into a full-scale
revolt. On the day after the night shift had walked out, the Oxford Party

sent to London for Abe Lazarus. He proved an inspired choice. The strike leaders from Pressed Steel had previously been members/activists of the Fed and the AEU. They accepted Lazarus' recommendation to opt for the TGWU. (The Oxford AEU branch took a conservative craft attitude towards recruiting Pressed Steel semi-skilled workers. By a quirk of fate, the progressive ODD who might have successfully pressurized the local branch officers into accepting semi-skilled members was on holiday at the time of the strike.)

Lazarus and the Pressed Steel leaders formed a model 'rank-and-file strike committee' which conducted the strike with determination and flair, working amicably with the same TGWU full-time officials from Birmingham who had assisted at the Hope's strike. After six weeks during which the conflict became increasingly bitter, Bevin intervened behind the scenes. The company negotiated a settlement with the TGWU National Engineering Officer Andrew Dalgleish which conceded union recognition and shop steward organization. The *Daily Worker* observed:

> Most important of all [concessions] is trade union recognition, which, provided a strong rank and file leadership is organised, will maintain and augment concessions now gained ... This Pressed Steel strike is a splendid example of what the workers can accomplish provided the fight from the first is under the control of the militant rank and file ...
>
> [A] mass meeting elected the works committee and the shop stewards etc. Many of the strikers had put forward the suggestion that Cde. Lazarus . . . should be appointed full-time secretary [of the TGWU branch inside Pressed Steel]. Cde Lazarus replied pointing out that it would be better for someone inside the works, and in intimate contact with the conditions there, should have this job (*sic*). His statement that as a member of the Communist Party he had thrown his weight into the strike was greeted with great enthusiasm. Bro. Packwood, organiser of the TGWU, said that he had been proud to work beside Cde. Lazarus. He spoke of the splendid work of Communists in other strikes in which he had recently participated – Tom Roberts at Hope's and Finley at Withers. The strikers generally realised the magnificent work put in by the Communist Party from the first moment of the strike.

The leader then drew the moral:

> When the Labour leaders tell the workers a) that a united front was impossible and b) that it would bring no strength to the workers anyhow, the Oxford strike gives them the lie . . . This is an example of the *united front in action* and it proves conclusively that those who are opposing the building of that front are preventing the advance of the working class.[6]

Despite these advances achieved through a strong rank-and-file organization working with union officials, the Young Turks and their supporters continued to act in a different way to pursue the goals of Independent Leadership. In 1934 Party activists in south west London precipitated revolts against the Bedaux system among the young women workers at Mullard's radio valve factories in Balham and Mitcham. The Party activists themselves adopted an 'independent' attitude towards the TGWU officials whom they had invited to assist in union recruiting, and encouraged the young women to do the same. The workers' walk-outs ended in disarray, and the officials denounced the Party and refused to have anything more to do either with Mullard's or the Party. The Party activists were apparently powerless to prevent many workers from being victimized, and they were unable to foment further conflict inside the factories without the union's support.[7]

Elsewhere in London Party activity in engineering remained firmly anchored in the AEU. In 1933 Jack Little was elected AEU President, the union's most powerful full-time office. He had been an active member of the BSP and convener at the giant Vickers-Armstrong Elswick works during the 1914–18 war. His roots were the same as we have already observed in Pollitt, Tanner, Hannington and the rest of the foundation Communist proletarian cohort: the union, Marxist socialism and factory organization.

It is hardly surprising to discover that there was little difference between AEU officials' and Party engineering activists' perception of the situation facing the union: both believed it was essential to rebuild strong shopfloor organization in order to restore the union's fortunes; but the Party activists also felt that a strong 'shop steward movement' would also prove the key to the working class taking state power.

Functioning within the highly elastic definition of 'rank-and-file movement' offered by Pollitt and Campbell, Party engineering activists began to rebuild and extend shop steward organization, and described their activities as recreating the 'shop steward movement' *inside* the AEU coincidentally as the AEU national officials were addressing the serious decline in the AEU's membership. As economic activity expanded, this *de facto* alliance produced results and the AEU's fortunes revived steadily, though many branch lay officials remained committed craft conservatives and actively obstructed the new factory-wide approach.[8]

Little appreciated the practical flair of the AEU's National Organizer, Charles Lamb, and worked closely with him to develop a strategy which accepted the changed realities of the inter-war engineering industry. Both men recognized that the union could no longer rely on craft exclusiveness to maintain its bargaining position, and that strong factory organization (including the increasing numbers of semi-skilled workers) was the most effective means of ensuring that employers continued to recognize the union and negotiate with it. Their views found support from most of the eight full-time executive councillors over whom Little presided as chairman, though many of them still hankered after the days when skill and craft-consciousness had been sufficient to win significant concessions.

In September 1934 the London District Committee and local full-time officials launched a recruitment campaign to inspire existing shop stewards to expand their activities, to get new shop stewards apppointed, and finally to take the union and the shop steward system into hitherto unorganized factories. Their campaign made use of an organizational innovation introduced by Charles Lamb, Area Committees, which functioned as sub-committees of District Committees to promote recruiting.[9]

Party engineers sallied forth to organize the new engineering sites proliferating around London's rim which produced consumer goods. They also turned their attention to revitalizing union organization in aircraft and other factories where it had been allowed to fall away during the economic slump. A new 'rank-and-file' newspaper, *Engineers' Bulletin*, was published to serve the campaign. The Party Centre and London engineering activists were optimistic that this 'shop stewards movement' would not only restore factory organization, but would also gather workplace support for a substantial wage claim and national wages battle with employers to avenge the engineers' defeats of 1922 and 1931.

Party activists had dominated the AEU London District Committee since 1920. (Within the terms of the AEU's thoroughly democratic constitution, District Committees which were annually elected usually from among branch lay officials and shop steward activists, still wielded considerable power and could also exercise substantial initiative.) The two ODDs who operated in London, Jack Tanner and W. Howell, and Tommy Knibbs the full-time London District Committee Secretary, were all sympathetic towards the Party activists and had worked closely with them for many years.[10]

The AEU London District Committee held a conference to promote the campaign in October 1934. It was attended by 230 delegates who listened to speeches by Joe Scott, Claude Berridge and Jack Tanner. Charlie Hoyle, a wartime revolutionary shop steward in Liverpool, recent Lenin School graduate and currently trying to organize new engineering factories, summed up the mood: 'There is represented here the true spirit of the Dorchester Labourers, the Tolpuddle Martyrs . . . Nothing can stand in our way if we carry this spirit back to the branches and factories . . . carrying forward an intensive campaign in "preparation for action" '.[11]

Hoyle's speech was redolent with the culture of trade union activism in which rank-and-filism and union loyalism were intertwined. Not all of the London Party engineering activists, including Percy Glading and Vic Parker, still accepted it. They now leaned towards the left of Class Against Class, and argued that the Party should be directly challenging 'reformist' union officials rather than working alongside them. Though they would not have publicly opposed the campaign, it was probably their disapproval which prompted Ted Taylor, Party activist and secretary of the District Committee's Organizing Sub-Committee to point out that the campaign had scored 'successes which could be repeated in factory after factory and district after district. The strength of the union was the strength of the rank and file, which must have its primary basis in workshop organisation.'[12]

London Party engineering activists continued to develop Pollitt's and Campbell's new approach with positive results. They believed that the rank-and-file were keen to fight at factory level and in national strikes for higher wages. They could make the rank-and-file's will prevail by utilizing the AEU's extensive democratic machinery. This meant Party activists and their allies mobilizing the rank-and-file vote in support of candidates for lay and full-time office who promised to follow militant policies – as many of them had been doing since their days as ACM and Metalworkers' MM activists.

Party engineering activists outside London also resumed their old habits, and soon the loose national coalition of Party activists and other militants were again organizing motions for AEU National Committee. They sought to tie the AEU Executive Council to militant policies, notably substantial wage demands in national negotiations with the Employers' Federation. They efficiently produced and gathered support for these motions and others which reflected the whole range of Party political and economic priorities.

This militant network linked those districts where the Party was influential and functioned at all levels of the union's organization from branch, through District Committee to Divisional Committee and finally the policy-making National Committee. Involvement in these institutions meant that engineering activists had to commit vast amounts of time and energy to ensure that the rank-and-file will prevailed inside all of them. (At this time, branches usually met weekly and District Committees sometimes also met weekly, although mainly fortnightly. Divisional Comittees usually met twice yearly, before and after the annual National Committee.) Even in South Wales, the Party finally showed signs of a complete recovery from the deep internal rift between supporters of the Young Turks and adherents of 'Hornerism'. After being exonerated by the Comintern, Horner had assiduously mended his Party fences. He had participated in the organization of a 'South Wales Miners Rank and File Movement'. This was another rank-and-file movement conceived along traditional lines, being parallel/complementary to the official union structure. Its fortnightly paper, *The South Wales Miner*, edited by Horner, appeared in June 1933 and preached the necessity of organizing the 'rank-and-file' inside the Fed. The Party mining activists who had never ceased to work inside the union knew how much ground the Fed had to make up, and enthusiastically welcomed Horner's return to active union work.

Since 1926 the Fed membership had declined disastrously due to a combination of high coalfield unemployment, a withdrawal by miners disillusioned with trade unionism altogether, and an expanding 'non-political' (Non-Pol) yellow union, the South Wales Miners Industrial Union (SWMIU). The SWMIU had emerged from the events at the end of the 1926 Lock-out and was now led by a calculating, ambitious general secretary who was more than willing to accept the assistance of the coalowners who viewed the 'Non-Pol' as a preferable alternative to the 'Communist-dominated' Fed. Party mining activists' first priority was to get Horner elected a full-time union official. This involved his moving his field of operations westwards away from the Rhondda Fach where coalowners had substantially contracted production to the Anthracite coalfield where pits were still profitable. In November 1933 he was elected an agent for Sub-Area No. 3, after supporters had conducted a vigorous campaign on his behalf.

From this official position, Horner now began a single-minded crusade against the SWMIU, which he viewed as presenting a potentially fatal threat to the Fed and the South Wales working class. Early in 1934, the Fed Executive sanctioned his secondment to conduct a campaign to dis-lodge the SWMIU from the Emlyn colliery, which was located conve-niently near his agent's patch. Emlyn was a Non-Pol stronghold, and the Fed's previous efforts had proved fruitless against it. Horner scored a stunning success against considerable odds, inciting the miners at Emlyn to fight fiercely and tenaciously.

The victory at Emlyn restored the unity and morale of South Wales Party mining activists. It also cemented good working relations between the Party and Fed officials. Party activists who had remained sceptical of Horner's revolutionary credentials now flocked to his side. They wanted to be part of this serious fight under Horner, even though he made com-mon cause with 'reformists'. Later in 1934, the Fed Executive gave Horner further leave to organize the Fed at the Taff-Merthyr colliery, near Bedlinog in east Glamorgan. Taff-Merthyr was not just a larger pit: the battle for the men's allegiance there was also viewed by all involved sides as a strategic trial of strength between the two unions.

Horner proved again to be both charismatic and tactically shrewd. Though the victory was by no means as clearcut as at Emlyn, there was no doubt that the Fed forces had inflicted severe damage on the SWMIU, and the coal-owners recognized they would have to rethink their own anti-Fed strategy. During the course of the valiant fight, Horner and the 'militants' had shown themselves capable not only of militancy but also of serious negotiation and substantial compromise. The *Daily Worker* observed that the struggle had been characterized by unity between 'reformists and revolutionaries' and 'employed and unemployed' who had 'written a page in working class history which is a striking example to all British workers and a fitting reply to the reformist leaders of the TUC who aim to sabotage such examples of unity as displayed at Taff Merthyr.'[13]

The pragmatic side of Horner was clearly visible in the course of negotiations between the Fed officials and the coal-owners for a wage agreement. Party activists who believed in the RTUO wanted to mobilize the Rank-and-File Movement to oppose the agreement, which was concluded in September 1934. Arthur Horner denounced the officials at a Fed delegate conference for their failure to win better terms, but he stood by the conference vote in favour of the agreement. He then pre-empted Party activists' attempt to call an unofficial strike in the Rank-and-File Movement's name. The South Wales' Party leadership stood by Horner and was publicly criticized by Party activists for reneging on Independent Leadership. The District Party formally acknowledged its error, but continued nevertheless to countenance Horner's 'Hornerism'.[14]

By the end of 1934, two years after the 12th Congress, Pollitt's and Campbell's new approach had produced outstanding results. The Party had literally come in from the cold. The decline in Party membership had been halted, and the membership's activities now revolved around trade unions. The 13th British Party Congress had been scheduled for early 1935 on the assumption that the 7th Comintern World Congress would take place in September 1934.[15] The Party Centre was confident that the Comintern would signal a decisive change at the World Congress. The shift, which the CPGB and Pollitt in particular had done his utmost to promote, was expected to make Communists' main priority fighting the threat of fascism and war by means of forging a united front not only from below but also with social democratic and 'reformist union' leaderships.[16]

Because other affiliated Communist Parties were critical and even downright hostile to the change in line, the 7th World Congress was postponed. The British Party leadership evidently felt no need to delay the British Congress as well. Preparations went forward along with their intention to announce a move away from Independent Leadership and the RTUO and the need to concentrate on building the united front. No doubt the terms in which they signalled this change were somewhat diluted compared with the rhetoric which would have been deployed had the 7th World Congress taken place on schedule. Nevertheless, the movement away from their 12th Congress position was clear enough.

The pre-13th Congress discussion in the *Daily Worker* began in November 1934. In contrast to the dispute about trade unions preceding the 12th Congress, there was no conflict inside the leadership. Indeed, the substantial shift away from their 1932 position was openly acknowledged and analysed. Palme Dutt himself justified the Party's 'new tactics' by reference to events in Europe since 1929, that is the rise of fascism.[17] Johnny Campbell observed:

> We could have a rank and file movement in every industry in the country on these (*old minority movement* [Campbell's parenthesis, my emphasis]) lines, but in three months everyone would be out of the unions and we would be further away from the *rank and file movement* in this country. This does not mean that if we have won a branch to a militant policy that we cease to organise rank and file supporters. On the contrary, we must back this up so that our hold in the existing conditions in the branches, district committees and sub-districts can be extended and solidified.[18]

Discussants stressed the need for daily mass work at the workplace, building factory shop steward organization, and intervening in union elections. Members were not cautioned about the 'left sectarian' and 'right reformist' errors, but simply exhorted to activism. There was the clear expectation that 'Life Itself' would take care of the rest.

> Communists must put forward concrete demands . . . to wring concessions from capitalism by a struggle of the working class, showing in practice that we are honest conscientious workers and comrades . . . Not by raising the question of Soviet power as an issue for the *united front*, not by putting forward ultimate aims, but taking the questions that are uppermost in their [the masses'] mind as a starting point. This is *building the united front*. *Life itself* is going to force this question of Soviet power to the front, the changes that are taking place in the Socialist world and the capitalist world are being felt and will be more and more understood by the masses.[19]

The 13th Party Congress was held in Manchester in February 1935. Activists' turn towards trade unions was reflected in Congress delegates' union affiliations: 234 out of the 294 delegates were in trade unions; 41 were in the TGWU (reflecting the Party's strength in London on the docks and the buses and in the recent Pressed Steel strike in Oxford); 25 were in the AEU; 19 were in the NUGMW; 18 were in mining unions, including eight from the Fed and eight from the UMS; 15 were in the National Union of Railwaymen (NUR).[20]

The Resolution which Congress adopted on the Party and the Economic Struggle omitted all mention not only of the RTUO, but also of rank-and-file movements as discrete organizations separate from trade unions, that is, along the 'old minority movement' lines. It committed members to concentrate on trade union work and take the lead in:

activising the branches, district committees, and areas committees of the various unions and, where it exists, the workshop organisation of the unions.[21]

> The improvement in our trade union work has been gained despite the fact that all the Party is not yet mobilised for work in the trade unions, and we have made little progress in mining, as a whole . . . and in the new industries, chemicals, aeroplane and artificial silk . . . The absence of this systematic work in the unions, combined with the slow development of basic units in the factories, has enabled the trade union leaders to control the wages movement of the workers, directing it into channels of arbitration.[22]

Even though the 13th Congress had resoundingly endorsed the concentration on trade union work and building the united front, many Party activists remained hostile to these and resisted the abandonment of Independent Leadership. Despite the empirical evidence that the class struggle in Britain had stabilized, they remained convinced that Communists could still make the revolution. They were also impervious to the broad hints from the Party Centre that the Comintern's position was about to change, and felt betrayed by increasingly rare allusions to and then the actual disappearance of the Revolutionary Trade Union Opposition.

These unreconstructed Young Turks staged a concerted *démarche* at the London Party District Congress in June 1935. Clive Branson from south west London proposed a motion condemning the change in the District's 'tactical line', opposing its neglect of 'the mobilising of the valuable existing Party forces for the independent organisation, initiation and leadership of class fights, of economic struggles which take on such great importance at the present time'. He was supported by Hugh Slater from 'Far East' London. The other delegates were evidently content to follow the Party Centre's lead. The *Daily Worker* reported that delegates had 'decisively rejected' the motion and had instead emphasized 'the urgent need for the development of a wide mass popular movement against war and in support of peace and for reinforcing of the peace policy of the Soviet Union.'[23]

Noreen Branson does not mention this rearguard opposition to the united front against fascism in her official history. Instead, she paints a bright picture of the British Party's untroubled transition away from the Third Period in which the foreground is uncluttered by empirical detail. In fact, the Party Centre had encountered serious practical difficulties in implementing the 'new tactics' at the end of April when, only weeks after the 13th Party Congress, Peter Zinkin seized the opportunity of an aircraft strike to establish an independent rank-and-file movement for aircraft workers with the clear intention of ignoring official union structures when they restricted 'revolutionary' activity. When challenged by Party

AEU activists, he was forced to postpone his project. Meanwhile, he confidently asserted that not only would his Aircraft Shop Stewards National Council (ASSNC) achieve the goal which Pollitt set members at the 12th Party Congress, it also conformed to the aims set forth at the 13th Party Congress. He was not anti-trade union, but merely against 'reformist' trade union activity which betrayed the 'rank-and-file'.

Zinkin's revolutionary opportunism took advantage of the efforts of Party engineering activists to rebuild the shop stewards' movement inside the AEU. Many of the London Party activists had worked in aircraft factories in the early 1920s and were well aware that they had great potential for union shopfloor organization. They had been painstakingly rebuilding trade union and factory organization in the west London aircraft companies since 1933. The numbers of union recruits and shop stewards had both increased as a result of successful shopfloor skirmishes. They planned an official lay aircraft committee covering all aircraft unions in London and the south-east, a London aircraft 'rank-and-file movement' *inside* the unions.

The opposition of the Party AEU engineering activists, led by Joe Scott and Claude Berridge, compelled Zinkin to seek support for his new rank-and-file movement. He went to the London District Industrial Organizer, Johnny Mahon, still a serious Young Turk, and probably a close associate of Zinkin since 1930–31. Mahon convened a meeting between Zinkin, Scott and Berridge at which he imposed the official Comintern line in both name and spirit and backed an independent aircraft rank-and-file movement. Scott and Berridge had little choice but to acquiesce, and the ASSNC belatedly saw the light of day in mid August, perhaps the same day that Dimitrov was making his speech to the 7th World Congress heralding the new line.

When the Seventh World Congress was finally convened in July–August 1935, its importance was signalled by the attendance of all three key British leaders, Pollitt, Campbell and Dutt. While they were in Moscow, however, Joe Scott could not resist making his case publicly at the *Labour Monthly* rank-and-file conference, convened to marshal support for the Party Centre's united front *démarche* at the TUC in September. There were 330 delegates from 142 trade union branches present. They heard Scott make a thinly veiled attack on the ASSNC by deploying the loose definition of 'rank-and-file movement' used by Pollitt and Campbell in their propaganda.

> There are a dozen and one various unions over the various sections of the workers in this country and we must visualise these as being the rank and file movement of the working class of this country . . . Our job is not scrambling about looking for new forms of movements.

Scott's intervention provoked Bert Papworth, who had recently been accused by Party and ILP busmen activists of betraying the principles of the London Busmen's Rank and File Movement. He sprang to the defence of true rank-and-filism:

> I am taking the line of . . . showing Scott and this conference the definite need of rank and file movements. Hear, hear! . . . After all is said and done, do you think a rank and file movement could exist under any circumstances if there was not a cause, if it was not reaping for its class at least some benefit?[24]

Seasoned Party veterans Julius Jacobs, a furnishing trades union militant, and Arthur Horner intervened to stop the conflict, but to no avail. Scott had taken up a position from which there could be no face-saving compromise. He 'vigorously contested the contention that trade unions are part and parcel of the capitalist machinery. He said he wanted to protest against this idea permeating the conference and that such loose ideas must be dropped.'[25]

With the conflict out in the open, the London District leadership was forced to address it publicly. The Labour Monthly Conference was recalled on 21st September for the ostensible reason of hearing a report back from TUC delegates. Scott and Berridge presented their fully developed case against the ASSNC in a paper written for the London Party Industrial Fraction meeting, called to establish a Fraction line for the recalled conference.

> Has it [the ASSNC] sought Union recognition; does it want Union recognition? Has any concrete results been accrued by them since formation [sic]? How many shop stewards are there connected with it? How often do they meet? What do they discuss? These are pertinent questions that need answering, for without the backing and support of the Union (branches, District Committees, etc.) the extension of its activity into organised shops, exercise of leadership on the problems of industry cannot exist, it is doomed to become an 'opposition' group or fraction which will be without influence or power at any crucial moment.

The paper then proceeded to elaborate a view of the 'economic struggle' which I have described as 'constitutional militancy' to distinguish it from reflexive union loyalism. The pioneer constitutional militants, Scott and Berridge, had already moved beyond the pre-war and wartime 'rank-and-filist' culture in their practice. Peter Zinkin's challenge now forced them to justify their pragmatic adjustments to the new conditions of 'the economic struggle' within Communist rhetoric. They used Pollitt's and Campbell's creative fudge to good effect.

> rank and file movements, must and can, only be useful or successful to the extent to which they embrace existing organisations of the

workers, officials (paid and otherwise) and all the best customs, practices and traditions of the workers in the industry. They must work harmoniously each with the other in giving *organised expression* to the demands of the workers' immediate requirements (and most time [*sic*] they will apparently be very limited), and by such activity lead the movements of the workers on to that plane so urgently necessary at the moment.

These movements are here, right here amongst us – so there is no need to go scratching and searching about for rank and file activities, nor to contemplate for one moment 'setting up rank and file movements'. Such a suggestion would only serve to show colossal ignorance of the situation, or what is more serious a deep seated sectarianism.

[Union structure] allows for organised expression of the rank and file within the given Union; and by affiliation of federation, locally and nationally allow for collective organised expression.

Even if other unions were less democratic than the AEU, 'there are enough rank and file movements within the structure of the AEU to provide scope for all'. But these union rank and file movements were now shunned 'as though they were the plague, we keep ourselves aloof from them and fail to play any part in them, because so many comrades are busy on "Party work" (whatever sins of omission that corrects) . . .'[26]

Scott and Berridge were by no means rejecting the old rank-and-filist traditions. Their evolving world view was first a reaction to Zinkin's own creative development of those traditions for quite different ends, and second a response to the changed conditions of inter-war trade unionism. They had already discovered that the greater centralization of collective bargaining meant that militants had to operate differently in order to be effective.

However, the *overt* issue in the conflict was whether separate rank-and-file movements were necessary to achieve militant aims. Most Party activists related to it in the same way as Bert Papworth: they perceived only an unwonted attack on the heart of rank-and-filism. Unlike Scott and Berridge they had not reflected on the changed conditions of post-war trade-unionism, and accordingly could not conceive that separate movements might prevent Party members operating effectively inside the official union machinery.

When the Party leadership returned from Moscow, steps were swiftly taken to mend fences on the rank-and-filist side. If King Street had closed down the ASSNC or pressed the London Busmen to wind up for the reasons urged by Scott, they would have been seen to be condoning a radical departure from the militant tradition which stretched back to the 1890s and Tom Mann. The London Busmen's leaders sincerely declared their allegiance to the TGWU, in the same breath as they insisted on the caveat that the union could never be trusted without the Rank-and-File

Movement. *Both* the union and their rank-and-file movement were essential to the Busmen's continuing victories. Zinkin had the additional justification of the multi-union situation in aircraft. He argued that the ASSNC was essential not only to make the leadership fight, but also to 'coordinate' union activity.

Nevertheless, on their return the Party Centre took full advantage of the International's imprimatur to reinforce what were now not merely 'new tactics', but the new line.

> The defence of the immediate economic and political interests of the working class must form the starting point and the main content of the united front in all capitalist countries . . .
>
> It is necessary to strive at the same time both for short-term and for long-term agreements providing for joint action with Social Democratic Parties, reformist trade unions and other organisations of toilers against the class enemies of the proletariat.

Arthur Horner was quick to utilize the ideological rationale provided by the 7th World Congress to wind down the South Wales Miners' Rank-and-File Movement.[28] But Pollitt's and Campbell's official position remained that all existing rank-and-file movements were loyal supporters of official trade unions, so there could be no question of dissolving any of them.

The *Labour Monthly* Recall Conference provided the occasion for a conspicuous display of unity amongst all militants about the need to concentrate on a united front for fighting fascism. Having firmly re-established the *status quo ante*, the Party Centre allowed a strictly theological dispute about the correct definition of 'rank-and-file movement' to proceed in print over the next six months. They recognized that it was counter-productive to suppress the conflict, but took care to see that the dispute did not affect the practical conduct of Party members' daily mass work. They made it clear to both sides that they were expected to operate the inextricably intertwined imperatives of trade union loyalism and rank-and-filism.[29]

However, Pollitt and Campbell proved unable to suppress the conflict for long. The public row between Scott and Papworth at the *Labour Monthly* conference reflected the real situation. In the pre-1914 world, rank-and-file/reform movements had coexisted with official union structures, often uneasily and sometimes with great tension, but occupying the same continuum. The development of collective bargaining in the post-war world meant that this coexistence was no longer possible. In the 1930s a rank-and-file movement which claimed to possess the inalienable right to decide whether to accept an officials' judgement presented a clear threat to union authority. Because union officials expected to negotiate comprehensive package agreements involving the totality of working practices, they had to be able to guarantee their members' adherence to their side of the bargain. Observant Party activists, who were most involved in trade union activity, could sense the incompatibility between the new negotiating culture and separate rank-and-file movements.

The constitutional militants' premonitions were eventually vindicated in May 1937. The London Busmen's Rank and File Movement and the ASSNC had serious confrontations with their respective trade union executives which had potentially damaging consequences for the movements, their activists and the CPGB. The vicissitudes of each were played out publicly and messily on the national political stage. We will return to their fates in Chapter Six. Meanwhile, we follow the development and advance of the Real United Front.

Notes

1. *Daily Worker*, 24 February 1934. There were 1,420 delegates, including representatives from 227 union branches. The TGWU had the highest representation with 81 delegates from 43 branches, probably mostly from the London Busmen. During 1934 the Communist Party played an important part in the campaign against the National Government's changes and reductions in unemployment assistance and the reorganization in its administration. There were major disturbances precipitated in Sheffield. United Front activity in South Wales burgeoned around these issues.
2. *Daily Worker*, 26 May 1934.
3. *Daily Worker*, 13 April 1934.
4. *Daily Worker*, 9 May 1934. For the 1934 Lucas events, see *Daily Worker*, 2, 3, 4, 5 May 1934.
5. These strikes await serious research. There are short reports in the *Daily Worker*, 21 April 1933 (Everetts and Phillips, Smethwick); 13 and 27 April 1934 (Withers); 26 January 1935 (Postlethwaite's, West Bromwich; mainly women workers); 18 March; 4, 12 and 18 April 1935 (Chance's Glass Works, Stonehouse's and Maple's Foundry, West Bromwich; 17 January 1936 (Jordan Enamel Works, Bilston); 11 April 1936 (GKN Bolt Mill, Birmingham). For Geobey and Varley, see Hyman, R., 1971, *The Workers' Union*, Clarendon Press: 50.
6. *Daily Worker*, 30 July 1934 (my emphasis). The most comprehensive account of the Pressed Steel strike is McEvoy, D., 1972 'From Firm Foundations, A Study of the Trade Union Recognition Strike at Cowley, July 13 to July 28 1934', paper for Westminster College of Education, Oxford.
7. See *Daily Worker*, 16, 19, 23 and 24 May 1934; 25, 27 and 31 July 1934; 1, 6, 9, 11, 13, 14, 16, 21, 23 August 1934. A strike at Balham occurred at the end of July just before the Olympia radio show. The company made concessions but refused union recognition. Busmen from the nearby Merton garage where the Busmen's Rank-and-File Movement was strong and had Marxist roots led a deputation of Mullard's girls to the TGWU Clapham office to demand help.
8. Claydon, T., 1981, 'The Development of Trade Unionism among British

Automobile and Aircraft Workers, c.1914–1946', University of Kent at Canterbury PhD: .360–1 and 368–9.

9. For a homily on the London campaign, see *Daily Worker*, 13 September 1934.

10. W. Howell had been a Party member in the early 1920s. Charlie Wellard remembered that he had continued to be extremely helpful to Party activists. He publicly supported the CPGB's application to affiliate to the Labour Party in 1936. Tommy Knibbs lived in Brixton where he was in the BSP. He may actually have been in the CPGB as a passive, 'old style' socialist. He had been elected District Secretary in 1926.

11. *Engineers' Bulletin*, 1934, No.2, October. Tanner praised the conference in his ODD's report in the *AEU Journal*, October 1934.

12. *Daily Worker*, 1 October 1934.

13. *Daily Worker*, 16 November 1934. These events are described in Fishman, N., 1991, PhD, op.cit., ch. 7.

14. For some of the background to this incident see Francis, 1980, The Fed, op.cit., pp. 198–200. See also *Daily Worker*, 15, 27, 29 August 1934; 19, 26, 29 September 1934; and 1, 5 October 1934.

15. Branson, 1985, *History of the CPGB*: 124–5. For the troubled gestation of the 7th World Congress and the new line, see Carr, 1982, *Twilight of the Comintern,*: 392–9, and Urban, 1986, *Moscow and the Italian Communist Party*: 113–20.

16. Mahon records that in November 1933 Pollitt attended the 13th Plenum of the ECCI, which had been convened to prepare the way for the new line. The Comintern's consultations continued into 1934. In January 1935 he spoke at the ECCI on the United Front. (Mahon, J., 1976, 'Our Work in the Trade Unions', p. 525) 'Pollitt [had criticized] . . . the practice of making united action dependent on conditions unacceptable to Labour and Social-democratic workers' (p. 195).

17. *Daily Worker*, 2 February 1935.

18. *Daily Worker*, 4 February 1935 (my emphasis).

19. *Daily Worker*, 28 November 1934 (my emphasis). There are other discussion articles on union elections, *DW*, 2 November 1934; another by Johnny Campbell, *DW*, 18 November 1934; and one by Emile Burns, *DW* 21 November 1934.

20. See Appendix 1.

21. Report of 13th Party Congress, p. 60.

22. Ibid., p. 59.

23. *Daily Worker*, 17 June 1935. Hugh Slater had attacked the 'new tactics' in an article in *Communist Review* which had made concessions to the importance of united fronts. (June 1935, p. 117.) 'South West' and 'Far East' London were areas where the Young Turks had been strong. The 'Far East' included the active enclave of Party members on the LCC Dagenham estate. It is likely that the south-west London members were influenced by their surrounding Marxist antecedents which included the BSP and the Balham group.

24. *Daily Worker*, 26 August 1935. *Labour Monthly*'s report of the conference had no reference to this exchange.

25. Ibid.

26. 'Statement on a "Rank and File" Movement in the Metal Industry'. The 'statement' was appended to a letter from the London District Party addressed 'to all industrial fractions and instructors. to all factory cells', dated 4 September 1935, in Lovell Collection, Marx Memorial Library.

From the context, it is clear that the authors were Scott and Berridge, with Berridge providing the intellectual gloss.

27. Dimitrov's Report to the Seventh Comintern Congress, *Inprecorr*, Vol.15 No. 37, 20 August 1935: 964.

28. The South Wales Rank and File paper, *The South Wales Miner*, had published an article by G. Griffiths, probably a pseudonym for Horner, in February 1935, which stated that the aim of a Rank and File Movement was 'to transform the Trade Unions from organs of class collaboration into organs of class struggle'. The article was a reply to a letter from 'Anthracite Miners' who argued a rank-and-filist case against the Fed's new 'rank-and-file' Executive. It concluded, 'in actual fact the Fed. has become a movement of the rank-and-file fighting for improvements in wages and working conditions of the miner and politically carrying out the policy of class struggle against the capitalists in general'. And, when a Lodge 'has been decisively won for the policy of the Rank and File Movement, and has become the organ of struggle, the lodge *itself* is the expression of the Rank and File Movement.' (*The South Wales Miner*, 6 February 1935). The last issue of the *South Wales Miner* appeared in July 1935.

29. A letter from an anonymous tramworker from New Cross supporting separate rank-and-file movements was published in the *Daily Worker* on 10 September 1935. E.D. Sheehan was probably its author. He was a branch officer at New Cross and had a signed article in *Labour Monthly* in December 1935 which attempted to integrate rank-and-file movements into the post 7th World Congress position. The first issue of a new Party periodical, *Discussion* had an article by 'P.J.', probably the veteran AEU activist Peter Jenkins, entitled 'Why We Don't Want Rank and File Movements'. This supported a full constitutional militant position. Three subsequent articles were published, two against and one in favour of 'P.J.' A subsidiary controversy emerged about the nearly dormant Railway Vigilance Movement in the March issue. See *Discussion* Nos. 1 and 2, January and March 1936. Noreen Branson's reference to this conflict is oblique. See Branson, 1985: 177–8.

CHAPTER FIVE

Waiting for the National Militant Upsurge

The dominant historiographical assumption is that the 'united front' line enunciated at the 7th World Congress enabled Western European Communists to adapt to the non-arrival of proletarian revolutions. British historians further assume that British Communists accepted a situation in which outbreaks of serious class struggle were unlikely. It was now official that 'Life Itself' was *not* going to present the possibility of seizing state power in Britain; indeed the principal question for the CPGB was accommodation and cooperation with 'reformist' leaders over questions of common interest.

Whilst the united front for peace and against fascism was certainly a more immediate and more credible goal than revolution, it did *not* entail abandoning the expectation that the British working class would rise up in revolt as a class. At the time, Palme Dutt made it clear enough that Communists were merely forging a new set of alliances in order to wage the class struggle in the changed circumstances.

> Where before the dream of democracy was a counter-revolutionary opiate, to-day the fight for democratic rights against fascism has become a mass fight against the main attack of finance-capital . . .
> . . . The real fight is the fight for the line of independent class struggle, for the independence of the Labour Movement against the line of collaboration with the National Government.[1]

The practical meaning of the new line was not *less* revolutionary for British Communists who had followed the logic of Pollitt's and Campbell's leadership from the 12th British Party Congress. From that time they had schooled British Communists not to rule out a militant upsurge in the class struggle, but to anticipate its occurrence inside the trade union movement. The significance of the post 7th Congress line was to confirm their vision of the *organized* working class rising up in a united front composed of both Communists and 'reformists'. Once the trade union movement was engaged in a full-scale battle in the 'economic struggle', the power of its fighting 'rank-and-file' would ensure that Communists played a dominant role.

Since at least 1930, the revolutionary expectations and zeal of Pollitt and Campbell had been directed towards just such a militant upsurge of trade unionists. They had ceased to envisage any other seizure of power in Britain. Therefore, far from dampening their revolutionary ardour, the 7th World Congress actually reinforced and legitimated it. The tactics which Pollitt and Campbell were now able to urge on their members without qualification might seem 'reformist' to superficial observers. Pollitt declared:

> In the Trade Union movement when we are defeated by majority votes in the unions we will accept such decisions, but we will continue with our propaganda and education to try and win the workers on to our side.[2]

He invoked a *Daily Worker* expression:

> It was that the Communist Party is the fighting champion for a mass trade union movement in this country. This should become a popular expression . . . We have in mind certain black spots in this country, notably Nottingham, Birmingham and the new industrial area that is rapidly developing round London . . . where trade unionism is weak. Our Party must come out especially strongly in those areas for the improvement of wages and conditions of the workers in the factories, and must win those workers into trade unions, so that wherever there are Communists, trade union organisation is strong.[3]

But the importance of adopting these tactics was not to accommodate to the lack of working-class militancy and spirit of revolt. Instead, these tactics were vital to ensure that this potential for revolt and the will to fight the economic struggle in full-scale battle were actually realised. For Pollitt and Campbell, the significance of the 7th World Congress was not to delay the militant upsurge, but instead to better prepare the ground for its successful prosecution.

> The Communist Party has no interests save those of the working class struggle. The wide body of trade union organisations are increasingly recognising this in their experience . . . The role of the Communist Party is more indispensable than ever before in the present united fight. There can be no illusions as to the character of the struggle before us. That struggle can never be settled in Parliament . . . We can only be prepared if we have a powerful revolutionary party of the workers leading the united mass movement . . . The workers are ready to listen to the message of Communism with a new mass response and sympathy.[4]

The response of the 'reformist' trade union leadership to the British Communists' 'new' line of the united front was predictably low key. By the summer of 1935 there had been ample opportunity for full-time union officials to observe that Party activists were not only union militants, but also loyalists who usually observed not only the letter but also the spirit of union rules. Trade union leaders showed no inclination to expose the ulterior motives behind Communist Party initiatives when these yielded significant increases in union membership and improved members' morale. We shall observe that union leaders responded to the Party's propaganda which stressed the importance of 'rank-and-file' activity and the need for a united front by adapting their own rhetoric to include these slogans.

There was clear evidence at the Trades Union Congress in September 1935 that union leaders were in no mood to disturb the *modus vivendi* between themselves and the Party members active inside trade unions. Harry Pollitt had written to Walter Citrine in March 1934 offering to place the Party's services at the unions' disposal in return for a formal united front alliance between the TUC and CPGB. Citrine responded by persuading the TUC General Council to send out two circulars that autumn, one to affiliated unions and the other to trades councils. They recommended that members of the CPGB and any fascist organization should be debarred by rule from holding union and trades council office. They also sought information about Communist 'infiltration' in official activities.

The Party dubbed them the 'Black Circulars' and mounted a high pro-file campaign for their rejection. Twelve unions, including the TGWU, NUR and AEU took a positive decision not to operate the circular addressed to affiliated unions.[5] The AEU and the MFGB each placed motions on the agenda for Congress in September 1935 opposing them. Party trade union activists had evidently been able to reap abundant moral indignation from non-Party union activists. The AEU motion expressed the 'rank-and-file' reaction succinctly: 'The recommendations [in the circulars] deny the full rights of membership of many active trade unionists, are undemocratic and . . . constitute a gross interference with the rights of members of affiliated unions.'[6]

The MFGB motion was debated first because it proposed the reference back of the section in the General Council's report dealing with the Circulars. It fell to Citrine to defend the section: 'The General Council have conceived it to be their duty . . . to explain to their unions the fact that disruptive tendencies are evident and that in the view of the Council these disruptive tendencies are organised.'

For the MFGB, Will Lawther retorted that the real disruptors in the labour movement were not 'what are presumed to be our enemies of the Left'. He continued: 'We do know that there are disruptive elements within our organisation. Where do we find them? We find them in the people who went with Macdonald at the last General Election.'

The reference back failed narrowly on a card vote, 1.427 million for and 1.869 million against.[7] The AEU motion called for both circulars to be rejected. Jack Little's speech described them as dictatorship which 'does not appeal to us one little bit, and when we see it appearing in the guise of the General Council we do not want it from that source either'.[8]

Bevin's reply on behalf of the General Council conceded most of the ground which Little had claimed. He denied any attempt to interfere with unions' internal affairs, pointing out that affiliates were not bound by the circulars to change their rules. He noted that trades councils had to be on their guard against 'subversion', but also protested:

> If there is one thing I would regret it would be the introduction of a
> political or religious test in this Movement . . .
>   There is nothing in this Circular that I have seen, and I would be
> no party to it, about excluding a Communist or Fascist as such. A
> trade unionist has the right to his political freedom. I do not want the
> Continental business to come up.[9]

Bevin went to considerable lengths to distance himself from the circulars which he was supposed to be defending. He revealed that he had not been present at the General Council meeting which adopted the circulars, implying that they would have been quite different in content if he had been. Bevin had damned the circulars with faint praise; he had also practically given his word that the General Council had no intention of launching an anti-Communist crusade. He then felt able to declare that the General Council regarded the AEU motion as a vote of confidence. It was duly rejected by 539,000 to 1.944 million votes, a tactical victory the size of which owed much to Bevin's candour.[10]

The proof of the General Council's hollow pudding could be detected in the subsequent failure of both unions and trades councils to put the circulars into practice. No affiliated union changed its rules; the National Union of General and Municipal Workers (NUGMW) remained the only union which banned Communists from holding office, a prohibition which dated from 1927.[11] Despite the formal operation of the second circular concerning trades councils, Party members regularly continued to serve as presidents and secretaries of trades councils, notably the councils which were most active and strategically important, London – Newcastle-upon-Tyne, Birmingham, Coventry and Manchester.[12]

Instead of active hostility, party trade union activists had to deal with the response from 'reformist' union leaders that British unions were *already* a united front, in which Communists were free to participate. As Johnny Campbell observed ruefully in August 1935: ' "The trade unions and the Labour Party are the real United Front." How often have we heard that phrase? We do not accept this phrase as being true, but the majority of delegates to [the Trades Union] Congress do.'[13]

Pollitt and Campbell skilfully counter-attacked by painting a picture of the 'real united front' which closely corresponded with earlier syndicalist conceptions. First, the current trade union movement was disunited because its was fragmented:

> The illusion that it [the trade union movement] is united arises from the fact that there is only one trade union centre, the TUC . . . But in daily practice what happens . . . Rivalry, inter-union quarrels, demarcations, competition for members . . . There is no common policy on the questions of wages, hours, and working conditions. There is not a semblance of a united movement when big issues arise.[14]

Second, they made the point that the 'real united front' would only occur when the whole of the organized working class was mobilized as a *class entire* in active struggle against the employers. This militant upsurge of course could only occur when Communists were in the van – at the front leading the assault alongside 'reformist' union leaders. Johnny Mahon proved an excellent propagandist for this vision. Having been a leading Young Turk, his late, but total conversion to the united front enabled him to infuse copious amounts of revolutionary spirit into homilies which incited Party members to take mundane trade union activity seriously. He wrote with absolute conviction about the qualitative difference between members' daily activities in the *apparent* united front of trade unions and the *real* united front, which would only appear when members had done their mass work correctly. 'We want to see class unity organised – that means getting 100% trade unionism, amalgamating the competing unions, affiliating the Communist Party to the Labour Party, forming one all inclusive trade union international.'[15]

He provided a catechism calculated to stir Party activists who thought they had already applied the new line satisfactorily.

> Why are the majority of our Party organisations still passive on trade union questions?
>
> Why are so many trade union branches led by Communists no different in their day to day practice than any other branches?
>
> Why are thousands of the most class conscious trade unionists, once organised in the Minority Movement, still outside the ranks of our Party?
>
> Why are the most active Communist trade unionists repeatedly absent from Party Conferences and discussions?[16]

Pollitt, Dutt and Campbell had returned from the 7th World Congress with the intention of building a 'united people's front' led by the CPGB along with the TUC and Labour Party. Dimitrov had declared to the Congress delegates that:

> . . . the defence of the immediate economic and political interests of the working class must form the starting point and main content of the united front in all capitalist countries.
>
> . . . it is necessary to strive at the same time both for short-term and for long-term agreements providing for joint action with Social Democratic Parties, reformist trade unions and other organisations of toilers against the class enemies of the proletariat.[17]

The Party Centre were still sanguine that a national militant upsurge would occur by virtue of a national wages movement. In the heat of class battle, they were confident that Party union activists would assume leading positions and that the Party would then gain a legitimate place in the labour movement leadership in its own right, making the 'united people's front' a reality. Their evidence for these sanguine expectations was that the sustained economic recovery had recreated the conditions necessary to successful skirmishing in factories and pits. The economic situation also gave the union side an advantage in national conflicts.

In October 1935, the *Daily Worker* observed:

> From below the movement is growing for joint action of the workers. At this moment, when the miners, engineers and railwaymen are putting forward demands for wage increases, the National Miners' Conference can make a big advance towards united trade union action for those common demands. There can be no doubt that such a lead will have a response never before equalled in the trade union movement of this country.[18]

The Party Centre confidently predicted strike action and urged activists to prepare the rank-and-file for the impending conflict. The *Daily Worker* issued periodic warnings that the fight must continue until the unions' full demands were achieved. Throughout 1935–36, however, national wage bargaining produced compromise results. Communists were active in marshalling support for union leaders' threats of strike action, which were never fulfilled and probably uttered only in tactical sincerity.

The post-war post-General Strike generation of union leaders had drawn very practical conclusions from the national confrontations of the 1920s. They evolved a strategy of presenting the employers with an impressive show of the militant intention to strike, a credible deterrent. Throughout the 1930s a credible threat of national strike action induced employers to make concessions before they were under actual duress. In these circumstances employers also felt it unnecessary to organize a counter-offensive in retaliation or 'self-defence'. If the 1930s were marked by the absence of militant national strikes, they were also characterized by a lack of national lock-outs, which were capable of inflicting serious damage on 'overmighty' unions.

Moreover, when the 'reformist' leaders organized compromises and marshalled orderly retreats, the Party Centre did not denounce them. In contrast to the fierce denunciations of 'class traitors' in CPGB propaganda of 1927–30, there was a notable absence of personal attacks on union leaders who compromised. The *Daily Worker* used a highly diluted rank-and-filism to explain the non-appearance of the anticipated national wages strikes, while also administering a powerful appeal to union loyalty.

A good example of this pattern is the national wages dispute in mining. Beginning in 1932, there had been a gradual accession of younger men to the official positions in the MFGB who proved able to assimilate the new 'Mondist' approach and adapt it to the difficult conditions of coalmining where district collective bargaining still prevailed. Joseph Jones of the Yorkshire Miners' Association (YMA) succeeded Peter Lee as President in 1934. He had been Vice-President from 1932 and this national experience combined with pragmatic determination to restore national negotiations and reassert the MFGB's hegemony over its affiliated coalfield unions. The MFGB's other officers were the Secretary Ebby Edwards from Northumberland and Vice-President Will Lawther of the Durham Miners' Association. Both had long-established friendly relations with the Party and now showed that they had no intention of maintaining the post-1926 vendetta against the Party.

In July 1935 Joseph Jones persuaded the MFGB conference to approve a strike ballot over the question of a national wage increase of two shillings per day. The officers staked their reputations on being able to win the ballot, although most observers were highly sceptical that the miners would vote to strike in their continuing state of demoralization. Jones and Edwards patiently built support in a gruelling campaign of coalfield meetings. They convinced and inspired miners who still bore the scars of 1926 to vote 'yes' so that the MFGB could stand up for them and win concessions.

The Party Centre enthusiastically committed all available Party resources into assisting the MFGB campaign, but did so in the patent spirit of helping the officials rather than trying to outflank them from the left. The Party Centre's most conspicuous contribution was to positively enforce the dissolution of the red union, the United Mineworkers of Scotland (UMS), despite the democratically expressed wishes of its members. Though the UMS had failed to gain formal recognition from the coal-owners, its officials had nevertheless been the only effective force fighting for miners' wages and conditions in Fife, where its own membership was concentrated. Moreover, UMS members throughout the Scottish coalfields felt a strong loyalty to *their* union which they did not view as a revolutionary Communist vehicle but rather as an expression of genuine 'rank-and-file' trade unionism. Given the continuing weakness of the 'reformist' Scottish regional mining unions, members' wish to keep the UMS in existence may have been parochial, but it was hardly surprising.[19]

Pollitt's and Campbell's determination to close down the UMS received powerful reinforcement from the 7th World Congress line which stressed the need for unity. In November 1935, Willie Gallacher was elected Communist MP for West Fife. His victory was the combination of fortuitous circumstances and six years of carefully nurturing the constituency. This political triumph by the Party made the dissolution of the UMS easier to bear for the Party activists who had been its poorly paid and highly committed officials.[20] The removal of this awkward thorn in the Scottish mining unions' side certainly made an immense difference to the overall morale of the other coalfield union activists. There was only one remaining gap in the miners' battle line, the breakaway Nottinghamshire Miners' Industrial Union (NMIU).

Ebby Edwards publicly acknowledged 'the Communist section and their service in delivering our literature' at an MFGB delegate conference.[21] His unspoken tribute to the Party Centre for managing the disappearance of the UMS was no less eloquent for not being spoken. In November 1935 MFGB officers' and activists' efforts were rewarded by a substantial majority in the strike ballot. Early in the New Year the Party Centre expected a strike:

> Everyone knows that this [1926] General Strike could have been a victory . . . The Mondist policy of the TUC led the trade union movement almost to the depths of despair . . . Today the working class movement is faced with a new situation which can make history of a new kind . . . Victory for the miners will inspire three million workers into action for their demands. It will lead the way to the downfall of this National Government . . .
>
> Workers! Pour in resolutions of solidarity with the miners' fight. Railwaymen and Engineers! Join in the common fight with the miners. Trade Unionists! Send in demands to the General Council of the TUC for a Special Conference of trade union executives to decide on united action in support of the miners.[22]

Joseph Jones led the national negotiations for the MFGB. He manoeuvred the MFGB forces to the very brink of a national strike. Having skilfully marshalled public opinion to support the miners' case, he then pushed the Government to apply pressure on the coal-owners. The coal-owners conceded substantial wage increases, and were also persuaded to agree to national consultative machinery, an important first step towards the principle of national negotiations, which they had abandoned in 1926.[23] Having marched his troops to the top of the hill, Jones marched them briskly down again to the palpable relief of the more realistic mining activists who had feared that they might actually be called on to deliver a real strike. The *Daily Worker*'s reaction was distinctly muted:

> The main lesson to be learned from this [settlement] was that negotiations must be accompanied by an active campaign amongst the rank and file to prepare them for action. This is the lesson also for workers in other industries who are making claims for wage increases, shorter hours, and demanding the restoration of cuts.[24]

Engineering provides further evidence, first of Party activists' general expectation of an imminent militant upsurge in the form of a national wages movement and second of their adherence to union loyalism at the expense of rank-and-filism when 'reformist' leaders reached compromise settlements. In April 1936, soon after the Baldwin Government's White Paper on Rearmament had been issued, a meeting was convened in London for metalworkers from large engineering centres, and particularly those with armaments factories. The *Daily Worker*'s prominent report did not credit any organization with responsibility for the meeting, presumably to avoid arousing the AEU Executive's hostility. The main speaker was Johnny Campbell. He delivered a speech which was full of militant optimism: 'the whole position in the metal industries had been revolutionised. Workers were developing new organisation where none existed before. Shop stewards were being elected, new interest was being aroused.'[25]

As the AEU Executive concluded a compromise settlement with the Employers' Federation in May, the *Daily Worker* criticized them for 'sitting tight, watchful of the membership, ready to damp down every tendency to fight the tyranny of the [Employers'] Federation by interposing their authority at every stage by repeated and prolonged negotiations which everyone knows beforehand will be fruitless.'[26]

Party activists, however, made no attempt to organize any 'rank-and-file' opposition to the deal. Official conferences about the settlement were sponsored by the London and Manchester AEU District Committees, at which Party activists encouraged a spirit of revolt. They were well attended, but failed to spark off any further activity.[27] Party engineering activists acquiesced, and made no attempt to organize further against the AEU Executive. Indeed, Peter Zinkin's bold bid to mobilize a national aircraft wages movement under the auspices of the thriving Aircraft Shop Stewards National Council (ASSNC) was peremptorily curtailed by the Party Centre, despite clear evidence that it had aroused 'rank-and-file' interest and support.

Pollitt's and Campbell's decision to stop the gestation of a thriving national unofficial movement was open to question since the AEU Executive had not held a democratic membership ballot to approve their compromise settlement. Pollitt had pledged Party members to loyally accept 'majority' decisions with the clear implication that this meant a majority of members not full-time officials. Nevertheless, the ASSNC declined to follow up the overwhelming 'yes' vote in its unofficial ballot for a national aircraft wages agreement, and the AEU Executive's authority remained unchallenged.[28]

The constitutional militants in the London District were now in the ascendant. Joe Scott had been elected Organizing Divisional Delegate (ODD) in September 1935 in succession to Jack Tanner who won election to the AEU Executive. Party engineering activists now proceeded to try to counter the Executive's 'reformism' by organizing a wages movement *inside* the union, following the outlines presented by Scott and Berridge in their 1935 paper for the London Metal Fraction.[29] The resulting activity precipitated a reaction from the AEU Executive in early 1937. Interpreting AEU rules extremely narrowly, the Executive threatened expulsions. The Party's National Metal Bureau decided to curtail even this constitutional militant wages movement for the sake of unity.

The Bureau's decision was influenced by the fact that, apart from Manchester, Party members had been able to excite little enthusiasm or even interest at the prospect of a militant confrontation with the employers over a national wages agreement.[30] AEU activists were evidently prepared to accept the compromise negotiated by the Executive readily enough, even though it did not reflect the ability of many engineering employers to pay. In those sectors of engineering which were expanding, militants had been scoring notable victories through carefully prepared workshop skirmishes and factory-wide unofficial strikes. The concessions gained for their members produced further recruitment to the union and kept their own local forces in good heart to fight another day. Zinkin's success in engendering an 'aircraft consciousness' and a spirit of offensive attack highlights the variation in outlook among the different engineering sectors. By contrast, the AEU District Committees in Glasgow and Greenock continued to battle against demoralization and profound apathy. The political commitment of Party, ILP and other socialist activists made no impact on this depressing situation.

Nevertheless, in addition to the numerous compromises, there were sufficient examples of the success of organized militants to keep the Party Centre sanguine. In May 1936 the leaders of the London Busmen's Rank and File Movement locked the official machinery of the TGWU in a collision course with London Transport over the busmen's demand for a seven-hour day. Bert Papworth addressed a Rank and File meeting of 1200 busmen. He appealed for patience and unity while the official negotiations continued. His charismatic speech was enthusiastically received.[31]

In addition, there was a palpable response from below to the Party Centre's propaganda which argued for a 'real united front'. With fascism gaining ground on the Continent, the idea of a powerful alliance to fight it appealed strongly to non-Party union activists. Party activists found it easy to pilot resolutions through their unions in favour of 'working class unity' and supporting the Communist Party's renewed application to affiliate to the Labour Party. During 1936–37, the sheer volume of 'real united front' motions making their way through official trade union machinery was daunting.

While the Party-inspired motions were usually passed, they had little apparent impact on the leadership's policies either in the trade unions or Labour Party. Union activists who supported 'unity' were expressing a reflexive moral sentiment in favour of the culture of solidarity which characterized the British Labour movement. They had been offered no practical vision of how the Communist Party's inclusion on the plinth of official leadership would actually alter events either domestically or in Europe.

When the Labour Party Executive rejected the CPGB's application for affiliation during 1936 there was no outcry from below, despite the impressive number of resolutions passed supporting affiliation. Nor did the Party Centre try to foment a revolt against the Labour Executive's decision. Rather than risk an all-out confrontation with the Labour and trade union leadership, Pollitt and Campbell bided their time full of confidence that the national militant upsurge would eventually appear.

As the period of waiting for Life Itself to deliver the desired result lengthened, the Party Centre had to steady its own troops behind the united front line. In November 1935, the *Daily Worker* had to administer a stern caution against accepting the superficial conclusion that trade union activity *in itself* was sufficient to produce the real united front. Many Party members had apparently concluded that with the prospect of revolution postponed indefinitely, there was no longer any pressing necessity to build the Communist Party itself.

'There is now a tendency to regard the United Front as a substitute for building the Communist Party. This idea can only harm the United Front, for the stronger the Communist Party the more quickly is it possible to establish the unity of the working class.'[32]

The *Daily Worker* carried a statement from Pollitt refuting arguments for the actual dissolution of the Party in May 1936. Evidently, members had not yet grasped the 'real united front' catechism that the Communist Party *per se* must be formally in the van of the labour movement.

> The Communists are carrying forward a powerful drive for improved methods of trade union organisation and struggle. This can only be carried through by an organised Party which groups around it the most progressive elements inside the trade unions. If we dissolve the Communist Party this would be obviously more difficult and the trade unions could easily stagnate. Secondly a revolutionary party is necessary to raise the level of the working class consciousness and to prepare the workers for revolution ... If the reformist leaders were really prepared to admit Communists as individuals and allow them to carry out their propaganda, they would have no valid reason for refusing the affiliation of the Communist Party to the Labour Party.[33]

And as the momentum of rearmament increased, the *Daily Worker* had more local strikes, Communist-inspired union motions and Communist victories in union elections to report than ever. When Arthur Horner was elected to succeed Jim Griffiths as President of the South Wales Miners' Federation in May 1936, the *Daily Worker* found it a portent:

> 150,000 Welsh miners cannot be wrong. His [Horner's] election is the reply to the disruptive 'Black Circular' of the TUC General Council. It is the reply to all who oppose the affiliation of the Communist Party to the Labour Party. It is a clear call to the TUC General Council to drop once and for all the policy of class collaboration and industrial peace and the attacks on militants in the trade union movement.[34]

Then came the wave of strikes which enveloped France in the summer of 1936 bringing in its wake a dramatic increase in the French Communist Party's membership and influence. The French events greatly intensified British Communist expectations. In October 1936 the *Daily Worker* observed:

> Well over one and a half million workers, engaged in five great industries, are pressing forward through their trade unions for increased pay, shorter hours and improved working conditions ... The determination of the workers in these great industries to force improved conditions from the employers is reflected in a great growth of membership of all the unions concerned. The national membership for all unions increased by 246,000 during 1935. During the current year, membership has increased at an even greater rate. The trade union army is on the march for improved wages and conditions. Militant leadership and unity will make that army invincible.[35]

During the first five months of 1937 the Party Centre's convictions finally seemed confirmed. Communist Party members played a prominent public role in a remarkable concatenation of events. The pace and incidence of industrial conflict quickened simultaneously in engineering, coalmining and on the London buses, the three sectors where Party trade union activism was strongest. There was a national class battle of epic proportions in the wings and apparently awaiting the call of Communist activists to precipitate its entry on to centre stage. The British equivalent of the French Popular Front Government was sure to follow.

In February 1937, AEU grinders at the Rolls-Royce Derby works went on unofficial strike, with the active support of their District Committee. The substantial Party presence on the shop stewards' committee helped to nurture the grinders' sense of grievance. The dispute remained confined to the grinders, despite attempts to bring the whole factory into the fight. Claude Berridge, the newly elected AEU London District President, was one of the early casualties of the strike. He travelled to Derby and spoke at a strike meeting. The AEU Executive unhesitatingly expelled him for intervening in another district's affairs without official sanction.

The Derby strike was sufficient encouragement for Peter Zinkin to promote another aircraft national strike ballot inside the ASSNC, in spite of the strictures against national unofficial action which had been imposed on them by the National Metal Bureau in 1936. Pollitt and Campbell acquiesced in Zinkin's throwing over the traces and stoking the fires of aircraft militancy. The evidence appeared overwhelming that the militant upsurge was gathering momentum. The *Daily Worker*'s rhetoric reflected this optimism from the beginning of March.

> While the union leaders speculate and quibble as to just how far they are prepared to co-operate in the defence plan, the Government and employers are united and are striking heavy blows at trade union-ism. The situation calls for immediate and united action on the part of the engineering unions who, together with the TUC are in a favourable situation to not only secure the immediate demands of the workers, but to effectively safeguard the trade union movement in the period of colossal war preparations.
>
> This [an unofficial strike in the de Havilland's toolroom at Stag Lane, Hendon] is the fifth strike that has occurred in aircraft facto-ries during the past few days and is another indication of the deter-mined efforts the employers are making to undermine trade union conditions and practices in the factories. General unrest in the indus-try has been brought to bursting point by news of what is happening in the big Rolls-Royce factory at Derby, and a growing demand is rising for action to be taken on the part of the Executive of the AEU.[36]

Then, on 27 March, a protracted, convoluted dispute at Beardmore's Parkhead Forge in Glasgow galvanized into a solid strike of 1300 AEU members.[37] Against the background of local union demoralization, the men at Parkhead Forge fought tenaciously. Exceptionally for Glasgow, Beardmore's had retained a well-organized shop stewards committee from the 1920s, and it had been continuously dominated by Party activists. The AEU District Committee mobilized strong support from members in other works who became increasingly involved and enthused as the strike remained solid. The ODD, Harry Luckhurst, told a district meeting of 2000 men that 'in his opinion, the issue of Parkhead would solve in one way or another the wages question for the whole of the Clyde engineers'.[38]

An engineering strike in a large Clydeside armaments works evoked unsettling memories in the London political establishment and media. The *Daily Worker* gloried in their reaction:

> Press propaganda has a wider and deeper aim than the normal one of discrediting the strikers and distorting their claims . . . [The] very 'national emergency' of which the newspapers now scream, if it

exists at all, has been deliberately manufactured by the employers to evade payment of legitimate demands raised by the workers ... Support for the Beardmore strikers will not lead to a national stop-page unless the employers force things to this stage. If they do this, it will be because they, together with the Government desire a national trial of strength with the trade unions. Such challenge, if made, must be met by the united strength of the whole Labour movement if that movement is to continue to exist.[39]

The Beardmore's strike did have a domino effect for the Glasgow Young Communist League (YCL). The highly political YCL activists there had taken union activity extremely seriously since the 7th World Congress had enjoined them to work for 'partial demands'. The national wage increase of three shillings per week conceded by the EEF in June 1936 was the second consecutive national wage increase won by adult engineers. The fact that neither had been paid to youths provided the YCL with a ready-made grievance to exploit. The 1936 increase was paid in three one-shilling instalments over six months with the last one occur-ring at the end of December. In mid-March 1937 apprentices in Paisley staged isolated skirmishes which produced local concessions to 'even up' youth's wages to the men's. Probably keen to emulate the Paisley success, YCL activists on the Clyde produced a remarkable strike wave in the wake of the Beardmore's strike.[40]

Five hundred apprentices at Fairfields shipyard came out on strike three days after the Beardmore's men. They 'established a mass picket to bring out all the apprentices of the closely-packed shipyards and factories in the Govan area.'[41] On 5 April, the *Daily Worker* reported that 3700 apprentices were on strike to win the same wage increases as the adults. The strike wave widened with more lads coming out along the Clyde. The AEU Executive recognized the strike after a fortnight, and there was a reasonably successful one-day strike by adult workers in the Clyde shipyards in support on 16th April. The Beardmore's and apprentices' strikes were cross-fertilizing one another and rekindled feelings of union loyalism which had long lain dormant.[42] The *Daily Worker* was jubilant:

> The Clydeside general protest strike is a warning to the Government and the employers that the working class is resolved upon its justifi-able needs and demands being met. It is also a signal to the Executive of the AEU and the rest of the trade union leadership that the work-ers are not only ready for action, but impatient at the failure and delay on the part of the leadership of the movement to buckle to and get ahead with the necessary measures. For make no mistake. The Clyde strike is not merely a gesture of protest on the workers' part intended to be left at that. Throughout industry as a whole a great wave of discontent and unrest is spreading ... The working class of Britain is rapidly swinging forward into action and the urgent need of the moment is to effect the closest possible co-ordination of its ranks and effective leadership as the guarantee of success.[43]

Meanwhile, the miners were marshalling their forces once again for a national battle. After months of patient and undercover activity by Party mining activists from Sheffield, a bitter strike broke out at the end of 1936 at Harworth colliery in Nottinghamshire against the NMIU. The MFGB officials provided strike pay since they believed that confrontation was the only means of dislodging Spencer and re-establishing the 'real' union, the Nottinghamshire Miners' Association. The strike had reached a stalemate in March, but MFGB officials intervened to escalate the conflict. At the beginning of April, an MFGB delegate conference voted by a large majority to hold a national strike ballot in support of the Harworth strikers.

On 2 April, the day the MFGB conference met to discuss the Harworth battle, the Party Centre issued a Special Statement which signalled the Party's intention to assume its legitimate place at the front of these 'immediate struggles' and the 'united movement'.

> The trade unionists in Britain, in line with their comrades in France, Spain, America and India, are now moving into action . . . Now is the time for the launching of the greatest united effort the Labour movement has ever undertaken, in order to enforce all-round advances in wages and the remedy of outstanding grievances in each industry, together with the placing on the Statute Book of this country of the 40 hour week, holidays with pay and adequate retirement pensions for the veterans of industry.
>
> Trade union leaders, who conceive it to be their first duty to hold the workers back, instead of to inspire them and lead them forward, are the real disrupters of the trade union movement . . . The trade unionists must see that only those who represent this policy [of united action] are elected to the Union Conferences this year, that only those who represent this policy are elected to executive office, so that the British working class will, in this critical period, have a leadership worthy of its dauntless fighting spirit, a leadership that will rise to the height of the great opportunities now confronting the workers.
>
> We call upon the whole working class movement to rally behind the immediate struggles of the Harworth miners, and Beardmore engineers and to prepare their support for the London busmen, as the first practical steps towards the united movement that can avenge everything that the National Government and the FBI [Federation of British Industries] have carried through since 1931.[44]

The MFGB conference decided to hold a national strike ballot. Palme Dutt welcomed this result in the *Daily Worker* on 3 April.

> Here in Britain we have not yet achieved any comparable advance with the United States and France in the industrial field, although all the conditions are now ripe for advance. The barriers to unity, the refusal of a united lead, and the moves of the Government in conjunction with a section of the trade union leadership to throttle all

strikes, are heavily hindering the development of the movement. Nevertheless, in response to the urgent needs of the situation, the advance is beginning. Trade union membership is rising ... If a united Labour movement were realised, that figure could be rapidly doubled, as the example of France has shown.[45]

On the following day, 4 April, Ernest Bevin gave London Transport four weeks' notice of an official London bus strike. The *Daily Worker* asserted:

It is a tribute to the unity the busmen have built up within their own ranks that the notices were handed in by Mr. Bevin, chairman of the TUC. They have broken with the stigma of 'unofficial dispute', so often attached by union leadership to disputes at the present time. There are reports that the decision for strike action has shocked the LPTB.[46]

The rapid succession of events prompted the *Daily Worker*'s page one headline on 6 April 'Press "Plot" Scare Fails. Millions Ready for Action.'

The story continued:

A great popular movement in support of claims for increased wages and improved conditions of employment is sweeping through the trade unions ... Thoroughly alarmed and scared by the strength and power of this great movement the Press has once again discovered a 'Communist Plot' ...
    Here is no 'plot' but a determined mass movement of British trade unionists to secure a little more food, a little more leisure, and a little better life for themselves, their wives and their children.[47]

One week later, the front page headline declared: 'Arms Strike Fund Extending. Boy Apprentices Leading Fight. Aircraft Men Want Ballot.'

The story continued in the same vein:

The whole trade union movement is pulsating with life and the will to fight. With a militant leadership at the top, such an army would prove unconquerable. Let every trade union and Labour worker redouble his efforts to build unity. Increase the pressure on leadership. Victory can be won. The time for action is now.[48]

Despite appearances and the London media hype, King Street's escalating expectations would have been pricked if the Party Centre had addressed the right questions to Party activists involved in the conflicts. While the Beardmore's men had settled in for a long fight, by mid-April their strike had failed to ignite other disputes of adult engineers in emulation either in Glasgow or other engineering centres. Many Clyde employers were already making wage concessions sufficient to induce apprentices back to work. Even though the ASSNC was preparing for an unofficial national strike ballot, other key Party activists in the AEU were adamant that there must be no unofficial action. They were taking all the necessary steps to pre-empt any unofficial strike which the ASSNC might call.

It was evident that the most likely outcome to the Battle of Harworth was not a national strike but another compromise settlement achieved in the wake of the national ballot presenting another credible deterrent in the form of a majority of 'yes' votes. Arthur Horner was already arguing the need for a compromise solution. Joseph Jones and Ebby Edwards with Horner's support, were aiming to maximize the pressure on the Nottinghamshire (Notts.) coal-owners through public opinion and the national coal-owners' association, and also to involve the Mines Department more closely in the strike.

It was well known by Party activists on the London trams that the impending bus strike would be highly problematic. They had warned the Rank and File leadership and the Party Centre that the London Bus Strike would not be supported by the Tramwaymen. But the busmen and King Street chose to believe that the London busmen could win an all-out strike on their own, because rank-and-file busmen were solidly behind their Rank-and-File leaders who would never sell out.

The official London bus strike began on the highly symbolic 1 May. The ASSNC met on 2 May and were inspired to give two weeks' notice of their own unofficial aircraft strike. Apart from the ASSNC's rush of blood to the head, there were no other signs that the national militant upsurge had gained in momentum. Indeed, nemesis followed hard on the busmen's heels. London Transport offered a compromise settlement on 6 May which Bevin wanted to accept as the best offer available in the circumstances. The Central Bus Committee stood firm and the busmen remained solid, but London Transport were determined not to give further ground.

During the first week of the bus strike more Clyde apprentices drifted back to work. On 7 May the MFGB suspended the handing in of strike notices to allow more time for negotiations about Harworth. The Beardmore's strike was settled on 18 May. The impending unofficial aircraft strike disappeared completely from view.

By 19 May the troubled London bus strike was the only remnant of the expected national militant upsurge. In the face of this depressing reality the Party Centre invoked the catechism of the real united front. The *Daily Worker* recited and defiantly disagreed with Bevin's declaration that the British Labour movement was the greatest united front the world had ever known:

> It is precisely because the Communists are for a *real united front* of the working class that they are out for full rights for all trade union members, and the fullest united support of the movement being

ranged behind the miners fight. And it is because they are real and genuine champions of trade unionism that they are striving their utmost to rouse the necessary backing and support for the miners and busmen in order to bring to an end the tyranny of the employers.[49]

In the following week, the TGWU Executive ordered the London busmen back to work and revoked the plenary powers it had given to the Central Bus Committee/Rank and File Movement to conduct the strike. The 14th British Party Congress convened in London four days later. By that time Party activists had actually led orderly retreats at Beardmore's and Harworth after achieving compromise settlements. Party activists had also persuaded London busmen to return to work, despite the fact that the Rank and File Movement's promise of total victory had not been achieved. This 'reformist' behaviour was not questioned at the Congress, either from the platform or from the floor.[50]

The *volte-face* which Pollitt and Campbell had to perform at the 14th Congress was dramatic enough. They had confidently anticipated a national militant upsurge. Nevertheless, Pollitt's and Campbell's practical approach to 'the economic struggle' proved flexibly capable of coping with the 'vicissitudes' which actually occurred. We have observed how the Party Centre had adapted policy and propaganda to the evolving pattern of 'Mondist' industrial relations in 1935–36, albeit wordlessly, without overtly acknowledging the need for compromise and retreat. In the *extremis* of three weeks in May 1937, Pollitt and Campbell were faced with a situation in which they could not avoid choosing between the two imperatives of revolutionary pragmatism, union loyalism and rank-and-filism. They unhesitatingly assigned priority to union loyalism. Pollitt's report to the Congress declared:

> In the credentials report we noticed the splendid fact . . . that out of 397 delegates who are trade unionists, 203 occupy official positions. I am proud to say that this came as a surprise to the representatives of France and Belgium, who did not think we had such a position here.[51]

He cited the TUC Tolpuddle Medal won by over a hundred Party members for recruiting trade union members:

> . . . comrades, the Tolpuddle Medal to a Communist is not a mere bauble, is not a Coronation medal, it is the highest order for Labour that can be possessed in the trade union movement, for it typifies the sacrifices of those who built the foundations of trade unionism in this country . . . We want the Congress next year to be one where we can announce not a few hundred Communists, but a thousand, who can display the highest honour that trades unionists can possess in this country.[52]

Instead of the compromises brokered and accepted by Party activists, delegates' attention was drawn to Bevin's perfidy and the heroism of the Harworth strikers. For the first time, the Party Centre also assigned some responsibility for failure to the 'rank-and-file' itself. Pollitt's report observed:

> The basis of our campaign for unity is not one of personal motives, but of the carrying out of a policy that is in the interests of the whole working-class movement. The fact that the general line of the Labour Party and Trades Union Congress is not based on the class struggle inevitably leads to the adoption of policies that in their practical results represent gains for the class enemy. They disrupt the workers' ranks, lead to doubt and confusion, dampen down struggle and prevent the united power of the working-class from being exercised.
>
> We oppose to this the line of working-class unity and struggle against the class enemy for the strengthening of every phase of the daily struggle against capitalism, and for the winning of the workers' final aims.
>
> But to bring about this change, the rank and file of the Labour Movement have to face their responsibilities. The chief responsibility undoubtedly falls on the dominant Labour leaders, but not sufficient fight is made to change the policy.[53]

Pollitt's and Campbell's *de facto* decision to give union loyalism higher priority than rank-and-filism was accepted by most Party union activists. By 1937, experience in fighting the 'economic struggle' in British conditions had caused them to discover that 'Life Itself' usually turned up *not only* the occasion for militant struggle against their employer, *but also* the necessity for compromise and orderly retreat. They could see that leading the fight for concessions and organizing for an expedient retreat were co-requisites for their own survival as union activists. Nowhere did Party activists attempt to lead the 'rank-and-file' in continuing struggle against the employing class.

It is notable, however, that while the events of May 1937 had compelled the Party Centre to make union loyalism an absolute imperative, the experience had not reduced their faith that 'Life Itself' would ultimately cause the revolution to appear. At the 14th Congress, Johnny Campbell acknowledged that Communists were accused of not being interested in increased wages but only revolution. He rejoined cutely that the question was like being asked whether he wanted jam or marmalade, and that he wanted jam first.

> We are for increased wages and we are for the revolution. It is because we are the irreconcilable partisans of the proletarian revolution that we are the most consistent fighters for increased wages as the way to mobilise the working class and lead them towards the conquest of power.[54]

Campbell argued that the increased exploitation and immiseration of the working class had produced the strike wave of 1936–37, not the temporary prosperity engendered by rearmament. Strikes would recur with even greater frequency because, as Marx had predicted, exploitation and immiseration would intensify. With more strikes, the Communist Party would find more opportunities to lead the working class. Having established that Life Itself was actually hastening the revolution, he reminded members not to commit the Communist sin of hubris. Life Itself would only produce its promised fruits if Party members fulfilled their daily mass work.

> ... the growth of the Party's membership is not reflected in a growth of the number and size of the factory groups. Without the growth in number and size of the factory groups as a stimulus of all round workshop organisation we cannot play an effective part as a Party in stimulating the great movement of the workers.[55]

> We want to see those people who tell us that the trade union movement is a real united front, establishing a joint committee in every industry, with agreement on a joint campaign in every industry, systematically working to bring those workers into the orbit of the trade unions.[56]

> Our main task is not to ensure that the working class will fight, but to ensure that when the working class does fight it will fight in a powerful and united movement that will enable it to gain victory comparatively quickly and painlessly. There are obstacles in the working class itself, but these obstacles would be trivial if they were not reinforced by the whole class collaboration policy of the leadership.[57]

Apparently against all the odds, the 14th Party Congress concluded amid much self-congratulation. There were no mutual recriminations or heart-searching, only unanimous certainty that the Party had never strayed from the right road. Nevertheless, the collapse of the great strike wave of 1937, so full of militant promise at its beginning, produced a permanent change in British Communist strategy. Pollitt and Campbell never again based their own calculations on predictions of social flux or class conflagration in Britain. They took care to see that the Party was never again publicly committed to such expectations. They were unwilling to jeopardize the Party's existing strength in the movement for the sake of hypothetical events. The logic of their decision was the Party's tacit acceptance of the *status quo* in the overall balance of class forces.

Despite the traumatic conclusion for activists involved in the strikes and the disappointment of everyone who had expected a national militant upsurge, there is no evidence that either King Street or members engaged in daily 'economic struggle' were depressed or beset by doubts about the future. Pollitt's and Campbell's approach to the 'economic struggle' remained unchanged and Party activists' conduct of it also continued as before. Party membership increased during 1937 and in subsequent years. There can be no doubt, however, that Party activists leading the strikes of April–May 1937 had done much hard thinking and endured much agonizing and conscience-searching during their course. The pull of rank-and-filism remained very strong. The three crucial disputes, the London bus strike, the ASSNC unofficial aircraft strike and the Harworth strike, are examined in detail in the next two chapters. They provide ample evidence that the edifice of revolutionary pragmatism built by Pollitt and Campbell since 1930 was capable of withstanding the substantial stress imposed by the compromises and retreats of May 1937.

Notes

1. Dutt's report on the Seventh Congress, *Labour Monthly*, October 1935: 595.
2. Pollitt's Report on the Seventh Congress, *Labour Monthly*, November 1935: 682.
3. 'Harry Pollitt's Report to Central Committee, 4–5 January 1936', CPGB pamphlet: 10.
4. *Daily Worker*, 15 November 1935.
5. *Labour Research*, September 1935.
6. TUC Report 1935: 269.
7. Ibid.: 261–2.
8. Ibid.: 269.
9. Ibid.: 275.
10. Ibid.: 280. The General Council received only a small numbers of replies to the circulars' request for information, and these contained very few examples of disruptive activities (Ibid.: 111–112).
11. The NUGMW had prohibited both CPGB and Minority Movement members from holding any union office, and Party activists were vigorously winkled out of the union's district organizations in London and Lancashire (Clegg, 1985, *British Trade Unions*, op.cit.: 420).
12. Interviews with Sid Atkin about Birmingham, Bill Warman about Coventry and Eddie Frow about Manchester by N. Fishman, and interview with Jock Gibson about Coventry by Peter Caldwell. Eddie Frow remembered that the Manchester Trades Council had decided to sacrifice two or three Party members to the ban. The 'victims' were chosen, accepted their martyrdom, and the Trades Council proceeded to function with the rest of its Communist personnel intact. See also Clinton, A., 1973, 'Trades Councils from the beginning of the Twentieth Century to the Second World War', University of London PhD: 262–4.
13. *Daily Worker*, 17 August 1935.
14. Harry Pollitt in the *Daily Worker*, 7 September 1935.
15. Trade Unionism and Communism, An Open letter by John Mahon', CPGB, n.d. *ca* 1936.
16. John Mahon, 1936, 'Our Work in the Trade Unions', *Discussion*, April: 13.

17.   Dimitrov's Report to the Seventh Congress, Inprecorr, Vol. 15 No. 37, 20
      August 1935: 964. For the 'united people's front' at the Seventh Congress
      see Degras, 1960, *The Communist International*, Vol. III, op. cit.: 375–6.
18.   *Daily Worker*, 17 October 1935.
19.   See N. Fishman, 1991, PhD: 311–325.
20.   Ibid.
21.   Arnot, R. Page, op.cit., Vol. III, p.178 quoting Ebby Edwards at an MFGB
      delegate conference on 24 January 1936. The UMS had held a ballot of
      members at the end of September 1935 to promote its plan for UMS
      branches and members to join the Scottish federation of coalfield unions.
      No public reports of the ballot result exist, and it is likely that members
      voted against unity. However, on 29 December 1935, 65 delegates unani-
      mously voted to achieve unity by 'advising all [UMS] members to immedi-
      ately join up in the county unions', (*Daily Worker*, 31 December 1935).
      Edwards's effusive praise for the CPGB occurred barely a month after the
      UMS dissolution.
22.   Front page statement from Party Secretariat, *Daily Worker*, 8 January
      1936.
23.   For the national wages dispute see R. Page Arnot, op.cit., Vol. III: 149–52,
      166, 169 and 171–8. For the Party's response see *Daily Worker*, 2 July; 5,
      15, 19 August; 18, 19, 24 September; 17, 19, 29 October; 16, 21, 22
      November; 2, 9, 13, 14, 20, 21 December 1935; and 4, 8, 10, 13, 14, 15,
      23, 27 January 1936.
24.   *Daily Worker*, 25 January 1936.
25.   *Daily Worker*, 6 April 1936. There were no attendance figures given.
26.   *Daily Worker*, 12 May 1936 .
27.   See *Daily Worker*, 11, 12 and 14 May 1936. Wally Hannington spoke at
      the London conference which was attended by 300 engineers and also dis-
      cussed rearmament.
28.   See pp. 144–7.
29.   See pp. 77–8.
30.   The National Metal Bureau had been formally constituted in mid-1936.
      The Party Centre evidently judged that there were now enough Party
      activists to make the need for coordination imperative, and also recognized
      the need for an authoritative voice to deal with the situations where rank-
      and-filism and union loyalty conflicted. In January 1937, the National
      Bureau established local metal bureaux in engineering centres to ensure the
      national wages campaign took root. The minutes of the Manchester Metal
      Bureau from 1937–39 are in the Working Class Movement Library; and
      the National Bureau's directives can be traced through them. Scott and
      Berridge were its leading forces, though Zinkin also served. For the instruc-
      tion to close down the wages movement, see Manchester Metal Bureau
      minutes, 16 and 30 April 1937.
31.   *Daily Worker*, 21 May 1936. See p. 119.
32.   *Daily Worker*, 19 November 1935.
33.   *Daily Worker*, 21 May 1936.
34.   *Daily Worker*, 25 May 1936.
35.   *Daily Worker*, 21 October 1936. The industries included clothing, woollen
      textiles, the Scottish miners and the railwaymen.
36.   *Daily Worker*, 2 March 1937.
37.   For a full description of the dispute, see AEU Executive minutes, Vol. 2,

1937: 101–12, Special Meeting held on 17 April to receive deputation from Glasgow. Luckhurst, James Docherty,the Beardmore's Convener and W. Irvine, leading District Committeeman and chairman of the Strike Committee, attended. The AEU rulebook required the District Committee to hold a ballot vote in the factory before sanctioning the strike. Luckhurst told the Executive 'that it was a widespread impression in Glasgow District – confirmed by many old members to whom he had spoken – that the taking of a Ballot Vote was not absolutely necessary'. Tom Clark, Executive Councillor for Glasgow, 'confirmed what Bro. Luckhurst had said regarding the practice on Clydeside in past years'. (p. 107).

Docherty was a Party activist, and Irvine a reliable sympathizer. Croucher observes that the Forge was the factory in which the Party had 'by far' the greatest strength. ('Communist Politics and Shop Stewards in Engineering, 1935-46', University of Warwick PhD: 319.) Peter Kerrigan had worked there at one time. The dispute was greatly complicated by the fact that Beardmore's were *not* members of the EEF when it began, but joined during it.

Luckhurst explained to the Executive that 'Messrs. Beardmore's are the only firm wherein our members have been able to maintain 100 per cent. Trade Union conditions and an efficient Shop Stewards' organisation throughout the period of the depression; and they were the only Firm where our Stewards were able to lay it down that Trade Union membership is a condition of employment.' The EEF had 'quite naturally, been after Messrs. Beardmore's for a long, long time. In fact, he was aware, as a result of information received from private sources, that the desire had been to enrol the Firm ... and ... then endeavour to break down the strength of the Union.' 'What he wanted to emphasise was that, if Beardmore goes down, then the Union's position on Clydeside generally would also go down (pp.105-6). Tom Clark and Davy Kirkwood MP, leading members of the Clyde Workers' Committee, had both worked at Beardmore's in the 1914–18 war.

38.   *Daily Worker*, 5 April 1937.
39.   *Daily Worker*, 30 March 1937.
40.   For the 1936 wage increase, see *AEU Journal* July 1936. For the Paisley strikes see McKinlay, A., 1986, 'From Industrial Serf to Wage-Labourer: The 1937 Apprentice Revolt in Britain', *International Review of Social History*, Vol. xxxi, Part I: 10. There was a substantial Party presence in Paisley engineering. (Interview with Bill McQuilkin by N. Fishman.)
41.   McKinlay, 1986, op.cit.: 11. McKinlay's view of the Glasgow Apprentices' Strike differs from mine. He emphasizes the centrality of the non-wage demands. In fact, the YCL 'rank-and-file' were the principal proponents of demands for union recognition, better training and treatment by management. The course of the strike shows that wages remained the principal grievance. Most employers had conceded wage increases for apprentices by the end of April, and a general resumption of work followed forthwith. The Apprentices' Charter produced by the YCL to articulate more general corporate demands about training, status and union recognition did not appear until most of the lads had returned to work. (See *Daily Worker*, 4 May 1937.)
      The strikes await a comprehensive treatment which examines the Paisley and Clyde outbreaks in relation to one another and also to their

local adult labour movements. Historians have taken YCL activists' propaganda at its face value and assumed that the outbreaks were hermetically sealed from events going on simultaneously in the adult economic conflict. The local link with the strike at Beardmore's Parkhead Forge is clearly established in contemporary accounts.

42. *Daily Worker*, 8, 9, 12, 17, 23 April 1937. An AEU district aggregate meeting set up a sub-committee to help the apprentices and established a membership levy of one shilling a week for the Beardmore's strikers. Stewards at the Albion works were already collecting this weekly levy. The Confederation of Shipbuilding and Engineering Unions (the Confed.), on which the AEU was not represented, provided the greatest support for the apprentices' strikes, probably because AEU officials and activists remained pre-occupied with Beardmore's. Nevertheless, the AEU benefited. Luckhurst reported that 400 apprentices had joined the AEU in May (*AEU Journal*, June 1937).

43. *Daily Worker*, 17 April 1937.

44. *Daily Worker*, 2 April 1937.

45. *Daily Worker*, 3 April 1937. The 'refusal of a united lead' refers to the TUC and Labour Party leaderships' failure to cede the CPGB a legitimate place either through affiliation to the Labour Party or a formal alliance.

46. *Daily Worker*, 5 April 1937. See p. 121.

47. *Daily Worker*, 6 April 1937.

48. *Daily Worker*, 13 April 1937.

49. *Daily Worker*, 19 May 1937 (emphasis mine).

50. The reports of Congress debates are in *Daily Worker*, 28, 29 and 31 May and 1 June 1937.

51. *It Can Be Done*, 1937, Report of the 14th Party Congress, CPGB: 195–6.

52. Ibid.: 198. The Central Committee Report stated that scores of other members could have received it if they had actually applied. (ibid.: 146). The medal was awarded for trade union recruitment: a gold medal for 100 members; a silver medal for 50 members and a badge for 20 members.

53. 14th Party Congress Report: 55–6.

54. *Daily Worker*, 31 May 1937.

55. 'It Can Be Done', 1937, loc.cit.: 100–1. Resolution on Industrial and Trade Union Work, introduced by Campbell.

56. Ibid.: 107.

57. *Daily Worker*, 31 May 1937.

CHAPTER SIX

Rank and File Movements: Communist Myth and Practical Reality

The London Busmen's Rank and File Movement

This chapter analyses the Communist Party's contribution to the two substantial rank-and-file movements of the 1930s, the London Busmen's Rank and File Movement and the Aircraft Shop Stewards National Council (the ASSNC). Both movements reached their climax in May 1937 when they embarked on collision courses with the TGWU and AEU Executives. The conflicts which ensued were resolved in the Executives' favour, but not exclusively. Pollitt and Campbell took care to ensure that the Party activists involved also emerged with their bona fides inside the trade union movement intact. They continued to lead skirmishes and strikes in the 'economic struggle' and to occupy lay trade union offices. Indeed, the London Busmen's leader, Bert Papworth, became the first Communist Party member of the TUC General Council.

We have observed that Pollitt's and Campbell's approach to the 'economic struggle', revolutionary pragmatism, contained two essential but contradictory elements: trade union loyalism and rank-and-filism. We have noted the ubiquity of the rank-and-file/reform tradition in pre-1914 British trade unions and also its expedient utility for Pollitt and Campbell in 1931–32. Pollitt argued then that rank-and-file movements constituted the embodiment of Independent Leadership in British conditions.

At the 12th Party Congress in December 1932, he held up the London Busmen's Rank and File Movement as a model for Party members to emulate. He acknowledged that the movement did not represent '100% the basis of the platform and principles of the British section of the RILU, namely the Minority Movement', [nevertheless it and other rank-and-file movements like it], 'represent the first beginnings towards that and therefore inside those Movements our Communist fractions have got to try and deepen the political understanding of those who are associated with them, have got to try and broaden them out . . .'[1]

The London busmen's victory over Ernest Bevin in 1931–32 proved fortuitous for Pollitt's and Campbell's new approach. We have seen how Busmen's Rank and File leaders forced Bevin to withdraw from a

'Mondist' deal which he had negotiated with the London General Omnibus Company (LGOC). He had miscalculated their ability to organize pressure from below inside the official union structure. Even though the Rank and File leaders were lay officials inside their garage union branches, they felt in no way bound to confine their activities inside official procedure. Indeed, the busmen's strong rank-and-filist culture enabled them to organize a full-scale revolt in good conscience: they did not feel they were sinning against their union by overturning Bevin's agreement.

Under such overwhelming pressure, Bevin had promptly given ground, and returned to the negotiating table and induced the LGOC into making substantial concessions. Though Rank and File leaders spoke against accepting the improved deal, they accepted the union delegate conference vote in favour, while vowing to continue their campaign for better working conditions. In 1932, with the enthusiastic support of the Party Centre and the more pragmatic Party bus activists, the Rank and File leaders established the London Busmen's Rank and File Movement on a permanent basis. It was endowed with an Organizing Committee (not the more hierarchical Executive) and a monthly newspaper, *Busman's Punch*, inherited from the pragmatic Party bus activists, edited by the Communist intellectual Emile Burns.

The Movement adopted the set of demands which Burns had set out in the best-selling pamphlet 'The Busmen's Case', issued during the conflict with Bevin: a Seven-hour Day; No Spreadovers; and No Standing Passengers. *Busman's Punch* described them as a 'fighting programme', and 'Militant trade unionism – a fighting policy against the employers vs. the policy of Mondism and wage reductions'.

> As far as our organisation is concerned the [TGWU] Executive Council and officers have received a lesson to which there is no parallel in bus history. It was a solid demonstration by the men that *they are the Union*, that *they pay the piper and will call the tune*.[2]

Bevin responded with characteristic vigour and determination to the Rank and File Movement, which he saw as a threat to the union's inviolate authority. His reaction was almost identical to the AEU Executive's response to the ASSNC three years later. Bevin, like most of the AEU Executive, had been on the militant left wing of the trade union movement before the war and into the 1920s. They had revised their own approaches to collective bargaining as a result of the traumatic events of the 1920s, but they were still capable of understanding and even sympathizing with the militant impulse which stressed the need to wage a serious fight against the employers to secure substantial concessions. However, both Bevin and the AEU Executive Council had also faced serious challenges from Communist Party activists in the 1920s. They were unwilling to tolerate an organized 'rank-and-file' presence which shadowed their union institutions.

At Bevin's instigation, the General Executive Council (GEC) prepared a report on the London Busmen's Rank and File Movement, condemning its attitude of putting the Movement before the union, and concluding that there was no place for an 'unofficial' movement alongside the union. The report was tabled at the TGWU's Biennial Delegate Conference (BDC) in July 1933. The Rank and File Movement had made thorough preparations for the BDC. Rank and File candidates had captured ten out of 13 London bus places at the BDC. Their average vote was 3507 compared with the other three winners who received an average of 1469.[3] (The importance of the Rank and File Movement's trans-London organization for mobilizing votes was clearly vital.) Busmen's delegates responded to the Executive Report condemning them with sincere protestations of union loyalism intertwined with unrepentant rank-and-filism.

> [Frank Snelling] was asked why they insisted on keeping their organisation in being after this particular dispute was over. Because, he answered, they distrusted the officials and disagreed with the reformist policy which they and the Executive were pressing. They felt it necessary to set up a vigilance committee. The Rank and File Movement . . . was the spontaneous expression of discontent and of a demand for a more aggressive policy on the part of the men. 'It is only by continued combat with the boss class that you can do any good.'[4]

Given Bevin's ascendancy over the union, it is unsurprising that BDC delegates voted to accept the Executive's report condemning the London Busmen by 215 to 30. They also approved a rule change which 'committed any member taking office to accepting the constitution of the Union and working through its machinery.'[5] Nevertheless, Bullock observed that Bevin's speech on the Executive report did not attack militancy or unofficial strikes *per se*, and indeed 'welcomed a more militant and critical spirit as a sign of health far preferable to apathy. What he objected to was the artificial fostering of discontent by setting up a permanent 'counterorganisation' within the Union which deliberately worked to destroy confidence in the Union's leadership and policy.'[6]

Bevin's conference victory proved purely formal. In the months following the BDC, he made a strenuous effort to draw out the Rank and File leaders, but signally failed to engage them in conflict over their ambiguous constitutional position in the light of the rule change and the GEC Report. Under the Party intellectual Emile Burns' editorship, Busman's Punch stressed the Movement's indissoluble devotion to both union loyalism and rank-and-filism:

> Every man connected with the movement, either as a rank and filer, a member of the [Rank-and-File Movement] Committee or of the Editorial Board of the *Punch* is a loyal member of the TGWU, as is proved by the record of prominent Rank and Filers in making and keeping members. Members who usually turn out not cardboard members, but active trade unionists. And the vote on the Biennial Conference delegate election proves without any shadow of doubt whether or not the London busmen subscribe to the policy of the Rank and File Movement.
>
> Our policy – and we wish officials to take particular note – is dictated to us by our members at properly constituted meetings composed of delegates elected at the [union] branches in a constitutional manner . . . The measure of success we have had justifies our continued efforts.[7]

The Rank and File leaders were implacably immune to his formidable moral pressure and remained in full possession of their lay positions. Indeed, they moved to reinforce their representation on the London busmen's formidable lay institution, the Central Bus Committee (CBC).[8] At the end of 1933 Bert Papworth, Frank Snelling, Bill Hayward, Bill Ware and Bernard Sharkey were all elected to the CBC, leaving only one garage branch seat unoccupied by the Rank and File Movement.[9] Snelling, the Chairman of the Rank and File Movement, was subsequently elected CBC chairman. The Movement now commanded a strong position from which to retaliate to further challenges from Bevin and to launch counter-offensives against him.

Faced with this apparently unshakable majority, Bevin desisted from further attacks on the Rank and File and refrained from any manoeuvre designed to entrap the Rank and File leaders on the CBC for their infringement of the TGWU's new rule even though they were clearly its intended objects.[10] Instead Bevin discovered that he could co-exist with these Rank and File leaders. From its inception in 1932 Bevin had encouraged the newly nationalized London Passenger Transport Board (LPTB) in its 'Mondist' tendencies. The Board proved a willing convert. It was keen to cultivate close relations with the union and continued the virtual closed shop granted by the LGOC, its largest constituent.[11] Consequently the Rank and File leaders were able to utilize their newly consolidated base in the CBC to win substantial concessions from the Board in local disputes. In the face of this practical reality, they evinced no desire either to precipitate unofficial strikes or to pursue a vendetta against Bevin.

No Rank and File leader incited workers to strike in order to extract an additional ounce of flesh from the bosses. They initially accepted the logic of their position as CBC officers and presided over the day-to-day 'economic struggle' played under these new 'Mondist' rules. Playing the game produced reasonable concessions in return for honouring the discipline of 'observing procedure' and pre-empting unofficial action in garages where militant rank-and-filism had previously been the rule. Comparative industrial peace reigned under this regime, instead of the increased numbers of disputes which Rank and File leaders had predicted Bevin's 'Speed Agreement' would bring.

Nevertheless, amid this apparently dramatic change in behaviour, the Rank and File leaders continued to use, feel comfortable in and believe their own rank-and-filist rhetoric. They also searched for rank-and-filist justifications for settling grievances through the official procedure for avoiding disputes. The CBC instituted changes to its procedures which provided for greater communication between local garage lay officers, the CBC and full-time officials, ensuring greater accountability to these 'grass roots'.[12] *Busman's Punch*'s reporting reflected the view that when disputes were settled peacefully, rank-and-filism had still triumphed because the officers had gained the substance of the men's case. In April 1934 *Busman's Punch* described a dispute at Romford where the CBC/Rank and File leaders had conducted protracted negotiations:

> The CBC met the Board as promised, and as the guarantees demanded [against speed-up] were not forthcoming at present the offending schedules and rotas have been removed. Thank goodness, we have at last found a CBC prepared to carry out the wishes of the membership.[13]

As the CBC's unbroken record of wins over the LPTB lengthened, there was a corresponding upward revision in branch officers' rank-and-filist expectations. In August 1934 *Busman's Punch* reported on a dramatic dispute at Upton Park garage which had culminated in a cliff-hanging finale. The branch committee had been so near to calling an unofficial strike that the heady odour of open conflict, so long absent from the London Transport scene, had reappeared and hovered in the air whilst the CBC/Rank and File leaders extracted a settlement. The mere whiff of this powerful scent with its accompanying stimulant effect revived powerful memories. *Busman's Punch* extolled the thorough preparations which the virtuous branch committee had made:

> . . . they have set up the Strike Committee, picket captains . . . they sent telegrams to all Branch Secretaries in the Fleet inviting them to a meeting . . . The meeting with the Board resulted in a complete victory . . . although the Board complained bitterly of the CBC going outside the machinery set up to deal with complaints of this character.
>
> The great victory that has been achieved in this case must be followed up. We on our part have always insisted that negotiation without agitation plus militant action is useless, and serves to defeat the aims and objectives of our fellow workers in the long run. The receiving of a deputation [by the LPTB] as a matter of urgency, a

> discussion with the deputation on the decision, an invitation to the Secretary and Chairman of the [Upton Park] Branch to accompany the CBC to an immediate meeting with the Board, which was accepted, the case put, demands met and results reported to branch officials from 22 garages, with a full CBC in attendance the same evening, only go to show the departures [from previous undemocratic procedure] and precedents that have been made and set up. This was made possible because we have elected a CBC who are militant members of our Union.[14]

Despite the provocative effect of being able to push the Board into disregarding its own rules and making concessions under duress, the two principal CBC/Rank and File leaders, Bert Papworth and Frank Snelling, continued to play the 'Mondist' game. The combination of their consummate negotiating skills buttressed by rank-and-file branch officials' increasing audacity produced escalating concessions but no outbreaks of unofficial action. However, the moment that Papworth and Snelling went to the Isle of Man to attend the TGWU BDC in July 1935, there was an unofficial strike at Nunhead garage, a Rank and File stronghold. It was precipitated by a comparatively minor incident in which the 'rank-and-file' felt a crew were being unjustly disciplined. The speed with which other garages voted to join the strike showed that the CBC/Rank and File leaders had certainly not presided over the neutering of 'real' rank-and-filism. At its height there were 5000 busmen out. Keen party members were mobilized by the London District Party leadership to offer enthusiastic support.

Three Rank and File leaders and the TGWU national bus officer flew back to London from the BDC to pre-empt a *fleet-wide* strike. Their presence produced an emergency conference which resulted in the LPTB lifting all disciplinary charges against the Nunhead crew.[15] In the aftermath of this conciliatory result, the *Daily Worker* reporter could not forget the atmosphere of struggle hanging in the air:

> At every bus stop stood young men. They gave out pamphlets entitled 'Bus Strike'. They shouted: 'Facts About the Bus Strike!' These were the Communists. At each place I went I saw these workers mobilising at the bus stops giving our leaflets. It was the same all over London . . . The Communist party mobilised quickly; they played their part well as the vanguard of the army of the working class; they drew in many Londoners into that army that night.[16]

The shock of this embarrassingly public climb-down produced some sober stock-taking at the LPTB. The Board determined to break the habit which they had acquired of yielding progressive amounts of ground in the face of organized union pressure. Bevin was informed that they were no longer prepared to negotiate during an unofficial strike, and that they would sack any men who 'broke their contract of service by taking part in an unofficial strike'.[17] Bevin hinted to the GEC that the Board had been pressurized by the Government into taking this hard line, but signified his intention to take them at their word.

The Board's decision to reclaim the terrain of managerial prerogative which it had conceded to the union proved to be a catalyst for the internal conflict which had been simmering for sometime inside the Rank and File leadership. The two dominant Rank and File leaders, Papworth and Snelling had fallen into the pattern of expecting to negotiate compromises. The other Rank and File leaders welcomed the concessions they gained, but had also begun to regret the dilution of 'rank-and-filism' which the lack of overt conflict with the Board had produced.

At the Rank and File Committee meeting in April 1935, Bro. Arlotte called for a return to doing things, 'the way we did when this movement was first formed'.[18] The vital need to revive 'rank-and-file' unity and prevent the Movement from disintegrating had evidently been recognized amongst the leaders. They applied their minds and astutely recognized that the Movement's internal conflicts could be sublimated in an all-out battle. Accordingly they began preparing the ground inside the official union machinery. On 25 July the *Daily Worker* reported that the busmen's delegate conference had voted almost unanimously to give three months notice to the LPTB to end the 1932 'Speed Agreement'. The vote was 'a reflection of the great discontent existing throughout the fleet, and the rising militancy which is demanding improvement of conditions'.[19]

Once a means of addressing the internal conflict had been found, *Busman's Punch* was able to record its symptoms. In August, *Busman's Punch* reported a brutally frank statement from Bill Payne, a veteran Rank and Leader, at the July Rank and File Committee: 'It was time the CBC came out before the membership with a positive programme of demands. He wanted to go back to the spirit and methods of 1932–3.'[20]

In fact, the moves to effect unity in the Rank and File Movement came too late. At the same time as the delegate conference was agreeing a return to the Movement's roots and its 'fighting programme', there was an unofficial strike at the Slough Green Line garage. Even though the Green Line was outside London bus jurisdiction, Bevin reacted immediately by using Bert Papworth and Frank Snelling to persuade the strikers to return to work. Papworth and Snelling had little choice but to comply with his request for them to use their good offices. On 27 July Slough garage branch officers told their full-time officer they expected the CBC's full support for their strike after a meeting of the Rank and File Movement Committee due to take place that evening. Bevin taxed Papworth and Snelling with these revelations, reminding them that the CBC could not officially support an unofficial strike and that if a fleet-wide unofficial strike were called it would end in defeat for the bus-men.[21]

The Rank and File Committee meeting which the Slough garage offi-cers had expected to support them instead became the occasion of a furi-ous onslaught against Papworth and Snelling for doing Bevin's business for him. When other Rank and File leaders accused them of naked betrayal, Papworth and Snelling protested that they had been hemmed in by their position as CBC leaders. They had taken their action in good faith, according to the Rank and File creed which held that union loyal-ism and rank-and-filism were indissoluble.

Papworth and Snelling refused to endure the continuing accusations coming from men who had been their close associates. They withdrew and resigned from the Rank and File Committee. Their own personal standing was so great that the other leaders quickly retreated. Papworth and Snelling probably also confronted the other leaders with the unpalat-able truth that Bevin now possessed not only the will but also the oppor-tunity to break their Movement. Following hard on the heels of Slough, an unofficial strike occurred at the Romford garage, within the CBC's jurisdiction. Bevin ordered the strikers back to work[22] and they duly returned without the Rank and File Movement uttering any protest against his 'tyranny'. The opprobrium of such mute acceptance of Bevin's violation of rank-and-filism deepened the already grave crisis inside the Rank and File leadership.

In the midst of this impasse, Bert Papworth was provoked by Joe Scott's veiled attack on the ASSNC at the *Labour Monthly* conference. Smarting under the accusations of treachery over Slough, Papworth pas-sionately believed that he had been true to both union loyalism and rank-and-filism. He asserted at the conference that a rank-and-file movement could not exist 'if there was not a cause, if it was not reaping for its class at least some benefit'.[23] And indeed, given Bevin's determination to staunch the fresh flow of unofficial strikes, the Busmen's Rank and File Movement needed to deliver some big results if it was to avoid fresh charges of refusing to lead the rank-and-file in fighting the boss.

In August strenuous steps were taken to resolve the issue of Papworth's and Snelling's resignations. *Busman's Punch* reported that the Movement's organization would be tightened up. Only affiliated branches would be able to attend Committee meetings, and each branch would only have its requisite six delegates. This expedient was presum-ably designed to pre-empt another Slough: since Slough was on the Green Line, its garage branch did not qualify for affiliation. The new rule meant that there could be no future possibility of branches outside the CBC's jurisdiction making requests for support which openly flouted the TGWU's demarcation lines.

Affiliated branches would qualify for only one delegate on the Organizing Committee. This change made it more difficult for keen militants to pack meetings to ensure support for strikes. When news arrived of an impending strike in a London or Green Line garage, the Organizing Committee must meet to decide Rank and File policy. No Rank and File leader could make a public statement about the strike before this meeting had been held. This policy was evidently designed to prevent CBC/Rank and File leaders being pressurized by Bevin without counter-pressure being exerted by the Rank and File.

These measures aimed at containing future rank-and-file militancy within the official union structure *and* maintaining the CBC/Rank and File leadership's independent initiative. Having done their best to ensure that another conflict of interest like Slough did not take place, a general reconciliation became practical. Papworth's and Snelling's resignations were duly referred to the Organising Committee[24], and a face-saving compromise was found. On 30 September, the Rank and File Committee accepted that Papworth and Snelling believed in Rank and File policy and that they had acted in good faith over Slough. A moratorium was imposed on accusations over Slough. The Committee agreed that blame for Slough could not be assigned to particular people, but was due to the general state of disorganization in the Movement. Punch reported: 'the movement goes forward all the stronger for the full and frank discussions which have taken place'.[25]

Nevertheless, the underlying contradiction between rank-and-filism and trade union loyalism remained unresolved. Most of the Rank and File leadership were temperamentally unable to countenance violation of the rank-and-filist principle of always supporting the rank-and-file in any fight. If Papworth and Snelling followed this principle unswervingly, they could never again agree another retreat and the Movement would quickly forfeit both power and position inside the union. Bevin's vigilance would ensure that Rank and File leaders who held union office would be unable to shirk their union responsibilities.

It was in search of resolution for this contradiction that Rank and File leaders now returned to the collision course with the LPTB which the delegate conference had set in train in mid-July. An official fleet-wide battle would enable the CBC/Rank and File leaders to fulfil their 'proper' role. A conviction of this battle's imminence and inevitability took collective hold on the Rank and File leadership; the chronic bouts of mutual suspicion and soul searching finally ceased. The Rank and File leadership set their course confidently, even complacently, and with dogged determination, towards the precipice of an all-out strike.

The leadership's certainty of a confrontation with the Board arose from their strategy of formulating immediate demands which they knew

London Transport would not meet except under extreme pressure. If the Movement's 'fighting programme' were pursued seriously, it was sufficiently Utopian to ensure that the Board would have to offer serious resistance. Not surprisingly, Bevin and the TGWU Executive operated from a different perspective. Neither had reason to share the Rank and File leadership's ardent desire for war. Moreover, the London busmen's current terms and conditions were already better than those of most employees in comparable jobs elsewhere.[26] Though Bevin and the GEC might consider the 'fighting programme' unrealistic and even self-destructive, if the busmen's delegate conference insisted on pursuing it the union's rules gave them little option but to accept its decision or else face a full-scale insurrection.

Though the Rank and File Movement dominated the CBC and important garage branches, the leadership were not complacent about the scale of the task ahead. They understood that it would be much more difficult to marshal men to fight a distant, as yet hypothetical, battle in cold blood than to incite them to support an unofficial strike already in full swing. However, they had to mobilize enthusiastic and concerted support for their 'fighting programme' in the form of sympathetic and committed garage delegates reinforced by good majorities in the branch votes mandating them. They needed this 'rank-and-file' back-up to counter the serious opposition to their plans which they knew would be mounted by Bevin and the GEC.

Accordingly, the Rank and File leadership made thorough preparations for the first round of their all-out battle with Bevin and the Executive. The Rank and File Organizing Committee announced a series of meetings to gather support for the delegate conference's vote against the 1932 Speed Agreement. *Busman's Punch* concentrated on propaganda for their ambitious immediate demands.

> It is true that from time to time opportunities have occurred to put forward and win certain of the other demands of the Rank and File Movement, as for example, the 12 days' annual holiday and the regular rotation of rest days. But experience has shown the fleet that in spite of concessions won in certain directions, the job as a whole is getting harder . . . The minor concessions won in certain directions are only a fleabite compared with the Board's extra profits, especially as traffic receipts have at the same time been increasing.[27]

The general preparations for all-out confrontation with the LPTB enabled Papworth and Snelling to continue their daily compromising activities on the CBC. The other Rank and File leaders knew that it was good generalship to conserve forces for the big battle. It was imprudent to allow local disputes to either dissipate essential supplies of energy and enthusiasm or threaten the TGWU's official involvement. Thus union loyalism was maintained unconditionally in the short run, while the rank-and-filist right to repudiate union officials' actions was held in pristine hypothetical reserve. Rank and File activists were not collaborating with Bevin. They had decided voluntarily to 'keep their powder dry' in pursuit of the day of reckoning with London Transport.

The Organizing Committee also initiated prudent building operations to strengthen their striking forces. The significant number of garages which had never affiliated to the Rank and File Movement were canvassed to join up. *Busman's Punch* reported successful affiliation votes from the summer of 1935. But the Movement's reputation was evidently not wholly positive inside the LPTB, and votes for affiliation were lost in some garages.[28] A leaflet was published to explain why London busmen outside the Rank and File should come in.

> Militancy is the stepping stone to Progress. Organised Militancy makes Progress certain. The Rank and File Movement is organised militancy . . . The Rank and Filer . . . stands for a 100% trade union, yet you know that Permanent Officials need gingering up. The Rank and File Movement puts the 'G' into ginger. You want the Union to carry out your wishes, so add *your ginger* by voting . . . for affiliation to the Rank and File Movement.[29]

Finally, the Rank and File leadership made an effort to include the tramwaymen in their projected offensive. *Busman's Punch* noted Bill Ware's observation that the bus section had declared its policies, but had not concentrated sufficiently on going to the tram branches and explaining them. It was a question of the CBC and the Trams Council getting down to a definite agreement, which they could only do when the tram branches understood the busmen's policy.[30] The problem to which Ware had drawn attention was, however, not merely a matter of explanation. LPTB tramwaymen's wages and conditions were substantially lower than the busmen's. Nevertheless, having identified the need for tram support, the Rank and File Movement made no move to formally request it, probably because they were well aware that tram support would be forthcoming only if the busmen moderated their own parochial demands in favour of helping the tramwaymen to move up to busmen's levels.

Bevin and the GEC withstood the pressure from the London busmen for a full 18 months. Throughout that time the Rank and File leaders remained single-minded in the pursuit of their objective. They were able to produce a succession of massive majorities in favour of a show-down. At the beginning of 1936 Bevin deemed it prudent to begin damage limitation measures against the eventuality of a fleet-wide bus strike. He proceeded to wring the reluctant admission from the CBC that the delegate conference proposals 'were impossible of realisation, representing as they did a colossal sum'. He subsequently tabled somewhat revised, more credible demands to the Board for a new agreement.

> The problems associated with the London Passenger Transport Board continue to take up a great deal of time . . . I have examined the demands and as far as I can see from the calculations I have made, they represent far more than the total surplus on the buses without allowing for any capital charges or overheads. I am certain these demands cannot be obtained, and I believe it would be misleading for the Members to put them in. I have always been of the definite view that it would be fatal to this Union to lead men to believe they can obtain something and then disappoint them.[31]

Bevin next took great care to have the CBC acknowledge their conduct in 1934 when the case for levelling up tram wages to bus levels had first been raised. At that time the CBC declined to abstain from making their own separate bus demands to assist the tramwaymen. He observed: 'obviously the Union could not go to the Board one day and argue for equal wages and conditions [for the tramwaymen] and the next day for a separate application for "Busmen".'[32]

He required the CBC to reaffirm this position and they gave an undertaking that they had no intention of including the tramwaymen in their demands. If the Rank and File Movement had been willing to mark time until the tram workers' wages and conditions level pegged their own and acquiesce in the disappearance of the differentials, then a united demand could have been put to the LPTB. But despite their rhetorical solidarity, Rank and File leaders could not afford to wait.

Armed with this disclaimer, Bevin approached London Transport with a brief which he felt he could defend. They agreed that the union and LPTB would *jointly* consider the LPTB's financial situation, opportunities for altering schedules, etc., examining 'the problem in all its phases'.[33] Joint determination had been part of Bevin's negotiating strategy since the Mond–Turner talks. He was evidently determined that the Rank and File leaders should dirty their hands in an analysis of the practical implications of their revised demands.

The CBC reported the outcome of Bevin's approach to the Board at a delegate conference on 23 April 1936. Bernard Sharkey responded with a motion requiring the CBC to convene an emergency delegate conference to decide on future action if the Board had not conceded the 7 Hour Day by Whitsun. The Rank and File leadership had probably concerted this strategem to force Bevin's hand. Bevin was evidently not the only player capable of self-interested calculation.

Sharkey's act of rebellion was carried by the delegate conference, and Bevin immediately insisted that the CBC dissociate themselves from the Whitsun deadline contained in his motion. However, he simultaneously

applied sufficient pressure on London Transport to move the dispute a
long way forward. On 4 May, the Board agreed that the Joint Committee
examining the case for a new agreement should commence work. They
also accepted that the period of notice for ending the existing agreement
should be shortened from three months to one.[34]

The delegate conference convened on 14 May, ostensibly to consider
Armageddon in the light of the Board's failure to concede the 7 Hour
Day. Instead, the conference accepted the Board's concession of the Joint
Committee with the face-saving caveat that *it should begin its delibera-
tions on the new agreement by Whitsun.* It was clear that the Rank and
File Movement had finally won the first round of their battle against
Bevin and the TGWU GEC. The momentum of the dispute with London
Transport was now unstoppable.

On 19 May a mass meeting of the Rank and File Movement took place
at which Bernard Sharkey welcomed the compromise result of his
motion. All the Rank and File leaders on the CBC spoke. Bert Papworth's
oratory welded the audience into one committed, excited mass. He
reminded the audience that he was speaking in three capacities, as Rank
and File Movement Organizing Committeeman, CBC member and
TGWU Executive Councillor.

> We have reached the unique position which all three [offices] are
> united in this demand, for the 7 hour day. If I thought you could get
> the 7 hour day by Whitsun with a complete and successful stand-
> down, I would say, 'I'm leading a strike'. I do not believe this is the
> way to do it. If we lose in the negotiations, you don't want me to tell
> you what to do next. Our position today is to show the Board that
> we are united, and that there is no room for arguments . . . If you
> show the loyalty to this platform that it deserves from you, in return
> we will show you just how much we appreciate it by leading the fight
> in the negotiations.

The *Daily Worker* observed that everyone had declared it was the best
meeting since the early days of the Movement. *Busman's Punch* was
reminded of 'the great days of 1932'.[35]

Having achieved this pinnacle, the Rank and File leadership discovered that they were still a long way from the summit. An additional com-
plication emerged in the autumn of 1936, when a rash of unofficial
strikes erupted in garages which had still not affiliated to the Movement.
These were mainly garages which the LPTB had gained from Thomas
Tillings and other smaller bus companies. Despite the Organizing
Committee's good resolutions in October 1935 to extend garage affilia-
tions, the leadership's attention and energy had been concentrated on
CBC activity. They failed to enlist most of the garages outside the
Movement's initial nucleus, which was still largely confined to the cluster

of ex-LGOC garages which had been the strongholds of the Red Button Union and wartime Vigilance Committee.

Even though they had not affiliated to the Rank and File Movement, garage branch officers at the non-LGOC garages had gauged the possibilities of emulating 'rank-and-filist' methods within the new secure environment of 'Mondism' accurately enough. The non Rank and File garages were also strongly affected by the heady martial atmosphere generated by the CBC in preparation for its all-out battle. In 1936–37, these garage branch officers became skilled exponents of rank-and-filist militancy. Papworth and Snelling found it difficult to deal with the consequences of this new enthusiasm for unofficial action. They had little choice but to respond to this opportunist militancy as responsible 'reformist' officials.[36] In November 1936 Bert Papworth observed:

> Many garages who took part in recent strikes had nothing to do with the Rank and File Movement. They had decided policy on their own. But they loyally accepted the decisions of [the official TGWU!] delegate conference, and we met with success [in settling the strikes speedily].[37]

As the weeks stretched into months, the Rank and File leaders on the Joint Committee, particularly Bert Papworth, evidently found it difficult to extricate themselves from the conventions of collective bargaining which presumed compromise on both sides to avert the outbreak of war. The Joint Committee's examination of the problem in all its phases confirmed Bevin's estimation that the Board was strictly constrained in its capability for concessions. How could Papworth manufacture a credible *casus belli* when his excellent practical judgement told him the result of a battle must almost certainly be defeat?[38]

It was an ominous portent when the busmen's delegate conference voted in January 1937 to accept the CBC's routine report of negotiations with the Board by an unusually close margin of 32–18.[39] Instead of disguising it, *Busman's Punch* chose to escalate this internal division in February by publishing an article by Bill Payne and Bill Jones prefaced by an editorial committee statement that it represented the true views of the Movement's majority.

> We believe that the time has arrived when the Rank and File Movement should take stock of its position and face the responsibilities for which the Movement was formed ... During these last few months doubt and uncertainty has [*sic*] crept into our ranks, and among the members clearness and clarity regarding the line of the Movement has vanished ...
>
> If the right course is taken the Movement will ... perform its rightful function for which it was intended – the furtherance of Militant trade unionism ... We know that it may be necessary sometimes to retreat. The time comes, however, when we advance. That time has come. Advance. Advance!!![40]

When news of the imminent breach in the Rank and File Movement reached Bevin he responded on 16 February by abruptly terminating discussions with the Board, declaring that their pre-conditions for a negotiated settlement were unacceptable.[41] He apparently calculated that it was preferable to keep the busmen united in an expensive and explosive official strike, over which he and the GEC exercised overall control, rather than precipitate unofficial action. It was clear that the Rank and File leadership would call an unofficial strike, with or without Papworth, unless the union's official machinery was placed on a wartime footing.

Bevin achieved the desired result by throwing down the gauntlet. The Rank and File Movement became conspicuously quiet. Evidently satisfied that the die had been cast, they were careful not to give Bevin any cause to renege. At the end of March 1937 Bevin attended a special delegate conference which voted unanimously to give one month's notice to terminate the existing agreement. To take account of the Joint Committee's deliberations, the conference agreed to moderate the hitherto sacred demand for 7 Hour Day to $7\frac{1}{2}$ hours. *Punch* acquiesced in the compromise as a 'minimum demand'.[42]

The TGWU Executive duly granted plenary powers to the CBC to conduct the strike if the last-minute negotiations between Bevin and the Board failed to produce a settlement.[43] *Busman's Punch*'s page one headline in April read:

> Prepare for Action.
>
> Everyone within the Section is now quite clear on the following points: ... The determination of the membership not to make any further compromise, but to stand firm and solid for the whole of our present demands ... We most strongly urge the members at their coming Branch meetings to make it clear beyond doubt to the General Secretary, the Executive Council, the CBC and Delegate Conference that the substantial concessions already made in the course of the negotiations, in order to avoid a dispute, are final.[44]

The *Daily Worker* reported Bevin's fruitless attempts to win concessions almost sympathetically. 'Pressure is particularly directed against Mr. Ernest Bevin, who in the course of long negotiations with the Board, has become convinced of the justice of his members' claims.'[45] Once the official one month's notice of strike action had been given, *Busman's Punch* concentrated on the need for branches to make it 'clear beyond doubt' that no further concessions would be made. The Rank and File leaders looked forward, as Bill Ware wrote, to never again attending a branch meeting 'with a view to preventing strikes. If there is one thing that I have detested doing, it was appealing to men not to take strike action, especially when I have known they were right.'[46]

On the eve of the strike Party tram activists warned that the tramway-men could not be relied on for support. Under Bevin's terms of engage-ment, they stood to gain nothing for themselves by solidarity action. Tram branch officers would never call on their members to make sacri-fices for the busmen when the busmen had refused to help them. E.D. Sheehan, a veteran militant and tram branch officer for New Cross garage, was very outspoken at a pre-strike meeting of the union's Regional Passenger Transport Trade Group, probably attended by both Papworth and Snelling: 'If they joined in [the bus strike], they wanted to be fully associated with the busmen's demands. They were not willing to take part in a struggle merely to push the busmen even further ahead of them.'[47]

The all-out London Bus strike began on 1 May 1937 and the busmen themselves were 100 per cent solid. On 2 May the Ministry of Labour applied the predictable emollient and established a court of inquiry into the dispute. Bevin presented the busmen's case himself with all his cus-tomary flair and conviction. The Court's Interim Report appeared on 6 May. It found a prima facie case for further examination of the shorter working day, thereby affirming the principle behind the busmen's demand. The Board immediately accepted the report.[48] In view of the weakness of the busmen's disposition of forces, this conciliatory action showed the Board's strong commitment to 'Mondist' collective bargain-ing and its eagerness to avoid a protracted dispute.

An additional feature in everyone's calculations was the coronation of George VI taking place on 12 May. Both the Ministry of Labour and London Transport were anxious to assist in the smooth and unblemished unfolding of this ceremony. This fortuitous additional inducement for the LPTB to make concessions and for the government to countenance them was of limited duration, expiring at midnight on 11 May.

Bevin calculated that the Interim Report upheld 75–80 per cent of the busmen's case. He recommended that the CBC accept the Board's con-cession as the basis for negotiation and call off the strike.[49] But the CBC and a subsequent delegate conference flatly refused to accept anything less than unconditional surrender from the Board. Meetings of the garage branches convened to consider the Interim Report had record atten-dances. Having heard their delegates' explanations of Bevin's and the CBC's opposing positions, only three branches voted with Bevin.[50] This show of defiance inside the union caused the TGWU Executive to send individual letters to all London bus members with Bevin's case for rec-ommending the Interim Report and ending the strike.[51]

As the date of the coronation approached, branch meetings were recalled to reconsider their earlier decision to continue the strike. The Daily Worker observed: 'With the rejection of the Board's offer a new stage has been reached in the human struggle. With the impossibility of securing a resumption of work in time for the Coronation, there is now talk of a "prolonged struggle"'.[52]

Rank and File leaders were seriously alarmed that the combined effect of the Executive's letter and the coronation's conclusion would produce a breach in their united front. They produced a Rank and File Movement leaflet which was distributed at the recalled branch meetings. It argued the case for standing firm on the 7 ½ Hour Day from first rank-and-filist principles, and made no attempt to address Bevin's pragmatic points.[53] In the event, the leaflet was probably superfluous; only one garage had changed its vote in favour of Bevin.[54] London busmen had always followed their own leaders' advice, and been amply rewarded for their loyalty. They were scarcely worried about flouting Bevin's judgement at this juncture.

After this second rebuff, the TGWU Executive bided its time, evidently hoping that the CBC would recognize the overwhelming strength of the Board's position and accept Bevin's settlement. Rank and File leaders had certainly acquired the survival reflexes of compromise and retreat through their dominance of the CBC from 1933. In May 1937, however, they experienced a temporary loss of these reflexes. Their inability to retreat at this critical juncture was not due to a fatal desire for self-destruction. Instead, the need to prove their bona fides as Rank and File leaders proved overwhelming, sufficiently strong to suppress all other considerations. Since 1935 they had argued against Bevin that total victory was attainable in an all-out battle with the Board. They were unable now to admit to their members that Bevin had been right all along.

The Rank and File leadership sincerely believed they would win because the rank-and-file were solid and their cause was just. The evidence hardly sustained their conviction. Previous concessions from the Board had been achieved in mere skirmishes against a management which was genuinely concerned to avoid disputes and therefore susceptible to pressure to settle unofficial disputes quickly by concessions and compromise. There were very different rules of engagement now that the Rank and File leaders had turned down the conventional settlement of compromise and honourable retreat and opted to stay in the field and fight for the higher stakes of total victory and unconditional surrender.

To achieve movement from the LPTB in this new, deadly serious phase of the battle, the busmen needed to seriously impair the London public's ability to travel. If the travelling public tolerated the strike's effects, the LPTB would be seen to be ahead. If they rebelled, the busmen would have advanced. In this situation the attitude of both tramwaymen and underground workers was crucial. The London busmen had fought and won parochial conflicts without having to take into account trams or tubes. They had a critical need now for the TOT (Tram, Omnibus, Tube) alliance, which had been rhetorically invoked by busmen as their goal ever since the pioneering syndicalist days of the Red Button Union.

In the absence of any serious impairment to the travelling public's ability to move around London, the strike unfolded more or less as tram activists and Ernest Bevin had foretold. The busmen remained solid, and sustained by an amazingly ebullient, self-confident mood. But they continued without support from the tramwaymen. (The tube workers were organized by the railway unions and their negotiations with the LPTB were totally separate from the TGWU's. The busmen had evidently never approached the railway union underground branches to discuss the strike.) The public continued to travel about London reasonably easily, tolerating the inconvenience of no buses, using trams and the underground when possible.

The CBC became immured in desperate schemes to bring the tramwaymen out on strike. When they came to nothing, the CBC still refused to acknowledge the need to compromise.[55] Throwing caution to the wind, the London District Party intervened to activate the London Trades Council and the 'real united front' Unity Campaign on the busmen's behalf. On 13 May, the Unity Campaign issued a statement under Stafford Cripps's, Papworth's and Snelling's signatures instructing local London Unity Campaign committees to offer their services to the busmen. Such overt 'interference' by the CPGB in the TGWU's internal affairs was inviting retaliation from Bevin and the Executive.

The London District Party also organized two demonstrations for Sunday 16th May in Hyde Park. Bert Papworth was their star speaker. He promised that all 26,000 busmen would picket tram, tube and railway stations if necessary, and even lie across the lines.

> The London busmen call on you, the public, to do your share alongside them. They look to you to help them, just as Madrid looks to the International Column. We are not fearful of the outcome of the strike, but we wish it could be won along ordinary trade union lines.[56]

On 25 May, the TGWU Executive finally concluded that the unrepentant CBC was incapable of rational calculation. The GEC revoked the CBC's plenary powers to wage the strike and instructed Bevin to enter into negotiations with the LPTB for a 'reasonable settlement'. On 26 May he presented terms which the Executive accepted and ordered the busmen back to work.

Bevin had evidently counselled the need for extreme caution and the Board had responded with an offer which was remarkably conciliatory given the duration and intensity of the strike. The Board reaffirmed its acceptance of the Interim Report; any new agreement would be retrospective to 8 May, the day on which the Board had signified its acceptance of the Report; there would be no victimization and no break in service declared for busmen returning to work on 28 May; and the joint investigation into the effects of speed suggested by the inquiry would proceed immediately.[57]

The busmen's return to work on 28 May was united, but marked by great bitterness and confusion. They went back under duress, feeling betrayed by their union. They had believed the Rank and File/CBC leaders and been confident of winning 100 per cent of their demands. They had been out on strike for over four weeks and were now going back on the basis of the same compromise settlement they had been offered in the very first week. At first none of their leaders could produce a convincing explanation for this turn of events.

Frank Snelling and Bill Payne soon provided rank-and-filist reasons for the débâcle: Bevin and the TGWU were responsible for betraying the busmen and their treachery could not be forgiven. Bert Papworth, Bill Jones and *Busman's Punch* did not seek to justify Bevin's behaviour. But they argued that despite official treachery, union loyalism made unity essential; the busmen had to settle their scores inside the TGWU.

On 28 May, the *Daily Worker* published a statement from the London District Party:

> We appeal to every busman not to drop out of the fight, but to make up his mind to play an even more active part in the Union. We appeal to every busman to maintain 100% membership and militancy in his branch, so that the London bus section, together with the rank and file of the other sections of the Union, especially those employed by the LPTB, can bring real leadership to the TGWU.[58]

The London busmen were caught in the middle of these mutual recriminations. Nevertheless, the Rank and File Movement had become the union and the busmen's first loyalty remained to their Rank and File/union leaders. When this leadership split, it was not clear where the busmen would place their allegiance. As a result, the TGWU's future on the London buses hung in the balance for the following two years.

Snelling and Payne attracted a substantial knot of supporters, many of whom were branch officers, often from the non-LGOC garages who had been attracted by the Movement's high profile of militancy. These neophytes rejected the TGWU because they reckoned it had forfeited their allegiance. Snelling and Payne approached W.J. Brown for help. Brown was General Secretary of the Civil Service Clerical Association. Having been a Labour MP between 1924–31, he had flirted with Mosley's New Party and was now a keen advocate of non-political unions. He unhesitatingly offered his support.[59]

Bert Papworth, Bill Jones and the Party Centre mounted a fierce resistance to Snelling's and Payne's attempts to woo busmen into a 100 per
cent rank-and-filist union. On 21 June 1937, the day after Brown had
publicly pledged to assist a new union, the Party Secretariat issued a
statement which declared that London busmen would resist the TGWU
Executive's attempts to punish the Rank and File Movement, but

> they will do so in a manner that does not imperil the working class
> movement, does not weaken the union, does not lead to a fall in
> membership; they will assert that the union is theirs and not Bevin's
> or the Executive Council's. [Communist members of the TGWU Bus
> Section] will urge all busmen to remain in the TGWU and increase
> their activity therein, to beat back every attack on their rights. They
> will show the world that the union is theirs, and that not Bevin nor
> the spineless Executive, but trade union unity, on the basis of trade
> union democracy, shall prevail.[60]

Since the strike Ernest Bevin and the TGWU Executive had indeed been
preoccupied with eradicating the Rank and File Movement inside the
union. The BDC convened in early July and received an Interim Report of
the Inquiry into Unofficial Movements which the Executive had
appointed as soon as the strike had finished. The debate on the Report
lasted for a full day. Rank and File leaders who were delegates provided
their own eloquent defence. Bill Payne asked why Bevin had not spoken
to the busmen during the strike. Bevin 'retorted, if I had, I should have
attacked you for continuing the strike. Why did you let it go on so long?
Because you were afraid to "carry the can" and take responsibility for
calling it off.'[61]

The Interim Report concluded that the Rank and File Movement had
tried to exert undue influence on sovereign union bodies. In addition, the
Communist Party was somewhere lurking in the background. The
inquiry had been unable to find *any* direct evidence of Communist Party
control; but Emile Burns' editorship of *Busman's Punch* and close links
with Rank and File leaders established the Party's 'guilt by association'.[62]
BDC delegates adopted the Report by 291 to 51 votes.[63] The *Daily
Worker* reported the result without comment.[64]

The Final Report of the Inquiry was presented to the Executive in mid-
July, soon after the BDC had concluded. Its full recommendations were
adopted. They included the expulsion of Bert Papworth, Bill Payne and
Bill Jones on the ground that their continued membership would 'constitute a danger to the stability of the Union'. Bill Hayward, Bernard
Sharkey and Bill Ware were debarred from holding union office until
1942.[65] (Frank Snelling had been seriously injured in a motor accident
soon after the strike. He was unable to give evidence to the inquiry, and
his status in the union was not dealt with until his full recovery at the end
of 1937.[66]

Having removed the source of the unofficial contagion, Bevin and the Executive evidently expected to reassert their authority. They discovered that their writ still did not run inside Rank and File territory. The October issue of *Busman's Punch*, which turned out to be its last, asserted confidently that London busmen would force the GEC to give a full pardon and restore the rights of Rank and File leaders. *Punch* was right. The CBC elections at the end of 1937 returned a solid phalanx of delegates committed to the full reinstatement of the punished Rank and File leaders. They communicated their demand for the restoration of the punished men's union rights to the GEC, and then conspicuously abstained from any further participation in the union's affairs.[67]

The new CBC's demands for a restitution of the wrongs done to the Rank and File leadership were made in good faith. Papworth and Jones had no intention of continuing the Rank and File Movement; it was made perfectly clear that they had abandoned their belief that a separate rank-and-file movement was necessary to provide the 'G' in ginger for full-time officials. The Rank and File Movement continued in nominal existence, but the TGWU Executive received abundant evidence that it was no longer conducting serious business. In fact, Bevin and the GEC had urgent need of the qualified assistance which the Party and loyalist Rank and File leaders were providing. Though the Snelling/Payne faction was marking time during Snelling's long convalescence, a Rank and File Committee meeting in December 1937 considered a motion to form a breakaway union. It was only narrowly defeated.[68]

The Party Centre campaigned vigorously for loyalty to the 'real' TGWU, which acknowledged its mistaken judgement and restored the Rank and File leaders' democratic rights. The *Daily Worker* reported on a meeting followed by a concert with turns at Shoreditch Town Hall attended by over 800 London busmen and their wives. Bert Papworth, Bill Jones, Bill Ware, Bernard Sharkey and other Rank and File leaders had been given a presentation. Speakers urged busmen to stay in the TGWU:

> there was no good to be obtained by tearing up their cards and breaking down the splendid organisation that had succeeded in winning many concessions.[69]

The London District Party judged it to be 'about time' to recruit both Papworth and Jones into the Party. They joined enthusiastically.[70] King Street realized a considerable amount of moral capital from their adherence and redoubled the Party's efforts to prevent a split in the TGWU.

On 7 January 1938, after their sweeping victory in the CBC elections, the Busman's Rank and File Movement was formally disbanded on a triumphant note, repeating its call to all busmen to belong to the TGWU.[71]

It was now Bevin and the TGWU Executive who were confronted with an unpalatable choice. They faced continuing demands from the busmen's union machinery bodies for clemency for loyal Rank and File leaders. Then on 24th February, W.J. Brown himself, along with Frank Snelling, Bill Payne, Bill Hayward and eight other TGWU branch officers, announced the formation of a new union, the National Passenger Workers' Union (NPWU).[72] On 25 February, the CPGB Politburo issued a Statement condemning the breakaway, which was an artful blend of trade union loyalism and rank-and-filism. This qualified support for Bevin further forced his hand.

> The Communist Party takes up this attitude not because it wants to make the interests of the busmen 'play second fiddle to the political interests of the Communist Party', but because the whole of British working class experience condemns the policy of seeking to remedy discontent with the bad policy of an Executive by forming a breakaway union. Amongst the miners, the clothing workers and the seamen breakaway unions were formed under great provocation. The result has been uniformly disastrous. Do not believe that the busmen will be an exception to this rule ... United with the tramwaymen, with the provincial trasnsport workers, the London busmen can force even the most reactionary officials to move ... Unity will defeat the Board. Unity will defeat reaction in the TGWU.[73]

In order to staunch the haemorrhage of his members into the NPWU, Bevin had to make common cause with the CPGB and the loyalist Rank and File leaders. Bevin had no hesitation in persuading the Executive to reconsider their expulsions of Bert Papworth and Bill Jones in March. It was decided to readmit them immediately on their own assurances of loyalty, though they could not hold lay office for four years.[74] The loyalist Rank and File leaders must have felt the scores were somewhat evened when Bevin and the Executive swallowed this humble pie. The Rank and File loyalists now concentrated on rebuilding the union and refused the new breakaway union any quarter. Despite the formal dissolution of the Rank and File Movement and Papworth's and Jones' ineligibility for office, the loyalists maintained their own personal influence inside the TGWU lay machinery unchallenged.

Pollitt and Campbell declined to exploit Bevin's enforced retreat. Amidst the deepening European crisis, glorying in Bevin's reverses probably seemed both gratuitous and unnecessarily divisive. Moreover Pollitt and Campbell had never viewed trade union loyalism as an opportunist tactic. They had not opposed the breakaway union for short-term gain. Union loyalism was a Communist imperative, a corner-stone of the 'real united front' against all threats, not only the employers but also fascism not least because W.J. Brown was not above suspicion of fascist political sympathies.

The rank-and-filist breakaway continued to function, despite the LPTB's refusal to recognize it in any way. The busmen's loyalty to full-blooded rank-and-filism and the scars incurred during the 1937 strike created the conditions in which Snelling and Payne gathered a core of ex-TGWU branch officers around them. The NPWU had some thousands of members and branch officers who administered its affairs locally while continuing to recruit members. Membership of the NPWU peaked in 1943; new recruits were probably put off the TGWU by Party bus activists' propaganda about the need to work harder for the war effort.[75] When the Labour Government repealed the 1927 Trades Disputes Act in 1946 the TGWU claimed a closed shop in the LPTB. Confronted with LPTB's determination to enforce TGWU membership as a term of contract, the NPWU finally faded away.[76]

The Aircraft Shop Stewards National Council

We have observed that the Aircraft Shop Stewards National Council (ASSNC) was founded in March 1935 as a result of Peter Zinkin's revolutionary opportunism. Between 1933–34 he had striven unsuccessfully to fulfil Pollitt's 12th Congress injunction to build separate, 'independent' rank-and-file movements with post office workers, nurses and civil servants in London. His ambition to lead the 'economic struggle' in a truly revolutionary direction was finally realized in early March 1935. At this time Zinkin described himself as being in charge of the Trade Union Information Bureau – the emasculated successor to the National Minority Movement.[77] His autobiography records the exact time, 4.30 p.m. and date, Thursday, 7 March 1935, when a Party member rang in to tell him about the toolroom workers walking out and stewards bringing the rest of the airframe workers after them at the Hawker Aircraft Company, Brockworth, near Gloucester. (Hawker's had recently taken over the Gloucester Aircraft Company; its Brockworth site continued to be known as 'Gloster's'.)[78]

Zinkin advised the Party member that the Gloster's stewards should try to spread the strike to Hawker's Kingston site. The Kingston shop stewards' committee duly brought their members out and Zinkin travelled to the strike committee headquarters at the Kingston Labour Club. He found a functional shop stewards committee with AEU, Sheet Metal Workers' Union and Brass and Metal Mechanics stewards. His autobiography describes how he became their self-appointed commissar with characteristic immodesty.

> Introducing myself as coming to report for the Daily Worker I was warmly welcomed, my offer to assist in any way possible was gladly

accepted and I was co-opted on to the Strike Committee. This was the first of many other strike committees in which I officiated. They had no previous experience of conducting a strike and were receptive to well intentioned advice, and so we got down to work.[79]

The tinder which had sparked the unofficial strike was the refusal of a toolroom worker, Mr. Hamlin, to join the AEU. However, the well-organized shop stewards committee had been fruitlessly pursuing other site grievances through official procedure for some months. They took the calculated risk of using the toolroom workers' walk-out to bring other trade unionists out on unofficial strike in order to hasten the progress of their general grievances. The tactic of exploiting a parochial skirmish in one shop to bring out a whole workforce was familiar to experienced shop stewards and particularly to Party activists who were stewards.

Hamlin applied for a union ticket after three days, by which time the Gloster's AEU stewards were already engaged in using the strike to exert maximum leverage on Hawker's to take their official agenda of grievances more seriously.[80] If the strike had not spread to Kingston, it is likely that management would have signalled their intention to make concessions at a works conference, to be properly convened through procedure once the strike had been called off. Having achieved its purpose, stewards would have led a return to work at Gloster's within the week. This had been the pattern of skirmishes in West London aircraft firms which Party AEU activists had recently been leading with great success.

In some West London aircraft factories, notably Handley Page in Cricklewood and de Havilland's Stag Lane, the militant tradition of the wartime shop stewards movement had continued unbroken through the straitened economic circumstances of the 1920s and early 1930s.[81] Joe Scott and Claude Berridge had worked at Handley Page in 1920 and then had gone to de Havilland's, Stag Lane where in 1923 they were joined by Bob Lovell. George Crane and Berridge served on the West London Lock-Out Committee in 1922.

From 1934 increased aircraft orders generated by rearmament produced markedly favourable conditions for the 'economic struggle'. However, veteran militants had learned from the earlier, leaner times to move carefully. They observed their union duty as shop stewards to work inside the apparently restrictive official procedure, the 'notorious' York Memorandum imposed on the engineering unions after the 1922 Lock-Out. They exploited the substantial gaps and lacunae at the workplace level in the Memorandum to develop flexible and favourable collective bargaining conventions. As a result of their tactics, management found themselves under some duress to make concessions, which in turn enabled the activists to gain union recruits and extend shop steward organization.

Zinkin's zeal to spread the Gloster's strike to Kingston showed his initial innocence of the tactics for fighting the 'economic struggle' in engineering being developed by Party engineering activists. When Zinkin observed their concern not to move too far from official procedure he reacted with the principled opposition of a revolutionary. His abiding conviction that union officials were essentially class traitors was in no way modified by experience. Despite his genuflection towards union loyalism, he remained a pure rank-and-filist at heart.[82] In fact, the AEU stewards at Kingston were very hesitant at leading their members out of the gate in cold blood, without any immediate local provocation. It was the more sanguine Sheet Metal Workers' stewards who felt no inhibitions about taking unofficial solidarity action.[83]

The Hawker's and Gloster's strike (as it was alliteratively described by those involved), continued for nearly three weeks and was waged with great élan. The fruits of Zinkin's opportunism were mixed. The concessions gained by the Gloster's strikers were not substantially better than they could have got after a week. Hawker's workers returned to work without any significant gains. Nevertheless, there were no serious victimizations and the unions involved had recruited large numbers of members. Full-time AEU union officials welcomed the increase in membership but were seriously alarmed by this sudden tendency to fan small skirmishes into protracted full-scale battles in which they felt constrained to offer strike pay.

For Zinkin himself, the main result of the Hawker's and Gloster's strike was his manoeuvre to form an independent rank-and-file movement in aircraft. To successfully execute it, he was required to subvert the carefully laid foundations which the Party AEU activists had been preparing for an aircraft rank-and-file movement *inside* the unions. From their base on the AEU London Distict Committee, they had been patiently surmounting the official hurdles to gain the AEU Executive's approval for a standing London Aircraft Committee with a remit to extend union organization. As ODD, Jack Tanner had been their firm ally, and the Executive's sanction finally appeared imminent when the Hawker's and Gloster's strike occurred.[84]

There were ample precedents for this official multi-union initiative in the joint union committees which the AEU Executive had promoted to fight the Lock-Out and to campaign for the shorter working week in the later 1920s. AEU shop stewards routinely cooperated with stewards from other engineering unions on the shopfloor. Scott and Berridge assumed that their aircraft movement would operate in the same spirit of class solidarity, with the AEU as the main engineering union routinely providing its foundation.

Zinkin used his base on the Kingston strike committee to convene a conference of London aircraft shop stewards in 'an immediate move...for extending the united front of aircraft workers'. The conference formed a Permanent London Aircraft Committee.[85] The Committee was evidently a compromise, an admixture of Zinkin's desire for an independent rank-and-file movement and Scott and Berridge's projected London aircraft committee under AEU auspices. Not surprisingly, the Committee never became operational.

As the Hawker's and Gloster's strike reached its zenith, a national air-craft conference was convened. It was addressed by the Party's leading AEU militant, Joe Scott. Claude Berridge also spoke and described the AEU London District Committee's plan for an official multi-union air-craft committee. It is likely that both men urged delegates from outside London to emulate their example of forming a rank-and-file movement inside unions. Zinkin's revolutionary intentions were evidently stymied as the conference ended in high spirits but without any more tangible result.[86]

Then, at the end of April, a month after the strike, there was a second national aircraft conference attended by delegates from 12 aircraft facto-ries. Scott's absence from the second national conference may have enabled Zinkin to realize his aim without further obstruction. Nevertheless the Daily Worker's report, probably written by Zinkin, noted merely that delegates from 12 aircraft sites had elected officers and decided to publish a pamphlet of their conference proceedings.[87]

It was not until four months after the April national conference that the Aircraft Shop Stewards' National Council finally emerged. A report in the Daily Worker on 20 August noted that the Aircraft Shop Stewards' National Council had met and approved plans for a monthly paper, New Propellor, '[to] assist in mobilising the workers and strengthening the connections between the factories'.[88] (The title recalled The Propellor, a rank-and-file paper produced by the West London aircraft shop stewards in the early 1920s.)

Compared to the report of the April conference, the August story was notably circumspect in advertising the new movement's rank-and-filism. The April report had proclaimed that 'We have to end the neglect of the trade unions of the aircraft industry, and by building up strong shop stewards movements we can end this situation'. The Hawker's and Gloster's strike had shown the need for a strong shop stewards move-ment 'which will also be able to destroy the operation of the York Memorandum'. The August report confined itself to observing that:

> In all factories wage-rates of large numbers of workers had been raised as a result of the activity in the shops. Important and unani-mous decisions were taken as to the best method of securing the first part of the aircraft workers' programme [the 2d/hour wage increase

which was the AEU's official wage claim for engineering as a whole]
... the delegates dispersed to all parts of the country inspired by the
proceedings and the wonderful solidarity shown, the guarantee that
the movement would accomplish its programme.[89]

Zinkin's autobiography described the decision to found the ASSNC as
'momentous', but made the typically circumspect observation that it was
taken 'after some discussion'.[90] His determination to use the Hawker's–
Gloster's strike to establish a national aircraft rank-and-file movement,
met with fierce opposition from Party AEU activists and he was only successful after appealing to Johnny Mahon, the Industrial Organizer at the
London District Party. Mahon convened a meeting with Zinkin, Scott
and Berridge at which he upheld Zinkin's initiative to form an independent national aircraft rank-and-file movement.

Zinkin does not give a date for this meeting. It probably occurred in
early August. It is possible that Zinkin and Mahon planned to hold it
then because they knew Pollitt and Campbell would be attending the 7th
World Congress in Moscow. They may well have feared that Scott and
Berridge would be able to appeal over their heads to Pollitt and Campbell
to interpret the Party line against Zinkin and Class Against Class. Zinkin
remained a dedicated line-follower of revolution, not pragmatism. He
dismissed Scott because he had never studied Marxism–Leninism, had
not been to the Soviet Union, and was ignorant of how to make the revolution.

By contrast, Claude Berridge was a Lenin School graduate, and Zinkin
now sought to drive a wedge between him and Scott by appealing to his
superior 'theoretical' knowledge. At the meeting with Johnny Mahon,
Scott's strong opposition to the ASSNC had only the 'half hearted support' of Berridge who 'readily accepted' that Zinkin's action was vindicated by the Party line.[91] Nevertheless, Berridge failed conspicuously to
provide any subsequent practical assistance to the ASSNC.

Scott's public attack on independent rank-and-file movements at the
Labour Monthly conference at the end of August was probably
unpremeditated. Clearly directed at Zinkin and the ASSNC, Scott was
moved by immense anger that Mahon had conferred his imprimatur on
what he believed to be a dangerous initiative for the Party. His outburst
escalated and re-opened the internal divisions within the Party, and
forced Scott and Berridge to develop and refine their case for rank-and-
file movements *inside* unions. The approach which I have described as
constitutional militancy was the result.[92]

Scott and Berridge regarded Zinkin as an interloper who admitted that
he was ignorant of engineering and the AEU. For foundation Party members who were skilled engineers, the AEU was the putative industrial
union which they had fought for in the pre-war 'syndicalist'

ACM/Reform Committee campaigns. For Hannington, Lovell, Gallacher, Percy Glading, Ted Taylor, Scott, Berridge, Ted Bramley, Charlie Hoyle, Jack Longworth, George Crane, etc., the AEU's foundation in 1920 marked a giant step along the road to one big industrial union capable of taking on the big battalions of engineering capitalists. It is hardly surprising that Scott and Berridge envisaged their aircraft movement with the AEU as its anchor.

Scott and Berridge remained intimately involved with the problems encountered in the day-to-day engineering 'economic struggle'. They also took the lead on behalf of the Party inside the AEU London District Committee. Their pragmatic response prompted them to adapt the pre-war Reform and wartime model to suit the changed circumstances which they and 'their stewards in the field' were encountering.

The AEU Executive continued to give clear indications of its willingness to deal with perceived challenges to its authority, even when these came from 'rank-and-file' sources professing loyalism. They refused the London District Committee's request for a multi-union aircraft committee and allowed them only to continue with their own Aircraft Sub-committee which could not communicate directly with neighbouring AEU districts about common aircraft problems. In early May 1935 the Executive issued a circular which deplored 'a growing tendency to involve the union in unofficial disputes'.[93] They had been thoroughly alarmed by the Hawker's and Gloster's strikers' dogged disregard of full-time officials' advice to return to work. The apparent equanimity with which the strikers flouted engineering procedure was deeply threatening to union authority. Even the TGWU, which routinely used strike pay as an incentive for recruiting members in unofficial disputes, decided not to pay up at Hawker's and Gloster's.[94]

In June 1935 the AEU National Committee endorsed the Executive's circular 'by practically a unanimous vote'. The *AEU Journal* noted that: 'Disruptive elements within our ranks received very sharp and rapt attention, and opinions were expressed that such should be eliminated and every action taken to prevent their recurrence.'[95] The Executive now had adequate justification for taking punitive action against members who were seen to be provoking unofficial action.

AEU Party activists were unwilling to spend their time fighting expulsions from the union when they were already achieving results within the boundaries of official procedure. They had learned to bend and extend the formal rules and judged it inexpedient to bypass or ignore them. For example, Party activists won concessions by leading skirmishes so as to maximize the advantages of speed and surprise. In April 1934, the *Daily Worker* reported a dispute in the Handley Page machine shop over a fortnight's bonus. It had been won *without a formal strike*; the men had simply stopped work momentarily in unison behind their shop stewards' demands.

> Within five minutes the management came to the shop saying 'tell these blighters they shall have their two weeks' bonus'. It is as well to remember in noting this victory that two years ago there were only one or two trade unionists at this firm. Now it is 80% organised, which speaks well for the work of the militants employed there.[96]

The *Daily Worker* and *Engineers' Bulletin* can be culled for other instances of creative 'economic struggle' from which Party activists did not seek primarily to escalate conflict, but rather were concerned to win tangible concessions which would induce more workers to join the union and back their stewards in further skirmishes. Scott and Berridge could cite a multitude of occasions on which the 'rank-and-file' had gained victories without the advantage of an independent rank-and-file movement. Peter Zinkin was not impressed. He had a barely disguised and enduring contempt for Party trade union activists like Joe Scott whom he did not consider understood Communism.

Zinkin remained convinced that without his bolshevik intervention, there would be no advance in aircraft. He denied that the AEU activists' work in West London aircraft factories had met with any success before he stepped in with the ASSNC.[97] This travesty becomes comprehensible in the light of his unswerving commitment to follow the Class Against Class line as he had experienced it in the Soviet Union of 1931–32. He dedicated the ASSNC to the Comintern's pre-7th World Congress goals: building the united fighting front from below against fascism and strengthening independent working-class organization.

The 7th World Congress had moved the International Communist Movement away from the pursuit of independent leadership about a fortnight after Zinkin's London triumph in its favour. On their return from the Congress in Moscow, Pollitt and Campbell moved to ensure that Zinkin understood the new rules which now prevailed. Nevertheless, they judged it inexpedient to close down the ASSNC. To Party members who were mere spectators, Zinkin appeared to have conjured up a rank-and-file movement from nowhere, a feat worthy of admiration and bolshevik emulation. They confined their intervention to the injunction that the ASSNC must disseminate and promote trade union organization.

As we shall see, Zinkin followed Pollitt's and Campbell's instructions after his own fashion: his genuflections towards trade union loyalism were genuine enough, but always qualified by invoking what he believed to be the more sacred ark of rank-and-filism. The clear apprehension of the irreconcilable contradiction between serious union loyalism and the fullblown rank-and-filism of many of his South Walian mining colleagues decided Arthur Horner to disband the South Wales Miners' Rank and File movement after the 7th World Congress. He justified his action with the same gloss as Scott and Berridge had used at the London District Industrial fraction; the Fed subsumed within itself both rank-and-filism and union loyalty.

Horner as the Fed's Communist President and his protégés in the Fed invariably opted for union loyalty when it was necessary to make the choice. Zinkin's conviction that rank-and-filism was the inevitable choice for Communists *in extremis* foreshadowed the ASSNC's messy end. For Zinkin, aircraft workers' participation in their unions was a mere means to his desired end, a fully-fledged national confrontation with aircraft employers from which the Comintern's aim of a united front with Party members in the van could be achieved. We have already observed him operating with this order of priorities in the Hawkers'– Gloster's strike. He continued to encourage aircraft workers to flout the conventions of engineering collective bargaining.

Zinkin deemed it prudent to base the ASSNC on union activists outside the AEU. The developed Party networks in aircraft were concentrated inside the AEU and his freedom of action was circumscribed by the influence of constitutional militancy there. AEU stewards from the London aircraft factories probably attended two sets of meetings: the ASSNC National Committee and the AEU London District Aircraft Sub-Committee. Their membership of both official and unofficial bodies provided an effective means for Scott and Berridge to monitor the ASSNC's affairs.

Zinkin built up his own network with the help of the militant stewards whom he had encountered at Hawker's Kingston. The first ASSNC chairman was Jimmy Boyle, convener of the Sheet Metal Workers' Union (SMW) at Kingston. Sheet metal workers had the strong democratic rank-and-filist impulses associated with their craft outlook. Zinkin encouraged their rank-and-filism whilst choosing to ignore their craft union exclusivism. His autobiography acknowledges his debt to sheet metal workers with unaccustomed candour. The 'tin-bashers' had evidently warmed his Leninist heart, usually immune from such undisciplined attachments.

> [Boyle] played an important part in helping to consolidate the movement through his contacts with other Sheet Metal Worker Union activists in several factories so that these highly skilled craftsmen were the main influence in attracting support to the ASSNC. They supplied the names and addresses of their members they considered most likely to assist, and these I visited at their homes throughout the country to evaluate the situation in their factory and to get them to arrange meetings for me to address with shop stewards, or when this was considered a better approach, with militant trade unionists.[98]

The first ASSNC secretary was Bill Corrigall, a leading militant at Kingston who successfully organized the National Brass and Metal Mechanics Union (B&MM) there. Engineering employers were often reluctant to recognize the B&MM, a direct though much smaller rival of the AEU, since its members were usually a tiny minority in any one shop. The B&MM survived because its subscription was lower than the AEU and semi-skilled workers were often denied admission to the AEU by craft conservative branch officers. Corrigall may well have joined the B&MM because the AEU District Committee at Kingston refused admission to Hawker's semi-skilled workers who were not earning the union's minimum hourly rate. By the spring of 1936, the B&MM had become the dominant union at Hawker's and militants turned their attention to the Vickers site at nearby Weybridge.[99]

The ASSNC's secretary's job was actually done by Peter Zinkin, who unblushingly recalled: 'He [Corrigall] felt it would be too much for him but he finally accepted when I undertook to do all that was necessary, acting in consultation with him, dealing with the correspondence as well ... he accepted and the arrangement endorsed [*sic*].[100]

Both B&MM and SMW activists were less constrained by full-time officials than their AEU counterparts. There were fewer B&MM and SMW full-time officials and moreover employers were accustomed to calling in the AEU District Secretary to resolve any difficulties. Zinkin quickly perceived and effectively exploited the difference between the unions' cultures.

It was the AEU full-time official who was seen by the 'rank-and-file' as the man who pulled stewards back inside procedure. This presented little difficulty to veteran AEU militants who perceived their union as providing the heavy artillery in economic battles. There was substantial space for rank-and-filism within engineering procedure, on terrain accepted as legitimate by both union and management. Particularly in the south-east and the Midlands, AEU militants effected an elastic development of engineering collective bargaining at factory level. They knew that their full-time officials would connive at limited skirmishes and even unofficial strikes when they themselves were willing to settle for limited concessions and to take responsibility for leading their members back to work and inside procedure.

The ASSNC's overt progamme contained none of the provocative rank-and-filism which Zinkin was routinely dispensing in person. He was scrupulous in observing the letter of the new Seventh World Congress line of the need to work for partial demands with 'reformist' trade unions: The ASSNC's Aims and Objects stressed union organization:

a) To establish and maintain 100% trade unionism in all aircraft factories. To elect shop stewards in each department of the factory, such shop stewards to form a Works Committee. b) The enforcement of all trade union agreements. c) To co-ordinate the activities of all workers in the aircraft factories and the trade union branches in order to secure higher wages and better conditions. To secure through the trade unions a national agreement relating to rates of pay and conditions of employment. d) To publish a Monthly Bulletin for all aircraft workers.

The ASSNC's Immediate Demands were proudly displayed each month on *New Propellor*'s masthead. Zinkin was content to appropriate the entire shopping list which AEU Party activists were promoting for the whole of engineering.[101]

Zinkin found fertile ground on which to build a rank-and-file aircraft movement. As well as sharing in the general economic recovery from 1934, aircraft had the additional financial security of Air Ministry contracts. Orders from the Ministry increased dramatically from 1934 with the recognition of German superiority in the air. Claydon reckoned that in 1935, employment in aircraft was 30–35,000 and that by 1939 the numbers had grown to 350–370,000.[102] An indefatigable activist, Zinkin described his daily routine:

> Careful study of the specialist magazines, The Aeroplane and Flight, not only provided news about developments in the industry, but occasionally they would reveal the name and location of some factory of which we were unaware . . .That would be a signal to try to find someone to approach to make the desired connection. In most such cases there was no contact so there would be a journey to the town to discuss with the local branch or Communist Party District Committee what to do. Usually they did know someone either working in the factory or a trade union activist who could be approached and with their advice, some success was chalked up.[103]

Zinkin proved a gifted editor of *New Propellor*. His propaganda emphasized the 'large profits' of aircraft firms and promoted aircraft consciousness. For skilled workers, craft exclusiveness remained an important part of their identification as 'aircraftsmen'.[104] *New Propellor* skilfully utilized their pre-occupations without pandering or encouraging them. It reported the endemic and usually successful disputes over trainees without the requisite skills as wins for the trade union side without ever commenting on their potentially divisive terrain of craft exclusivity.

Prior to Zinkin's entry into aircraft rank-and-filism, Party AEU activists had cultivated an 'aircraft consciousness' in keeping with the AEU's segmented approach to the diverse 'engineering industry'. The AEU negotiated separate agreements for its members who worked in ship repair, for those who worked on board ship as marine engineers and for engineers in Ministry of Defence establishments, to mention but a few. Party AEU activists on the London District Committee of the AEU argued that aircraft engineers also merited a separate agreement. Zinkin appropriated their argument to justify the ASSNC's immediate demands: 'Agreements covering separate sections of the engineering industry, districts and sections of industry within districts, already exist, and there can be no valid argument as to why the Trade Unions should not now open up negotiations with the British Society of Aircraft Constructors for such an agreement.'[105]

In fact, the British Society of Aircraft Constructors included airframe makers only. Companies producing aero-engines were members of the EEF, and their workers were already covered by general engineering agreements. Airframes had been made with metal rather than wood comparatively recently. Companies manufacturing airframes were still coming to terms with being part of 'engineering' with its attendant collective bargaining procedures.[106] While a separate aircraft agreement remained an attractive slogan, there was little prospect of its being achieved. Party AEU activists would probably have ceased to pursue a separate agreement under pressure of these practical considerations. Despite its flimsy dubiety, Zinkin had little choice but to take a separate aircraft agreement seriously. Without its *raison d'être*, there was no ground for the ASSNC's continuing existence.

In addition to its lack of practicality, Zinkin's separate aircraft agreement had no aircraft-specific features. We have seen that the ASSNC's Immediate Demands were the same as those being pursued by engineering activists elsewhere. Neither Zinkin nor the Party AEU activists would have tolerated an aircraft parochialism based on gazumping workers in the rest of engineering. It is hardly surprising that the ASSNC's fervent propaganda for a separate aircraft agreement had a somewhat hollow ring.

The core of Zinkin's propaganda line was the claim that all militant trade union activity in aircraft was due to the ASSNC. The ASSNC accumulated a high-profile charisma as a result of his copywriting skills, which Scott and Berridge were unable to challenge publicly. Claydon observed: 'From 1924 to 1935 trade unions maintained their position in the aircraft industry'; and estimates that there was 50 per cent trade union organization in 1935 which was 'noticeably higher than it had been amongst the much larger, more heterogeneous labour force in wartime'.[107]

New Propellor announced:

> We all of us know that had it not been for the ASSNC, the aircraft industry instead of being the best organised section, would have been still the worst organised section of the engineering industry,

> with rotten conditions and wages. Once more we must state, that to our supporters and to the policy which we have advocated and which is now the official policy of the trade unions, namely improved wages and working conditions in an aircraft agreement, belongs the honour and responsibility for the matter now becoming the subject of negotiations, and belongs the credit for the tremendous growth in trade union organisation.[108]

In fact the ASSNC's main function was to provide networks for strike collections on the few occasions when skirmishes developed into actual strikes. This role could have been performed equally well by existing Party engineering networks. Nevertheless, aircraft activists outside the circles of AEU constitutional militancy began to believe the claims of Zinkin's advertising campaign. *New Propellor*'s style was notably snappier than other 'rank-and-file' papers, including *Busman's Punch* which was frequently lugubrious. It was invariably a good read.

The centrepiece of *New Propellor* were its monthly reports of aircraft skirmishes which Zinkin gathered from his travels and expanding network of militants. New Propellor's litany of concessions won provided fresh inspiration about new targets to aim for and examples of new fighting techniques. Zinkin transformed the smallest gain into a noteworthy advance, achieved without the help of union officials. He tried to reinforce the will to emulate the most militant practices of which he approved and omitted to praise the more pragmatic reflexes such as the need to retreat. Aircraft militants must have enjoyed reading about themselves clothed in his purple prose. They probably conducted the 'economic struggle' more confidently feeling part of a potent movement.

New Propellor's scorecard for February 1936 comprised:

> *Armstrong Siddeley*, Coventry: Since March 1935, union membership was up 50% at the Parkside Works with the Sheet Metal Workers being 100%. An active works committee and shop stewards had gained a 1d/hour increase in the aero engine test shop with smoking from 11.0–11.15 a.m. and 4.0–4.15 p.m. and on overtime and nights.

> *Parnall*, Yate: There was nearly 100% trade unionism in three departments with stewards and shop committees. A new canteen was being built and there was a new lavatory. They had 1/6 per hour basic rate in all departments, and piece rates yielded time and a third on a basic rate of 1/3 per hour.

> *B.A.C.*, Bristol: Management had agreed to build a bike shed and improve the canteen. There was mutuality in the sheet metal shop which was 100% organised.

> *Handley Page*, Cricklewood: There were now new cycle racks and a new canteen being built. Two members were on the AEU District Committee and another two were branch secretaries.

de Havillands, Hatfield: Fitters were getting 1/6 per hour plus bonus. Toolmakers were earning from $1/7\frac{1}{2}$ to $1/9\frac{1}{2}$ per hour plus bonus. There were two district committee members and one branch secretary.

Fairey's, Hayes: Earnings were up 10% with piece rates in the machine shop and on the bench being determined by mutuality with ratefixers. (There was a shop pricing committee in the sheet metal shop.) There were two members on district committees and a third was a branch secretary.

Hawker's, Kingston: Unions were practically 100% and the bike shed was a source of great annoyance.[109]

During 1936 Zinkin and the constitutional militants learned to co-exist with one another in the aircraft 'economic struggle'. The ASSNC and *New Propellor* intensified pressure for an Aircraft Agreement and criticized full-time union officials' 'unconscionable delay' in achieving it. The constitutional militants continued to pursue an aircraft agreement through AEU channels, but registered slow progress. The paucity of their achievement lent credence to Zinkin's arguments that the ASSNC would have to take matters into its own hands before union officials would respond. A knot of ASSNC activists, encouraged by Zinkin, seriously contemplated leading an unofficial national aircraft strike to get their aircraft agreement.

In fact, the AEU Executive Council's discussions reveal that Executive Councillors took a lively interest in aircraft issues. Aircraft sites were comparatively dispersed throughout England and aircraft issues affected most Executive divisions. The AEU Executive were keen to extend their predominance in engineering to this rapidly expanding sector. Some Executive Councillors, including Jack Tanner, were suspicious that the other aircraft unions were trying to usurp the AEU's 'natural dominance'. They counselled that the AEU's policy should be directed at ensuring its paramountcy.[110] Zinkin's propaganda and the constitutional militants' official pressure for a separate aircraft agreement combined to induce the Executive Council to actively explore the possibilities for a separate *airframe* agreement. The Executive Councillors had every self-interested reason for succeeding in this project.

ASSNC militants sought to magnify and escalate their skirmishes to precipitate a national aircraft strike. In March 1936 *New Propellor* reported on two minor disputes. At de Havilland's, Hatfield, workers went on unofficial strike for four days over a payments-by-result system. Workers at de Havilland's Stag Lane site came out in sympathy.[111] At Fairey's, Stockport, there was an unofficial strike over 'dilutees'. Fairey's Hayes workers had come out in sympathy, and many girls in the dope shop joined the TGWU.[112]

Soon after the Fairey's Stockport strike had begun, a national meeting of the ASSNC was convened at three day's notice. Thirty four delegates attended from thirteen sites 'to discuss the growing movement in the aircraft industry for a national agreement.'[113] They agreed that the ASSNC's Immediate Demands were having a powerful influence. 'Everywhere the question is being asked, "How can we get such an agreement quickly", before we miss our opportunity.'[114]

Zinkin's ambitions for spreading the two strikes were not realized because they had both been settled by shop stewards and full-time officials bending the 'rigid framework' of the York Memorandum sub-culture. De Havilland's workers went back after a week, having obtained promises of an early works conference at which concessions would be made and no victimization. The Fairey's strikers returned to work after 11 days with the same two pledges of an early works conference plus concessions and no victimization. Nevertheless, New Propeller concluded portentously that the two disputes had assumed 'national proportions, extending far outside of aircraft and even of the engineering industry . . . They were recognised by most sections of the organised working class as being of somewhat more than ordinary importance, and their success has even greater significance.'[115]

The ASSNC's first AGM was held on 10 May 1936. Delegates from 15 sites agreed to hold mass meetings to consider strike action to enforce the negotiation of an aircraft agreement by union officials. New Propellor reported that many delegates had hailed an unofficial strike at Handley Page, Cricklewood, as the spark which would set off a national aircraft strike. '[But] A very strong feeling was expressed, that the forces of Handley Page workers should be conserved for what they hope is to be a National Stoppage of all aircraft factories in the very near future, in order to enforce the negotiation of an aircraft agreement.'

The Secretary's report recorded 28 factories affiliated to the ASSNC.

> No one can honestly dispute the fact that it is the existence and work of the ASSNC which has been largely responsible for this great desire for unity, for strong trade union organisation; not a milk and water, ineffective trade unionism, but a strong effective, powerful movement of the aircraft workers.[116]

Zinkin clearly meant what the ASSNC and New Propellor were saying. The Fairey's and de Havilland's strikes prompted the Executive to re-issue their 1935 circular deploring unofficial strikes.[117] Zinkin was undeterred by the threat of action against Party AEU activists. He continued to hare around the country inciting aircraft workers to wage open-ended offensive action.

On 11 June 1936, the AEU Executive discussed a dispute at Parnall Aircraft in Yate, Gloucestershire. The President, Jack Little, reported that the Director of the EEF, Alec Ramsay, had 'admitted that their member, who had only recently joined the Federation, and was therefore new to the procedure, had not acted as he might have done'. Ramsay was prepared to instruct Parnall to remove the three 'dilutees' from skilled work and thus remove the grievance which had precipitated the dispute, if the ODD would in turn arrange a return to work, 'a Works Conference to be held immediately therafter for the purpose of discussing the whole question and other outstanding matters'.

But the ODD had

> directed attention to the hopeless position in which he found himself, due to the interference by representatives of the National Aircraft Shop Stewards Council, who were practically dominating the dispute.
> ... a Bro. F. Peters [Peter Zinkin], acting on behalf of the National Aircraft Shop Stewards' Council had been on the scene of the dispute, spending practically the whole of his time urging the members to remain solid, pointing out the attitude taken by the Executive Council in recent unofficial disputes, and also quoting the voting of E.C. in regard to the payment of benefit.
> He further asserted to the men that if sufficient pressure was exerted by them and they were able to get branches to flood the General Office with resolutions, the Executive Council would pay benefit after they had returned to work. In evidence of this allegation he cited the cases of Fairey Aviation Co., and de Havillands, Stag Lane, disputes.[118]

The AEU Executive's concern over the palpable intensifying of aircraft disputes was not solely motivated by a desire to preserve their own authority. They recognized that unofficial disputes often provided an opportune recruiting ground and had shown themselves prepared to tolerate them for that reason. They had also become accustomed to paying strike benefits in short unofficial disputes to new members even though they did not yet qualify for payment. The Executive had accepted the need to pay, because other unions, notably the TGWU, routinely offered strike pay to new recruits. But the Executive was now fearful for the AEU's solvency when confronted with the prospect of paying dispute benefit to growing numbers of new recruits in unofficial strikes of lengthening duration.

In addition, the effect of Zinkin's interventions had seriously disturbed the *status quo* in which unofficial strikes were confined to the flexible, but comparatively narrow gap in procedure at the factory base of the York Memorandum. The Executive were fearful that the disequilibrium caused by the escalation in aircraft economic conflict would be eventually resolved in the employers' favour and that the gap at the local base of engineering procedure would be closed. The Handley Page strike in May 1936 is an apt case in point. From 1920, AEU full-time officials in the two London divisions had been notably more tolerant of unofficial strikes than officials elsewhere. The Executive had acquiesced in this local tradition.

The Handley Page management had quickly conceded a works conference to Joe Scott who was the presiding ODD for Cricklewood. When Scott had tried to arrange the return to work which was the expected response to management's move, Peter Zinkin had appeared to escalate and spread the strike. He incited the strikers to organize a model rank-and-file strike committee with appropriate sub-committees. Scott's counsels of prudence were disregarded. Mass meetings were attended by 550 people in Cricklewood Trades Hall and money was raised 'in all directions'.[119]

Party AEU activists had organized all-out battles accompanied by intense rank-and-filist activity in exceptional circumstances, for example the fight to gain uion recognition at Ford's Dagenham in 1933. They failed to see why such a response was required at Handley Page for a merely routine skirmish conducted by well-organized trade union forces. Moreover, the open-ended strike placed Scott's credibility in jeopardy not only with the AEU Executive but with local employers as well.

Pollitt and Campbell swiftly enforced a temporary retreat on Zinkin and consequently the ASSNC. The June meeting of the ASSNC included a discussion on strike tactics which was remarkable for the disappearance of rank-and-filism. In fact, the meeting appeared to have been a model of constitutional militancy. It had been agreed that while strike action was necessary on some occasions,

> we need to be very careful in making such decisions. There were many methods of struggle open to us, tactics of guerrilla warfare, bans on overtime, working day work instead of piecework, etc., etc. It was necessary for us to exercise our imagination and initiative, so that we could fight all along the line, and strengthen our forces in the process.[120]

Despite this change in attitude, the ASSNC's preparations for a national aircraft strike continued. Protesting their union loyalism all the while, in the late summer of 1936 the ASSNC laid its plans for a ballot of aircraft workers. Zinkin ensured that the ASSNC had publicly staked its bona fides on the ballot and achieving a favourable outcome. However, he also was well aware of the need for caution. The operation of the rank-and-file ballot proceeded discreetly at factory level. There was almost no publicity either in the *Daily Worker* or *New Propellor*. Then at the end of August, the *Daily Worker* observed:

> Mass meetings in various [aircraft] factories have been strongly attended, the claims have been endorsed and in many cases demands for strike action have been adopted . . . It is expected that the results

of the ballot vote which is now being taken amongst the aircraft
workers of this country will show a majority in favour of strike
action to enforce the workers' demands.[121]

At the meetings, militants had put the ASSNC's Immediate Demands and
encouraged workers to vote for an aircraft strike, basing their case on the
ASSNC's pamphlet 'The Aircraft Workers' Case'. It was vintage rank-
and-filist Zinkin:

> It would be true to state that no rank and file movement has devel-
> oped so rapidly before or during the postwar period as has the
> 'ASSNC'. It was born out of the conflict of the aircraft workers with
> the employers just 16 months ago, and has grown so rapidly that
> there is hardly an aircraft factory of any importance that does not
> elect its representative ... It has directed more strikes during the
> past months than some trade unions have during an equal number of
> years, and as a consequence workers have gained more concessions
> in that period.[122]
> We claim that the wages paid in the aircraft industry are not com-
> parable with those in other trades, and in no case are other trades
> paid too high a wage. We demand a much higher standard of living
> than we have been accustomed to over the periods of economic
> depression ... We demand a share in the huge profits which the
> employers are able to realise from the unpaid labour of those
> employed in the industry.[123]

The AEU Executive responded with predictable speed to this direct challenge. It is notable, however, that most Executive Councillors did not
want a witch-hunt against aircraft militants, nor did it occur to them to
stop paying dispute benefit in unofficial strikes. Executive Councillors
who favoured punitive measures were an isolated minority. Everyone
agreed with Jack Little that their Executive's authority had to be force-
fully reasserted. But most also recognized the force of Tanner's observation:

> the Movement [ASSNC] had developed very largely from what was
> considered by its adherents as being the 'delay' in the matter of offi-
> cial Union action. There had been a great change in the outlook of
> many of the men, even within the past twelve months, their desire
> being to get something done.

Executive Councillor Openshaw commented:

> He [Tanner] had repeatedly succeeded in securing [Executive]
> Council's approval for the payment of Benefit to members partici-
> pating in unofficial disputes, and, in this respect, Council had been
> exceedingly generous. For his part, he was prepared to support the
> continuation of this generous treatment, but not if it is to be taken as
> an indication of any 'weakness' on the part of Executive Council.[124]

On 2 September, Jack Little told the press that the Executive had instructed district committees to caution shop stewards that AEU members taking part in the ballot or a strike would be acting against rule and liable to expulsion. He reminded the public that the AEU National Committee, *'a body representing the rank and file'*, had decided to open negotiations with the EEF for an aircraft agreement as soon as this was possible under the existing national wages agreement.[125]

The *Daily Worker* reported the strike ballot result on 10 September: 6258 workers had voted for strike action and 2527 against. The ballot had been held at nineteen aircraft sites; between one quarter and one fifth of all aircraft workers had participated.[126] Despite this favourable outcome, the ASSNC meeting in September decided not to call a strike. A flurry of vague militant rhetoric camouflaged the *volte face*. The Party Centre had evidently intervened to pre-empt a strike which would certainly precipitate a chain of adverse consequences for Party AEU activists. Once the prospect of a national aircraft strike appeared unlikely, the AEU Executive forbore to take any disciplinary action against the many AEU shop stewards and members who had participated in the ballot.

The September ASSNC meeting postponed any decision on strike action for a month, stating that time was required to make preparations. The October ASSNC meeting postponed a decision on strike action for a second time, offering the reason that they were allowing the AEU time to begin official negotiations! *New Propellor*'s account emphasized the need for militants to pressurize their trade unions to take action. Face-saving plans were made to extend the ASSNC's influence, including provision for taking up the case for an aircraft agreement through official machinery.[127]

After the second postponement of the strike decision, the ASSNC failed to meet for three months. It was clearly easier to maintain the pretence of an imminent strike when there were no monthly meetings which would have to re-postpone it. When the ASSNC finally met, in January 1937, delegates had no progress to report on the ambitious plans laid in October to carry the movement to unaffiliated aircraft sites. They preserved the fiction of an impending national action by making a new plan for affiliated works committees to present the ASSNC Immediate Demands to their respective managements on 1 February.[128] Such synchronised local collective bargaining evidently represented the limits of feasible action.

The ASSNC failed to hold its next scheduled meeting on 14 February. Despite the apparent atrophy of the rank-and-file movement, the union forces continued to win local skirmishes in aircraft. In addition, the AEU submitted its claim to the EEF for a national agreement covering airframe manufacture.[129] Zinkin's claim that the ASSNC was the vital ingredient for success in aircraft militancy was being disproved.

The aircraft ballot and the campaign promoting it in the summer of 1936 proved to be the ASSNC's zenith. The campaign with its promise of an impending strike had been espoused by aircraft stewards from all aircraft unions in 19 factories. Workers had been caught up its momentum. Zinkin had evidently been able to convince successive ASSNC meetings that their rank-and-file movement could bend union executives to their will and that strike pay would be dispensed for a national dispute to win their just demands. When the campaign yielded a majority for a strike, stewards and workers expected it to happen. When it fizzled out instead, they learned from the experience and routinely discounted the flamboyant claims still made in *New Propellor* about the ASSNC's strength.

Peter Zinkin remained irrepressible. The February ASSNC meeting was probably abandoned after the AEU Executive threatened AEU members involved in the ASSNC with disciplinary action. They were responding to reports received at the end of January that 'Bro. Peters' had turned up at an unofficial strike at Boulton and Paul, Wolverhampton:

> the D.O. [Organising Divisional Delegate] reports on his attendance at a [shop stewards'] Meeting held on the 25th instant, when questions had been asked regarding the attendance of an individual named Zinkin, believed to be the Editor of 'The Propeller', objections being taken to his presence. He had asked for a hearing, however, and presumably because he had brought a grant in aid of the Dispute from the National Aircraft Shop Stewards' Council, he was allowed to address the Meeting. [The ODD had asked] to have an E.C. Representative on the spot to combat the interference by the individual named Peters or Zinkin.[130]

The AEU Executive subsequently wrote to members whose names had been furnished by the General Secretary, Fred Smith, who cautioned 'that he hoped E.C. would not press him to disclose the source of his information, which – should they do so – would inevitably dry up'. Members were asked whether they had attended meetings of the ASSNC, an unofficial body 'which cannot be recognised' and '[it was pointed] out that if they attend any further Meetings of the kind, E.C. will have to take steps to deal with them in accordance with Rule.'[131]

On 22 February, the Executive minutes noted the receipt of replies to the letters which had been sent to Percy Glading, Billy Stokes, Claude Berridge, George Crane, Joe Scott 'and others'; and 'in each case that E.C. accept[ed] the personal assurances contained in the letters and the writers' disclaimers of having any connection with the Body [ASSNC] in question'.[132] The *Daily Worker* reported the Executive's letter on 23 February, presumably after Jack Tanner had conveyed the news of the

Executive's decision not to take disciplinary action against Party activists. The story made no attempt to arouse readers or 'the rank-and-file' against this interference with union members' democratic rights. Pollitt and Campbell were evidently prepared to countenance the official restriction of organized rank-and-file activity.[133]

The progressive atrophy of the ASSNC was interrupted by the imminent official London bus strike, the escalation of the MFGB's Battle of Harworth and the Rolls-Royce grinders' strike in Derby. The example of these militant confrontations revived Zinkin's bolshevik impulses. A special meeting of the ASSNC was suddenly convened for Sunday 28 February, and the *Daily Worker* graced its deliberations with the headline: 'Complete Aircraft Stoppage Threatens'.[134]

In fact, the ASSNC meeting had promised merely to organize affiliated sites to provide their usual financial support. Sympathy strikes had been discussed, but not agreed. The formal demand was also made for union executives to ballot their aircraft members if the EEF made an offer for an airframe agreement. The press statement which Zinkin issued after the meeting had probably amplified the possibility of sympathy strikes, and the *Daily Worker*'s sub-editor had absorbed its spirit in composing the headline. During these heady February and March days members working close to the Party Centre were all experiencing a similar quickening of their revolutionary heartbeat.[135]

In this atmosphere, Zinkin took his chance. The Party Centre expected the imminent arrival of a national militant upsurge which would result in power moving away from 'reformist' union officials towards Party activists. Zinkin hastened to resuscitate the ASSNC so as not to miss being in the vanguard. He was careful to continue with the full regalia of the real united front and union loyalism.[136] Nevertheless, the *Daily Worker*'s sub-editor had correctly detected that the substance of Zinkin's press release lay in its militant tone rather than the union loyalism of its formal content.

In April, the sanguine mood at the Party Centre was reinforced by the deeply stirring spectacle of strikes on Clydeside and Ernest Bevin handing London Transport one month's official strike notice.[137] Zinkin responded by completely sloughing off the rhetoric of the union loyalism. On 11 April, the ASSNC met for the first time since 28 February. However, reports of the meeting in the *Daily Worker* and *New Propellor* conflicted on one crucial point.

The *Daily Worker* noted that the meeting had agreed that unions should ballot their memberships if the engineering employers had not replied within a fortnight, i.e. by 25 April, to the AEU's claim for an airframe agreement. *New Propellor* reported that the ASSNC meeting had given the employers two weeks to respond to the union claim. If they failed to do so, then a strike ballot would be held within a week to secure the ASSNC's demands. There was no mention of *union* ballots.[138]

The conflicting reports indicated that a serious breach had occurred. Some delegates had agreed with Zinkin that the time was ripe for an unofficial aircraft strike; others had asserted the need to confine action within their official union structures. It is also likely that London AEU aircraft stewards who normally attended ASSNC meetings failed to attend this time in view of the AEU Executive's recent threats of expulsions. *New Propellor*'s leader referred to the breach obliquely when it justified the ASSNC's decision to hold a strike ballot, which it acknowledged was normally the sole prerogative of unions' official machinery. 'It is the duty of leadership to lead. A leadership that tails behind, and tries to drag back the forward movement when the time is ripe, is no leadership.'[139]

That Zinkin's revolutionary zeal had survived untempered by the practical realities of British 'economic struggle' can only elicit the scholar's awe and incredulity. His belief that aircraft workers were ready and willing to go on indefinite national strike for the ASSNC's Immediate Programme was belied by the dominant pattern of small-scale and intermittent economic conflict in aircraft over the two years which he had been intimately associated with it.

The union activists leading the aircraft skirmishes had gained the self-confidence which comes from success and the knowledge that their members would follow them when asked. Had Zinkin called a national unofficial aircraft strike, many of them would have brought their members out and experienced the adversity of defeat. Zinkin had been saved from the logic of his extremism by the Party Centre, and the aircraft stewards' reputation with their members had accordingly not suffered.

Even at this juncture of mounting excitement, the Party Centre took care to restrain Zinkin. The *Daily Worker* chose to studiously ignore the ASSNC's plans for an aircraft ballot and strike. Zinkin evidently calculated that Pollitt and Campbell would tolerate his activities. While the Party Centre did not suppress his strike preparations, they made no attempt to stop AEU Party activists using the National Metal Bureau networks against the ASSNC.

The 25 April deadline set by the ASSNC passed without any report of an aircraft ballot being held. The Manchester Metal Bureau met on the 25 April and discussed the situation at AV Roe's, a large aircraft firm on their patch: 'The big issue is the ASSNC demands. We anticipate that the [ASSNC] Council meeting next week-end will decide for strike action and have a big job to get a solid front here.'[140]

A week later, the Manchester Metal Bureau had further intelligence of ASSNC developments: 'It was reported that Handley Page's have circulated resolution for strike action. That certain moves have been made locally to get unions to decide against strike action and that any strike action will be unofficial.'[141]

The ASSNC met on 2 May, the day after the London bus strike had begun. Tom Schofield's remarks from the chair set the tone:

> [He referred] to the busmen's strike, the splendid contingent of aircraft workers which marched in the London May Day demonstration the previous day, that the Handley Page workers had a day's strike for May 1, and to the fact that the miners had decided to give in their strike notices to the employers so as to enforce recognition of the MFGB at Harworth. These factors were an indication of the growth in the active spirit, militancy, amongst the working class, and an indication that any action decided upon by this meeting would receive the sympathetic support of the workers.

A busmen's representative spoke, probably Bert Papworth, and his passion must have had its effect. Delegates would have been reminded of the parallels between the sister rank-and-file movements and felt inspired about their own projected strike. Reports were taken from aircraft factories which had decided to strike on 25 May. Caution was eventually thrown to the winds. *New Propellor* acknowledged that there had been a heated discussion, and the majority, which had not yet held strike meetings, agreed to hold their own ballots for strike action to commence on 25 May unless the employers made an acceptable offer.[142]

The *Daily Worker* did not carry a report of the ASSNC meeting on 2 May. Indeed, apart from a passing reference on 3 May, the Daily Worker did not mention any aircraft events until 26 May, the day after the ASSNC's national aircraft strike should have taken place.[143] But the Special Issue of *New Propellor*, which Zinkin rushed out after the meeting announced that the ASSNC's London-based Acting Committee had met

> and has prepared the plan of campaign, and a start has been made on setting up the necessary organisation. These proposals . . . will show that . . . plans to cover the great degree of organisation involved, are now made which will give every aircraft worker a great deal of confidence in our ability to wage a successful fight.[144]

Pollitt and Campbell probably calculated that the AEU Executive would publicly denounce the proposed strike and awaited their intervention before taking any action themselves. This expedient allowed them to use the overriding need to maintain the united front as their justification for pre-empting the ASSNC's unofficial action. Nevertheless, their hedging also allowed the Party Centre to keep its options open. If the London bus strike had actually transformed the mood of a critical mass of trade union activists into offensive militancy, then an unofficial national aircraft strike would certainly have appeared to be the logical next step.

The London bus strike was increasingly isolated. There was no rush of blood to the head from other trade union activists. By the middle of May, it was evident that calculations of a national militant upsurge were misplaced. When the AEU Executive made its expected move against the ASSNC the Party Centre was prepared to enforce the abandonment of any unofficial aircraft action.

On 19 May the AEU Executive received reports from the Stockport District Secretary and the Portsmouth District Committee 'to the effect that Ballot Papers were being circulated by the National Aircraft Shop Stewards' Council, inviting aircraft workers to vote for or against the tendering of notices on the 19 May, to be followed by a cessation of work on the 25 May.' The Executive decided to re-issue their circular of September 1936 dealing with the ASSNC's first strike ballot. Fred Smith was authorized to issue a suitable press statement.[145]

Executive Councillors felt compelled to take action to safeguard the union's authority because they believed the AEU remained the members' best defence of their economic interests. They felt they were fulfilling their responsibility as union officers by ensuring that their members in turn took their own responsibilities and duties to the union seriously. Nevertheless, they opted for a comparatively mild response to what was arguably an immense provocation. They threatened expulsions in the confident expectation that they would not have to carry them out. It transpired that Executive Councillors had a more realistic view of their members' likely behaviour than Zinkin. They were confident that their activists wanted to remain loyal to the union, and would not lead members on strike in answer to 'rank-and-file' calls for all-out national battles.

Pollitt and Campbell now made certain that the ASSNC aborted its strike plans, though these were evidently in an advanced state of readiness. Zinkin acquiesced and the Party Centre and the ASSNC both offered a public version of events from which all evidence of the ASSNC's strike decision of 2 May was expunged.[146] The flat denial that an unofficial aircraft strike had ever been even considered allowed aircraft activists to play the injured innocents in response to the AEU Executive. Zinkin spoke at the 14th Party Congress about the fight of the aircraft stewards which was 'uniting the workers not only against the employing class but also against the National Government'. He concluded that the 'real attack is being made on *trade unions* in the aircraft industry and this is a warning to us all . . . They are singling us out because they want to disrupt the unity which has been built up in these last few years.'[147]

The Party Centre connived with the fiction that there had never been any plans for a national strike or strike ballot, and that the AEU Executive were engaging in unwarranted witch-hunts. It was a wise expedient. Since they had never promised to hold one, the failure of an unofficial national aircraft strike to materialize could hardly be blamed on union officials' treachery or betrayal. It would have been equally embarrassing to explain that the strike had failed because there had been almost no support for it in the face of official union opposition. A cover-up was the most politic option.

It transpired that the AEU Executive were also anxious to forget about the aborted strike. AEU Party activists were providing so many new recruits, including apprentices, and being so successful in elections to union lay office that it was inexpedient for the AEU Executive to desire their pound of flesh from Zinkin. Consequently they made no attempt to realize any moral capital or extract revenge from the whole episode. The mutual discreet but rigid silence has continued. Peter Zinkin's autobiography omitted any mention of the 1937 events. Noreen Branson also failed to address the strike that never was. Non-Party historians who have examined the interwar rank-and-file movements have failed to detect the incident, and it remains shrouded in the mists of the AEU's still potent culture of union loyalism.

Following Zinkin's climb-down, Pollitt and Campbell recognized that the Communist Party's situation was too serious for the ASSNC to be left to its own devices and Zinkin's independent judgement. They cooperated with Scott and Berridge to impose rigid boundaries for the ASSNC's activity. The ASSNC must not only profess trade union loyalty, but must also be seen to practice it. The magnitude of the changes which the Party Centre had effected were soon clear. Only the shell of a separate rank-and-file organization remained.

The constitutional militants used their consequent internal Party advantage to take control of the Party's conduct of engineering affairs in all sectors of the industry. They enforced on all Party activists the pledge which Joe Scott had given the AEU Executive in March 1937:

> Bro. Scott said that, if and when the time arrived – and, for his part, he was unable to see it – when he found that his Union official interests were in conflict with his activity on behalf of or membership in the Party, he had his liberty to leave the Party. He had the same liberty in an A.E.U. connection. For example, there are many Provisions in our Rules with which he does not agree, and in regard to which he would use all his influence and power to bring about a change. Again, if the National Committee laid down a Policy with which he found it impossible to agree, he would still have his liberty to choose which course he should take.

Executive Councillor Hutchinson summed up ODD Scott's 'understanding of his position . . . he attends to all his official duties, but claims freedom of conscience and the right to take part in any activity which, in his opinion, seems designed to further or promote working class interests in general'.[148]

The National Council of the ASSNC, which Zinkin had fostered so assiduously as an independent fighting leadership, ceased to meet regularly or even frequently. When they did meet, Council delegates no longer took decisions. *New Propellor* continued to be published, and its circulation even increased. But Zinkin's flair for propaganda was now put to the service of trade unionism *per se*. *New Propellor*'s columns no longer reverberated with the persistent refrain of rank-and-filist caveat. The achievements of shopfloor and factory action were imaginatively praised, but always within the confines of union loyalism.

New Propellor comprised the most tangible embodiment of the ASSNC. Unofficial 'coordination' of economic conflict in aircraft undoubtedly continued. But it was now conducted through the Party's engineering networks, not the ASSNC. This arrangement permitted Scott and Berridge to oversee developments and pre-empt any incipient challenges to official union machinery. The contacts which Peter Zinkin had built up during his tenure as aircraft supremo were pressed into the service of the Metal Bureau's grand designs. And now that the ASSNC was firmly subordinated to the Party Centre, the constitutional militants recognized that a token rank-and-file movement had its uses.

In September 1937, *New Propellor* reported on a 'national meeting of representatives from aircraft factories' about 'shadow factories'' threat to aircraft wages and conditions.[149] The rapid expansion of aircraft 'shadow factories' in 1937–38 presented AEU activists with a serious challenge. Rather than try to induce aircraft companies management to transform their batch/craft production techniques in order to increase aircraft production, the Air Ministry commissioned car companies, including Rover, Standard and Austin, to open 'shadow' aircraft factories utilizing their mass production methods.[150] From the perspective of skilled aircraft workers, this development was unacceptable dilution. In addition, most car factories remained poorly organized; the conventions of engineering collective bargaining had yet to penetrate them. The contrast with healthy and growing membership and shop stewards' committees in aircraft factories could not have been greater.

Once the ASSNC had made a token contribution, local activists took over. Party activists, other AEU loyalists and capable AEU ODDs combined their forces to organize the newly recruited, volatile workforce in shadow factories. *New Propellor* closely monitored their successful skirmishes and strikes. At the third AGM of the ASSNC in May 1938, the secretary noted that real progress had been made in organizing the shadow factories. In contrast to previous years he made no attempt to claim the credit for the ASSNC.[151]

We will examine the development of union organization in two Birmingham shadow factories in Chapter 8. By September 1939 activists had made significant inroads on managerial prerogative on this new terrain. It is interesting that the difficult spectre of demarcation disputes and skilled parochialism never appeared to haunt shadow factory shopfloors. Evidently, in a new factory, when the pioneering AEU activists did not raise these difficult problems, their skilled members were content with maintaining craft privilege within the confines of their own shops, and did not view the new semi-skilled production methods as any of their concern.

*   *   *

The Party Centre's handling of the London busmen's strike and the ASSNC's planned strike in May 1937 showed that Pollitt and Campbell had no hesitation in placing union loyalty before rank-and-filism when the two imperatives came into public open conflict. But their choice was highly embarrassing and potentially damaging for King Street's credibility. The Party's approach to the economic struggle was seen to be contradictory and therefore unreliable as a guide to action.

Pollitt and Campbell had been drawn unwillingly into the crises faced by the two rank-and-file movements in 1937. The London Busmen's Rank and File Movement and the ASSNC had both placed rank-and-filism first. Pollitt and Campbell intevened to enforce union loyalty as the first imperative. They acted in a way which appeared identical to 'reformism' and 'Mondism', contrary to bolshevik principles. Their conduct under fire was supported by the majority of Party members at the 14th Party Congress, held immediately after the strikes had collapsed. At that time the defeated and humiliated busmen and the hastily aborted aircraft strike were still painfully present in delegates' hearts and minds. The smoke-screen of Bevin's betrayal and the barefaced denial of the planned ASSNC strike had not yet become received Party mythology.

Pollitt and Campbell moved swiftly to mend the rent in the seamless garment of revolutionary pragmatism by camouflaging the choice of union loyalism which they had just imposed. Their exercise in damage limitation was routine political stuff. Conservative or Labour leaders were accustomed to cover their tracks in the same way when their ideologies broke down while trying to cope with unexpected vicissitudes. By 1938 Pollitt and Campbell had sedated Party activists into forgetting the painful events of May 1937. They behaved as if trade union loyalty and rank-and-filism had never clashed, and presumed that they were the only true champions of the 'rank-and-file' in the 'economic struggle'. The *Daily Worker* persisted in drawing the distinction between the 'reformist' and 'Communist' approaches when it had to report a union executive's compromise and/or retreat.

The *Daily Worker*'s counter-argument to the executive's pragmatic defence was invariably that if greater reliance had been placed on the rank-and-file and more care taken to marshal their forces, then no compromise need have been made. We shall observe in the next chapter that the Party Centre took care to distance the Party from Arthur Horner's strong support for a compromise solution to the Harworth strike in 1937. However, they were simultaneously solicitous in seeing that Horner was not accused of betrayal by other mining Party activists.

Pollitt and Campbell sublimated their own disappointment at the failure of a militant upsurge to appear in May 1937 in the emergency of having to cope with the AEU and TGWU Executives' threat to the Party. They then had to heal the wounds of others inside the Party caused by bruising encounters with Life Itself. They managed to salvage the Party's influence and power inside the official trade union movement. They also established that the imperative of trade union loyalty superseded the imperative of rank-and-filism when they openly clashed. Having piloted the Party successfully through this serious trial, Pollitt and Campbell could now reliably assume that Party members had learned to respond to the 'economic struggle' with the same order of priorities as they themselves. During the testing times, their own reflexes had been imprinted on the Party's collective culture.

Notes

1. Pollit, 1932, 'The Road to Victory', op.cit.: 48.
2. *Busman's Punch*, No. 10, August 1933. Burns moved over from the Labour Research Department during 1932 to work more closely with Pollitt at King Street. (Branson, 1985, *History of the CPGB*, op cit.: n.17, p. 94.) His membership of the clerical section of the TGWU enabled the Rank and File Movement to accept his editorial services with a good conscience.
3. *Busman's Punch*, No. 8, June 1933.
4. Bullock, 1960, *Ernest Bevin*, Vol. I, op. cit.: 522.
5. Ibid., p. 524.
6. Ibid., p. 522.
7. *Busman's Punch*, No. 8, June 1933. In early 1932, Bert Papworth was awarded the TGWU's silver medal for recruiting 170 new members. Clegg, 1950, *Labour Relations in London Transport*, op. cit.: 29. Burns was a member of the clerical section of the TGWU.
8. For the genesis of the CBC out of the busmen's rank-and-filist traditions see pp. 51–2.
9. The election results were reported in *Busman's Punch* No. 12, December 1933. There were eight seats on the CBC, two members elected from each of the three geographic LPTB districts by busmen; two inside staff reps

were elected by shop stewards, Clegg, 1950, op. cit.: 38. The Rank and File never gained adherents among the inside staff.

10. See Bevin's article in *The Record*, September 1933 and the rebuffs in *Busman's Punch*, Nos. 9, 10 and 11, September, October, November 1933.

11. The first Chairman of the LPTB, Lord Ashfield, had been head of the LGOC and an enthusiastic participant in the Mond–Turner talks. Clegg, 1950, op. cit.: 9–13.

12. See *Busman's Punch*, No. 16, February 1934.

13. *Busman's Punch*, No. 18, April 1934. The dispute concerned the transfer of routes from the London bus network to Green Line country services, which militants believed had the ulterior motive of removing them from the more democratic procedures of red London buses.

14. *Busman's Punch*, No. 22, August 1934. Editorial Committee Statement.

15. For the Nunhead strike, see Clegg, 1950, op. cit.: 111–2. Observing the TGWU's policy of denying Rank and File leaders credibility, neither Bullock nor Clegg name the three delegates who flew back; they were probably Papworth, Sharkey and Snelling. *The Daily Worker* made no mention of the fact that the TGWU delegates who had flown back were Rank and File leaders. (*Daily Worker*, 4 July 1935.)

    Rank and File delegates to the 1935 BDC increased their average number of votes compared to 1933 (Barrett, 1974, *Busman's Punch* op. cit.: 105.)

16. Ibid.

17. Bevin's Report to TGWU GEC meeting, 19 August 1935, GEC minutes: 223. Bevin took a very close interest in London bus affairs, presumably because he felt the need to be on his guard. See for example TGWU F&GP minutes, 21 January 1933, loc. cit.: 16–17.

18. Report in *Busman's Punch*, No. 31, May 1935.

19. *Daily Worker*, 25 July 1935.

20. *Busman's Punch*, No. 34, August 1935.

21. Bevin's account of events is contained in his report to the TGWU GEC, GEC Minutes, 19 August 1935: 223. If the CBC had called a fleet-wide unofficial strike to support Slough without GEC sanction, the GEC would doubtless have seized the opportunity for a trial of strength with this troublesome subordinate body. The *Daily Worker* offered only a partial account of the Slough strike (*Daily Worker*, 29 July 1935), and *Busman's Punch* did not report it at all.

22. Bevin's Report to TGWU GEC meeting, 19 August 1935, GEC minutes: 223. There was no report of the Romford dispute in either the *Daily Worker* or *Busman's Punch*.

23. See pp. 76–7.

24. *Busman's Punch*, No. 35, September 1935.

25. *Busman's Punch*, No. 36, October 1935. The 'full and frank discussions' were not, however, reported in any detail by *Busman's Punch*. There were no reports of this conflict in the *Daily Worker* and Branson chose not to disinter its skeleton. It appears that the resignations were tendered at one meeting, but not accepted. The challenge from Papworth and Snelling probably lay on the table awaiting resolution for over a month.

26. Clegg, 1950, op. cit.: 96–7.

27. *Busman's Punch*, October 1935.

28. *Busman's Punch*, June, August, September, October, November 1935. In June 1936 *Busman's Punch* noted that one of the pleasing features at the mass meeting of the Rank and File Movement had been the presence of so many union representatives, including many branch officers from garages not associated with the Rank and File Movement. It had evidently been normal for garage branch officers to attend Rank and File Committee meetings as 'fraternal delegates' without their garage having voted to affiliate to the Movement. The lack of formal affiliation made it much more difficult for the leadership to enforce collective discipline on the Movement.

29. *Busman's Punch,* October 1935.

30. Ibid.

31. Bevin's Report to January 1936 GEC, TGWU GEC minutes, 1936: 82.

32. TGWU GEC minutes, Appendix, Memorandum by the General Secretary re Central Area Busmen, adopted under Council Minute No. 369, 11 May 1936: 131–3. The Memorandum summed up events in the dispute.

33. Ibid.

34. Ibid.

35. Report in *Busman's Punch*, June 1936 and *Daily Worker*, 21 May 1936. Papworth had been elected to the TGWU Executive in 1935.

36. Clegg, 1950, op. cit.: 119–20.

37. *Busman's Punch*, November, 1936. Bill Jones commented that 'They [the busmen] were becoming so confident that they were having strikes for very unreal reasons.' (quoted in Barrett, *Busman's Punch,* op. cit.: 102.) There are reports of strikes in the *Daily Worker*, 8 and 9 October 1936.

38. Bullock records that on the Executive Papworth and Bevin 'watched each other like hawks – a situation which did not prevent each expressing a wry regard for the other's qualities', Bullock, 1960, *Ernest Bevin,* (op. cit.: 607).

39. *Busman's Punch*, January 1937.

40. *Busman's Punch*, February 1937.

41. TGWU GEC minutes 1937, F&GP, minute no. 82, p. 28.

42. *Busman's Punch*, April 1937.

43. TGWU GEC minutes, No. 266, 31 March 1937: 93.

44. *Busman's Punch*, April 1937.

45. *Daily Worker*, 26 and 27 April 1937.

46. *Busman's Punch*, April 1937.

47. Corfield, T., 1964, *The Record*, March: 42. The *Daily Worker* had flatly refused to believe these warnings and published a sanguine prediction that both tram and trolley-bus workers would support the strike on 30 April. For Sheehan's faithful adherence to rank-and-filism, see note 27, Chapter 4. He became a TGWU organizer in 1937.

48. Bullock, 1960, op. cit.: 610.

49. Corfield, 1964, op. cit.: 42.

50. *Daily Worker*, 11 May 1937.

51. TGWU GEC minutes, 11 May 1937, minute no. 333, p. 120.

52. *Daily Worker*, 11 May 1937.

53. The leaflet is reproduced in the Report on Unofficial Movements, GEC Minutes 1937, p. 209. The events surrounding its production are discussed on pp. 203–4. The report elicited the information that Emile Burns had helped to write the leaflet and that he had taken part in regular consultations with Rank and File leaders. The CBC presumably felt unable to produce the leaflet in its own name.

54. TGWU GEC minutes, 11 May 1937, no. 333 p. 120; 23 May 1937, No. 354; p. 128; *Daily Worker*, 13 and 15 May 1937.

55. See TGWU GEC minutes, 11 May 1937, Nos. 332 and 333, p. 120; 23 May 1937, minute no. 354, p. 128; No. 356, p. 129. See also *Daily Worker*, 11, 13, 15, 17, 21, 24 May 1937.

56. *Daily Worker* 17 May 1937. No attendance figures were reported, an indication that the demonstrations had not provided mass support of the bus strike. For the Unity Campaign, see p. 228.

57. TGWU GEC minutes, Nos. 358–60, pp. 130–1; No. 361, p. 132; No. 364, p. 133.

58. *Daily Worker*, 28 May 1937. A pamphlet, 'The London Bus Strike. What Next?', was published by the London District Party making the same points.

59. See *Daily Worker* and *Daily Herald*, 21 June 1937.

60. *Daily Worker*, 21 June 1937.

61. Bullock, 1960, op. cit.: 613.

62. Branson noted that in April 1937 there were 83 active Party members on the London buses, organized in fourteen garage groups (Branson, 1985, op. cit.: 174).

63. Ibid. There were 13 London bus delegates. A motion for the reference back of the Report was defeated by 269 to 63 votes (Clegg, 1950, op. cit.: 127).

64. *Daily Worker*, 7 July 1937. The *Daily Worker* noted the inquiry's statement that 'This unofficial action [of the Rank and File Movement's] must be distinguished from what sometimes occurs, such as sporadic difficulties due to some disturbances which might arise from time to time.'

65. Report on Unofficial Movements, loc. cit.: 207. Bullock, 1960, op. cit.: 613.

66. Clegg, 1950, op. cit. and *Daily Worker*, 6 August 1937.

67. See Clegg, 1950, op. cit. and *Daily Worker*, 30 August; 3 and 18 September; 4 November; 29 December 1937, and 8 January 1938.

68. Barrett, 1974, op. cit.: 134. Barrett does not give his source, but this information probably came from Bill Jones.

69. *Daily Worker*, 14 December 1937.

70. Interviews with Bert Papworth and Ted Bramley by N. Fishman. It is likely that their formal entrance into the Party had been indefinitely deferred from 1935–6 because of the perceived need not to give Bevin evidence of 'Communist infiltration' of the Rank and File Movement.

71. *Daily Worker*, 8 January 1938.

72. *Daily Worker*, 25 February 1938.

73. *Daily Worker*, 26 February 1938.

74. *Daily Worker* 7 March 1938 and Clegg, 1950, op. cit.: 127.

75. Clegg, 1950, op. cit.: 129. Corfield states that the NPWU had between 4000 and 5000 members and was influential at those garages where breakaway Rank and File leaders had been TGWU officials. (*The Record*, June 1964: 45–6.)

76. Barrett, 1974, op. cit.: 137 and 144–5.

77. Zinkin, 1985, *A Man to be Carefully Watched*, op. cit.: 99–109. Zinkin states that he had previously been London Industrial Organizer. His efforts to form rank-and-file movements evidently qualified him for this appointment in a Party district where the Young Turks were still influential. In

February 1933, the Information Bureau had taken over the NMM office, typewriter, files, and its network of contacts. Pollitt and Campbell had probably agreed to its formation in order to preserve some kind of continuity with the NMM's supporters and activities. Winnifred Renshaw recalled that George Renshaw, who was a keen Young Turk, had also worked for the Information Bureau. Zinkin continued to serve on the London Party secretariat after moving to the Information Bureau.

His belief in the critical importance of bringing revolutionary politics to the shopfloor had been evidently instilled by his observations and experiences of the beginning of the first Five Year Plan during ten months spent working on a lowly rung of the Comintern between September 1931 and July 1932 (ibid.: 87–90).

78. Ibid.: 116.
79. Ibid.: 118.
80. For the pre-strike grievances at Gloster's see reports from the ODD, E. Porter in the *AEU Journal*, July and August 1934. The new Hawker's management were evidently keen to weaken the union's power. Gloster's had been an AEU stronghold since the 1920s (see Claydon, 'Development of Trade Unionism', 1981 op. cit.: 171).
81. For West London aircraft strikes in 1918, see Hinton, J., 1969, *Rank and File Militancy in the British Engineering Industry*, University of London, PhD: 390–4. There were various rank-and-file committees of aircraft and engineering workers in West London during the 1914–18 war (ibid.: 385 and Claydon, 1981, op. cit.: 142 and 154–5).
82. Zinkin, 1985, op. cit.: 117.
83. For the strike see *Daily Worker*, 9, 11, 14, 15, 16, 18, 19, 21, 25, 26 March 1935 and Claydon, op. cit.: 186. The *Daily Worker* observed that the TGWU had gained 150 members at Hawker's Kingston and 160 members at Gloster's. (*Daily Worker*, 27 March 1935).
84. The London District Committee of the AEU had been negotiating with the AEU Executive for nearly a year for permission to organize a multi-union London aircraft committee. An additional bureaucratic complication was the District Committee's intention to include all the aircraft sites around London, which meant drawing in the outlying AEU District Committees surrounding London. See *Engineers Bulletin* No. 5, n.d., c.a. February 1935; and Jack Tanner's ODD Reports, *AEU Journal*, February and April 1935; *Daily Worker*, 11, 25 March 1935.
85. *Daily Worker*, 16 March 1935.
86. *Daily Worker*, 18, 25 March 1935.
87. *Daily Worker*, 29 April 1935.
88. *Daily Worker*, 20 August 1935.
89. Ibid. The report noted that over 8000 copies of 'Aircraft', the pamphlet describing the April conference (no doubt written by Zinkin), had been sold. The 2d per hour wage increase had first been proposed by the London divisional committee and approved by the AEU National Committee in June 1934 for inclusion in the union's claim.
90. Zinkin, 1985, op. cit.: 120. Zinkin identifies the second national conference on 28 April as being the date of its foundation. This is self-serving hindsight. The *Daily Worker*'s report made no mention of the ASSNC, and nothing more was heard of an aircraft rank-and-file movement until its report of 20 August. Zinkin obliquely acknowledges this hiatus when

he states that '[Joe Scott made] an attempt to kill the ASSNC before it had time to get firmly established' (ibid.: 132–3).

91.   Ibid.
92.   For the *Labour Monthly* conference and Scott's and Berridge's response, see pp. 76–8.
93.   *AEU Journal*, April and May 1935.
94.   TGWU Finance and General Purposes Committee minutes, 11 April 1935: 96.
95.   *AEU Journal*, August 1935. Opposition to the Executive was confined to a resolution from the London District Committee. The *Daily Worker* made a very restrained comment on the circular during the National Committee meeting (3 June 1935). In July the Final Appeals Court, usually no friend to the Executive, had supported the circular by handing down a decision in the Executive's favour in connection with an unofficial dispute.
96.   *Daily Worker*, 14 April 1934. See also *Engineers' Bulletin*, No. 2, October 1934. The *Bulletin* noted that four new stewards had been elected at Handley Page.
97.   Zinkin, 1985: 121.
98.   Ibid.: 138. Boyle worked in the Rosyth Naval Dockyard as an apprentice before the 1914–18 war. E. and R. Frow, 1982, *Engineering Struggles*, op. cit. He was elected on to the London District Committee of the SMW in 1935. The second ASSNC chairman was Tom Schofield, a sheet metal worker at de Havillands, Hatfield. Originally from Rochdale, he had served on the London District Committee since 1931. The SMW had a strong left-wing political culture accompanying their craft rank-and-filism in London. (Interviews with Benny Rothman, Bill Warman, Johnny Mansfield and Bert Pankhurst by N. Fishman.)
      I have used the generic term 'Sheet Metal Workers Union' to refer to the two main unions which organized sheet metal workers. At the beginning of 1921 the Amalgamated Society of Sheet Metal Workers had joined with a number of local societies and unions of sheet metal workers, tinplate and brassworkers to form the National Union of Sheet Metal Workers, (Claydon, 1981, op. cit.: 483.) The National Union had a working agreement with the Birmingham and Midlands Sheet Metal Workers Society (ibid, p. 487).
99.   Information on Kingston from John Foster, AEU National Organizer, in interview with N. Fishman, additional information from Benny Rothman.
100. Zinkin, 1985, op. cit.: 124.
101. *New Propellor*, Vol. II No. 3. The shopping list had hardly changed since Party engineers formulated a minimum programme in the aftermath of the 1922 Lock-Out and the reductions in piecework and overtime rates imposed by the employers in 1931. *New Propellor* listed: '1) An immediate wage advance of 2d/hour on the basic rate, the consolidation of the war bonus into the basic rate, and the establishment of a minimum rate of wages for adult workers of 1/4s. 1/2d/hour. 2) Where a system of payment by results prevails, the workers shall be able to earn at least $33\frac{1}{3}$% above the basic rate of wages and the abolition of all 'debt systems'. 3) No change in workshop customs and practices shall be made until negotiations have been completed with the Shop Committee, subject to the approval of those concerned. In all factories, records of piecework shall be

available for inspection by the Shop Stewards and Works Committee. 4) 40 Hour Week, with no reduction in pay. 5) A minimum outworking allowance of 7s.6d./day. 6) The restoration of the cuts in overtime and piecework rates of pay made in 1931. 7) Payment for all statutory holidays. 8) Every aircraft worker a trade unionist.'

102. Fearon, P., 1974, 'The British Airframe Industry and the State, 1918–35', *Economic History Review*, Series 2, Vol. 27: 243–8. Claydon, 1981, op. cit.: 177.

103. Zinkin, 1985, op. cit.: 139.

104. Fearon, 1974, points out that airframe companies relied on batch production methods which in turn relied on skilled craftsmen (op. cit.: 240).

105. *New Propellor*, Vol. I No. 6. n.d., c.a. February–March 1936.

106. See Robertson, A.J., 1975, 'The British Airframe Industry and the State in the Interwar Period: A Comment', *Economic History Review*, Series 2, No. 28: 649–52 and Fearon, P., 1975 'A Reply', ibid.: 660–1.

107. Claydon, 1981, op. cit.: 167.

108. *New Propellor*, Vol. II No. 5, February 1937.

109. *New Propellor*, Vol. I No. 6, n.d., *ca* January–February 1936. By 1937 *New Propellor* was selling 15,000 copies. (NP Vol. II No. 7 April–May 1937).

110. See AEU Executive Council minutes, 1 August 1935: 127–8; 22 October 1935: 94; and 4 February 1936: 191–4. The threat of the ASSNC was often subsidiary in the Council's collective mind to the problem of 'interloping' unions. For constitutional militants' pursuit of a separate aircraft agreement through AEU official machinery, see resolutions on an aircraft agreement in *AEU National Committee Reports*, 1935, 1936 and 1937.

111. *Daily Worker*, 21, 28, 29 February and 2, 3, 5, 6 March 1936 and *New Propellor*, Vol. I No. 7, n.d. *ca* March 1936.

112. *Daily Worker*, 6, 7, 9, 10 March 1936 and *New Propellor*, Vol. I No. 7. A speaker at Hayes, probably Zinkin, had offered 'full support' from the ASSNC.

113. *Daily Worker*, 9 March 1936.

114. *New Propellor*, Vol. I No. 7.

115. Ibid. The strikes coincided with the Government's announcement of the rearmament programme and their intention of seeking discussions with trade unions to ensure its speedy fulfilment. Pollitt and Campbell were keen for the Party to lead a working-class reaction to these plans and Party AEU activists in London were active in organizing a trade union response. See p. 91.

116. *New Propellor*, Vol. I No. 9, June 1936. The Handley Page strike lasted five days and occurred because youths had replaced adults working a machine. Forty-six delegates and visitors attended the meeting.

117. *AEU Journal*, April 1936.

118. AEU Executive Council minutes, 11 June 1936: 259–60.

119. See *Daily Worker*, 12 May 1936, and *New Propellor* Vol. I No. 9, June 1936.

120. *New Propellor*, Vol. I No. 10, July 1936.

121. *Daily Worker*, 27 August 1936.

122. Copy in Marx Library, n.d., p. 3. The *Daily Worker* said on 3 September that 14,000 copies had been sold and 12,000 more would be arriving for sale shortly.

123. Ibid.: 11.

124. AEU Executive Council minutes, 1 September 1936: 281–5.

125. *The Times*, 3 September 1936 (my emphasis). The AEU rules covering strike action unauthorized by the Executive were very concise and any infringement would have provided clear grounds for expulsion (*AEU Rulebook*, 1945 ed. Rule 21, para. 1, lines 10–15).

126. *Daily Worker*, 10 September 1936. The report stated that the ballot had been counted by union district committeemen, shop stewards and London factory workers.

127. *New Propellor*, Vol. II Nos 1 and 2, October and November 1936 and *Daily Worker*, 10 September 1936.

128. *New Propellor*, Vol. II No. 5, February 1937. The meeting was attended by delegates from 18 sites. This was only three fewer sites than had been represented at the October 1936 meeting and showed that there was still interest in hearing about an aircraft agreement and what stewards in other places were doing.

129. See *New Propellor*, Vol. II Nos 2, 5 and 6, November 1936 and February, March 1937.

130. AEU Executive Council minutes, 26 January 1937: 152–3.

131. AEU Executive Council minutes, 26 January 1937: 153.

132. AEU Executive Council minutes, 22 February 1937: 403.

133. *Daily Worker*, 23 February 1937. For similar problems which the National Metal Bureau was encountering at this time with its National Wages Movement *inside* the AEU, see pp. 91–2.

134. *Daily Worker*, 2 March 1937. Delegates from 20 sites attended the meeting.

135. See pp. 94–8. From the ASSNC's inception, Zinkin had issued press releases after meetings in an effort to obtain the widest possible publicity. The *Daily Herald* and the *Daily Telegraph* used them in regular news stories about the ASSNC.

136. For example, in March 1937 *New Propellor* reported that eight aircraft workers had received the AEU's Gold Medal for recruiting, and then claimed their achievement for the ASSNC. 'That we [ASSNC] are not a recognised part of the trade union machinery is simply due to the fact that there are forty seven trade unions in the engineering industry today . . . There is strong rivalry between the officials of these trade unions, and the only way in which we can ensure continuous joint working between the members of all trade unions, is by medium of the ASSNC.' (*NP*, Vol. II No. 6).

137. See pp. 96–8.

138. *Daily Worker*, 13 April 1937 and *New Propellor*, Vol. II No. 7, April–May 1937.

139. *New Propellor*, Vol. II No. 7, April–May 1937. Unusually, *New Propellor* gave no attendance figures for this meeting, which probably indicates that there had been comparatively few delegates.

140. Manchester Metal Bureau minutes, loc. cit., 25 April 1937.

141. Ibid., 1 May 1937.

142. *New Propellor*, Vol. II No. 7 Special Issue, May 1937. The Special Issue was rushed out after the May meeting and was numbered 7, like its predecessor April–May. May Day fell on Saturday in 1937, facilitating an afternoon strike at Handley Page. It is highly unlikely that there was a day's

stoppage. Workers who attended the May Day march had simply chosen not to work overtime on Saturday afternoon.

143. A story on 3 May referred to the mass meetings being held in aircraft factories 'at which the proposal of the ASSNC for a national strike ballot on the wages issue has been endorsed'.

144. *New Propellor*, Special Issue, Vol. II No. 7. It was reported that 250,000 copies of a leaflet with the ASSNC case were being printed and that there would also be a public statement. I have seen no copies of a leaflet or evidence of a press statement.

145. AEU Executive Council minutes, 19 May 1937: 275–6. The Stockport District Secretary had received a report on the ballot from an AEU member employed at Fairey's. Both Stockport and Portsmouth District Secretaries had already written to their aircraft shop stewards explaining that the ballot was unconstitutional, and the Stockport District Secretary sought the Executive Council's approval for his action. Fred Smith's Press Statement was reported in the *Daily Telegraph* and the *Daily Herald* on 20 May.

146. See *New Propellor*, Vol. II No. 8, July 1937 and *Daily Worker*, 25 and 26 May 1937.

147. *Daily Worker*, 1 June 1937.

148. AEU Executive Council minutes, 2 March 1937: 327–8, see also pp. 334–5.

149. *New Propellor*, Vol. II No. 10, September 1937.

150. See Robertson and Fearon, op. cit.

151. *New Propellor*, Vol. III No. 5, May 1938.

CHAPTER SEVEN

The Battle of Harworth

The third major industrial conflict to reach its climax in May 1937 was the strike by members of the Nottinghamshire Miners' Association (NMA) at the Harworth colliery. From the outset, it was clear that the strike would settle the question of the survival of the 'breakaway' union, the Nottinghamshire Miners' Industrial Union (NMIU), which had been established in 1926 in the aftermath of the General Strike. The Miners Federation of Great Britain (MFGB) President Joseph Jones and Secretary Ebby Edwards convinced their Executive to stake both money and reputation on the Nottinghamshire Miners Association (NMA) men winning at Harworth. It was the MFGB's involvement which invested the dispute with more than parochial significance. The Nottinghamshire Coalowners' Association stiffened the opposition of the Harworth owners, Barber-Walker. As the strike settled into a bitter siege, it aroused painful memories and deep forebodings inside the National Government and Labour Opposition.

The NMA's principal strategist on the ground was Mick Kane, a Communist mining activist based in South Yorkshire. He became President of the Harworth Branch of the NMA in June 1936 and led the men out on strike in December. The pit was located

> in the extreme north of Nottinghamshire quite near the Yorkshire border ... It was thirty-five miles from Nottingham (where the Nottinghamshire Miners' headquarters were situated), eight miles from Doncaster, and a similar distance from Worksop. It was a new community of miners isolated and remote; numbers of men had migrated from the Durham coal-field, and with their families had settled in this new village of Bircotes to work at the Harworth pit ... The description of 'Durham in Notts' could rightly be ascribed to Harworth pit and Bircotes village.[1]

In an endeavour to break the stalemate, an MFGB delegate conference voted in January 1937 to hold a national strike ballot over Harworth. Sceptical delegates were swayed by Arthur Horner's speech proposing the ballot in which he declared that the MFGB had to prepare for war against Spencer, the NMIU's general secretary.[2] Despite an overwhelming national vote in favour of strike action to support the Harworth men, the complicated dispute dragged on. The settlement eventually achieved was a tribute not only to Joseph Jones' negotiating acumen but also to Horner's inspiration in guiding Party mining activists through the difficult manœuvre of leading a full retreat while the mining community's fighting spirit and will to win a 'just' settlement remained strong.

The terms accepted by the MFGB officers on behalf of the Harworth men were far less favourable than those which Ernest Bevin negotiated for the London busmen. Their strike had left the busmen in a substantially weaker position, but the London Transport Passenger Board (LPTB) guaranteed that there would be no victimization for busmen who returned to work immediately; they also received the full offer of improved terms and conditions made by the Board nearly three weeks previously. At Harworth, Barber-Walker would yield no further than giving an undertaking to consider employing the strikers again when the occasion arose. They made no agreement to alter the arbitrary and anti-union management practices which had precipitated the strike. Nevertheless, the Party Centre described the Harworth strike as a victory for the miners while arguing that the TGWU Executive had betrayed the busmen.

It was because the strike achieved the end of the NMIU that both Joseph Jones and Harry Pollitt hailed it as a great victory. Harworth miners were martyred, albeit willingly, in the service of the trade union cause. This profoundly negative outcome cannot have been surprising to either the MFGB national officers or the Party Centre. But despite their perception of the likely end, they both showed no hesitation in inciting the Harworth mining community to stand fast in the heat of battle and exhorted miners in the other coalfields to stand up and do their duty for the sake of their fighting comrades.

The willing sacrifice and steady courage under fire of the Harworth miners and their families were remarkable by any standards. Their example inspired full-time and lay officials who were quiescent and sceptical in other coalfields to campaign for a 'yes' vote in the national strike ballot. They also induced George Spencer to abandon the union in which he had invested so much time and personal credibility. This chapter will examine the genesis of the Harworth strike and analyse the way in which MFGB officers and Party mining activists conducted this epic battle.

The origins of the battle

The continued existence of NMIU posed a serious threat to the MFGB's ability to engage in collective bargaining. During the 1935–6 coalmining national wages dispute George Spencer had promised that his members would continue to produce coal.[3] The size and productivity of the Nottinghamshire coalfield made this pledge a serious factor in the calculation of both sides in the dispute. A major outcome had been the concession by the Coalowners' Association of a national framework for discussing wages. Under substantial pressure, the Coalowners' Association had accepted that mining trade union officials had adapted themselves to the changed 'Mondist' terrain for collective bargaining.

The Notts. coalowners refused to participate in the national consultative machinery established after the dispute because they continued to deny recognition to the MFGB's affiliate in Notts., the NMA. They viewed the 'Spencer' union as their bulwark against a return to the offensive militancy of coalmining unions. The national consultative machinery was likely to remain a dead letter for the MFGB unless it could bring the Nottinghamshire coal-owners into the scheme. Without them, the Coalowners' Association would have no incentive to move towards meaningful national negotiations on wages.

The 'Spencer' union provided the key to unlocking the MFGB's dilemma. If the Notts. owners could be forced to abandon the NMIU and recognize the NMA, their participation in the national consultative machinery would be assured. During the national wages dispute MFGB officers and leading Party activists had expended copious amounts of time and energy in the Notts. coalfield to encourage miners to revolt against the NMIU and rejoin the NMA. 'A number of rallies were held (at which such speakers as Bill Betty of South Wales, Herbert Smith of Yorkshire and Joseph Jones . . . appeared); the Red Flag was sung and broadsheets issued by the thousands.'[4]

Pollitt and Campbell enthusiastically followed suit. They sent the veteran Scots miner George Allison to Nottinghamshire with the 'radio van'. He toured for weeks, holding impromptu meetings and 'generally rousing the miners and their wives to a pitch of enthusiasm.'[5] Two series of meetings were conducted in parallel, one organized by the NMA and one organized by the CPGB.

The *Daily Worker* reported from Mansfield, 'At towns and villages throughout the Notts coalfield audiences gathered by hundreds in some places and by tens in others . . .' Speakers at the Party meetings included Lewis Jones and Dai Lloyd Davies who described how the 'breakaway' union had been defeated in South Wales.

> The most prominent amongst the speakers at all meetings were the members of the audience. This is a county where even talk, wherever two or three are gathered together, is as dangerous as the companies and the strongest company union West of the Rhine can make it.[6]

On 1 December 1935 Party activists organized a Unity Conference in Nottingham with 100 delegates from Labour Parties, trade unions and co-ops. They demanded a campaign against Spencerism by the Nottingham Trades Council and others. Pollitt spoke and pointed the Unity Campaign, one of the first fruits of the 7th World Congress line, towards addressing this difficult problem: 'I am convinced that Maxton,

Lansbury, Pollitt and Gallacher can initiate a campaign which would be the death-knell of "Spencerism" in the Notts coalfield.'[7]

The *de facto* joint efforts of the MFGB and King Street at least effected a greatly improved morale amongst the small knot of NMA loyalists in the coalfield. Val Coleman, the Secretary of the NMA, told the *Daily Worker* that the present campaign

> has produced a friendly confidence amongst the men that has not been seen since 1926 ... you get men now standing up in a meeting and saying: 'I have been in the Spencer Union because I could not help myself. I am not going to stay in it any longer, and if anyone wants to go and tell that to the boss, he can go ahead and tell it.[8]

However, the actual increase in NMA membership was small. The numbers gained in no way justified the amount of time, energy and emotional capital which had been expended. At the end of the national wages dispute, the nagging problem of the Spencer Union remained and was evidently no further towards being resolved. Ebby Edwards observed candidly but somewhat ruefully at the MFGB delegate conference which ended the dispute: 'Nottinghamshire cannot be won unless the people themselves are prepared to fight. Let us be frank because some of us have been there weeks and know the difficulty.'[9]

The MFGB leadership were in no mood to underestimate the magnitude of the problem which the 'Spencer' union posed. A number of breakaway unions had been formed in the coalfields towards the end of the 1926 Lock-Out reflecting the disgruntled reaction from many of the 'rank-and-file' at activists' implacable refusal to seek a compromise settlement and expeditious retreat. Most of the coalfield unions had been able to retake the membership lost to these 'scab' unions, in Durham with the connivance of the local coalowners.[10] The NMIU and its sister union the South Wales Miners' Industrial Union (SWMIU) had both survived with continuing support from their respective Coalowners' Associations. Neither the NMA nor the Fed had recovered their lost membership through moral appeals to the men's trade union principles in well-intentioned but ineffectual membership drives. The SWMIU had only appeared vulnerable after Arthur Horner had the audacity and strategic skill to lead successive frontal assaults against it.

The NMIU had an advantage which its South Walian counterpart did not share. Its General Secretary, George Spencer, Labour MP, had been the long-serving General Secretary of the NMA during the General Strike. He answered appeals from members returning to work to follow them out of the MFGB and negotiate a local settlement on their behalf. Many Notts. miners were convinced that they had remained loyal to their union because Spencer had gone with them. They had simply transferred their union allegiance away from the MFGB intact and in good faith through the medium of Spencer's person.

Before the General Strike, the Notts. owners had offered a district set-tlement substantially above the MFGB's demand for a national wage deal. Notts. miners came out in answer to their union officials' appeal for solidarity; they stood to gain nothing from the General Strike. The Notts. owners stood by their offer throughout the Lock-Out. Not surprisingly, Notts miners were among the earliest returners and they went back to work in the greatest numbers.[11]

When in the summer of 1926 Spencer answered the returning miners' request to represent them he took much of the vital fabric of the official union with him. Notts. miners joining the NMIU could feel justified in asserting that they had never left their own union.[12] The Notts. coalown-ers encouraged the new union, and determined to rid themselves of the strikemongering, troublesome MFGB. Every colliery company united in withdrawing recognition from the NMA and refusing its lay officials employment until they broke with the union. 'Most of the active branch leaders were now out of work and were likely to remain so . . .'[13]

There was widespread resentment against the coalowners' victimiza-tions. Spencer's secession along with the first 'strikebreakers' was hardly greeted with universal approval in the coalfield. During 1927, the NMA's membership actually increased from 7000 up to about 13,500 compared with the Spencer union's 4–5000.[14] Griffin observes:

> It is perfectly understandable that men who had been members of the NMA since boyhood should wish to rejoin it once they were set-tled in to work once more. On the other hand, even those who stayed out of the NMA would resent pressure being brought to bear on them to join the Industrial Union, and the bulk of them resisted this pressure for a long time.[15]

However, the owners' continuing refusal to negotiate with the NMA meant that miners who remained NMA loyalists had nothing tangible to gain. They were also risking the sack if they were identified by manage-ment as NMA. In these circumstances, membership of the 'old union' fell into permanent decline until the national wages dispute in 1935.

> Much the strongest [NMA] branch was Kirkby, many of whose members were Welshmen . . . Apart from Kirkby, the strongest branches were in the old mining districts . . . At the other end of the scale, many of the new mining villages had only a handful of adher-ents . . . Gedling where the butties were very powerful also had a very weak branch (35 members) whilst the Huthwaite and Welbeck branches had no members at all although there were 50 members working at New Hucknall colliery.[16]

Spencer evidently enjoyed exploiting the advantage which the coal-owners' favour gave him in waging the 'economic struggle'. He regularly conjured up the spectre of the bolshevik NMA to drive a much harder bargain with the Notts. owners than they had intended to concede.[17] There was, however, no collective bargaining taking place between the owners and the NMIU at pit level. Waller observes that the NMIU was 'top-heavy' in its structure, and that Spencer was reluctant to allow branches to hold meetings. Instead of negotiations, the local everyday problems were addressed by a deputation from the NMIU waiting on management to present their grievance for redress.[18] This device was redolent of a return to an earlier culture in which the union was the supplicant seeking justice rather than an equal in the bargaining process.

Before 1914–18, Independent Labour Party (ILP)/syndicalist influence had been centred around Mansfield, in North Notts., near to the more volatile South Yorkshire coalfield. Marxism arrived in Mansfield via a spoiled priest Jack Lavin. He went from Ireland to San Francisco where he had been active in both the Marxist Socialist Labour Party and the Syndicalist Industrial Workers of the World. He went to Yorkshire in 1914, and then found work in the Notts. Welbeck Colliery in 1915–16. He organized the SLP and addressed meetings in Mansfield marketplace and surrounding towns.

During the 1914–18 war, it was Derbyshire miners, the Hicken brothers, Phil and Henry, who were the best known Marxists and syndicalists in the East Midlands coalfields. Phil Hicken became a foundation Party member and was active throughout the 1930s. Henry became secretary of the Derbyshire Miners' Association in 1928, while remaining sympathetic to left-wing politics. Lavin's SLP branch joined the CPGB on its formation.[19] Otherwise the Communist Party in the Notts. coalfield had a meagre inheritance.

The hothouse atmosphere of the early 1920s produced a late flowering of militancy in the Notts. coalfield from these inauspicious beginnings. Political conflicts inside the NMA suddenly took root and became deadly serious. A serious trial of strength took place on the Mansfield Area Committee. ILP activists, notably Herbert Booth, lined up with Party mining activists in the 'left-wing' camp against the 'right-wing' and quickly drove them to the point where they began to contemplate secession. In 1924 Arthur Cook campaigned strongly in Notts. for the general secretaryship of the MFGB and helped to enflame the local conflict.[20]

The small number of Party mining activists threw themselves into the task of defeating the 'Spencer' union. Their commitment and perseverance were matched by their left-wing colleagues, the ILP and Labour activists who remained loyal NMA officials, Frank Varley, Val Coleman, Bernard Taylor, Charlie Brown, Herbert Booth and Jesse Farmilo. Shared adversity brought the men in this rump even closer. They were a small band resisting a detested common enemy in the face of great hardship. In stark contrast to other coalfields, there was no division between Party and other leftwing activists during the Third Period. In 1928, the NMA nominated Horner for MFGB Vice-President.[21]

After a while, the band of NMA loyalists developed a siege mentality which reflected the situation in which they found themselves. Bernard Taylor recalled that they had identified their own fight against Spencer with the Spanish Republicans' war against Franco and other European workers' resistance to Fascism.[22] It was hardly surprising that the remaining NMA officials and their loyal members continued to be receptive to initiatives coming from their Party comrades in arms. In 1936 the NMA joined the Fed in supporting Communist affiliation to the Labour Party.[23]

In the period immediately following Spencer's breakaway, Herbert Booth had advocated 'fusion' between the NMIU and the NMA as a pragmatic way out of their dilemma. He had attracted 'a certain amount of enmity' from NMA loyalists on a speaking tour of the county and also been rebuffed by Spencer. Frank Varley was the only other NMA official advocating the need to compromise with Spencer. After his premature death in 1932 the self-righteous badge of suffering isolation proudly worn became the NMA officials' identifying feature.[24] 'No surrender' was another strong bond holding NMA loyalists together, even though as a strategy it held out no prospect of regaining Notts. for the MFGB. Herbert Booth continued to support 'fusion', but he did so at great personal cost. He became NMA President and served throughout the Battle of Harworth. Nevertheless, many of his colleagues believed that he had been a Spencer spy in the NMA camp throughout their long years in the wilderness.[25]

The NMA could not have survived on its depleted membership base after 1927. The MFGB had provided financial support for the contracted complement of full-time officials who maintained a skeleton organization for the NMA loyalists and also tried to do some recruiting. However, the MFGB officers had not addressed the 'Spencer' problem seriously for some years. Their forays into the Notts. coalfield during the national wages dispute provided the opportunity for fresh assessments. When they returned to this difficult terrain, the MFGB officers recognized that 'fusion' with the Spencer union remained the only feasible option. The unpalatable facts remained: the NMIU's substantial membership in pockets of the coalfield, the owners' apparently unshakeable support for Spencer and Spencer's stubborn commitment to running a 'proper union'.

The problem for the MFGB officers was that the NMA Council remained adamantly opposed to 'fusion'. Jones and Edwards felt morally obliged to respect the opposition of this democratically elected body.

Their opportunity to intervene more effectively occurred in February 1935. The national wages dispute was beginning to gather momentum, and activists in other coalfields were enjoying a resurgence of optimism and energy from the patient confidence-building campaign of MFGB officials. The NMA loyalists felt excluded and isolated. The NMA Council 'had complained [to Jones and Edwards] that since 1926 the Federation had not given them the help to which they were entitled'. The MFGB officers responded by requesting the NMA Council to give them 'plenary powers to obtain recognition . . . It was made perfectly clear that would include power to discuss fusion with Spencer.' The Council had agreed, 'and we have travelled on those lines ever since . . .'[26]

The NMA Council had little option but to accept the MFGB officers' view of the situation. They had approached Jones and Edwards with the complaint that the *status quo* was unacceptable, but had no practical alternative to suggest to their *de facto* strategy of wearing Spencer down through attrition. Most delegates had agreed to grant MFGB officers plenary powers in the confidence that Spencer and his subalterns would never agree to merge with them. They had accepted 'fusion' as a hypothetical possibility which would never actually occur as the price to be paid to get the money from Jones and Edwards for a fresh campaign against the NMIU.

Fusion was feasible for the first time because Arthur Horner had evolved a practical strategy for weakening 'scab' unions. The series of engagements against the SWMIU which Horner led had allowed the Fed to regain the initiative. The Fed membership's self-confidence had grown accordingly, enabling their leadership to deploy greater strength in subsequent battles. The strikes had forced South Wales owners and William Gregory, the SWMIU General Secretary on to the defensive for the first time since the General Strike. The Fed had regained the advantage and Horner was using it to undertake fresh initiatives and manoeuvre to good effect.

But fighting total war for an issue of principle was a high-risk undertaking. The mining communities in the South Wales coalfield had been willing to stand up and be counted for the Fed, a position from which they stood to gain little materially in the short run. The atmosphere in which such sacrifices were made had not materialized out of thin air. As experienced union officials, Jones and Edwards recognized the magnitude of the Fed's achievement. As Griffin observed, the 'average Notts. miner' had shown no willingness 'to run the risk of martyrdom'.[27]

Nevertheless, it was evident that attrition and moral superiority had failed. If the stakes in total war were high, great gains were also possible. If the NMA could mount an all-out battle, they could disorientate and demoralize the coal-owners and Spencer sufficiently to flush them out from their entrenched positions. Nerve and considerable audacity were required from the men who led the conflict. Careful strategic skills were also needed to recognize the point when the moment for retreat had arrived and then to supervise a united and orderly falling back. An important feature of the South Wales strikes had been Fed officers' meticulous attention to maintaining morale during retreat. Even though they had returned to work without having achieved their most substantial demands, Horner ensured that the strikers' displays of heroism were accepted as fitting sacrifices to gain the Fed's 'victories'.

Ebby Edwards told the MFGB annual conference in 1936 that the Notts. miners had to be prepared to fight.[28] He knew perfectly well that the will to go over the top and risk everything for the union did not materialize spontaneously in miners' breasts. His unspoken wish was for someone to appear in Notts. who could emulate Horner's achievement in mobilizing and motivating miners. In fact, Party mining activists had already begun preparing for the fight ahead. However, they were not the Party miners in the band of NMA loyalists. They remained stuck in the rut of their siege mentality, unable to contemplate any fresh approaches to the problem of Spencer. And when the breakthrough finally came, it was not Notts. miners who made it. They too remained entrenched in their passive acceptance of a divided coalfield. It was emigrants who provided both the leadership and the foot soldiers for a fresh assault on the NMIU.

Party activists apply their minds to the 'Spencer' problem

During their visits to the Notts. coalfield in the national wages dispute, Pollitt, Allison, Horner and others would have used the occasion to visit Sheffield and meet mining activists there with whom they had worked closely since the early 1920s. The question of whether Horner's successes in South Wales could be repeated in Notts. would have been exhaustively examined. Jock Kane, the current Sheffield Party Secretary, would have taken part in these discussions. His brother Mick had been in London for some time but is likely to have returned to help with the Party's mining campaign.

The Kane brothers had been leading Party mining activists since their arrival in the East Midlands coalfields in 1928.[29] Jock Kane recalled: '. . . we all worked at Harworth for a few months before the second shaft [was sunk]'.[30]

Mining activists were still able to function energetically because economic conditions favoured militancy in the East Midlands. There were no well-established patterns of collective bargaining here and Class

Against Class reinforced the strong rank-and-filism which the Kanes had acquired in Scotland. In the East Midlands, the pattern of ownership and the social geography enabled miners to escape victimization by moving from one district, even county, to another with comparative ease. Following the Comintern's agitprop instructions enthusiastically, East Midlands Party mining activists also published rank-and-file pit papers wherever they were working and agitating.

A letter in the *Harworth Spark* in July 1931 described the situation there:

> What I would like to know is how can we get things altered at this pit because it seems to be overrun by lambs, men running after chargehands jobs, they attend the Colliery classes and whist drives ... thinking they will touch lucky, you made reference in your paper to the Durham men, I think if we had some of the real Durham men down here things would get a move on. Northumbrian Miner[31]

After being laid off at Harworth, the Kanes had found work first at Shireoaks colliery near Worksop, Notts. They moved on to the Ireland colliery, a Derbyshire pit owned by the Staveley Coal and Iron Company. Employment involved entitlement to a company house, and Bridget and the family moved to the pit village of Staveley. Jock remembered that he and Mick were regarded as agitators by the local miners. 'Boys would hardly be seen talking to you on the street corner. That's the sort of town Staveley is.' The Kanes had raised issues at the branch over wages and tonnage rates, but to little avail. Their keen militancy was not emulated by the Derbyshire miners who were accustomed to the autocratic conduct of their management.

When Mick and Jock were sacked from Ireland in early 1933, the family was turned out of their company house. But they did not leave without a fight. The Staunton and Staveley company lawyer declared at a meeting that they could stay in the house if Mick stopped his agitating. Instead, the whole family marched to the local workhouse behind an NUWM banner.[32] Phil Hicken took up their case and was arrested while speaking in Staveley. He refused to be bound over and the legal expenses for his appeal were defrayed by the Derbyshire Miners' Association. He was defended by Sir Stafford Cripps.[33]

Having been roused by the company's vindictiveness and the Kanes' fighting spirit, some local citizens stood up to be counted. A widow who was a Salvation Army member immediately took Jock and his younger brother Pat into her council house, saying that Staveley couldn't touch her. A newsagent/grocer who was 'very well respected' then offered a three-storey house with room for everyone. He was active in the Liberal Party and had organized accommodation for the Hunger Marches on their way to London. The family was reunited here and eventually moved into three council houses in the village.

This time Mick and Jock didn't attempt to find a start at neighbouring pits. Mick continued with NUWM work, and probably stepped into Phil Hicken's place as the only speaker, at Sunday evening open air meetings in Chesterfield. The rest of the family would walk there to keep him company and were often his only audience. He soon found his way to London where he remained very active in the NUWM, becoming friendly with Wally Hannington.[34]

Jock attended the Lenin School in 1933–34, using his mother's maiden name, 'Higgins'. On his return, he found work at Bolsover with another Party member. The pit was owned by the Bolsover Colliery Company, but its management were as accustomed as Staveley's to getting their own way. If the coalface wasn't cut and ready, the manager expected men to come up to the pit top and wait around idle and unpaid until the coal was ready to cut. When they found their stall unprepared, Jock and his mate refused to come up. They also came out at the time when their shift should have ended. The undermanager sacked them, saying that he didn't mind them coming up at the proper time, 'but not when you bring the others with you'.[35]

After this encounter Jock somehow got a start at another Staveley's colliery, Markham. During the general election campaign in November 1935 he was unable to resist heckling the manager of the Staveley Coal and Iron company at a meeting. In retaliation, the manager vowed that no Kane would ever work for Staveley's again. Evidently concluding that he was unlikely to find other work, Jock commuted to Sheffield where he became Secretary of the District Communist Party. Chesterfield and Staveley were part of the Sheffield Party district, as was Doncaster and the South Yorkshire coalfield. It is likely that he concentrated his attention on mining activity since the national wage dispute was in full flow at this time.[36]

The discussions in Sheffield during the national wage dispute inevitably would have come round to examining the merits of Harworth as a possible site for battle against Spencer. The Kanes knew the pit and were familiar with its mainly emigrant workforce. Its pit village Bircotes was occupied by 'Geordie' miners and their families whose closest ties were to the strong culture of their native Durham Miners' Association. In addition, many miners commuted to Harworth from Yorkshire by bus. Back home, they were outside NMIU territory and amongst YMA members. Although the NMIU had a lodge at Harworth, the Party caucus decided that it could be dislodged.

The evidence certainly showed Harworth's potential for the NMA. During the national wage dispute the MFGB's campaign in Nottinghamshire reinforced by committed branch officials, produced an increase in membership from 10 to 100 in June 1935 and 40 men joined in July. However, due to Barber-Walker's policy of sacking miners whom they suspected were promoting the NMA, the new membership fell away. Herbert Booth told a public meeting in January 1936 that Barber-Walker had sacked successive branch officials holding office for the Harworth NMA.[37] The Durham men would join the NMA because it was a 'real' union like the DMA in their native coalfield. They resented Barber-Walker management's authoritarian attitudes. Regularly contentious issues such as 'dirt money' were settled according to strict conventions mutually enforced by the coalowners and the DMA in Durham. While at Harworth, Griffin observed that deductions for dirt at Harworth were 'unprecedently heavy'.[38]

Having agreed that Harworth was a favourable site for battle, the Party caucus would have considered the general staff for directing the fight. The difficult strikes in South Wales underlined the importance of leadership. It was clearly desirable to have seasoned veterans underground. Mick Kane was eminently qualified. He knew the pit; he had been out of local circulation for some years and hopefully out of mind for colliery managers; his notoriety as an agitator had been acquired at Derbyshire pits which were actually a long way from the Notts. collieries in *social* geography. It is likely that Mick Kane had already come to Sheffield to help with the CPGB's campaign for the MFGB national wage dispute and would have been party to the discussions.

In the event Mick Kane returned from London and found work at Harworth, probably in late 1935 or early 1936, living in Yorkshire and commuting to the colliery.[39] He re-established contact with men with whom he had worked before and began to recruit some into the Party. The small knot of NMA activists/Party members concentrated on gathering men about them whom they could trust. In contrast to his conduct in the early 1930s Kane did not agitate or wage 'economic struggle' openly. He emulated the South Walians in planning and laying down careful foundations for a battle of attrition. He nurtured the men's many grievances and then repeated the lesson with which they were already familiar: they could only stand up to this authoritarian management if they were solid inside a 'real' union and willing to fight.

The growing number of NMA members committed to a fight went about their chosen business with all the care of an undercover resistance operation.

> The atmosphere was quite unlike that of the old, settled mining communities of the Leen Valley . . . The radicals believed that their every action was reported upon to company officials, and this belief encouraged them to conduct their affairs in conspiratorial secrecy.[40]

Mick Kane's prudent determination got results. His band of NMA activists/Party members eventually transformed the atmosphere underground. Membership of the NMA increased, and this time the members remained. The secrecy observed in the fledgling branch was effective in preventing victimizations. Barber-Walker's apparently did not suspect that something was afoot. Kane was elected President of the Harworth NMA in June 1936. He had a running mate, Dave Buckley, who was elected Secretary. Their victory against an established incumbent who had done nothing to forfeit members' trust signalled that something unusual was in the air.[41] The previous President had been an outstanding union loyalist. Kane stood against him and explained that loyalty was not enough. Miners who voted for him knew that they were casting their lot in with a man who would lead them in revolt against the unwarranted infringements of their liberty as union miners.

Miners who had stayed outside the NMA understood the significance of Kane's victory well enough. His presidency had a stiffening effect on the men who had hung back. Recruiting for active service became much easier. More men decided they were fed up with their treatment by a management who were accustomed to exercising their prerogative unencumbered. At NMA branch meetings, Kane would have used the South Wales strikes to show that you could only beat the 'non-pols' and management by fighting. He preached the need for battle. By August 1936 the Harworth Branch of the NMA had 640 members. Joseph Jones recalled: 'It was at that stage that the revolt against the conditions that had prevailed in 1926 took shape at Harworth.'[42]

In early September, the *Daily Worker* reported the first skirmish. Kane tried to avoid a confrontation because his forces were slender and untried. But when the men responded to provocation in hot blood, he deemed it inexpedient to be seen to be damping down the more audacious members' resolution to resist managerial rule. The reporter explained:

> For several months now the men have been building up a branch of the [Notts. Miners] Association, in the face of great opposition, the manager succeeding in driving away the militant elements time and again. However, lately they have been successful and in the last fortnight there has been a real influx into the real union.[43]

The incident began when the chargehand ordered the evening meal at 4.20 instead of the customary 6.0 p.m. Men underground had agreed because the conveyor was broken, but those working on the surface refused. The management immediately sacked the six men who had started the walkout. A meeting was hastily convened and it was decided to call the nightshift out on strike. A mass meeting in Bircotes the following morning decided to organize mass picketing, the first time that mass picketing had been seen in Harworth 'for years'. Management played for time by agreeing to receive a deputation from the men on the following day and there was a return to work. When the men descended, however, management refused to meet the deputation and imposed a lock-out. Every miner had to sign on afresh for his job. Barber-Walker's refused to take back the six 'militants' who had first walked out and also sacked the members of the deputation who included most of the NMA branch officers, a total of 43 miners.[44]

The NMA had lost ground in the face of the swift management counter-attack. Kane had no alternative but to fight back from this weakened position. If the sackings had been passively accepted, the Harworth NMA's credibility would have evaporated. A mass meeting agreed to hold a strike ballot unless the men were reinstated. Meanwhile, 148 more miners joined the NMA. Feeling was running high and righteous indignation prevailed over fear. Management's intimidation succeeded initially in raising the temperature. It was clear their victimization had backfired when an NMIU meeting at the pit agreed to sponsor a deputation for the sacked men.[45] The 'non-pol' meeting would have had a complement of dual NMA/NMIU members to argue the sacked men's case. Horner's encouragement of dual membership in preparation for the battles against the SMIU at Emlyn and Taff-Merthyr was known to Kane and probably emulated by him.

The ballot revealed a large majority for strike action, 785–136. Membership of the NMA continued to increase; during the strike incident it had moved up from 300 to 700. But Kane had no money to support his members in a strike. He had approached the NMA Council for official support in taking on Barber-Walker. The Council had approached their paymasters, the MFGB. The wheels of union official business did not grind to the spontaneous rhythm of the men on the ground and there had been no decision taken. Kane and his fellow branch officers had little alternative but to counsel patience to their members. The 43 victimized men were supported by voluntary contributions from the Harworth miners still at work and MFGB subsidy.[46]

When the moment passed without battle being joined, management put strong pressure on men to enforce NMIU membership. They were 'zealously attempting . . . to find out who among these employees were walking past the Industrial Union Box at the Pit Head.' Men succumbed and stopped paying their NMA subscriptions to protect their jobs. However, Kane and his depleted forces did not give up and the MFGB responded to their evident will to fight. They found 'a spare bit of ground' and 'for the first time since 1926 the men walked without fear up to their own Union Box to pay into their own Union'.[47]

On 24 September, the MFGB Executive, on which Arthur Horner served as Fed President, discussed and accepted Jones and Edwards' report of their meeting with the NMA Council. The report recommended that the MFGB commit its resources to taking on Spencer and Barber-Walker under strict conditions. The NMA Council had to give the MFGB 'plenary powers'. There also had to be a ballot at Harworth about which union the men wanted to represent them. If the MFGB Executive were satisfied with the result, and if the dispute was still outstanding, they would sanction the tendering of strike notices and accept financial responsibility for supporting the strikers.[48]

The provision for a ballot on representation showed that much had been learned from South Wales. In January 1935, after a protracted, hard-fought but inconclusive strike, the SWMIU had organized a ballot at Taff-Merthyr colliery under the supervision of a firm of Cardiff solicitors. The result was a 5 to 1 majority in favour of the SWMIU and proved a serious embarrassment for the Fed.[49] Jones and Edwards wanted to be certain of their ground before committing the full weight and authority of the MFGB to the fight at Harworth.

The pace of events at Harworth quickened. The spirit of resistance had taken root and miners suddenly felt entitled to regard management's normal behaviour as unacceptable. Management also started proceedings to evict the sacked men from their company houses in Bircotes village, thus galvanizing the whole mining community behind the NMA men.[50] The Harworth men experienced a fresh rush of hot blood to the head after witnessing these fresh casualties.

Mick Kane acted to secure his supply lines. He arranged coalfield collections for the sacked men, and arranged for Joseph Jones to attend an emergency meeting of the Harworth NMA on 11 October. Jones was able to see the mood of the men for himself, and concluded reasonably enough that the MFGB either had to reinforce their will to fight now or lose the opportunity to attack Spencer. The time for prudence and proceeding by the official book had passed. On 22 October he obtained plenary powers for himself and Edwards from the MFGB Executive 'to obtain suitable facilities at Harworth to organise the resistance of the men'.[51]

Arrangements for the ballot over union representation were swiftly finalized. Kane probably felt that he needed to take advantage of the high tide of anger and determination among his forces. It was held on 4 November and a neutral member of the Notts. county bench supervised it. Its result was more decisive than the Fed had achieved in the two similar ballots in South Wales, 1175 for the NMA and only 145 for the Spencer Union.[52]

The ballot enabled the miners to express their feelings collectively and publicly in the ritual act of voting against Spencer. Its overwhelming result fuelled their expectations and there was a general feeling for striking straightaway. Kane and Joseph Jones kept them at work even though the atmosphere underground must have been very highly charged. Kane and Jones knew that the final outcome of the strike would not depend solely on the men's determination. The MFGB had to be able to marshal 'public opinion' and pressurize the political establishment as well as fighting the battle on the ground. This meant that the MFGB forces had to be seen to be following procedure, observing the rules and behaving honourably.

Jones met the Harworth men on the 8 November and they 'strongly expressed' their view that they wanted to tender strike notices immediately. He persuaded them to leave the matter in the MFGB's hands 'so that every possible opportunity could be given the Company of settling the issue by peaceful means'.[53] But the meeting decided that branch officers should begin collecting signed strike notices immediately from miners in preparation for the final battle.[54]

The Harworth men remained at work for nine more days. Barber-Walker were evidently unwilling to make the first move. But the men knew that all-out battle was imminent and insisted on challenging the established conventions in the pit. On 5 November a 4 to 1 majority was registered in a vote of No Confidence in the colliery checkweighman. When management refused to allow deputy checkweighmen freshly elected by the men to undertake his duties, a walk-out followed on Monday night, 15 November. On 17 November 2800 men walked out when management again refused to accept a deputy checkweighman in the checkweighman's box. The size of the strike showed that the spirit of revolt had spread even further underground than anyone had expected. Though Jones tried to induce the men to return to work, he had no intention of shirking the confrontation. On 19 November he obtained the MFGB Executive's authorization for the Harworth men to hand in their strike notices on the 23 November. The Executive decided to ask districts for a 3d. levy per member to support the Harworth men.[55]

The *casus belli*, the tinder which ignited the explosive mixture, was 'dirt money'. The checkweighman's job was guaranteed by law so that he could be an impartial umpire. Barber-Walker's refusal to accept the deputy checkweighman in the box was management's formal declaration of war. They could not allow the men to dictate matters which had always been part of management's absolute prerogative in this pit. For miners accustomed to Durham where the checkweighman would usually have been a DMA lodge official, the situation was intolerable. They suspected him of selling them short when he should have been taking their part in doing his duty of monitoring and challenging management's assessment of the amounts of good coal and dross in their tubs.

On 20 November a meeting attended by 1300 Harworth miners and their wives listened to Jones, Edwards and MFGB Vice-President Will Lawther arguing for a return to work to enable strike notices to be handed in and run their course. Mick Kane's speech was an impassioned plea to observe this rule of the game. The current strike was unofficial and 'unconstitutional'. Moreover, he knew very well that while there was an advanced guard of men eager to fight, the rest of his forces were far from prepared. The branch's decision to collect strike notices on 8 November had yielded little fruit. Not many miners had taken the irretrievable step of handing them in.

Walking out of work in hot blood was one thing, signing a strike notice in cold blood which committed a miner and his family to a strike for as long as necessary without any means of support except the union was a very different matter. Mick Kane preached loyalty to the MFGB injunction to return to work whatever men's 'private opinions' might be. His heart was with the men who wanted to stay out but his brain was dictating the moves. ' "For God's sake stand by the Association. There are men in this hall who have not yet signed their strike notices. Will they sign them now?" The notices came in first as a few, then as a flood.' After what was described as a long and heated discussion, the return to work was agreed. The numbers of notices in the branch's keeping went up to 900.[56]

Mick Kane had been taking his own steps to galvanize the miners. A Harworth miner who lived in Maltby, Yorkshire had taken Kane to court for intimidation. He said that Kane got on the bus with him on 19 November and said, ' "If you don't stop we shall – we'll come over to Maltby to your homes with the lads and we shall stop the bus." Kane added that he was not going to allow outsiders coming to Harworth scabbing.' Two miners and other passengers had given evidence. The miner and five others on the bus had stayed away from work on the 20th. The case was committed for trial at the Retford Quarter Sessions.[57]

When the men tried to return to work on 21 November, Barber-Walker's would only allow members of the Spencer Union to restart. They recognized it was foolhardy to cede the advantage underground to the NMA. Eight hundred men turned back at the gate and remained loyal to the NMA.[58] Jones 'authorized' the men still at work to hand in one-week's strike notices on Monday 7th. On 11 December he issued a statement which signalled the MFGB's intention to enter into total war:

> mineworkers throughout the country are asked not to accept employment at the Harworth Colliery as it is now stipulated by the management that an undertaking must be signed for deductions from wages as contribution to the Spencer organisation. This action of the colliery management not only resulted in the full support of the Federation [MFGB] being given to the Harworth men, but may

subsequently involve an extension of the dispute to the coalfields of Notts and Derby, and, should that not prove effective, it is possible that a conference of all the coalfields may be convened to discuss what further action may be taken.[59]

The strike notices expired on 14 December. The *Daily Worker*'s page one headline was 'Miners Patrol Streets':

> 700 miners formed into marching order this afternoon and in spite of drenching rain patrolled the streets of Harworth ... On the instructions of a superintendent, police tried to disperse the gathering and drive the workers off the streets. Witnessing this, a number of miners, who had continued working at the pit came forward and handed in notices to join the strikers.[60]

The immediate conflict centred around Barber-Walker's ability to keep the pit working. The chairman of Barber-Walker's was also chairman of Notts. County Council and chairman of the Standing Joint Committee which controlled the police in the county. Not surprisingly the forces of law and order were not spared in assisting the company's bid to get men through the colliery gates. On New Year's Eve the *Daily Worker* noted that police had been billeted in company houses in between strikers so as to be able to watch their every move.[61]

Bernard Taylor was sent to Harworth in early December by the NMA Council to represent them. He recalled: 'Many police were drafted into the village ... they were everywhere. It was advisable not to go alone [around the village] in case something happened; the evidence of more than one was important.'[62]

In the first week of the New Year management were still unable to resume normal working.[63] Though exchanges between strikers and the convoy of working miners became ritual, they remained deadly serious.

> every evening, at the time the night shift began, those still at work would assemble at a given spot ... a distance of at least half a mile from the pit-yard entrance. From this point, with police in front, at the rear and on either side, they marched to the pit-yard ... [They marched down] a long promenade which ran past the colliery entrance. On this stretch of road every night in the darkness, in all kinds of weather, hundreds of men and women congregated to watch this nightly march ...
>
> It was called the chain gang. Many of the strikers were apprehended by the police, rushed to the police station and charged ... Many of the arrests and summonses were not justified, for apart from vocal disapproval, there was no evidence of physical interference at this nightly happening.[64]

With so many men still cleaving to the NMA, there was no prospect of the strike collapsing. On Spencer's advice, the company tried to assuage 'public opinion' roused by the company's infringement of the men's free-born English liberties. Barber-Walker stated that while they only recognized the NMIU, they would employ men from either union. On 6 January 1937 the BBC broadcast the company's pledge to employ men of either union who came to work at Harworth.[65] The gambit failed.

Few strikebreakers answered the call and the strike held. Jock Kane recalled that it had been 'a terrific strike, solid as a bloody rock the lads were'.[66]

Jock was in a good position to remember. He had stepped in to help take his brother's place when on 12 January he was sentenced to two months hard labour for his 'intimidation' of the Maltby miner.[67] The *Daily Worker* reported that Jock Kane spoke to a packed meeting at Harworth arranged by the Communist Party to protest at the sentence.[68]

The NMA branch and its supporting leaders, Taylor for the NMA and Jock Kane for the CPGB, made its dispositions for a long fight.

> Every night of the week during the dispute, except Friday, there were meetings and social gatherings. They had, of course, to terminate in time to watch the chain gang being escorted to the pit . . . Every imaginable subject was discussed: Trade Unionism, Parliament and National Politics . . . and sometimes we had a 'question and answer' evening. The men and women from the north would sing the folk songs of their native county. They would talk of the struggles of their native Durham and Northumberland, and the part their forbears played in the building of the miners' organization. A lot of history they had listened to and learnt in their homes during childhood, and they felt and were convinced that they were carrying on the tradition of their fathers to try to establish the right to band together in the Union of their choice.[69]

The strikers formed a Bircotes Athletic Club and two of their number, a boxer and a gym instructor, provided organized tuition.[70] On Saturday evenings the branch committee organized a dance and social in the Market Hall. Having ministered to their worldly needs, the meetings on Sundays in the local cinema were conceived and used by the Communist Party and the branch committee as chapel services, to inspire and prepare the assembled men and their families for the trials of the coming week. Willie Gallacher spoke at one of the Party's Sunday morning meetings and Jock Kane would have continued to deputize for Mick. Sunday evening meetings were official NMA occasions. The NMA officers were regular speakers. Edward Dunn, the YMA sponsored MP for the Rother Valley, Ebby Edwards and Arthur Horner also played their part in ministering to the strikers. On Sunday 24 January Edwards paid tribute to the women: 'If the homes were safeguarded and the children fed, then the women would continue to be the most loyal fighters.'[71]

The fight on the ground settled into trench warfare. There was some respite for the NMA when a judge granted an extension of two months on the eviction summonses, stating that 'Blood cannot be got from a stone.'[72] Nevertheless, Barber-Walker's superior resources made them the more likely victors in a battle of attrition. The MFGB needed a national movement to maintain the momentum of their attack. South Wales provided the initiative. Arthur Horner's proposal for a national coalfield conference on Harworth was unanimously accepted by the MFGB Executive.

The delegate conference convened on 20 January and Horner moved the Executive resolution asking for the power to hold a strike ballot on the question of enforcing the principle of freedom of organization and trade union recognition in the Notts. coalfield.[73] On his return from the conference, Bernard Taylor told the Harworth miners how well Horner had done for them,[74] using all his missionary zeal to dispel delegates' doubts and scepticism. Like spectators everywhere, they saw the formidable obstacles more clearly than the desired aim of 'destroy[ing] Spencerism once and for all'[75] As in 1910, the other coalfields drew inspiration from the Fed's example of a mining union which had been fighting and winning battles.

Having been stiffened by Horner and listened to the descriptions of the 'chain gang' and the Notts. police from the NMA delegates, the conference endorsed the Executive resolution.[76] The MFGB officers had demonstrated their ability to win a national strike in the 1935 wages dispute. The Harworth ballot was more problematic because it involved an issue of principle and promised no immediate personal gain. 'Public opinion' was uncertain of the outcome. In the week following the conference a special MFGB message deployed the uncompromising rhetoric expected of a side prepared for conflict:

> The issue is one of fascism versus democracy in trade union affairs. Unless wiser counsels prevail than those now observed by the Notts. owners, the country may once again be plunged into the horrors of a coal war ... A general stoppage would not leave the Notts pits unaffected. There are means at our disposal of preventing Notts owners from putting coal on the market.[77]

The MFGB decision was swiftly augmented by a statement from the TUC General Council declaring that it would keep in close touch with events at Harworth and pledging its full support for any national action which the MFGB decided to take.[78] The full pressure of the trade union movement was now being applied to George Spencer, and it was sufficient to induce him to re-assess his position. He was nearing the end of his career and the Harworth strike had shown that he had failed even in the Notts. coalfield to supplant the MFGB with 'non-political' trade unionism. He suggested terms for fusion between the NMIU and the NMA to the MFGB through the good offices of the Department of Mines. While he intended to extract the maximum benefit for himself and his followers from a deal with the MFGB, he had no scruples about abandoning the Notts. coalowners. His bedrock allegiance had remained to the principle of working class self-organization, vindicating the judgement of the pro-fusion NMA loyalists.

Jones and Edwards began meetings with Spencer in mid-February at the Department of Mines. The Secretary for Mines showed himself keen to obtain the best possible terms for the MFGB.[79] He needed all his per-suasive powers. Spencer might be reluctant to become a pariah among his own people, but he remained determined to put the NMA in the weaker position in a fused union and preserve his own honour unblighted from 1926. His demand that the fused union guarantee all NMIU officials' jobs would make it financially difficult and politically impossible to maintain the NMA officials in post. He also demanded that there be elections for officials in the foreseeable future.

In the circumstances, the MFGB officers concluded, apparently with Horner's strong support, that they had to settle on these terms. Spencer's class loyalty could not be relied on if the Harworth strike ended before negotiations with him had concluded. They were well aware that the Harworth strikers' capacity for resistance was limited. They were also sceptical about their own ability to return a convincing majority in a national strike ballot. With Horner's help they prepared the ground for the Executive and a recalled delegate conference to be able to accept fusion on Spencer's terms as an honourable compromise and a victory for the trade union movement.

When the terms for fusion became public knowledge in early March, the Party Centre hesitated, and then publicly rejected them on 17 March. However, the Centre carefully refrained from attacking the MFGB offi-cers and Executive during their continuing negotiations with Spencer.[80] Pollitt and Campbell were caught in the horns of a dilemma of their own making. The Harworth strike was being fought for trade union loyalism on rank-and-filist principles led by branch officers who were Party activists. It had the support of the MFGB Executive and TUC General Council. According to the Party catechism, such a united front should have produced a national miners' strike and total victory. But the MFGB leadership, including Horner, were now arguing for compromise and retreat.

Before the MFGB officers could close the deal Barber-Walker publicly declared their refusal to take back any Harworth striker. This 'no surren-der' stand was strongly supported by the other Notts. owners who had reacted to the Harworth strike in the opposite way to George Spencer. Their conviction was reinforced that the NMA and MFGB were only interested in promoting insubordination, abetting bolshevik agitators, and condoning violence and civil unrest. The General Manager of the New Hucknall Colieries Ltd., Captain P. Muschamp, 'one of the most influential' of the Notts. owners,[81] used the occasion of the Nottinghamshire County Coalowners Association Annual Dinner on 19 March to speak about Harworth. He spoke to an audience of colliery owners, operators and the Deputy Chief Inspector for Mines who expected the usual after dinner anodyne oration. They heard a call to arms.

> This district – the Notts area – can take credit to itself for having smashed the national strike, and since then we have carried on very peaceably with the Industrial Union for ten years . . . This Industrial Union . . . has been the buffer which has prevented national strikes in this country.
> [The MFGB] have gone round the corner, and with the assistance of the Mines Department, I am sorry to say, are now trying to get in at the back door.
> We know – those of us who are in a position to know – how these strikes are initiated. They are initiated definitely by Communists. The working men of England do not want to strike. Generally speaking, they only want to be left alone. I say definitely that if the Government does not deal with the question of the Communists in a more definite way, there will be no peace in this country.
> We want to adopt the German idea. If the Government is to check future trouble, it must put its foot down and put it down strongly.[82]

At this point Jones and Edwards turned to the Secretary of Mines and the national Coalowners' Association for help. The Coalowners' Association were determined to bring the Notts. coal-owners back into the national fold to participate in the national consultative committee, and the Secretary of Mines agreed. Both had a vested interest in seeing the Notts. coal-owners taken down a peg or two by the MFGB and applied pressure on them to make concessions accordingly.[83]

Muschamp's speech transformed a problematic industrial dispute into an issue of political principle. The Westminster establishment concerned with the strike widened from the Department of Mines and mining MPs to include both front benches. Muschamp had tabled the desirability of Fascism as a means of dealing with the Communist menace in earnest. Serious democrats and defenders of English liberty could hardly forbear to take the offensive against him. They found themselves in good company alongside Arthur Horner and Harry Pollitt.

On 24 March the MFGB Executive met to consider the fusion terms. Horner was still supporting the fusion in the hope that Westminster and the national coalowners would push the Nottinghamshire owners into line on the Harworth strikers. The *Daily Worker* quoted him extensively without comment.

> ...there are several conditions [of the fusion deal] which are
> unpalatable, and which, in other circumstances, would be held to be
> unacceptable. My view of the present situation is that every effort
> must be made to establish trade unionism in the Notts coalfield
> within a reasonable period of time. The continuance of the past ten
> years in Notts cannot be thought of. But this situation cannot be
> regarded as settled unless and until the Harworth dispute is satisfac-
> torily terminated. Subject to a way being found to save the
> Harworth men from unemployment and victimisation, I am for a
> merger which . . . is necessary for the restoration of unity. . . [84]

Horner had correctly anticipated the Executive's mood; they were hardly
conciliatory. No one could consider compromise with Spencer until
Barber-Walker agreed to take back the Harworth strikers. The Executive
eventually accepted a proposal from Yorkshire, Lancashire and
Northumberland to convene a special delegate conference to consider the
terms of settlement. South Wales was conspicuous by its absence from
this manœuvre to escalate the situation. Horner may have considered the
situation far too serious to commit his union to making militant threats
which they might not be able to deliver. He may also have engaged in a
Machiavellian counter-manœuvre to push the other coalfield unions into
taking a stand.

Pollitt and Campbell were unequivocal in rejecting the fusion terms
with Spencer and urging an all-out national battle. The delegate conference met on 1 April, the same day that the TGWU Executive authorized
the handing in of the London busmen's official strike notices. The *Daily
Worker* stated:

> Acceptance of such slave conditions is unthinkable . . . Delegates at
> today's Conference should do more than reject the present terms.
> They should with the minimum of delay, put into practice their pre-
> vious decision to bring national aid to the men of Harworth in the
> fight to free the Notts coalfield . . . let the ballot for national action
> proceed in order that the full weight of the half a million members of
> the MFGB can be used to win victory for Harworth, unconditional
> reinstatement of all strikers, and re-establishment of a united union
> in Notts on the basis of full democracy. [85]

The Harworth terms of settlement comprised the overt conference
agenda. MFGB officers' hidden agenda was to orchestrate an impressive
display of miners' militancy and anger which they could deploy to good
effect in fresh negotiations. Delegates' outbursts of ritual indignation and
threats about ballots were the maximum credible riposte which they
anticipated making to Barber-Walker and Muschamp. Joseph Jones
reported that the MFGB had got everything possible from Spencer
'unless it be that any subsequent action we may take may change the attitude of Spencer and the owners'. [86]

The earlier delegate conference had been marked by self-doubt and hesitation. Nine weeks' later conference delegates found ample fire in their bellies. The Harworth strikers' stubborn resistance had caught their imagination and earned their admiration. Delegates reached down to find the rich vein of offensive militancy in the coalfield unions' culture and the conference erupted with an exhibition of working class pride equal to Spencer's. Delegates declared their commitment to fight, giving no quarter to the unrighteous.[87] The usually moderate Samuel Sales from Derbyshire chided Horner for concluding a compromise settlement with the SWMIU after a protracted strike at Bedwas.

> I remember what Comrade Horner had to say [at the January Special MFGB Conference]. He said we are not bluffing [about striking at Harworth]. We are in earnest in this struggle. I took up last week's *Forward*, and when I saw the terms made in South Wales, I came to the conclusion that the whole Conference was bluffed at the last Conference which was held and the biggest bluffer of all was Horner himself.[88]

Horner forebore to reply that the Fed's experiences of fighting 'scab' unions had shown that there was no cause for sanguine expectation that spontaneous militancy would vanquish the wicked. Nevertheless, the MFGB Executive responded to the mood of their delegates by taking a calculated risk. On 2 April Will Lawther introduced a fresh proposal that the strike ballot be held 'with the object of securing recognition of the MFGB and adequate assurances to prevent victimisation at Harworth Colliery'.[89] They were deploying their ultimate deterrent. If it failed to have an effect, there was nothing left.

The veteran Lancashire leftwinger, Joseph McGurk, seconded Lawther in a rare but exemplary exhibition of pre-1914 mining trade union élan. It is interesting that neither Jones, Edwards nor Horner spoke for the motion. They may have been concerned to minimize their association with this maximalist position so as not to prejudice their credibility in further negotiations. They may also have considered it expedient to remain publicly silent about the national strike ballot in order to leave themselves free to organize a retreat in the event of the ballot backfiring. McGurk reminded delegates that the government had recently launched an extended rearmament programme. If ever there were a favourable time in the history of the MFGB 'to choose the battle ground, that time is now. I am one of those who believe that the Government dare not and would not permit the mine workers of this country of Britain to lay down their tools'.

If the MFGB voted for a national strike, the Government would bring pressure to bear on the coal-owners, giving the MFGB the upper hand against Spencer. 'In other words, or in football phraseology, pass the ball back to Spencer . . . Speaking parochially, we should fight against any victimization in Lancashire. I do not think that any body of self-respecting men could accept these conditions.'[90]

Delegates voted by 503 to 32 to hold the strike ballot,[91] and then dispersed to their coalfields to do their duty. They understood well enough what was required in order to deliver the result. H. McKay of Northumberland expressed their expectations:

> If the leaders of the Miners at any time are prepared to go so far as to recommend their members to a given course, my experience has always been, that regardless of the difficulties, after you have given the men a lead as leaders, you have found the men enthusiastically behind you. That is my experience of the rank and file. They will almost follow you to the death. In the meantime you might in the ultimo have a similar result to 1926, and there may be breakaways, but if the National Committee give a lead you will always get about 90% every time in a ballot vote.[92]

The MFGB officers addressed 'A Message to the Miners of Britain':

> . . . certain principles are at stake of outstanding importance to every mineworker in the country. The first is the simple, but vital issue – shall mineworkers who desire to join and be represented by their own Federation be free to do so? The second – shall men be victimised because they have fought for their rights as Trade Unionists? If a definite answer in the affirmative cannot be given to the first question and an equally emphatic 'no' to the second, then we are no longer free citizens, and Trade Unionism has lost its meaning . . .
>
> . . . the heroic men of Harworth pit, who, for five months, have fought the battle of free Trade Unionism, are in grave danger of victimisation.
>
> By this ballot vote you are asked to record, not merely your detestation of the violation of the principles of free citizenship and free Trade Unionism, but your determination to fight for those principles if necessary and your Federation unhesitatingly recommends you to do this by recording an emphatic 'YES' to the question asked you. Armed with your authority in this way, the Federation will then make further efforts to achieve a peaceful and honourable solution of the dispute, but every man must clearly understand that if, after being armed with this authority, the Federation is still met with a stubborn and vindictive attitude on the part of the employers, then it may be necessary to close the ranks and fight bitterly and stubbornly for those rights which are of the very essence of our liberties.[93]

The ballot was held on 15–16 April. A turnout of 98.9 per cent of MFGB members voted by an overwhelming majority to hand in strike notices. The vote for strike action was relatively uniform throughout the coalfields, with Scotland having the largest minority voting against strike action.[94] However, as Joseph Jones had anticipated, the result failed to move either George Spencer or Barber-Walker. Neither were impressed by the mere threat of national strike action when they knew how swiftly the situation at Harworth was deteriorating for the MFGB.

The Harworth strikers had been out for nearly half a year. Well-organized and comparatively plentiful assistance had staved off physical hardship. But the strikers had endured the monotony of idleness, the stress of continual struggle and the worry of what the future would bring.[95] It was a tribute to Durham grit that they had remained solid for so long. When their morale cracked, Spencer would have a good prospect of regaining the advantage in Nottinghamshire. The Nottinghamshire owners felt they had nothing to lose by calling the MFGB bluff. In a national strike, Nottinghamshire coal would command premium prices.

Harworth at bay

In fact, the crisis at Harworth materialized quickly. The *Daily Worker* reported that on Friday night, 23 April, a 'busload of scabs from Dinnington Yorkshire' had behaved very provocatively at the pit gates. The small number of pickets at the pit gates had responded by throwing stones, and every window in the bus was smashed. The police called on 'blacklegs' in the welfare club for reinforcements. 'A pitched battle ensued, and the police and blacklegs retreated.'[96]

Such skirmishing had become quite routine.[97] The police may have escalated the conflict in order to avenge their defeat by a small force of pickets. They may also have been encouraged by their superiors to mete out more swingeing punishment because of the recent national ballot result. For whatever reason they called in reinforcements from Derby on Saturday morning. They then took the unusual step of delivering the usual summonses at the weekly dance and social in the Market Hall taking place on Saturday night. They threw down the gauntlet in an overt invitation for a fight. Once Mick Kane, who had been released from gaol since March, and four others were taken,[98]

> the whole thing flared up, and a running battle began . . . cars [were] overturned . . . The Market Hall even on the Sunday . . . looked more like a slaughterhouse than a dance hall. Men were bruised, cut and bandaged . . .
> Harworth was now national news. The radio and press gave prominence to it, and in all the coal-fields it became a talking point.[99]

About 30 men and women were arrested on this occasion and 16 were subsequently charged with riot. Though the violence in the Market Hall was newsworthy, it was the national ballot result which underpinned the interest shown in Harworth by the media. The national limelight made repeated punitive arrests by the police seem inevitable as long as the strikers were still putting up a game fight against the 'scabs'. Barring the unlikely occurrence of a spontaneous revolt by Notts. miners[100] the collapse of the strike could only be a matter of time. There were simply not enough people to replace the shock troops who would be incarcerated.

The MFGB officers clearly did not consider a national strike to be a feasible option. Nevertheless, the MFGB Executive could not be seen to draw back from their declared intention to take national strike action. On 30 April, the eve of the official London bus strike, the recalled delegate conference was told that talks were proceeding at the Ministry of Mines but that their details could not be revealed. It was unanimously agreed to hand in a fortnight's notice of strike action on 7 May to expire on 22 May.[101]

As the last few days ticked away, delegates who had forced the MFGB officers' hand over the national strike ballot were compelled to recognize that a national strike would be highly problematic, possibly fatal, for the MFGB's credibility. A national strike in all coalfields but Nottinghamshire would hardly put more direct pressure on Spencer and the Notts coalowners. The indirect pressure being applied on Spencer and the Notts. owners by the National Coalowners' Association and the Government would actually cease once national industrial action had begun. Moreover, both these institutions would in turn feel obliged to apply strong pressure on the MFGB to return to work. The only other potential gain to be made from a national strike would come from the miners' ability to inflict powerful damage on the general public and thereby precipitate a national political conflict. This was unlikely to occur in early summer when coal stocks were at their height and the Notts. owners were keen to supply coal to the domestic markets normally served by other coalfields.

The first days of May 1937 were a heady time for the Party Centre. It had high expectations of a militant national upsurge of the whole working class.[102] However, after Mick Kane's arrest at the Market Hall on 25 April, the Party Centre refrained from pressing its case for the strike ballot victory to be implemented in a national battle over Harworth. The *Daily Worker* argued for united action in rhetorical terms adopting the measured tone it had used during the 1935 national wages dispute when Joseph Jones was negotiating a compromise settlement.[103]

Pollitt and Campbell continued to offer solid support for Harworth and even kept up the appearance of expecting a national miners strike. They sent the loudspeaker van with George Allison back to Nottinghamshire to agitate in pit villages in favour of a national strike. It was said to have met with an excellent response, with questions being mainly about strike pay.[104] They had no intention, however, of organizing a serious revolt against the MFGB officers' strategem of holding out until the eleventh hour to obtain the best possible compromise.

There were improved terms of settlement, but they appeared by a circuitous and unexpected route. On 5 May 1937, two days before strike notices were due to be handed in, apparently without pre-meditation, Stanley Baldwin chose to accept the Leader of the Opposition's request for a debate on Harworth. Clement Attlee invited Baldwin not to take sides in the Harworth dispute, but instead to declare his support for the free democratic principles of collective bargaining. Baldwin responded to empty Treasury benches:[105]

> I agree . . . absolutely with what he [Attlee] said about collective bargaining. What is the alternative to collective bargaining? There is none except anarchy . . .
> And yet we all know in our heart of hearts that it may be a clumsy method of settling disputes . . .
> Some day when we are all fit for a democracy, we shall not need these aids, but certainly for my part, and as long as I can see ahead, unless there is that change in human nature which we are always hoping for, collective bargaining will be a necessity. . . .
> I appeal to the handful of men with whom rests peace or war to give the best present to the country that could be given at that moment, to do the one thing which would rejoice the hearts of all the people who love this country, that is, to rend and dissipate this dark cloud which has gathered over us, and show the people of the world that this democracy can still at least practise the arts of peace in a world of strife.[106]

The Secretary for Mines used Baldwin's appeal as a ploy for initiating another round of negotiations. The Industrial Officer of the Mines Department requested a broadly based committee, thereby recognizing that any settlement would stand a better chance of being accepted if officials from the main coalfield unions were associated with it. The MFGB included men from Durham, Yorkshire, Arthur Horner from South Wales, and James Bowman from Northumberland.[107] Spencer and Barber-Walker had been put at a slight disadvantage by Baldwin's arguments for conciliation and the virtues of collective bargaining and the MFGB side reaped the maximum possible advantage from his homilies.

MFGB officers duly came before the Executive at five minutes to midnight bearing a marginally more face-saving final settlement. The fusion terms were not so demeaning for the NMA officials and Spencer had agreed to elections for new officials. Barber-Walker pledged to take back strikers who had worked at Harworth as employment became available. The Executive pronounced the improved terms acceptable and instructed its affiliated unions not to hand in strike notices, though they were to continue collecting them. The Executive then recommended the settlement to a delegate conference on 27 May. Relieved delegates voted by a five to one majority to accept it.[108]

The Battle of Harworth was over at last. The flimsy substance of Spencer's and Barber-Walker's additional concessions made it a very Pyrrhic victory for the MFGB. Horner's crucial role in preparing the way for and promoting the settlement was an aspect which the Party Centre did not care to analyse too closely. Party and non-Party activists in the NMA continued to denounce the fusion agreement and muttered darkly that most of the strikers would not be re-employed. If the Harworth strikers had broken ranks and called on the coalfields to honour their votes for strike action, there would probably have been a serious split in the MFGB which would not have followed any political logic.

Pollitt and Campbell quickly drew the veil of myth over the Harworth events, and Mick Kane was accorded the Party's highest accolade by being elected to the Central Committee at the 14th Party Congress. In the circumstances, Pollitt's and Campbell's studied acquiescence in the MFGB negotiators' deal was crucial in maintaining union loyalism and upholding the primacy of unity inside the MFGB. The Daily Worker did not comment on the improved terms of the settlement except to offer the predictable observation on 28 May that: 'with an increased drive and a more centralised organisation of the Federation [MFGB] much better terms could have been gained'.[109]

On 30 May at the 14th Party Congress, Mick Kane proudly praised the Party's contribution: 'Today in Harworth the Communist Party and Daily Worker are looked on as the leadership of the working class movement'.[110]

On 26 June Mick Kane was convicted of riot for his part in the events at the Harworth Market Hall on 26 April and sentenced to two years' imprisonment with hard labour.[111] On his release from gaol in August 1938 he was blacklisted in every pit in the East Midlands.[112] Branson records his election to the Central Committee but not his other bitter reward. She reproduces a faithful version of the serviceable myth.

> The dispute came to an end only in May 1937 after the MFGB had threatened a national mining strike. The owners gave in and a compromise was arrived at, whereby the Spencer union was fused with the NMA and all the Harworth strikers reinstated.[113]

*   *   *

This chapter has shown how different the fight against Spencer was from Branson's monochrome gloss. By supporting the Durham miners and their general Mick Kane in the fight, the MFGB defeated Spencer and his union and assured its own survival. Joseph Jones conducted the MFGB's part in the dispute and his pragmatic judgement never faltered. He faced up to the need to compromise with Spencer, but also recognized the need to accept Mick Kane's views about how to keep the men on the ground in good heart.

The conduct of Arthur Horner's battles in South Wales against the SWMIU provided the initial inspiration for Party mining activists in Sheffield to take on Spencer and plan the Battle of Harworth. Pollitt's and Campbell's injunction to Party activists to put united front action and union loyalism first provided the ideological foundation for their crusade to dislodge Spencer and save the NMA from strangulation. Horner's determined support for the compromise settlement was crucial in ensuring its acceptance by the MFGB and Pollitt and Campbell.

Finally there was the willingness of Mick Kane and his hard core of activists at Harworth to risk victimization and imprisonment for the cause. They provided the courage and bold audacity without which the battle would never have been joined. They cheerfully incurred martyrdom in order to emancipate the working class by liberating it through struggle from the likes of Spencer and Barber-Walker. But it was not only the shock troops who were victimized. The majority of Harworth strikers never got back at the pit.[114] (The pledge given by Barber-Walker was probably never meant to be honoured.) The Battle of Harworth was a united front effort, but a richer and more complicated united front than the myth perpetuated in both Party and trade union annals.

Notes

1. Lord Taylor of Mansfield, 1972, *Uphill All the Way*, Sidgwick & Jackson: 65–6.
2. See p. 183.
3. Griffin, A., 1962, *The Miners of Nottinghamshire* 1914–1944, London: 256.
4. Ibid.
5. *Daily Worker*, 24 December 1935. Allison was familiar with the coalfield and its NMA stalwarts. He had tried to break the return to work in 1926 and remained to fight the Spencer union at its inception.
6. *Daily Worker*, 14 January 1936.
7. *Daily Worker*, 2 December 1935. Pollitt and George Crane had also spent time in the Notts. coalfield in 1926 trying to dislodge Spencer. Crane had found work as a colliery engineer and remained there until the early 1930s. For the Unity Campaign, see p. 228.
8. *Daily Worker*, 11 January 1936.
9. Quoted by Griffin, 1962, op. cit.: 257.
10. For Durham see Mason, A., 1967, 'The Miners' Unions of Northumberland and Durham, 1918–31, with special reference to the General Strike of 1926', PhD, University of Hull: 452–6 and Garside, W.R., 1969, 'The Durham Miners Association 1919–47', PhD, University of Leeds: 365.

11. Griffin, 1962, op. cit.: 205; Waller, R.J., 1987, 'Sweethearts and Scabs: irregular trade unions in Britain in the 20th Century', in *Politics and Social Change in Modern Britain*, Waller, P.J. (Ed.) Harvester: 217 and Williams, J.E., 1962, 'The Derbyshire Miners', Allen & Unwin: 720–1. Spencer remained an MP until 1929 but spoke from the Liberal benches.

12. Griffin, 1962, op. cit.: 192–3, Williams, op. cit.: 721–4.

13. Griffin, op.cit.: 207–9.

14. Ibid.: 209. Only one company, J. Oakes & Co., who operated Cotes Park, Pye Hill and New Selston collieries, continued to let NMA collectors on their premises to gather NMA subscriptions throughout the 11 years.

15. Ibid.: 210.

16. Ibid.: 249.

17. Ibid.: 251–2.

18. Waller, R.J., 1987, op. cit.: 219.

19. Griffin, 1962, op. cit.: 38–9, and Williams, 1962, op. cit.: 583–4 and 833–4.

20. Griffin, 1962, op. cit.: 116–8.

21. Ibid.: 236.

22. Ibid.: 249.

23. Ibid.: 236.

24. Ibid.: 243–8.

25. Taylor, 1972, op. cit.: 84. Although Taylor tries to be charitable to Booth he cannot resist repeating the spy rumour which he says was widely accepted by NMA loyalists after 1937. He implies that he believes it.

26. Joseph Jones' report to MFGB Special Conference, 24 March 1937. Conference Minutes, p.103. Council was the term by which the Executive was denominated, like its Yorkshire and Durham counterparts. I think it is probable that the MFGB's official attitude towards 'fusion' had been hostile until Jones' accession to the Presidency.

27. Griffin, 1962, op. cit.: 308.

28. Ibid.: 257.

29. Jock Kane interview with Charles Parker, tape in Charles Parker collection, interviews with Betty Kane and Bridget Kane by N. Fishman. Mick Kane was born in the West of Ireland in 1897 and had come to Perth with his family at the turn of the century. Jock was born in 1907 when his father and older brothers were working in a pit in West Lothian. After the war the Kane's father had joined the Reform Union and taken collections for it at the pit. Mick, his elder brother Martin and younger sister Annie were foundation members of the Communist Party. Martin had volunteered for the Irish guards in the 1914–18 war and been invalided out. Bridget Kane remembered that Jock had been the first miners' son to attend Bathgate Academy, but had to leave at 14 to go down the pit. Another elder brother Tam had done some enterprising gun-running for the IRA in the early 1920s. He would get soldiers drunk in Edinburgh, buy their guns and then send them to Glasgow for forwarding to Ireland.
    In the aftermath of the General Strike, the Kanes' father was the only one in the family who was taken back in the pit. Mick found a job in a Stirlingshire pit and a house; and the rest of the family moved with him. In October 1928 Mick served on a strike committee and helped to win a wage increase; he was then sacked. As employment in the pits in Scotland contracted, the Kanes joined many other miners in the trek southwards

for work. Jock had gone to Durham first in 1927 and lost heart when there was no work there either. He joined Mick in 1928 in Yorkshire where a pal, Barney McQueenie, helped them to find work at Hatfield. They sent for their sister Bridget who was now keeping house for the family and their younger siblings. The house they found was rejected by Bridget because it had bugs. Mick and Jock moved on to find work in Nottinghamshire and Derbyshire pits.

30. Jock Kane interview with C. Parker, loc. cit. In February 1932, the *Daily Worker* reported that some 600 men had been given notice at Harworth, and only 150 had been reinstated. A mass meeting was held on a Sunday, convened jointly by the Harworth NMA and the NUWM branches in Doncaster and Rossington. The *Daily Worker* (13 February 1932) explained that Harworth men signed on in Rossington, Yorkshire; the Doncaster NUWM was undoubtedly the most numerous and well organized of NUWM branches with mining members.

31. *The Harworth Spark*, No. 4, 31 July 1931. The editorial address was in Doncaster. An article stated that the Communist Party had been holding meetings on Sunday evenings for the previous five to six weeks. There are two issues of the paper, No. 7 and No. 9 in the Modern Records Centre of the University of Warwick. At no point is any mention made of the NMA. Other papers in the Modern Records Centre for the East Midlands are the *Edlington Lamp*, *The Kenneth's Hawk*, *The Barnsley Main Spark*, *The Askern Turning Point*, the *Bentley Turnplate* and the *Denaby & Cadeby Rebel*. The situation at Harworth in 1933 was described by Bernard Taylor as being a desert for the NMA (op. cit.: 67).

32. Interviews with Jock Kane and Bridget Kane, loc. cit.

33. Williams, 1962, op.cit.: 834–5. Williams does not identify the occasion of Hicken's meeting being the Kanes' eviction. Magistrates regarded his speech as 'a direct incitement to people to help themselves to things from the shops' (p.835).

34. He lodged with his sister Annie in Brondesbury Park, not far from Hannington's Edgware base. He helped her out in the Marble Arch café which she and her husband ran, but spent his evenings in the East End agitating. (Interview with Bridget Kane, loc. cit.)

35. Ibid.

36. Interviews with Jock Kane and Betty Kane, loc. cit. Sir Charles Markham, part of the family who had a major share of Staveley's was standing as the Conservative candidate in the nearby Belper constituency. (Williams, op. cit: 838)

37. Membership figures in Griffin, 1962, op. cit.: 259. Booth's speech reported in the *Daily Worker*, 14 January 1936.

38. Griffin, 1962, op. cit.: 258. Taylor concurs that 'dirt deductions' were an important grievance (op. cit.: 67). Both were ex-miners and viewed dirt money as a serious matter. The miners working at the face were paid piece-rates, according to the weight of the coal in their tubs. Dirt deductions were made for dross which they had hewed and put in their tubs but which was not coal (ibid. 258).

39. I have found no reliable evidence for the date of Mick's return to Harworth. At the beginning of the dispute, he was variously described by the *Daily Worker* as Councillor Kane (21 November 1936) and a Labour councillor (22 December 1936). Reference to his local councillor status

then abruptly ceased, and no other sources mention this connection. He may have been elected a Labour councillor in Yorkshire while retaining his Communist Party membership. When the Harworth dispute developed, the Sheffield Party deemed it expedient for him to quietly resign from the Council in order to avoid discovery of this ruse.

40.   Griffin, 1962, op. cit.: 258. This resistance mentality is similar to the conventions adopted by AEU activists at Briggs Bodies in Dagenham. See N. Fishman, unpublished paper on union organization at Ford's Dagenham, 1933–45.

41.   Griffin tartly records that there was 'a complete change in leadership of the Branch. Mr. J. Pickering who had done so much to build up the Branch was succeeded as President by Michael Kane, a Communist militant' (p. 259). For Buckley, see Taylor, 1925, op. cit.: 70. A Steve Buckley is mentioned in *The Harworth Rebel*, 5 September 1931 and they may either have been the same person or related.

42.   MFGB Special Conference Report, January 1937, loc. cit.: 26.

43.   *Daily Worker*, 10 September 1936.

44.   *Daily Worker*, 8, 10 September and 14 December 1936. Mick Kane described the incident somewhat differently on 14 December in the *Daily Worker*. He stated that the one-day strike had materialized after 50 men working in one section of the conveyor face refused to take their 'snap time while waiting for tubs'. 'Quite spontaneously their action was supported by men in three other parts of the pit.'

45.   *Daily Worker*, 8 and 10 September 1936.

46.   *Daily Worker*, 18 November and 14 December 1936. MFGB Executive Minutes, 24 September 1936: 335. The figures given by Mick Kane do not tally with Jones's statement that the Harworth NMA had 640 members in August. See note above.

47.   *Daily Worker*, 18 November 1936.

48.   MFGB Executive Minutes, 24 September 1936: 335. The Executive formally requested the NMA Council to grant the MFGB power to deal with Harworth.

49.   Francis, 1980, *The Fed*, op. cit.: 234. At the end of October 1936 a ballot was held at Bedwas in South Wales where there had been a fierce strike by Fed miners. The Fed cooperated in the ballot which produced a substantial minority of 309 still in favour of the SWMIU, compared to 1177 for the SWMF on a 91 per cent turnout. (*Daily Worker*, 30 October 1936.)

50.   *Daily Worker*, 18 November 1936.

51.   MFGB Executive minutes, 22 October 1936: 343–4.

52.   MFGB Executive minutes, 19 November 1936: 347–8 and *Daily Worker*, 14 December 1936.

53.   MFGB Executive minutes, loc. cit.

54.   *Daily Worker*, 18 November 1936.

55.   MFGB Executive minutes, loc. cit. and *Daily Worker*, 18 November and 14 December 1936 and Taylor, 1972, op. cit.: 68–9. Taylor's recollections are inaccurate in places.

56.   *Daily Worker*, 21 November 1936.

57.   *Daily Worker*, 27 November 1936.

58.   Mick Kane in the *Daily Worker*, 14 December 1936.

59.   *Daily Worker*, 12 December 1936. For events of the previous week, see *Daily Worker*, 8 and 10 December 1936.

60. *Daily Worker*, 15 December 1936.
61. *Daily Worker*, 31 December 1936. Arnot, Vol. III, op. cit.: 229. Barber-Walker's owned pits in the older Eastwood part of the coalfield as well as Bentley colliery in the South Yorkshire coalfield.
62. Taylor, 1972, op. cit.: 71.
63. *Daily Worker*, 7 January 1937. Taylor confirmed that there were not many men working (op. cit.: 72–3).
64. Ibid.: 73. MFGB officers believed that the coal-owners had pressurized the police to provoke the strikers. The National Council for Civil Liberties investigated and issued a report which condemned their tactics. The epithet 'chain gang' probably was inspired by the knowledge of the conditions of black convicts in the Southern USA.
65. *Daily Worker*, 7 January 1937. MFGB Executive minutes, 19–20 January 1937: 1.
66. Interview, loc. cit.
67. *Daily Worker*, 13 January 1937.
68. *Daily Worker*, 14 January 1937.
69. Taylor, 1972, op. cit.: 77.
70. *Daily Worker*, 2 February 1937.
71. *Daily Worker*, 21 January 1937 and Taylor, op. cit.: 73. The *Daily Worker* reported Dunn's speaking on 13 January and 16 February 1937 and Edwards' speech on 26 January 1937.
72. *Daily Worker*, 21 January 1937.
73. R. Page Arnot, Vol. III, op. cit.: 211–3 and *Daily Worker*, 21 January 1937.
74. *Daily Worker*, 22 January 1937
75. Joseph Jones' phrase in MFGB Executive minutes, 20 January 1937: 6.
76. MFGB Special Conference minutes, 20 January 1937: 26–36.
77. Quoted in *Daily Worker*, 26 January 1937.
78. *Daily Worker*, 28 January 1937.
79. See MFGB Executive Report, 12 March 1937: 72–3.
80. On 13 and 15 March, the *Daily Worker* reported the terms and discussed their pros and cons, continuing to stress the need for unity. Articles on 10, 19 and 26 February 1937 reported miners' determination to fight Spencer at Harworth and canvassed the importance of gaining wider labour movement support and holding the national strike ballot at once.
81. R. Page Arnot, Vol. III, op. cit.: 218 and Griffin, op. cit.: 267.
82. *Notts Journal*, 20 March 1937.
83. Griffin, 1962, op. cit.: 256–7.
84. *Daily Worker*, 24 March 1937.
85. *Daily Worker*, 1 April 1937. See p. 97 for the Special Statement by the Party Centre on 2 April about Harworth, the busmen and the Beardmore's Parkhead Forge strike.
86. MFGB Special Delegate Conference Minutes, 1 April 1937: 95.
87. The *Daily Worker* reported that delegates from South Wales, Yorkshire, Northumberland and Kent had spoken against the terms (*DW* 2 April 1937).
88. MFGB Special Delegate Conference Minutes, 1 April 1937: 116. *Forward* was the ILP newspaper.
89. R. Page Arnot, Vol. III, op. cit.: 219–20.
90. Special Conference minutes, loc. cit.: 129.

91.   R. Page Arnot, Vol. III, op. cit.: 220.
92.   Special Conference minutes, loc. cit.: 135.
93.   Quoted in R. Page Arnot, Vol. III, op. cit.: 220.
94.   Ibid.: 221. The voting was 444,546 to 61,445.
95.   Bernard Taylor remembered that every Friday men and women from Harworth 'were taken by bus to the pits in Nottinghamshire and Derbyshire to collect. The miners in the two county coal-fields responded generously'. 'Resources did not in any way provide luxuries but were sufficient to keep the wolf from the door, and this was a change from 1926. Ernest Marklew, who at one time was Member of Parliament for Colne Valley . . . daily sent a consignment of fish'(op. cit.: 74–5).
96.   *Daily Worker*, 26 April 1937.
97.   Taylor recalled: 'The taking out of summonses was as common as the buttercups growing in the fields', op. cit.: 75.
98.   *Daily Worker*, 26 April 1937. Frankie Jobson was arrested with Kane. A Durham man, he had been the *Daily Worker* agent during the strike. Bridget Kane remembered that Mick had lodged with the Jobsons at this time. (Interview, loc. cit.) See also Arnot, Vol. III, op. cit.: 222–3 and 236–40.
99.   Taylor, op. cit.: 75–6.
100. The Party Centre had periodically canvassed the possibility of the Notts. miners being roused in defence of their Harworth comrades. During the strike, the Party had organized intermittent meetings in the coalfield in an attempt to precipitate this 'united front'. See *Daily Worker*, 18 January 1936 and 21 January 1937. There had been no response.
101. *Daily Worker*, 1 May 1937.
102. See pp. 98–9, 122, 150.
103. For example on 22 May 1937 the *Daily Worker* argued that the TUC should call a special meeting of the General Council to discuss 'the mobilising of the whole movement' in the same article as it reported that talks between the owners and the MFGB on fusion might reopen. See also *Daily Worker*, 24 May 1937 and the reports of the settlement in *Daily Worker*, 27 and 28 May 1937.
104. *Daily Worker*, 27 May 1937.
105. *Daily Telegraph*, 6 May 1937. Page Arnot gives the misleading impression that the debate was a concerted, concerned *démarche* which Baldwin arranged to avoid the Coronation on the 12 May being marred by the prospect of a national miners' strike. He also states that 'the members of the House of Commons, according to contemporary witnesses, were visibly affected, partly by the knowledge that it was his swan song.' (p. 230). Baldwin bade farewell to the House of Commons on 27 May.
106. Quoted in Page Arnot, Vol. III, op. cit.: 230–1.
107. MFGB Executive minutes, 20 April 1937: 135.
108. Page Arnot, Vol. III, op. cit.: 232–5.
109. *Daily Worker*, 28 May 1937.
110. *Daily Worker*, 31 May 1937.
111. *Daily Worker*, 28 June 1937. The *Daily Worker* observed that it was one of the heaviest sentences ever inflicted for this charge.
112. Mick Kane finally found work in a Derbyshire pit after the war due to intervention of the former Labour mining MP for Pontefract, Tom Smith. Interview with Jock Kane, loc. cit. He went on to become an agent for the Derbyshire Miners' Association.

113. Branson, 1985, op. cit.: 185.
114. Taylor, 1972, op. cit.: 80.

CHAPTER EIGHT

Organizing the United Front against the Bosses

Despite the monumental disappointments of May 1937 the Communist Party finished the year much as it had begun. Pollitt's and Campbell's main domestic priority was still increasing the Party's power and influence on the shopfloor and inside trade union machinery. They had previously counted on the national militant upsurge to appear and create the conditions for the CPGB to assume a legitimate place in its own right alongside the other institutions of the British Labour movement. They had fully expected the British scenario would be similar to France where the PCF's dramatic increase in popularity had occurred during the great strike wave in 1936.[1] The PCF's sudden prominence had presented French socialist and union leaders with a stark choice: they either had to make some room for Communists or risked being outflanked by them.

Pollitt and Campbell had been encouraging party activists to build strategic positions inside workplaces and unions from which they would be able to direct great national strikes. The economic recovery did indeed produce a British equivalent of the French militancy, but we have observed that its outcome was very different than in France. There was never any point at which existing 'reformist' trade union leaders relinquished their hold on the leadership; in the event Pollitt and Campbell even ensured that party activists assisted in the achievement of compromise settlements within official procedure. The more developed conventions of collective bargaining in British industry evidently enabled British unions to represent workers more effectively, thereby lessening any opportunity for the Communist Party to move into the breach.

Unlike many Party members' reaction against 'reformist' unions in 1926 there were no attempts to turn against trade unions in the wake of the May 1937 disappointments. The CPGB remained bound by the Seventh World Congress injunction to play a crucial part in the proletariat's fight for partial economic demands and to carry this fight into 'reformist' unions. Evidence that activists were fulfilling this Communist duty was the continuing energy and flair with which Young Communist League activists propagated trade union culture and preached the 'economic struggle'. The Clyde apprentices' strikes had failed at the time to ignite similar action in England. But the well-organized YCL activists in Manchester and Coventry had been impressed by the Scots' success and learned from it.

The Scottish strikes had been precipitated by YCL members encouraging a sense of grievance over apprentices being denied the hourly wage increase given to adult engineers as part of the national wage award agreed by the Engineering Employers' Federation (EEF). A new national wage agreement had been signed in July, and on 23 August the first of its two instalments of one shilling and sixpence was paid out to adult engineers.

On 6 September there were apprentices' strikes in Salford which quickly spread to Manchester and other parts of Lancashire, and eventually at the end of September to Coventry. It was not only apprentices, but also young trainees and 'improvers' who went on strike. The youth strikes also occurred in Leeds and South London. This second wave of strikes were led and spread by YCL activists, ably assisted by AEU full-time officials and lay activists with other unions offering advice and mobilizing popular support.

In Lancashire and Manchester the YCL's relations with the adult labour movement were cordial and very proper, conducted under the dense umbrella of local trade union culture. Jack Munro, the Manchester Trades Council Secretary who had been a member of Openshaw British Socialist Party (BSP) along with Harry Pollitt, played an important role in helping to organize the apprentices' strike committee and gathering affiliated union branches' support. In Coventry, the lads' strike sparked off a spate of strikes by semi-skilled adult workers in textiles and electrical goods from which the TGWU made big recruiting gains. The trades council under Party leadership provided strong public support, buttressed by the Amalgamated Engineers' Union. A well organized campaign was launched including open-air meetings and marches during which the trade unions displayed an impressive public presence and excited popular interest.[2]

As on the Clyde, when individual employers granted wage increases to their lads the strikes ended in a piecemeal fashion. But this time the EEF finally conceded a demand which the YCL activists and the AEU had been pursuing since the Clyde strikes and granted the AEU limited recognition to negotiate on behalf of young workers and apprentices. The AEU Executive were well satisfied and forebore to make any attack on the highly visible Communist youths such as Johnny Gollan who were orating from the platforms of well-attended national unofficial apprentices' conferences.[3] In their turn, these firebrand revolutionaries did not maintain any unofficial youth organization outside the unions. Zealous rank-and-file pursuit of economic aims simply ceased and any youthful energies were channelled inside the official union structures.

Meanwhile Pollitt and Campbell were wrestling with their problem of how the Party could win its fitting and proper place in the van of the labour movement. They still needed to create a real united front. Their inclination to await the rank-and-file upsurge from below had misfired. There had been no breach in the flow of events to give an opportunity for the CPGB to step in. So the Party Centre now tried a new tack. They decided to take the initiative nationally, *in the Party's name* in pursuit of immediate demands for the whole working class.

The Party and its activists would embark on national campaigns for immediate demands which would in turn fuel the rank-and-file's desire to fight. Through its own efforts, the Party would find itself at the head of a popular movement. As a party, the CPGB had not taken immediate demands very seriously. A list of general partial demands had been appended to the Resolution on the economic situation at the 13th Party Congress in February 1935, but there had been no attempt to follow it up with any practical initiative. The list was widened and up-dated for the 14th Congress to reflect significant developments. Since 1935 there had been considerable progress made by Labour and the TUC in pursuing material goals. There had also been the spectacular advances enacted by the French Popular Front Government. After the Congress, the Party Centre launched a campaign around its immediate demands which was intended to mobilize rank-and-file trade unionists. It continued through the summer and peaked in time to influence the Trades Union Congress.

In fact, the immediate demands approved by the 14th Congress were virtually identical to the Labour Party's current Immediate Programme, published just two months previously. Both lists included holidays with pay, adequate retirement pensions, the 40-hour week and emphasized the need to concentrate on the particular problems of women and youth.[4] Despite their similarity, the Party campaign's message was that the trade union leaders would only deliver on the CPGB/Labour shopping list of demands after 'rank-and-file' pressure was applied and that only the Communist Party would ensure that this pressure was effectively organized and directed accurately towards its 'reformist' target. On 5 August, the *Daily Worker* reported that the preliminary agenda for the 1937 TUC contained one resolution which criticized the General Council for refusing to wage a joint, 'real united front', campaign for the TUC's principal demands, including the 40-hour week. It anticipated that 'in debate on this question the inactivity of the General Council will undoubtedly be criticised'.

> The employers, greedy for more profits, are sucking the life energy from the workers. They refuse to lessen the hours of labour . . . The nerve-wracking tension and exhaustion to which the worker is subjected today in factory and workshop makes both shorter hours and paid holidays an urgent and crying necessity . . . Backed by a powerful campaign with the full weight of the TUC behind it, these demands could be quickly achieved.[5]

An indication of the importance which the Party Centre assigned the campaign was the appearance on 21 September of a pamphlet by Harry Pollitt promoting the 40-hour week, for distribution at the Trades Union Congress in the following week. Pollitt had been increasingly pre-occupied with the European political arena and fighting Fascism. His activity had made him increasingly familiar to and admired by Labour and trade union activists. (He had been appearing with Stafford Cripps and Jimmy Maxton to packed audiences in a series of meetings organized by the Unity Campaign.)[6] 'From Friday Night Till Monday Morning' was evidently an attempt to use his growing popularity and rising reputation for the party's domestic political ends.

The pamphlet carefully anchored the Party in the heart of the trade union movement, emphasizing members' dual adherence to union loyalism and rank-and-filism.

> This idea of the five-day, 40 hour week is beginning to catch on. People are really talking about it ... Even here men are getting excited ... Our employers, of course, are not so sure. They need some gentle persuasion, and they'll probably get it soon, because when British workers want a thing hard enough, they usually find ways of getting it.
>
> It is very definitely practical politics – this five day week. It is one of the big points in the Immediate Programme of the Labour Party ... We shall have to fight the employers for it in any case – whether Labour is in power or not. Let's start now!
>
> 'United we stand'. That has been commonsense since the world began. It is the slogan and principle of trade unionism, and the Communist Party is working with Labour rank and filers to get that principle put into practice through the whole Labour Movement ... Join your union branch if you believe in good wages and a fair share of leisure ... Make sure your delegates consult their members on how they shall vote and act. Even the big ones like Mr. Bevin! ... We want to get on with the job of winning higher wages and the 40 hour week. That is why so many of us are impatient at the way some of our leaders spend their time hunting out and running down militant members instead of leading us against the ruling class ...
>
> For we Communists who are people who work as loyal but *militant* trade unionists ... We work at recruiting because we are determined that the great British trade union movement shall be brought into militant action again – as it was in the great days when Britain led the world to better working conditions.[7]

The pamphlet did not inform readers that there had already been an important TUC *démarche* on shorter hours culminating in 1936. Ernest Bevin had served on the TUC delegation at an International Labour Organization (ILO) conference convened in 1933 to discuss an international convention on the reduction of working hours. After attending a further ILO conference in 1935, at which

> ... he led the campaign for an international convention to establish
> the principle of a forty-hour week ... he told the delegates [in pri-
> vate session at the TGWU BDC] bluntly, with much support from
> the floor, that as great an obstacle to shortening the working week as
> the employers was the trade unionist who insisted on working 50, 60
> or even 70 hours for the sake of overtime pay and who refused to
> share the work.'[8]

Bevin's perceptions of the problems involved in this issue clearly differed
from the Party's public stance. He had given a discursive and frank report
to the 1936 TUC on the General Council's efforts to persuade Baldwin to
adopt the ILO Convention for a statutory 40-hour working week. The
Government accepted the employers' argument that any reduction in
hours was best achieved through joint voluntary agreements tailored to
suit each particular industry's circumstances. 'This, as Bevin admitted
... was an effective retort. There was much opposition in the trade-
union movement to any reduction in hours which might interfere with
the opportunity to earn overtime pay.'[9]

A candid trade union activist reading Pollitt's pamphlet might have
responded: 'We want to reduce working hours, but our members can't
afford to lose the money. The unions will never be able to stop overtime
for that reason.' The Party Centre apparently found it impolitic to admit
that it was not 'reformism' or 'Mondism', but the low hourly wage rates
and habitual overtime which prevented the TUC from putting strong
pressure on the Government to ratify the ILO convention. Too few union
leaders, of either left or right, had either the energy or will to face this
looming internal obstacle to change.

Bevin consistently argued that the low wage rates and long working
hours in engineering were linked. He believed that if engineering wages
were increased from low levels to a 'reasonable' base, employers would
have an incentive to reduce hours and overtime.[10] The more conservative
AEU Executive had never considered demanding that the EEF embark on
the thorough-going revision of the industry's terms and conditions which
this linkage would involve. Nor did Party engineering activists wield
their growing influence inside the AEU to support the connection
between higher hourly wage rates and shorter hours. Instead, they
doggedly pursued their anachronistic goal of mobilizing a rank-and-file
national wages movement in order to precipitate an all-out conflict with
the engineering employers.

It follows that if Pollitt and Campbell were serious about pursuing a
40-hour week, they would have to devise an approach to the latent
internecine conflicts which would emerge along the way which might
involve Party activists in opposing other militant union colleagues.
Because Britain had a developed trade union structure, achieving even

partial reform meant facing the fact that the 'rank-and-file' possessed substantial vested interests and would resist change inside union institutions. Bevin's frank admission of the internal divisions at the 1936 Congress indicated his willingness to contemplate a period of struggle and 'creative disunity' in order to galvanize the trade union movement behind a progressive stand on shorter hours.

If King Street had been determined to launch a Party-sponsored 'rank-and-file' campaign for shorter working hours which addressed the salience of higher hourly wage rates, Bevin would have had no reason not to utilize the opportunities it created to advance on this front. However, the Party Centre's reluctance to disturb the equilibrium inside the trade union movement ensured that its national campaign for immediate demands was purely rhetorical. A fine crop of Party-inspired resolutions on the 40-hour week and the need for working class unity were debated at the 1937 TUC. They reflected Party activists' diligence in attending union branch meetings, successfully moving resolutions, and then following them through the intricate network of union institutions to Congress. Nevertheless, after the Congress was over these same activists did not translate their formal victories into practical action.

The Party Centre proclaimed the need for a 'real united front' to fight for immediate demands. But they also avoided confronting the internal divisions which had to be overcome to achieve real unity. Their consistent refusal to address this awkward problem was determined in part by the Communist catechism under which 'reformist' leaders were the main brake on working-class advance. But there was the additional tactical consideration that Party activists would alienate some of their militant 'rank-and-file' allies who opposed radical change when it impinged on conservative union culture. For example, if Party activists had argued for the need to increase hourly wage rates and reduce working hours inside the AEU, they would have had to deal with the issue of wage rates for semi-skilled workers. In the process, serious divisions would have emerged inside the close-knit informal alliance of 'left-wing' activists many of whom retained an abiding craft hostility towards the increasing importance of semi-skilled work in the industry. A related example was the admission of women into the AEU, a matter of undeniable importance for the union since there were growing numbers of women workers doing semi-skilled work in light engineering who were being recruited by the TGWU.

Most AEU activists were opposed to the admission of women with varying degrees of vehemence for craft-conservative reasons. Party activists had moved that women be admitted to the union at the AEU's first Rules Revision Committee in 1926. They were punctilious in moving the admission of women at each successive meeting of the committee every five years. However, they were notably reticent in arguing the case for this rule change inside union institutions or on the shopfloor. They were evidently unwilling to deal with the conflict which would arise if they canvassed for support in the way in which they normally promoted other Party-sponsored motions. Because the informal militant networks were well serviced by Party activists, Party-inspired initiatives usually gathered substantial support inside the AEU's extensive lay institutions.

In 1930 the motion to admit women was proposed by Jack Tanner and seconded by Joe Scott. It was lost 44–6. In 1935 Claude Berridge proposed and Tommy Sillars seconded the same motion which attracted a total of 4 votes. Nevertheless, other Party-sponsored rule changes were passed. At the AEU National Committee, party-sponsored motions regularly mustered at least 12 votes.[11] Party members' support for women's rights remained abstract, isolated and apparently unsupported both inside branches and district committees or on the shopfloor. Neither the *Daily Worker* or *New Propellor* carried propaganda arguing for the admission of women until the war economy placed the issue firmly on the AEU's agenda.[12]

In the wake of the non-appearance of its national popular campaign for immediate demands, Pollitt and Campbell fell back on the vicissitudes of the 'economic struggle' to provide the 'real united front'. There was a downturn in the economy at the end of 1937 which some experts forecast would develop into a slump. The Party Centre argued that the recession proved Marx had been right and that the concessions won during the previous upturn were purely temporary. In December 1937 the *Daily Worker* reminded readers that capitalists were trying even harder to increase their rate of exploitation of workers. An editorial on 30 December 1938 repeated the previous New Year's message. The *Daily Herald* had reported an increase in living standards.

> This is a distortion of the true facts. True, due to the efforts of the trade unions, the workers in several industries have won wage increases, but these increases have been more than swallowed up by the higher cost of living ... The fact is that 1938 saw a definite hardening among employers, faced with the shadow of the on-coming slump, when pressed by the unions with demands for wage increases ...
>
> We would be the last to detract from the valuable services rendered by the trade unions in winning certain concessions from the employers. At the same time it would be wrong not to point out that greater successes could have been won had the trade unions been more vigorous in prosecuting their claims, and had the General Council of the TUC played its proper role of leading and co-ordinating the struggles of the organised workers for improved wages and conditions of labour ...
>
> The trade unions are stronger now than they have been for a

decade. A vigorous drive, properly conducted and led, can leave the mass of the people immeasurably better off at the end of 1939 than they are at the end of the year now drawing to a close.[13]

After reading this Communist lesson Party members were meant to be inspired to apply themselves with renewed dedication and diligence to waging the 'economic struggle' within their specific parochial boundaries. Despite the CPGB's strict adherence to Leninist democratic centralism in political matters, Pollitt and Campbell had never made any attempt to impose a general line for waging 'the economic struggle' from above. They had merely provided a framework, revolutionary pragmatism, within which Party activists had to make choices about their particular situations. Their activists had to judge their own terrain and decide their own conduct according to the culture and organization of their particular trade unions, the collective bargaining traditions of their workplaces and regions and the capabilities and character of the previous and current generation of local union activists and full-time officials.

The Party had been well served by the dissemination of revolutionary pragmatism as a general perspective combined with a lack of prescription about tactics in daily mass work. Party membership increased from 6500 in February 1935 to 15,750 in September 1938. At the 1938 Party Congress 367 of the 539 delegates were trade union members and 138 of them held official positions.[14] The *Daily Worker* observed with some satisfaction: 'The CPGB has entered 1939 stronger in experience, influence and membership than at any time in its existence. It is strengthening and unifying the forces of the Labour movement with increasing power and energy.'[15]

Neither the recession nor their propaganda about increased exploitation caused Pollitt and Campbell to revise the general framework of revolutionary pragmatism. They did not incite members to follow the logic of the propaganda by organizing all-out class battles to resist immiseration. They observed the priority of union loyalism compared with rank-and-filism which they had arrived at in May 1937. They assumed that Party activists would observe their unions' official negotiating conventions, bending and stretching them in the heat of struggle, certainly, but ultimately acknowledging their legitimacy. This meant fighting the 'economic struggle' about issues and conditions which were already inside the boundaries set down for 'joint determination' and not venturing too far beyond into terrain where the union writ did not run.

Trade union activists responded pragmatically to the slump in most cases, revising their horizons downwards accordingly. Party activists played their part in this belt-tightening exercise. They had received no instructions from King Street to lead the working class in mass protest against 'increased exploitation', nor did they expect any. Where union activists had developed operational collective bargaining, most employers refrained from using their temporary advantage to repudiate earlier concessions and retake prerogatives surrendered during the boom. Party activists were content to lead small skirmishes and win minor concessions through negotiation. The equilibrium between unions and employers was maintained despite the forebodings of the *Daily Worker* and some union leaders, including Bevin.

The specially favourable circumstances of the aircraft shadow factories produced remarkable gains for union organization in 1938–39. The automobile manufacturers Austin's and Rover's had begun preparations for aircraft shadow factories in Birmingham during 1936. In 1937 George Crane found work in one of Rover's two 'shadow' aircraft works at Acocks Green.[16] A young Party AEU activist, Les Ambrose started in the toolroom at Austin's 'shadow' factory in Cofton Hackett in 1938. Crane and Ambrose led brilliant forays within the limits of local engineering procedure. Their practical goal was the attainment of mutuality on piece-work pricing and the *de facto* ejection of the stop-watch for piece-work timings.

Shadow workforces proved notably willing to challenge managerial prerogative. Les Ambrose observed that his shadow factory workmates had a different attitude to the 'economic struggle'. Because they viewed their jobs as temporary, they were more receptive when activists suggested union organization and industrial action to remedy grievances. They felt they had less to lose than workers in 'permanent' industry. Shadow factories also had no previous histories of defeats and retreats which long-serving sceptics could throw in the balance to weigh up against union activists' prediction that management would concede ground under pressure.

George Crane had settled in Birmingham in 1934. He immediately became active in the AEU lay institutions, recording a good vote for the divisional delegate to the TUC in that year and actually being elected in 1935, 1936 and 1937. He was victimized at Lucas in 1934 because he had ventured outside the toolroom and commenced agitating among the women workers. Les Ambrose remembered wryly that George Crane would 'recruit anyone into a union'.

In late 1936 Crane had marshalled a 'progressive' majority on the AEU District Committee to support District Secretary Teddy Ager in a move to admit semi-skilled workers into Section V even though they were not earning the hourly wage rate prescribed by the District Committee. (The AEU Executive Council had encouraged District Committees to take this step; many had refused to do so and excercised their sovereign rights under the rules.) The District Committee had then emulated the Charles Lamb/London model and formed an Organizing

Sub-Committee which then formed local committees. They arranged recruiting campaigns with superannuated members leafleting factory gates at 7.30 a.m.[17]

These innovations netted substantial gains in AEU membership. Nevertheless, the recruits were mainly skilled men. It was Crane's freedom from any kind of craft reflex which enabled him to win the majority of semi-skilled workers in the Rover shadow factory into unions. In April 1938 he precipitated an unofficial strike at Acocks Green over new piece-rates. Miraculously for a site with 2000 workers and no previous history of union organization, the strike was nearly solid. Neither Rover's management nor Teddy Ager were alarmed by the strike's unofficial nature. During the 1930s a short 'demonstration' strike outside procedure was the conventional first move by unions in the evolving sub-culture of engineering procedure in both the Midlands and South-east.

After a week the new rates were withdrawn and the strikers returned to work in good heart and good order. Newspaper reports noted that 90 per cent of the strikers were organized, mostly in the AEU. The AEU ODD, Billy Stokes, commented in the *Birmingham Gazette* that the strike 'had provided an example of solidarity almost unknown in the Birmingham area, and through it the union had been able to accomplish work in other factories which it had been trying to do for long periods.'[18]

The fledgeling union organization flourished at Rover's. Crane evidently succeeded in inducing different departments to elect shop stewards whom management duly recognized. Shop negotiations commenced on contentious issues. *New Propellor* reported in August 1938 that chargehands at Acocks Green approached shop stewards to ask their permission for overtime to be worked, and that the new chief ratefixer who had been drafted in from the car works 'frequently consults with the convener on piecework prices, with the result that the prices on the new engine show an increase . . . Shop stewards now number twenty five and work together very well as a team . . . Trade union organising meetings are being held here in the dinner hour in the various departments.'[19]

During the strike, George Crane had taken care to hold a meeting outside Austin's shadow factory at Cofton Hackett, known locally as the Aero, which was attended by 3000 workers.[20] The strike's unqualified success and the stories of subsequent management retreats which filtered through to the nearby Aero reinforced activists' efforts to build union organization there. When Les Ambrose started in the toolroom, the 800 toolmakers were nearly 100 per cent organized and the sheet metal workers had declared a closed shop.[21]

In June 1938 two sheet metal workers were sacked at the Aero for refusing to have the stopwatch time them on a job; one of them was chairman of the shop committee. Both were reinstated after a threatened strike. The stopwatch soon produced another incident in the sheet metal shop in which the young women welders also participated. The offending rate-fixer and his stopwatch were withdrawn and the shop committee was recognized by management. *New Propellor* reported the news gleefully and observed that action might now be taken to get the stopwatch out of other departments.[22]

In August 1938 there was a nine days unofficial strike at the Aero. Shop stewards for skilled workers had been pursuing a dispute over hourly wage rates through official channels for sometime.[23] Management refused to go further than an offer of parity with their automobile site at Longbridge, where rates were below the AEU district rates.[24] After barely a week the AEU Executive swiftly made the Aero strike official, along with the other unions involved. They were understandably keen to pay dispute benefit. They all stood to gain many recruits, and officials had not observed the presence of 'irresponsible bodies. . . . whose primary objects are to advocate openly flouting the union's rules'.[25]

The strike ended in the manner appropriate to an unavoidable dispute which had been conducted by both sides according to the accepted rules of engagement. Shop stewards led a united return to work on the unspoken understanding that an official works conference would be convened immediately from which suitable management concessions would emerge. The initial grievance had concerned the skilled workers; shop stewards nevertheless incited the whole factory to come out. Management felt it incumbent to offer everyone concessions, proving that collective strength gained results.

If the strike had occurred in 1933–34, the *Daily Worker* would have written about the 'rank-and-file' strike committee and stressed that full-time union officials were fully cooperating with it. In 1938 *New Propellor* made no mention of a discrete 'rank-and-file' presence. It commented on the strikers' energetic range of activities and noted with approval the union recruiting and arrangements for electing shop stewards.

> Thousands of Strike Bulletins were sold at the engineering and other aircraft factories in the Midlands. On one occasion, a convoy of about 30–35 cars went to Coventry with mass sales of the Bulletin and to conduct three meetings . . . A pleasing feature of this dispute was the way in which the car workers in some of the shops contributed to the excellent collections. In the park opposite the [Cofton Hackett] factory, two loudspeakers were in use, broadcasting the speeches made at the frequent mass meetings.[26]

Thereafter, union organization prospered at the Aero. Les Ambrose recalled that the TGWU had some shop stewards and a lower subscription rate than the AEU Section V contributions. He set himself the aim of recruiting the whole male semi-skilled workforce into the AEU. Ambrose became convener of the Works Committee in 1939. He reckoned that by 1941 the majority of male semi-skilled workers were AEU members. The chairman of the shop stewards was Fred Fowler, a Communist sheet metal worker.[27]

The very poor state of union organization at Austin's large car factory at Longbridge presented a stark contrast to the Aero successes. Throughout the 1930s management barely tolerated the AEU's presence and then only inside the toolroom. AEU activists including Party members, confined their activities to the skilled shops, despite the large numbers of semi-skilled workers. They had to reckon on management's well attested hostility to collective bargaining and willingness to victimize.

In November 1936 National Union of Vehicle Builders (NUVB) members at Austin's were provoked by new timings for piece-work jobs into staging a walk-out. They were followed by the rest of the workers who were non-unionists ('nons') in the West Works. The AEU District Committee wanted skilled members at Austin's to fight for the union hourly district rate and enthusiastically supported the NUVB strike. But Party members in the toolroom were evidently unprepared for the NUVB action. Their *ad hoc* attempt to spread the strike inside the factory to the South Works was stymied by police action.

There was a scratch strike committee of 'nons' who evidently had little experience and proved unequal to the task of rousing the entire works. Management refused to meet union officials. Instead they accepted a 'deputation' of workers and withdrew the contested timings after three days. A return to work followed.[28] Engineering unions had all recruited members during the strike.[29] Nevertheless its speedy settlement and management's continued hostility to collective bargaining ensured that workplace conditions remained unchanged at Longbridge.

The union stalwarts in the toolroom were caught in a vicious circle. Management were unlikely to concede practical recognition unless pressurized by a full-scale *démarche* similar to the total stoppages at the shadow factories. However, the predominant AEU culture at Longbridge was orientated solely towards the skilled tradesmen. Communists did their daily mass work in the comparative security of their toolroom enclave and unlike Crane and Ambrose did not venture out to encounter the majority semi-skilled workforce, potential Section V recruits. From 1937 the toolroom activists displayed a new confidence. With skilled labour shortages prevailing in Birmingham, they perceived themselves to be in a stronger position and were anxious to test its bargaining potential. In the machine shops two non-Party skilled men also began to build up the AEU. One of them, Frank Key, had been recently recruited by George Crane. Both men were committed to union organization, but were only interested in their skilled workmates.[30] The AEU at Longbridge remained a 'skilled man's union'.

TGWU members and full-time officials tried to take advantage of the AEU's omission. By 1938 the TGWU had only managed to recruit 1000 members, 'a small minority of semi-skilled members at Austin'.[31] In the circumstances it was remarkable that the T&G was able to maintain a continuous existence inside the factory. There were two activists, Freda Nokes and Karl Kirton, who were undaunted by the unwelcoming terrain and continued to recruit women into the TGWU. Kirton had been recruited into the AEU initially by Party activists with whom he was friendly because of his left-wing views. He left the AEU when he found that his women colleagues could not join.

Freda Nokes had joined the Workers' Union (WU) during the 1914–18 war which had amalgamated into the T&G in 1929. She had been 'union-minded' because her grandfather had been prominent in the 1913 wave of strikes in the Black Country when the WU had established a strong regional presence.[32] As a result of their joint efforts, the TGWU established a viable bridgehead in the semi-skilled workforce at Longbridge from which it was never subsequently dislodged.

Where management were tolerant towards unions, the fortunes of Party activists were very different. This is illustrated by the renaissance in trade unionism at Napier's aero-engine works at Acton Vale in West London. Austin's management stifled every attempt to re-establish the effective shopfloor organization which they had been compelled to concede at Longbridge during the 1914–18 war. In Napier's the 1922 Lock-Out had probably precipitated the progressive atrophy of shopfloor organization. After a gap of over ten years, the outlook for unions on the shopfloor was transformed, first by the favourable economic conditions of rearmament and second by the arrival in 1936 of Fred Arter in the grinding shop.[33]

Arter was a Party veteran who had gone to the USA to work and agitate in the car factories. He returned to England after being blacklisted. He persuaded his fellow grinders at Napier's to elect him shop steward, an official with whom management had not had to contend for a long time. His success in winning concessions for the grinders in skirmishes with management were soon the main topic of conversation in the other shops on the site. The consensus was that Arter was a cheeky outsider. Despite this parochial response, the results he gained from being brazen and having a go induced other shops to nurture their own grievances.

Within 12 months, Arter had drawn energetic young men into union activity. Without warming to this battle-hardened and rather brittle man from the Midlands, they were impressed by his independence and determination. First the milling shop decided they needed their own shop steward. As other shops followed suit, Arter revived the shop stewards' committee and became its convener. The growing numbers on the committee met regularly after work in a nearby cafe. It was not until the war that Arter pressed management to reinstate the full panoply of the previous wartime engineering procedure with a joint works comittee.

Napier's operated on traditional engineering lines and there were a majority of skilled workers in the various shops. Unlike in car factories, there was not a polarized division between the skilled toolroom and the majority semi-skilled workforce. Management and the workforce accepted the AEU as the legitimate union and recruitment proceeded without the impediment of craft exclusiveness.

Arter and West London AEU branch officers were genuinely indifferent as to whether new members were skilled or not. They were also immune from the ASE tradition that craftsmen should show their commitment to the union by holding a Section I green card. Section I was only open to craftsmen and its higher subscription included the considerable friendly society benefits which the ASE had pioneered in the nineteenth century. However Ralph Fuller, a skilled miller, became a Section V red card holding member of Acton 2 branch in the late 1920s without giving it a second thought. The semi-skilled section subscriptions were considerably cheaper and he had a wife and mortgage.[34]

Arter preached the offensive and self-confident gospel of trade unionism as class war. In addition to his uncompromising convictions, he had acquired a marked reluctance to provoke battle. (In the United States he had presumably watched the loss of terrain and demoralization which usually accompanied hard-fought protracted strikes.) The pattern of his generalship in the 'economic struggle' consisted of leading prudently conceived and carefully executed skirmishes involving low risk.

There were nearby engineering and aircraft factories with Party activists, Handley Page's at Cricklewood, Douple's and AEI at Hendon, and Glacier Metal at Wembley, where sporadic militant strikes with mixed results had become almost routine.[35] Arter achieved the twin goals of building AEU activism and consolidating the Party as a visible presence with the minimum use of force. Although he introduced *New Propellor* into the works, he also apparently took care to keep Napier's away from active involvement in the Aircraft Shop Stewards National Council.[36]

Because most shops in Napier's operated on piece-work and had batch production, there were ample opportunities for confrontations involving the timing of jobs and rate-fixing. Ralph Fuller remembered that Napier's management would meet Arter with another shop steward on an 'informal' basis. As a new shop steward in the milling shop, Fuller had dealt with piece-work problems about twice a week. No miller had wanted to shoulder the onerous responsibility of being shop steward, so Fuller and another young colleague agreed to share the milling shop steward's job.

During 1937 Arter argued with management that rate-fixers should not use the stopwatch which could split seconds in piece-work timings. He was eventually successful and timings were done by the clock on the wall which only measured minutes. Arter also proposed that the time saved as a result of retimings should be compensated by workers being paid bonus not merely on half, but the whole saving. He pointed out that productivity would increase as a result. Management, after 'chewing it over' agreed. All jobs were then retimed, and 'everyone knew where they were'.[37]

Arter presided over a cumulative change in shopfloor attitudes. A critical mass of the workforce accepted his vision that their working life consisted of manœuvreing within carefully drawn battle lines between 'us' and management. Fuller reflected that Napier's workers had come to understand they had to choose between loyalty to management and trade union. They chose trade union loyalty and became 'class conscious'. By 1938–39:

> We had a great deal of influence in the factory from the point of view of friends in management. People in management were impressed by organised labour and realised that men who had worked at Napier's for 20–25 years had taken our stand on the side of the working class. That integrity got through.
>   We learned how to use our power. It was straightforward as long as you knew what you wanted. The transition to this position was smooth as long as the demand you were making was not extravagant.[38]

Napier's management accepted readily enough the conventions of collective bargaining which Arter practised and disseminated. They conceded substantial ground within the established boundaries of the 1914–18 workshop bargaining procedure and evidently did not feel their prerogative under serious threat. Moreover, the return of regular and restrained factory negotiations was not occurring only in Napier's. The Manchester Metal Bureau was receiving regular reports from factories where strong shop stewards' committees were recognized and were winning concessions from management.[39]

As the international situation worsened, keen young trade unionists at Napier's progressed from fighting their own grievances to develop a compelling interest in the rest of the world. The young millers all belonged to the Left Book Club, which was probably introduced into Napier's by Arter. During the mid-day break they enjoyed discussing the books in the large park across the road. Napiers' stewards went on the Arms for Spain demonstrations in 1939 and were active in collecting money for Spanish orphans. Arter had interceded with a sympathetic manager to find a job for an International Brigade veteran.

A Communist group operated inside Napier's by 1939. Like most other Party factory groups before the war, Napier's hardly conformed to the closely knit, tightly disciplined cell which the Comintern had envisioned.[40] British Party activists adapted the Comintern model to their own conditions. Factory groups did not agree a detailed strategy formally binding on members in a democratically centralist fashion. Nor was their membership usually confined to Party members.

Napier's factory group was not unusual in relying largely on self-selection. Any steward who felt committed to these aims was welcomed. Ralph Fuller recalled that when someone felt they had become 'one of us' at Napier's, they became part of the group. They were not asked whether they had a paid-up Party card. 'Many people thought they knew who had party cards, but they didn't.'[41] These 'sympathisers' might join the Party in the fulness of time but they were not pressurized to do so. Party shopfloor activists generally waited for evidence that someone was 'ready' before encouraging them to join.

They were in fact a development of the more informal groups of 'reform' and socialist union activists in factories and union branches before the 1914–18 war. The Metal Fractions in Manchester and Sheffield were also functioning on a non-partisan basis: any committed militant was admitted and treated equally. Bob Lovell's refusal to distance himself from the Party after his expulsion in 1938 is another indication of the continuity of this 'reform' tradition. Most union activists in south-east Essex continued to believe that Lovell was a Communist throughout the war. Neither Lovell nor local Party activists made any attempt to clarify this case of mistaken identity.[42]

Within the framework of revolutionary pragmatism Party activists used the factory group to advance trade unionism and engage management in disputes when the occasion arose to win concessions and encroach on their prerogative. They functioned as 'kitchen cabinets' and were perceived as subordinate and complementary to their shop stewards/works committees. There was a clear advantage in having an informal forum for talking through and digesting situations before binding decisions had to be taken in the shop stewards' committee. (Like the British cabinet, engineering shop stewards' committees operated the doctrine of collective responsibility, an unpluralist undemocratic but necessary practice if effective leadership was to be maintained.) The habit of reflecting collectively in a supportive atmosphere about the problems facing the factory and teasing out the wide variety of ways in which union forces could respond was invaluable. When this reflection proceeded under the guidance of veterans, a factory group could quickly become indispensable to the shop stewards committee's successful functioning.

There were audacious attempts in 1938–39 by Party trade unionists at Siemens' cablemaking works in Greenwich and Pressed Steel in Oxford to seize large amounts of territory outside the conventional limits assigned to unions in collective bargaining. Neither offensive came in response to worsened conditions or increased expectation and both were initially spectacularly successful. Management then counter-attacked with determination to retake the ground and without hesitation sacked the Party 'ringleaders' facing down the spontaneous opposition against the victimizations. When full-time union officials declined to sanction strikes, the Party Centre privately acquiesced in these decisions and ensured that Party activists organized ordered retreats at both factories.

It is notable that Pressed Steel and Siemens factory groups operated along the more orthodox democratic centralist model to which the Party Centre still officially adhered. The groups viewed their job as representing the Party inside the factory. They sought to emulate what they believed to be best bolshevik practice. Charlie Wellard organized formal Communist education classes for Siemens recruits after work on the local Workers' Education Association (WEA) premises. The Siemens and Pressed Steel factory groups also engaged in the serious business of promulgating battle plans. Instead of a kitchen cabinet, they functioned as a general staff. This meant that the shop stewards committees operating at the two sites were not fully sovereign; they carried out decisions arrived at beforehand by the Party factory group.

After the 1934 strike, the principal activists at Pressed Steel had joined the Party and set about building union organization. The TGWU 5/60 factory branch achieved virtually 100 per cent union membership with management reluctantly acknowledging the union's shopfloor clout. Ernest Bevin and the TGWU national engineering officer Andrew Dalgleish used to boast that 5/60 was the largest union branch in Europe.

> 5/60 Branch meetings were unique. They were held every Sunday morning in a big hall – but you couldn't get in unless you came early. Always full. Right through the 30s. It was fantastic discussions . . .
> We had the biggest [Party factory] group in the country . . . At the time of the Popular Front you could literally command thousands of workers to take part in demonstrations by just putting leaflets out. There was a 'Soviet Britain' pamphlet. We used to sell them hundreds at a time in the factory. During the Spanish War you could tell the lads to bring in a cart load of stuff and they'd bring it in.[43]

During April 1937 management were put under the duress of a strike and conceded the right to negotiate on the union side of the factory's collective bargaining machinery solely to the 5/60 branch officers without the previous sanction of their full-time officials. This was a radical departure from engineering official procedure which management immediately regretted, as did the T&G hierarchy. The TGWU GEC had only recently created a new full-time official's post in Oxford evidently because they were alarmed at the extent of branch officers' comparative immunity from official control. In a departure from the union's practice, its first incumbent, Jack Thomas, was appointed from outside the region.[44]

Thomas agreed with Pressed Steel management that the *status quo ante* must be re-instituted and shopfloor control rolled back. In the face of the evidence that management and Thomas were conniving at a counter-offensive the 5/60 branch officers remained self-confident and did not take any steps to defend their exposed position. In October 1938 the company duly gave notice that it was returning to the old procedure which vested negotiating authority in the full-time union official. The difference which their move made to shopfloor practice was that a local grievance could no longer be so easily escalated or swiftly followed through by the branch activists. The Pressed Steel branch officers faced a change in the balance of advantage back towards management's side.

It would have been possible for the 5/60 officers to retreat in an orderly fashion and await opportunities to retake their lost official power in a piecemeal fashion. We have observed that Party activists in established engineering factories were winning substantial concessions under this *ancien regime* easily enough. If Thomas was determined to crush not merely to curb their authority, this strategy would have been feasible. However, this strategy of damage limitation was evidently not contemplated by the branch or the Party factory group.

In November 1938, the 5/60 branch secretary, Tom Harris, was summarily dismissed for leaving his department to negotiate on a dispute elsewhere in the factory. Militant shop stewards and Harris led an immediate down-tools. Norman Brown remembered that

> they [workers] marched right through the factory from one end to the other. I nearly got killed. There was literally thousands of workers behind us, all marching . . . and all these workers were pushing us to get through to the other departments . . . They had a meeting in the Press Shop and there was workers everywhere – stenographers, typists, God knows what, all over the machines taking the stuff down that the workers who were the leaders, who were on the top of the presses were saying. And they turned machines over, they turned car bodies over. Just erupted.[45]

Management now had cause to summarily dismiss all the 'troublemakers'. With the core of 5/60 and Party leadership gone from the factory, the spontaneous protest petered out and the Party militants evidently made no attempt to organize an unofficial 'rank-and-file' strike from outside. Jack Thomas pursued the dismissals through the management appeals procedure, not surprisingly without result. The TGWU took no further action. Bevin and Dalgleish might have interceded privately for the men in view of their close involvement in Pressed Steel since 1934. If assurances of good behaviour had been forthcoming it is possible management might have reinstated some of their victims.

Bevin and Dalgleish evidently placed the union's central authority above humanitarian concerns however. 5/60 branch had been using the union's authority under the new procedure to systematically probe areas of management's sole prerogative, and where their defences proved weak to attack and occupy them. Bevin and his full-time officials recognized that their branch officers' success had destabilized the internal situation to the extent that management believed that the sackings were necessary to restore their credibility and shaken self-confidence. Bevin's other concern was to maintain the union's authority over its own lay machinery. 5/60 branch officers had chosen not to heed clear warnings from Thomas about their untenable position. In the circumstances, the TGWU GEC acquiesced in their sacrifice with a clear conscience.[46]

For its part, the Party Centre made no attempt to apply pressure on the TGWU to support its rank-and-file activists. Indeed the Centre apparently ensured that the local Oxford Party remained uncharacteristically passive in the face of the victimizations. The *Daily Worker* would normally have given the Pressed Steel events great prominence. However, nothing appeared in the paper and there were no reports in *Labour Monthly* or *Labour Research* either. The attempt to delay the news reaching militants and Party activists outside Oxford was apparently made to pre-empt opportunities for any unofficial sympathetic action to be organized and also to minimize the Party's loss of face for allowing the sacrifice of rank-and-file activists.

The Centre's conspicuous inaction and cover-up exercise should be viewed in the context of the tacit armistice which the Party concluded with Bevin in April 1938. Each side had given ground in order to forestall the threat of the breakaway union on the London buses. Bevin knew that without the Party's support the TGWU had no hope of fighting, let alone defeating, the NPWU, the London busmen's breakaway union. Pollitt and Campbell required Bevin's continuing support for London bus activists to be able to resume their full democratic rights inside his union.[47] The armistice was fragile but mutually necessary and withstood the stress imposed by the Pressed Steel events.

Almost a year after the Oxford martyrdoms, Charlie Wellard was sacked from Siemens. The *Daily Worker* reported his case sympathetically if somewhat circumspectly. Wellard was an AEU member and relations between the Party and that union were considerably easier than with the TGWU. The unofficial strike in his defence lasted much longer than the spontaneous revolt at Pressed Steel and news of it was more difficult to suppress because Greenwich was an integral part of the effective communications network of London AEU activists. The Pressed Steel events had been isolated from the normal 'rank-and-file' engineering links not only by social geography, but also because most AEU militants regarded the TGWU as outside their horizon.

Wellard was victimized for the same reason as the 5/60 branch officers, his invasion of management territory had been too successful. In common with most large manufacturing sites, Siemens had conceded shop-steward organization and workplace collective bargaining during the 1914–18 war. On his arrival in the firm in 1932 Wellard had found only three surviving and 'corrupt' shop stewards. His achievement in building 100 per cent union organization and a full complement of shop stewards over five years is all the more impressive, because he was a toolmaker in a minority union on the site. He was an exceptionally charismatic leader whose skirmishing and negotiating skills were virtually self-taught.[48]

Before Siemens, Wellard worked at the nearby Johnson & Phillips (J&P's) cablemaking works. Union organization there had remained in somewhat better order. He joined the Communist Party in 1931 in revulsion against Ramsay Macdonald's 'betrayal'. One of his older workmates at J&P's remarked, 'You're a Communist'. He had set out to discover more about this 'Communist thing' and never looked back. His local Party contained few union activists but he fondly remembered his first political mentors, two teachers Sandy and Kath Duncan. He successfully gingered up the union organization at J&P's, supporting the efforts of other Party members who had found work there. He retained an interest and influence in the factory after departing for Siemens.

Wellard asked the London District Party if there were a young woman who wanted to do daily mass work in Siemens. He was conscious of the need for a young woman to organize the large numbers of young women workers. The district sent Myf Hygot to see Wellard. She subsequently started at Siemens and became an effective shop steward. She was sacked soon after Wellard in 1939. Wellard recruited the majority semi-skilled workers into the NUGMW because Siemens was not an engineering factory and not a member of the EEF. He chose the NUGMW because the local TGWU official was a downright reactionary. (Dogged reaction was a common characteristic of South London TGWU officials in this period.) The NUGMW official was left-wing, helpful and sympathetic throughout the 1930s.[49]

Siemens' management were forced by Wellard's energetic harrying attacks to give ground steadily. They did so unwillingly and in bad grace.

But they had little choice when Wellard had organized the factory around a community trade union culture and loyalty to 'one's own'. The tight collectivity he created compares to the class-consciousness successfully preached by Arter at Napier's. Like Arter, Wellard's generalship produced concessions and increased union power through the deployment of minimum force. He led skirmishes and resisted temptations for a trial of strength with management through calling a set-piece battle.

The shop stewards' committee continued to make advances into management terrain right up to the moment of Wellard's sacking. The committee's full complement was 40 stewards of whom Wellard recruited a substantial number into the Party. Johnny Campbell was assigned to the Party factory group as a political instructor in 1936 when the London district was attempting to regularize factory organization. Wellard remembered that he had sat quietly smoking his pipe, content for the most part not to intervene in discussions about factory tactics.[50]

A measure of Wellard's unique position and manœuvring ability was the fact that Siemens and Johnson & Phillips were the only places in London where young lads came out to join the second wave of apprentices' strikes in October 1937. When the second wave of apprentices' strikes started in September 1937, Ted Bramley called leading AEU activists into the Party District office to urge them to precipitate similar action in London. They had all confidently agreed, but only Wellard fulfilled his promise. Wellard also worked closely with the AEU South London ODD to help union activists at the Standard Telephone Company (STC) in Woolwich to gain recognition. Every week for a period of some years the two travelled across on the ferry to meet AEU stalwarts from STC in a pub where they would discuss conditions at the works and plan the men's next move.[51]

Wellard was sacked on 5 April 1939, without warning, in the midst of a serious outbreak of lightning strikes in various shops. There was an unofficial strike organized in his defence which lasted until 24 April. In the midst of the strike, Wellard was summoned to see Harry Pollitt. Pollitt asked him whether he thought they would win the strike. He replied no, truthfully but somewhat reluctantly. Pollitt agreed and commiserated.[52] I think it likely that Ted Bramley and/or Joe Scott arranged Pollitt's intervention to see that Wellard did not break faith with union loyalism. He was well known to be his own man and no automatic supporter of the constitutional militants. London District relied on Pollitt's charisma to ensure that Wellard complied with the priorities of revolutionary pragmatism. Forty-five years later, Charlie Wellard's eyes still shone as he recalled his audience with Pollitt at this fateful juncture.

The *Daily Worker* reported the solid unofficial strike and the growing local support for Charlie Wellard with great enthusiasm. They also canvassed the case for official union support against Siemens, a German firm with 'Nazi shareholders'. On 11 April Wellard and Siemens strikers went to a dinner hour meeting of 2–3000 workers at J&P's. The *Daily Worker* reported the events. Charlie Wellard had declared: 'We in Siemens understand that we are in the front-line trenches in a general attack on the trade union movement. We feel that we are able to hold the fort until the whole organized movement is able to give us effective help.' He added that the

> destruction of the Siemens' Shop Stewards Committee would be followed by an attack on their own trade union officials. As they marched off, banners gripped firmly, the proud bearing of these men and youth, boys and girls alike, flung the lie into the teeth of those who say that the old spirit has gone out of the working class, that workers 'cannot stick together' . . . Speakers declared that the Shop Stewards Movement [at Siemens] since its inception had fought casualisation and the introduction of cheap labour. Had obtained one week's holiday with pay, and higher wages for some departments.[53]

However, when the AEU Executive ordered the strikers back to work, the *Daily Worker* duly invoked trade union loyalty and the need to present a united front. The strikers took a collective decision to return to work on Monday, 24 April at a Saturday afternoon meeting at the Woolwich Empire. Charlie Wellard himself put the strike committee's recommendation to return to work. 'When Mr. Wellard broke down with emotion, the whole of the audience rose and cheered him for several minutes.' The chairman assured the meeting that the fight had not ended; they were returning in a body to build and strengthen the shop stewards and the union.[54]

Despite Charlie Wellard's ringing appeals to the rest of the trade union movement, Party trade union activists were not stirred into action. They responded sympathetically but stoically to the victimizations as a regrettable but often unavoidable fate for union activists. They were accustomed to operating from positions of weakness and accepted the sack as being an occupational hazard for shop stewards. By 1939 most Party shopfloor activists in engineering had either been martyred or acquired a prudent survival instinct which kept them from moving too far beyond the conventions of engineering procedure. However, the Pressed Steel and Siemens sackings had not taken place in circumstances of trade union weakness.

Charlie Wellard and the TGWU 5/60 branch officers had occupied an exceptionally strong position, an unfamiliar situation for most contemporary activists. They had been stopped in their tracks because they had been not only audacious but also successful in taking new ground from management. Though the circumstances were atypical, the sackings raised a crucial question: whether workplace collective bargaining could function when the boundaries of sole managerial prerogative and joint regulation were disputed. Since most Party activists were still trying to establish shopfloor union organization on a secure foundation, the question might seem irrelevant. Nevertheless, until it was settled there could be no permanent advances made by the trade union side on the shopfloor. Shop stewards' committees might press their advantage home in temporarily favourable circumstances, but they remained vulnerable to management counter-attack when the balance of forces moved away from the union side.

It seems likely that Campbell at least was well aware of the need to address the question. We shall observe that in 1942–43 the Party and Campbell in particular argued that the unions had to place shop steward organization on a more secure basis. However, in 1939 neither Campbell nor Pollitt was able to devote much time to this domestic and indeed parochial engineering issue. They were pre-occupied by the growing crisis in Europe and profoundly concerned with how the CPGB ought to respond to the war which activists had been expecting since Munich.

Notes

1. For the PCF's fortunes, see Jackson, J., 1988, *The Popular Front in France*, Cambridge University Press: 85–112 and 215–34.
2. For the second wave of apprentices' strikes and the Coventry events see Fishman, N., 1987, 'The British Communist Party and the Trade Unions 1933–1945', unpublished manuscript, Warwick Modern Records Centre (MRC): 322–6 and 378–81.
3. But Fred Smith, the AEU General Secretary, was uneasy about the Party's visible presence in the strikes. He spoke in Carlisle at the end of October and said that AEU officers 'needed no assistance from those whose furious howling often clouds their pernicious movements under a guise of an explosive leadership, but who are seeking to undermine the constitutional authority of the union and degrading a serious problem by deceitful tactics' (*The Times*, 25 October 1937).
4. For the Labour Programme, see Bullock, 1960, Vol. I, op. cit.: 597–8. Bullock states that many of the programme's demands, in particular the new and comprehensive pensions plan, raising the school leaving age and reducing the working week to 40 hours had been first set out in Bevin's 'Plan for Two Million Workless', written in 1933.
5. *Daily Worker*, 5 August 1937.
6. For the Unity Campaign, see p. 228.
7. 'Friday Night till Monday Morning', CPGB pamphlet issued 21 September 1937.
8. Bullock, 1960, op. cit., Vol. I: 558. For the 1933 ILO conference, see ibid.: 506–8.
9. Ibid.: 575.

10. See for example TGWU GEC minutes, 17 April 1934 and 27 February 1939, General Secretary's Reports.

11. See *AEU National Committee Reports*, 1926, 1930, 1935.

12. The first article in the *Daily Worker* supporting the admission of women appeared on 2 April 1940. There was a leader on 9 April 1940. These were undoubtedly timed to influence the 1940 AEU Rules Revision Committee. This time the motion to admit women moved by Tommy Sillars and seconded by Vic Wymans was more narrowly defeated, by 25–14. (Two 'rank-and-file' delegates who regularly supported Party motions voted against admitting women.) The closer result reflected the Party's more public stand in favour, the AEU Executive's discreet support and also the vicissitudes of wartime circumstances which had resulted in AEU shop stewards recruiting women workers in large numbers into the TGWU. For the eventual admission of women in January 1943, see Fishman MRC, loc. cit.: 264–5 and 309–11.

13. *Daily Worker*, 30 December 1938. The same argument had been deployed in an end-of-year editorial on 8 December 1937. The author was probably Campbell on both occasions.

14. See Appendix 1. It is likely that the definition of 'official' used here denoted branch and district lay officials, but did not include shop stewards or conveners.

15. *Daily Worker*, 13 January 1939.

16. For the shadow factories see p. 153.

17. At the time, there were only two or three Party delegates on the District Committee. Ambrose joined George Crane and Ted Baker on the Committee in 1935–36. (Interview with Les Ambrose by N. Fishman.) Crane was elected Chairman of the AEU Distict Committee in April 1939. For Birmingham, see N. Fishman, MRC, loc. cit.: 359–63. In Coventry, the District Committee had to be bamboozled by national officials into abandoning its craft exclusiveness. For Coventry, see Carr, 1982, *Twilight of the Comitern* op. cit.: 435 and 448–9. For discussions of the AEU's record in recruiting semi-skilled workers to Section V before 1939, see Fishman, MRC, loc. cit.: 302–311 and Claydon, 1981, *The Development of Trades Unionism among British Automobile and Aircraft Workers, c. 1914–1946*, op. cit.: 360–1 and 368–9 and 498.

18. Quoted in Hastings, R.P., 1959, 'The Labour Movement in Birmingham, 1927–45', University of Birmingham MA, p. 87. See also *Daily Worker*, 13 and 18 April 1938. Billy Stokes was a leading Party activist in Coventry who in 1936 sought the Party's endorsement for his candidacy for Organizing Divisional Delegate. The National Metal Bureau supported George Crane who had moved to Birmingham from London in 1936. The Midlands Metal Fraction, however, backed Stokes on the grounds that he was better known than Crane. Stokes was also better liked by Party activists according to Harold Marsh (interview with N. Fishman). Stokes eventually managed to reverse the National Metal Bueau's decision and received the Party's endorsement. He won the election, but left the Party shortly afterwards. In the circumstances his positive verdict on the strike was hardly gratuitous.

19. *New Propellor*, Vol. 3 No. 7, August 1938.

20. *Daily Worker*, 13 April 1938.

21. Interview with Les Ambrose by N. Fishman. Claydon points out that the

numbers of skilled workers in motor car manufacturing actually increased in the interwar period, and presumably this was also true of shadow factories using motor car manufacturing methods. Op.cit., p. 331, fn. 1 and pp. 346–7. See also *Political and Economic Planning*, No. 140, 7 February 1939, 'Labour Relations in Engineering', p. 5.

22. *New Propellor*, Vol. 3 No. 8, September 1938. See also Hastings, op. cit.: 87.

23. Hastings, op. cit., p. 88 and *Daily Worker*, 8 September 1938. Before the strike Teddy Ager had already attended two works conferences over the issue of payment of the skilled district rate. Management had refused any concession.

24. It was managements' practice in the new car factories to pay hourly rates substantially below the union's rates in all shops. However, weekly earnings were considerably above the union's prescribed hourly rate. The difference was made up by the bonus paid on payments-by-result. Hence the vital importance of timings for a job, the rate-fixer and his stopwatch for car workers, both skilled and semi-skilled.

25. Fred Smith's description of the ASSNC at a meeting in Chester on 16 April 1937 (*Daily Telegraph*, 19 April 1937).

26. *New Propellor*, Vol. 3 No. 8, September 1938.

27. Interview with Les Ambrose by N. Fishman. The previous convener had been a TGWU grinder and an ex-music hall performer. The TGWU gained 300 members from the 1938 Aero strike. (Region 5 Committee minutes, loc. cit., 20 October 1938.)

28. See *Daily Worker*, 13 and 17 November 1936; Hastings, op.cit.: 70–71; and Claydon, 1981, op. cit.: 105–7. Austin's employed 20,000 workers at this time; the strike involved *c*. 5000.

29. The TGWU reported gains of 300 members. Region 5 Committee Minutes, loc. cit., 21 January 1937.

30. Interview with Harold Marsh by N. Fishman. The Party factory group also began to take itself more seriously at this time. Marsh remembered that they recruited new Party members and that six Party members had met regularly in a member's house near the works. He worked in the toolroom and had joined the Party in Wolverhampton where George Crane had worked in the late 1920s and had established a strong Party presence in the AEU district.

31. Claydon, 1981, op. cit.: 107. He quotes the TGWU National Organizer in November 1937 'Union organization and membership is on the upgrade in the Austin factory.'

32. Steven Tolliday, unpublished paper on trade union organization of women workers in the Midlands, LSE Carworkers Seminar, April 1983.

33. Interviews with Ralph Fuller by N. Fishman. Fuller's father was a coppersmith at Napier's and in 1922 found his son work there as a youth trainee; Napier's were saving money by cutting down on apprentices. His father was a union man and Fuller joined the AEU as soon as he was old enough. His branch met once a fortnight and there would be about thirty members in attendance. A local dispute would double these numbers.

34. Les Ambrose remembered that in the north-east of England Section I members in the craft shops could still refuse to work with red card holding members in the 1960s (interview with Les Ambrose by N. Fishman). Throughout this period and up to at least the 1960s activists standing for

election to higher lay positions inside the union structure, e.g. delegate to divisional committee or National Committee and to full-time positions, found it politic to hold a green card irrespective of the district where they were members.

35. See Jack Tanner's ODD reports in *AEU Journal*, January, March, May and October 1935. *Engineers Bulletin*, Nos. 6 and 7, n.d., *c.* April–May 1935. *Daily Worker*, 30 September 1935 and 11 July 1936.

36. Reports about Napier's appeared infrequently in *New Propellor*. For example, in August 1936, *NP* reported that Napier's had elected seven shop stewards (Vol. I No. 11). Zinkin established *NP*'s office above the café in Acton Vale where the stewards committee met. There is no evidence that Napier's had affiliated to the ASSNC, though Zinkin states that he had frequent discussions with Napier's shop stewards during their dinner hour. (Zinkin, 1985, op. cit.: 126.)

37. Interviews with Ralph Fuller by N. Fishman.

38. Interviews with Ralph Fuller op. cit.

39. See N. Fishman, Warwick MRC, loc. cit.: 313 and 342–6 and Minutes of Manchester Metal Bureau, *passim*.

40. Party factory groups were denominated 'factory cells' in the 1920s reflecting the desire to import bolshevik terminology into Britain. It was probably after the 7th World Congress that they were renamed 'factory groups'.

41. Interview with Ralph Fuller, loc. cit.

42. Lovell was expelled for his refusal to stand down in the elections for AEU National Organiser in favour of the candidates endorsed by the Party's National Metal Fraction, George Crane and Tommy Sillars.

43. Interview with Norman Brown by N. Fishman. Norman Brown started at Pressed Steel soon after the 1934 strike at the age of 20 having already led a strike in Bristol. The Pressed Steel strike leader, Dai Huish, who became chairman of 5/60, recruited him into the Communist Party in 1936–37. His father was a Wigan engineer and militant trade unionist at the Leyland works.

44. Thomas was from Swansea where the TGWU had contended with militant Party busmen practising 'rank-and-filism'. The Region 5 Committee decided that there were no suitable candidates from Oxford or the rest of the region for the Oxford post. (TGWU Region 5 Committee minutes, 22 October 1936). Norman Brown remembered that Thomas had been reasonable in his personal relations with Party activists and always described himself as left wing.

45. Interview with Norman Brown.

46. Interview with Norman Brown and Richard Whiting, 1977, 'The Working Class in the "New Industry" Towns Between the Wars: The Case of Oxford', Oxford DPhil: 185, 268–73. Harris became a coal merchant in Oxford.

47. See pp. 127–9.

48. Wellard's father was a blacksmith's striker in South London; his father and brothers were all union members. His political interest was awakened by reading one of his brothers' copy of *The Ragged Trousered Philanthropists* at the age of 16, interviews with Charlie Wellard by N. Fishman.

49. Ibid.

50. Ibid.

51. Ibid.

52. Ibid.
53. *Daily Worker*, 12 April 1939. See also *Daily Worker*, 13, 15, 17, 18, 20, 21, 22, 24, 25 April 1939.
54. *Daily Worker*, 25 April 1939.

CHAPTER NINE

Organizing the United Front against Fascism

Communists were not alone in their recognition of the Fascist threat to European security and democracy in the 1930s, but they were certainly in the van in Britain. Overt anti-Fascism was regarded as impractical by the Westminster political establishment who believed that ordinary people did not wish to be disturbed by rehearsals of the increasingly problematic situation in Europe. Politicians and journalists for the most part acquiesced in this *de facto* moratorium on public debate. The serious agonizing about how to deal with Hitler and Mussolini took place largely behind closed doors within the precincts of Westminster.

A few hardy individuals like Churchill and Aneurin Bevan insisted on the need to address civil society directly and did so by speaking very much out of turn in the House of Commons. Ernest Bevin and Citrine perceived the implications of Fascism for trade unions only too well from their participation in various trade union international forums. Both men were ahead of the Labour front bench in their forthright declarations of the need for Britain to oppose Fascism. However, in most working-class communities and factories Communists were usually the first and often the only political activists propagating the case for opposing Fascism at home and abroad.

Communists argued that a defensive alliance between Britain, France and the USSR was both necessary and sufficient to contain Fascism. The Party's agitation was aimed at a popular level and was intended to involve people at the workplace and local communities. It was received by an attentive audience, many of whom became sufficiently committed to participate in some 'united front' activity. Though Party activists' increasing involvement in European events was not unique, they devoted more time and energy to arousing popular interest than their local Labour or Conservative counterparts. In many places where Labour organization was thin on the ground, Party activists were the only missionaries against Fascism and for peace. Ben Pimlott quotes Richard Crossman lamenting in the *New Statesman* in May 1937 that Labour left-wingers were failing to reach the 'millions of people [who] still read the racing page . . . and they have not seen a Labour canvasser for five years, far less seen any signs of practical activity by the local Labour Party'.[1]

At the beginning of 1937 the CPGB joined with the Socialist League, a recent left-wing discussion/pressure group inside the Labour Party and the Independent Labour Party (ILP) to launch a Unity Campaign 'against the National Government, against Fascism, against War'. The Party Centre was confidently expecting the arrival of the national militant upsurge and Unity Campaign activities were accordingly orientated towards achieving unity in the domestic class struggle. On 7 April 1937, the *Daily Worker*'s leader rehearsed the evidence and berated the TUC General Council for denying 'its elementary duty to the movement . . . [and not] setting the whole of its resources and machinery to work to inspire and unite the workers' ranks'.

'It is precisely the uniting of the wages movement which the Unity Campaign is so vigorously engaged in pressing . . . In every area it is strongly raising the issue and meeting with an enthusiastic reception and response.'[2]

The Unity Campaign's instant success in attracting large audiences at public meetings and many concerned participants was inspiring, but proved short-lived. The Socialist League was riven by internal controversy about how to respond to the Labour Party Executive's and TUC's outrage at its alliance with the Communist Party. The collapse of the national militant upsurge in May had also frustrated the Campaign's ambitious plans. By June it was self-evident that Unity Campaigners were supernumerary on the domestic front. By the autumn, the Unity Campaign petered out amid disappointed acrimony in the same quarters which had welcomed it a few months previously.[3]

The failure of the national militant upsurge to appear and catapult the Communist Party into the forefront of the Labour Movement moved the British Party leadership to recast its previous interpretation of the composition of the 'united people's front' which the Seventh Comintern Congress in 1935 had enjoined affiliated parties to pursue.[4] As recently as the 14th British Party Congress in May 1937, Harry Pollitt had justified the Party leadership's virtually exclusive concentration on building working-class unity.

> In a country like Britain, where the industrial workers are the decisive majority of the population, where the most class-conscious section of the population is already organised industrially and politically, our first job is to bring about unity within the Labour Movement and when that has been achieved, you will have the irresistible magnet that will attract to its side all the progressive forces in this country.[5]

In the wake of the end of the London bus strike and the Harworth strike and the failure of engineering militants to ignite their industry into a national wages movement, the CPGB leadership evidently concluded that there was unlikely to be sufficient movement inside the trade unions to precipitate a 'real united front'. King Street examined the success of the Popular Front governments in France and Spain which were all-class alliances as an alternative political path and from 1938 adopted their strategy of inclusion. Everyone and every organization which supported democracy, including bourgeois and petty bourgeois individuals and their class institutions, qualified as an ally in the fight for democracy and against Fascism.

This new interpretation of the 'united people's front' did not mean that the Party Centre ceased to stress the importance of working inside the Labour Movement. Harry Pollitt's speech to an overflow meeting in the Manchester Free Trade Hall in February 1938 reflected the difference. He was giving the keynote speech in the Party's Crusade for Unity. The *Daily Worker*'s leader underscored his message:

> The whole future of Labour in Britain depends on this overwhelming mass enthusiasm [at Pollitt's meeting] becoming linked to a united Labour movement. This is the meaning of Communist affiliation to the Labour Party ... The Communist Party has no wish to exploit the mass enthusiasm it is able to arouse today for any sectional aim, but only to strengthen it for the common interests of *the whole Labour Movement and of the people of this country*. In the words of Pollitt at Manchester:- 'We have only one thought in our minds; no narrow party aims, only the interests of *the overwhelming majority of the British people and only the unity of the Labour Movement* can give us the guarantee of success for a General Election.'[6]

The new strategy of inclusion brought two main practical changes of direction for Party activists. Communists were now prepared to work publicly with the Liberal Party and its activists as well as members of the *petit bourgeoisie* – shopkeepers, farmers, etc. – and acknowledge them as honourable allies. There was also a renewed emphasis placed on recruiting intellectuals into the Communist Party. As representatives of the progressive bourgeoisie, they were potentially useful in building support for an all-class alliance.[7]

This inclusive permutation of the 'real united front' resonated with indigenous radical populism[8], a hardy political tradition which had last been effectively invoked in British politics by Lloyd George in 1909–10. Many Labour activists, including the MPs D.N. Pritt and Aneurin Bevan, were inspired by the enthusiastic mass support which the Popular Front governments in France and Spain had mobilizd. They agreed that 'the British people' had to force the governing class to fight Fascism in Europe through the application of strong pressure on Parliament and shared Pollitt's and Campbell's desire to mobilize 'the people' here. They believed passionately that it was the Labour Party's duty to take the lead in such extra-parliamentary activity. Disappointed in their attempts to persuade the Labour Front Bench, they channelled their thwarted populist impulses into 'real united front' initiatives which local Party activists were taking.

From the autumn of 1937, Pollitt and Campbell concentrated their own and their members' energies into responding to the rapidly worsening international situation, fighting Fascism, supporting the Spanish Republican Government and the International Brigade in the Spanish Civil War, and promoting an Anglo-French-Soviet peace alliance. Pollitt and Campbell had assumed an increasingly active role in Europe. Campbell was the British representative to the Comintern and until the outbreak of war he made periodic trips to Moscow.[9] In July 1937, Pollitt made his second visit to the British Battalion of the International Brigade. In September, he met French Communist leaders in Paris. In December he visited the British Battalion again, and then attended the PCF's 11th Party Congress.[10] It is hardly surprising that they called on Party trade union activists to muster support for the Party's initiatives in these new arenas in addition to their daily mass work in the 'economic struggle'.

King Street cannot have been disappointed by the response. Trade union activists' commitment to agitating around the Spanish Civil War, promoting the Peace Alliance with the USSR and fighting Fascism was as earnest and enthusiastic as Pollitt's and Campbell's. The Party leadership and activists both were determined that the British working class should play its part in European events. Their keen desire was reinforced by the interest which they encountered on the shopfloor and in union branches. On the last occasion when Party members had systematically broached international issues, in the early 1930s, they had used Comintern jargon and esoteric Marxist–Leninist rhetoric. The Communists' pristine message had failed to inspire widespread interest in the early 1930s. But the party's anti-Fascism and related 'real united front' activities now became a positive asset providing many new recruits with a powerful motive for joining.

Jessica Ambrose remembered her initial impression of Birmingham Communists as a motley collection of 'unwashed bohemians'. Then from the mid-1930s the Birmingham Party began to recruit serious-minded young men and women like herself and husband Les. Party members built up their influence on the Birmingham Trades Council in order to direct it towards mobilizing popular support for Spanish loyalist causes.[11] Sid Atkin, the Communist President of the Birmingham Trades Council, remembered that the Council had inaugurated a scheme whereby trade union activists from all parties sponsored Basque refugees. Basque orphans were also found homes in South Wales, and house-to-house food collections for Spain became a regular feature of activity in the mining communities.[12] This pattern of Party members spearheading trade union and community activity was replicated elsewhere.

It is not surprising that many of the new recruits to the Communist Party at this time joined because of its position on Fascism and European events. They were not being driven by their experiences of hunger, unemployment or a consciousness of community suffering to a millenarian/ revolutionary commitment. They were interested in European events and viewed their commitment to a political party as being bound up with its *political* stand rather than what it was saying about the economic struggle and trade unions. Their own experience had not led them to view the domestic class struggle as the crucial influence shaping their own lives.

Jim Forde was a young time-served toolmaker growing up in Hayes in the late 1930s. He joined the AEU only after he had joined the Communist Party because he had worked in companies along the Great West Road where unions were not recognized and had never encountered the union's presence on the shopfloor. He joined the Communist Party because of its vigorous campaigning in the West Middlesex area over Spain. His branch told him that he should join the AEU and become a union activist, both of which 'tasks' he then performed with enthusiasm and interest.

Dick Etheridge had received engineering training at the local technical college in Birmingham in the mid-1930s. He became a Communist through his regular conversations with leading city Party members who were habitués of his father's all-night café where their political discussions would continue late into the night. The Party then encouraged him to find work in an engineering factory and join the AEU. We have already observed that Ralph Fuller had joined the AEU as soon as he was old enough because his father was a union man. However, his commitment to the CPGB arose both from the shining example on the shopfloor of Communist shop steward Fred Arter and the Party's politics about which he read in Left Book Club selections and *Labour Monthly*.

Benny Rothman had joined the YCL as an adolescent, having been drawn by its strong presence inside the substantial Jewish working-class community in Manchester. Adult Communist mentors urged him to find a job in engineering, specifically inside Metro-Vic, to assist the Party's attempt to make it a factory fortress. His keen interest in rambling had drawn him into exciting populist struggles to liberate the footpaths. Nevertheless, he had viewed his main commitment to the Party as being fulfilled at Metro-Vic inside the AEU and on the shopfloor.[13]

Alan McKinlay established that the leaders of the Scottish Apprentices' Strike had met first during activity around the Spanish Civil War. They did not find their own work an interesting topic of conversation. One participant recalled:

> Well I had met Stuart Watson [later chairman of the 1937 appren-
> tices' strike executive] and a couple of others through the YCL and
> the Spanish campaign before we came out on strike . . . Of course,
> we were more interested in Spain than we were in talking about our
> own factories . . . There was a lot of muttering among us boys at our
> work, but nothing else.[14]

Despite the National Council of Labour's dogmatic hostility, local
Labour activists continued to work enthusiastically with their Communist colleagues to organize campaigns in connection with the Spanish
Civil War under the auspices of trade unions, trades councils and *ad hoc*
'real united front' committees. Many Labour activists were drawn
towards Communism as a result of their anti-Fascist campaigning. The
Party Centre felt justified in encouraging them to remain Labour activists
while also holding a Communist Party card and participating in regular
consultations with the District Party leadership.[15] The Labour Party
Executive consistently refused to allow the CPGB to affiliate to the
Labour Party as a socialist organization on the same basis as the Fabian
Society or the CPGB's predecessor, the BSP. It seemed meet that keen
individuals should realize the aim of the 'real united front' for
Communist/Labour co-operation in their own persons.

Inside the unions it became increasingly problematic to distinguish
between Party and non-Party activists' response to the worsening international situation and the Chamberlain Government's manœuvres. As
early as the spring of 1935, Jack Little used the occasion of his inaugural
address as AEU President to attack the Government over the Incitement
to Disaffection Bill employing the same rhetoric as Pollitt or his AEU colleagues Bob Lovell and Wally Hannington were using at the time. In view
of their common pre-war political formation inside the trade union
'reform' movements and the BSP, this coincidence of expression (and
feeling) is hardly surprising.

> When talking of fascism we are inclined to think of Mosley, but
> Mosley and his blackshirts were mere puppets of the game, and of
> little or no consideration at all. What we recommended delegates to
> do was to watch the Government. Observe the nature of the legisla-
> tion the Government was responsible for if they wanted to appreci-
> ate the real significance of fascism in this country . . . The
> Government did not pass a measure like that [the Incitement to
> Disaffection Bill] for nothing. It was not a measure to be held up in
> the archives, but a measure to be used when the Government find it
> necessary to use it.[16]

In April 1938 the AEU Executive issued a Circular requesting all
branches to support Voluntary Industrial Action for Spain (VIAS) a 'real
united front' initiative in which AEU Party activists were playing an
important part.[17] Joe Scott was the VIAS treasurer and Jack Tanner had

piloted the case for the AEU to take up VIAS cause through the Executive Council. The *Daily Worker* quoted the Circular approvingly:

> It is not a question of 'Having nothing to lose but your chains', but of preventing more chains being fastened on you . . . We must be prepared. The workers of Spain will not be the last to be attacked. Every anti-Fascist must begin – now – to play his part in building up an organization which will enable him then to be of maximum use.[18]

At the 1938 AEU National Committee the Party activists joined other delegates in endorsing the Executive Council's support for VIAS. This 'progressive' phalanx of delegates then recorded their congratulations to the Executive Council for refusing during the previous year to discuss the problems of the expanding rearmament programme with the Secretary for Defence, Sir Thomas Inskip.[19] Conventional historiography has overlooked or dismissed the evidence of a *de facto* 'progressive' bloc inside the trade union movement over issues of European politics, anti-Fascism and impending war. Nevertheless, Jack Little, and the Durham miners' Treasurer, Sammy Watson, willingly associated themselves and their unions with Party-inspired initiatives to support the Spanish Republican Government. Little joined the Executive of a Labour Party proscribed organization, the Labour Research Department (LRD), and with three AEU Executive Councillors and the National Organizer went to the Soviet Union on a fact-finding mission which was financed by Soviet trade unions.[20]

Watson and Little were deeply orthodox Labour loyalists. It was evidently a matter of indifference to them that their views on the Spanish Civil War and other political matters coincided with their Communist colleagues. They were not inhibited from subsequent cooperation with Party activists for fear of being labelled 'fellow-travellers'. Both men took their own viewpoint seriously and would attack or support Communist initiatives according to their merit. For example, at the 1937 AEU National Committee, Jack Little expressed ambivalent feelings about a Party-inspired motion on the united front and vigorously opposed another Party-inspired motion which tied the Executives' hands on the wages question, rendering it impossible for them to negotiate any compromise.

> 'I am trying to forget the Communist Party's history. If you approach the question of unity remembering its history up to twelve months ago you approach the question with suspicion. The Communist Party is an international movement and its headquarters is the Third International. If it were admitted into the Labour Party, what authority would there be – the international centre or the Labour Party in this country?' . . . Mr. Little's view is still that unity should be sought but that questions will have to be asked . . .[21]

'[On the wages question] I will tell you straight, you are not going to have me exercise the functions of a robot. If you think I am a fool you have got a lesson coming to you.'[22]

The men who were regarded by their anti-Communist contemporaries as genuine 'fellow-travellers', like Jack Tanner and Will Lawther, viewed themselves quite differently and behaved as independent left-wing agents.[23] Though they regularly allied with Party activists inside their unions, neither Tanner nor Lawther felt compromised by their long and close association with Party-sponsored activities. They were socialists and thinking, reflecting men who were not going to be told by Citrine and Bevin from Transport House what they should and should not do. Indeed, they probably saw the National Council of Labour's attempts to direct activists' lives as undemocratic and proto-Fascist!

The 'progressive' phalanx inside trade unions succeeded in getting increasing numbers of motions passed inside unions, and finally the TUC, about the Spanish Civil War and the need for 'real united front' activity in Britain. The slow pace at which official machinery ground out its business determined that commitment to the Spanish Republican Government was not translated into official policy until the union conferences held in the spring and summer of 1938. These resolutions were duly tabled at the 1938 Trades Union Congress in the first week of September.

Will Paynter had recently returned from Spain where he had acted as the Political Commissar to the British battalion of the International Brigade. He was a Fed delegate to the TUC and his speech in support of the MFGB pro-republican motion moved delegates to tears and unanimous support in defiance of the General Council's vigorous lobbying for the National Council of Labour's policy of non-interference in the Spanish Civil War. A motion proposed by the Tailors' and Garment Workers' Union supporting working class unity in general terms was also carried by Congress.[24]

Only some of the Party-inspired *démarches* at Congress succeeded. Nevertheless, Ben Francis observed in the *Daily Worker* on the following Monday:

> The agenda, on home affairs, was the weakest for many years and it is not too soon to start preparing for next year's TUC NOW! The Congress decisions on international affairs marks [*sic*] a considerable advance on decisions taken at the TUC during the last five years. Lastly. All decisions taken at this Congress are only of value if they are carried out. This it seems to me, is the task before the Labour and trade union movement now.[25]

After the Congress Sir Walter Citrine approached the MFGB and the train drivers' union ASLEF, whose 'fellow-travelling' general secretary J.R. Squance had seconded the motion on Spain, for guidance about how the General Council might implement its provisions. The guidelines 'were finally drafted by Lawther, Horner, and J.R. [Johnny] Campbell and accepted by Citrine as the lines of action to be followed'.[26]

During 1938 all British political parties were drawn increasingly, if reluctantly, to focus their thoughts and cares on Europe. People in 'public life' took sides in the internal conflict about how Britain should act to maintain peace in Europe and the related question of how and whether a stand should be taken against German revanchism and Fascism. The German Government's mounting pressure on Czechoslovakia during the summer of 1938, Chamberlain's flight to Munich on 29 September and Hitler's triumphant entry on to Czech territory on 5 October catapulted the whole of British civil society suddenly and unexpectedly into thinking about these portentous matters.

There was a slow but undeniable and unrelenting reaction within civil society to these events resulting in a readiness to contemplate war against Germany again, though with great reluctance. This remarkable sea change away from the inchoate but dogged pacifism which had dominated Britain since 1918 was unevenly communicated to the political establishment. Party activists were probably aware of it before most MPs and journalists. Their daily contact with 'the public' at organized workplaces enabled them to gauge the public mood routinely and accurately. As the realization of the country's new mood penetrated through to Westminster and Transport House, politicians and trade union leaders including the Communists began to prepare in one way or another for this new possibility.

The Communist Party's strong repudiation of Chamberlain's deal at Munich enhanced its standing among shopfloor activists and reflective workers who were compelled towards politics through being able to see clearly the logic of worsening events. The increasing popular interest in Europe meant that wherever the Party had a public profile it benefited from its uncompromising opposition to Fascism. Its influence and membership increased accordingly. Richard Crossman ruefully remarked that people who became Communists were those who tried to fight Fascism 'before it was respectable to do so'; people who 'were too honest to accept the prevailing belief in an automatic Progress, a steadily expanding caitalism, and the abolition of power politics'.[27]

The Manchester Metal Bureau secretary recorded the reports from activists that the Party's campaign around the Munich crisis had been the most successful ever in union branches and factories. Increased sales of Party literature and the *Daily Worker* were recorded in all factories. In one factory, a discussion circle had been formed; at another factory 25 workers had met and decided to hold a mass meeting. Recruiting to the Party had increased and new factory groups could now be established.[28] This success was replicated to varying extents up and down the country wherever the Communist Party had established a public presence.

The Manchester Party was particularly well organized and the foundations for its Munich propaganda offensive had been laid earlier in the year. An article in the first number of the revived *Party Organiser* appeared in August 1938 describing experiences at a Manchester factory where there had previously been little Communist activity. Party members had undertaken some intensive 'mass work' which transformed the situation.

> ... permission is given by the management for holding factory gate meetings, providing the shop stewards agree. It is worth noting that the shop stewards have never yet refused a Communist meeting and that one of them reported a marked improvement in trade union membership and activity after the last meeting. At this factory the men can actually sit on forms conveniently placed near the gates! It is very noticeable that whereas ten years ago Communist speakers were often greeted with hostility, the factory workers are no longer duped by the abuse and distortion of the Tory Press . . . In fact, in the dozens of dinner-hour meetings the Communist Party has organized recently at the great Manchester engineering works, no vocal opposition has yet been expressed.[29]

Recent historians have rightly questioned the mythologic view disseminated by Party and assorted labour historians that British Communists inspired the Labour movement into adopting a heroic stand against Fascism in the 1930s. Tom Buchanan has shown that the practical impact of the various trade union initiatives were marginal in their impact on government policy towards the Spanish Civil War and that the amount of aid contributed by British unions was very small compared with the Republican Government's actual needs. He has also drawn attention to the disparity between the actual response by workers to pro-Republican campaigns and the 'mass mobilisation' claimed by the Party at the time.[30]

It is certainly clear that Party trade union activists raised European and anti-Fascist issues on the shopfloor and in the pit selectively and with care. They were not always sure that their message and what they were asking people to do would be well received. Even then, initiatives like VIAS, collections for Basque orphans and campaigns to pressurize the Government over arms for Spain did not always meet with a positive response.

At Gardner's diesel engine factory in Manchester the Party chairman persuaded the strongly left-wing shop stewards committee to call a mass meeting to seek support for VIAS after tea-break. The Manchester Metal

Bureau minutes noted that there was 'a riot' because workers were unwilling to give up their pay for the half-hour meeting. The meeting was held the following dinner time. The Joint Works Committee proposed that Gardner's management would contribute facilities and material whilst the men contributed their unpaid overtime for making engines for lorries for the Republican forces; Leyland workers would make the chassis. They also proposed a levy to help VIAS. Both proposals were turned down by the workforce.[31]

Where domestic workplace battles were being fought on difficult terrain, activists' energies and commitments were often dominated by their own battles and there was apparently neither time nor energy for political 'real united front' campaigning. In south-east Essex, for example, Party activists concentrated exclusively on issues of union organization and recruitment. There is no evidence that the strong Party industrial fraction made any attempt to mobilize workers around European issues. The well-disciplined and highly political membership in south-east Essex evidently decided that their priority was the serious class struggle at Ford's Dagenham and surrounding engineering sites.

The Party engineering activists in the forefront of 'rank-and-file' activity around the Spanish Civil War worked mainly at the aircraft sites in West London with which we are already familiar through their involvement in the 1920s shop stewards movement and then the ASSNC. These activists formed the nucleus of the shop stewards' committee demanding Arms for Spain which emerged into the public gaze in early 1939. The committee organized two marches of engineering workers in central London within a fortnight to demand that arms be sent to the Spanish Republican Government. According to the *Daily Worker*, 600–700 workers stopped work early at 4.00 to attend the first march and over a thousand came the following week. They came from sites in North, West and South London where Party activists were prominent on operational shop stewards' committees.

The numbers indicate that those attending were mainly shop stewards accompanied by some curious and/or enthusiastic observers though *New Propellor* reported that Napier's shop stewards hired a bus to take their workers to the second march. The *Daily Worker* tacitly acknowledged the comparatively sparse attendance by describing many of the factories represented as sending 'delegates'. Presumably, shop stewards' committees had agreed to support the march and arranged for the keenest of their number to get off work early in order to be present. In most cases there would not have been mass meetings held to endorse the stewards' decision.[32]

The marchers were addressed by Harry Pollitt, Willie Gallacher MP, four members of the AEU London District Committee, Len Powell, a young Party shop steward from R&J Beck Instrument Makers of Kentish Town who was a protégé of the veteran Vic Wymans, the convenor of Beck's shop stewards committee, and a Handley Page shop steward.[33] Beck's workers were outstandingly active in VIAS. They worked unpaid voluntary overtime and the firm credited their pay towards the purchase of their own microscopes which were shipped to poorly equipped Spanish loyalist hospitals. It was their example which shop stewards elsewhere attempted to emulate.[34]

The marches are a good example of Buchanan's point. Bill Rust described them in the Daily Worker as examples of the London District Party's success in organizing mass activity, and enjoined other districts to replicate London's success. Buchanan quotes the Times' estimate of the the first march as being only 200 strong and also its observation that there had been no cessation of work at Handley Page while only a few had stopped work early at de Havilland's Stag Lane.[35] Even the Daily Worker's reports of numbers do not qualify them as 'mass activity' unless this definition is distorted to describe all marchers as 'delegates' on behalf of their respective factories.

Two subsequent marches were planned for the following weeks and announced in the Daily Worker. They both failed to materialize, even though the second one was arranged for 6.00 – presumably to enable workers to arrive without taking time off work.[36] Trade union activists' willingness to take time off, to lose pay or even to make the effort to go to Central London was apparently limited, particularly when the Government was clearly unmoved and highly unlikely to bend to this limited pressure.

Nevertheless, Buchanan's accurate observations need to be placed in context. His conclusion that 'rank-and-file' involvement in support for the Loyalist Government was not mass activity does not invalidate the evidence that these Party-inspired démarches reinforced the morale and self-confidence of trade union and Labour activists. Moreover, the activists had some justification for declaring that they were marching in the name of the 'working class' and 'the Labour movement'. The stewards who marched were atypical by definition because they cared enough to give up time and energy for Spain. But they also marched on behalf of their members.

News of the two marches would have filtered through their sites and and the stewards probably encountered many expressions of sympathy and admiration from workmates for the Republican Government and the Spanish people's plight. Buchanan does not cite any evidence of counter-activity organized at workplaces in favour of Franco's forces or support for Hitler's intervention on Franco's side. Though only a minority of factory and pit workers were actively involved in the 'mass campaigns', the rest usually watched sympathetically while the keen ones got on with it.

I have found no evidence of a general reaction in favour of Franco or of booting stewards out of office for supporting the International Brigade.[37] Party-inspired initiatives were neither 'mass' nor popular, but they enabled activists to feel that they were personally crusading against Fascism and reinforced their identity as elected representatives of the working class acting for the whole collectivity. The marches, collections and VIAS activity also precipitated the political socialization of many young men and women.

For example, Bert Pankhurst and Johnnie Mansfield were apprentices at Fairey's Hayes in the toolroom when they were offered the opportunity to convert motorbikes into ambulances for VIAS. Both lads bought *New Propellor* when their shop steward came round selling it. They had joined the AEU when they were sixteen when an adult colleague on the bench said 'it's about time you joined the union'. The chairman of their local AEU branch worked at the largest factory in West London, EMI at Hayes, and had volunteered his garage for use as a workshop for VIAS. The lads agreed to help VIAS because they were delighted to be able to tinker with motorbikes. In the course of their tinkering they became partisan supporters of the Loyalists and keenly interested in the course of the Spanish Civil War.[38]

The Spanish Civil War blooded the democratic forces throughout Western Europe in those countries which were not fascist. Through their participation in the pro-Loyalist activity with warlike rhetoric and militant commitment, Communists, Socialists and Radicals alike adjusted to a perspective in which it became possible to again contemplate waging war, an option which many if not most of them had vowed never to support again after the horrors of 1914–18. The CPGB's conspicuous place in mobilizing the Labour Movement in Britain for Spain significantly reinforced the efforts being made inside the political establishment to move the Government towards facing up to Hitler.

The increasing number of coherent clusters of Party activists functioning inside union branches and at workplaces meant that the Party's propaganda was disseminated more effectively than the Labour left-wing anti-Fascist campaign which deployed similar, if not identical, arguments.[39] However, there is little evidence that Party union activists used this opportunity to gain a sectarian advantage over their Labour left-wing colleagues. Moreover, most Party union activists also declined to exploit increased popular interest in politics as a recruiting vehicle with previously apolitical workers. They followed Pollitt's and Campbell's injunctions to campaign around anti-Fascist issues because they were moved by a genuine desire to bring them to the attention of workmates rather than score political points or gain members.

However, Labour left-wing activists usually had to make their desire to join the CPGB very clear to Party colleagues in the 1930s before they could actually gain entrance. Workers with no previous political affiliation found it similarly difficult to actually join the Party. Despite regular and determined exhortations from the Party Centre to build a mass party, the attitude of most union activists towards recruiting continued to be decidedly non-conformist. They felt strongly that the only workmates who ought to join the Party were those who had been called. New recruits had to show by their actions that they were suited to the vocation of being a Communist.

I encountered this self-conscious approach, articulated and evidently long reflected on, from Party union activists in all parts of the UK. Charlie Wellard was no élitist. Nevertheless, he declined to undertake indiscriminate recruiting for a 'mass Communist Party', even though he could easily have exploited his popularity throughout Siemens and J&P's to increase local Party membership manyfold. He confined his Party recruiting to proven shop stewards and interested young people. He explained his deviation from the Party Centre's demands by emphasizing the demands of a Party activist's life before the war. Not everyone could face the risk of victimization at work, financial insecurity and the large amounts of time spent away from home and family doing 'daily mass work' after work. He had been unwilling to assume responsibility for another individual by recruiting them to bear these burdens. He approached those men and women to join the Party whom he judged to be 'ready', who understood what being a Communist activist entailed and willingly accepted this difficult burden.

My interviews revealed that the same cautious approach was adopted by John McArthur in East Fife, Will Paynter in South Wales, Ralph Fuller in Acton Vale and Herbert Howarth in Sheffield. When someone was 'called', they were encouraged and welcomed into the fold; there was no pressurizing or hard sell.[40] This attitude entailed the recognition that not everyone was suited to being a Communist. John McArthur recalled to Ian Mac Dougall that

> Joe Stalin subsequently became known for the phrase that Communists were people of a new kind. But before we had read anything from Joe Stalin we were trying to get across similar ideas to our Party recruits. Probably it was because of our Calvinistic Scots upbringing . . . we claimed that members of the Communist Party should keep in mind that the Party's prestige was all-important, and how they conducted themselves in their private life had its reflection in support or otherwise for the Communist Party . . . In addition to that, if we were to win support and if our leadership was to be accepted where we worked, we should take every step possible to acquire the highest skills in our work. We should be all-round,

thorough, competent miners, so that if we were advocating a line of policy, it would not be open to management, or even to some work-men that disagreed with us, to say that we were arguing that way because we were unable to do the job.[41]

The interviews conducted by the South Wales Coalfield Project in the mid-1970s show that Communists who were activists in the 1920s and 1930s did not view Communism as having mass potential.

> Now we used to, well we had an opinion in those days that the Communist Party was the vanguard of the workers. You had to be honest, sober, industrious, a good citizen, those were the qualities we were looking for, and of course everybody doesn't come into that.[42]

> We accepted the fact that we were now professional revolutionists, in the same way that Stalin was see and all the old Bolshevik leaders they were professional revolutionaries, and the psychology that had developed in those [South Wales] valleys amongst the leaders now, not the rank and file, was that we were for ever to be unemployed and therefore we have to be professional revolutionaries.[43]

> A typical party member in those days was a fellow who . . . accepted that there was nothing else in this god-damn world that was more important than the building of the Party and the serving of the Party. And the endless sacrifices that men and women in the Party, that they were prepared to make during that period was such that look-ing back now I wonder how the hell they survived them.[44]

The growth in Party membership during its 'heroic' anti-Fascist period supports the impression that these union activists' aversion to indiscrimi-nate recruiting was not atypical. The CPGB expanded almost threefold from 6500 in February 1935 to 15,750 in September 1939. This figure is miniscule compared to the TGWU's 1939 membership of 694,474; the AEU's 1939 membership of 413,094; or even the South Wales Miners Federation's 1939 membership of 123,677. Though Pollitt boasted at the 14th British Party Congress in 1937 that the French and Belgian Com-munist representatives were surprised by the number of delegates who held official trade union positions, the Party Centre's ambition to make the CPGB as big as its legal continental counterparts remained un-fulfilled.[45]

South Wales proved the most consistent disappointment to the Party Centre. From the turn of the century its history was dominated by pat-terns of militant economic struggle, mining trade union activists' evange-listic, articulate and well-developed 'rank-and-filism' and the vigorous growth of organic Marxism, socialist culture and widespread indigenous working class education. Despite these high and oft-repeated hopes, the Party Centre never gained its point. Party activists continued to display a characteristic prudence towards mass recruiting. There was an imaginative and popular campaign waged by Party members in the South Wales coalfield around the Spanish Civil War.[46] This success produced a renewed expectation at the Party Centre that South Wales was finally making the breakthrough into mass membership.

It was probably the palpable lull in the domestic class struggle which gave Party activists the motivation and space to develop anti-Fascist politics. The dramatic staydown strikes which flared up in one militant pit after another in the autumn of 1935 proved the peak of the coalfield's inter-war militancy. Though further outbreaks of industrial conflict and battles over the 'scab' union, the South Wales Miners Industrial Union (SWMIU), followed, notably in the autumn of 1936, there was no collective upsurge with sustained momentum comparable to 1934–35. The circumstances which had produced the wave of strikes disappeared, in large part because Horner's manoeuvres to extricate the Fed from the impasses of the earlier epic battles succeeded.[47]

The South Wales Coalowners' Association abandoned its support for the SWMIU after the stay-down strikes. Then the SWMIU suddenly vanished in the summer of 1938, leaving most Fed loyalists and militants convinced that their morally superior forces had triumphed. Horner had actually ensured this outcome by clandestinely using Fed money to buy off the SWMIU general secretary who was very willing to be bribed to disappear.[48]

The economic struggle was further moderated by the comprehensive agreement which Horner concluded with the coal-owners in April 1937. Sitting down at the bargaining table with Horner, whom they had previously denounced as a dangerous revolutionary, signified the coalowners' new willingness to co-exist peacefully with the Fed. The Fed's deal was little different than the 'Mondist' packages which Ernest Bevin had pioneered in the early 1930s.[49] The union conceded orderly collective bargaining and rationalization of custom and practice, and gained substantial wage increases, a joint conciliation procedure and a grade structure within which wage levels could move steadily upwards.

Nevertheless, Horner's agreement also violated rank-and-filism by its surrender of substantial opportunities for 'rank-and-file' union initiative and militancy at the point of production. This Achilles heel was noted and exploited by the *Daily Herald* and leftwing Labour MPs. Their attacks provoked Idris Cox, a leading South Walian Party full-timer, into a semi-official defence in the *Daily Worker*:

> There must . . . be some system of negotiation and particularly in an industry like mining where a hundred and one disputes crop up every day. If strike action is the only answer to every dispute in the South Wales coalfield there would never be any work in the mines. Trotsky's theory of permanent revolution would live again in the theory of 'permanent' strike action![50]

As the agreement produced its promised rationalization at the pit bottom, sporadic outbreaks of militant unofficial strikes occurred, particularly in the Anthracite Area where favourable economic conditions had enabled local 'unofficial' custom and practice to be tenaciously maintained.[51] But nemesis did not follow this 'betrayal' of rank-and-filism. Horner defused the strikes without either disturbing the Fed's peaceful equilibrium or precipitating a reaction from Party activists. He was able to hold the ring partly because he now exercised formidable authority as the man who had led the battles against the 'scab' union. In addition, the wage increase he won was a substantial advance, certainly higher than anyone in the coalfield had previously dared to contemplate. For miners who had endured low wages and short-time working for nearly a generation, the increase was a powerful incentive to fall in behind their President's bargain.

Having arrived at their commitment through a variety of vicissitudes, by 1937 the cohort 'called to Communism' from the coming generation was clearly visible and being trained up by their elders. Young miners continued to join the South Wales Communist Party during the hiatus in the class struggle. Like the young engineers whose political socialization we have observed, they were attracted by the Party's all-round political position within which the 'economic struggle' was one element – the Spanish Civil War, anti-Fascism and impending war in Europe often proved equal if not more important factors in the decision to join the Party. Though the prolonged slump in the market for South Walian coal had resulted in a comparatively low level of both employment and wages in the pits, there had been neither general disaffection nor mass alienation. The existing communal institutions (including the CPGB) helped to ameliorate the hardship and the disorientation consequent upon unemployment and countered the creeping demoralization.

Throughout the 1930s the Communist Party in South Wales was only one of many avenues, including non-conformist chapels and the Labour and Liberal Parties, which young miners in search of their adult identities could explore. Lads and lasses joined the CPGB rather than (or perhaps in addition to) the Baptists or Calvinistic Methodists – or the local jazz band – because of their contact with a forceful personality and/or coherent lively group of young Party activists men and women. We observed that it was capable, motivated activist and local workplace tradition which transformed engineering firms into 'factory fortresses'. These same determinants produced the Party 'strong places' in particular South Walian mining communities and pits.

Horner's unique blend of Communist millenarianism, charisma and intellectual virtuosity attracted a small group of young, gifted protégés to his side. They attached themselves on to the small existing entourage of his trusted veteran allies in the Fed and Party. Nevertheless, many veteran Party activists, Jack Davies for example, kept their distance from Horner because of his consistent willingness to compromise his militant principles. They kept Party discipline and did not oppose him openly.[52] But they also kept their own counsels and conscience, recruiting into the Party miners who supported rank-and-filism.

There were other equally charismatic and creative figures besides Horner, such as Councillor Lewis Jones, who went their own quite different but also Communist ways under the remarkably catholic umbrella of the South Wales Party.[53] It is arguable that more young men and women joined the Communist Party to emulate Lewis Jones's memorable exploits as a popular resister and agitator than earnest rebels who admired Horner's more complicated example.

The gap between the leadership's pursuit of mass status and the membership's conception of Communism as a minority vocation was particularly evident in the 'real united front' revival campaigns organized by the Party Centre in 1938 and 1939. Revival meetings and campaigns had been part of British socialists' activity since the 1890s, another direct borrowing from non-conformism, the revival campaign. Socialist revivals before the 1914–18 war enabled activists to display, propagate and bear witness to their muscular socialist belief. Revival 'camp meetings' provided an important communal social occasion when enthusiasts could openly appeal to and legitimately win converts from the unbelieving 'mass'.

The Party Centre initially declined to win supporters in this old way. Party campaigns and agitation were linked to actual issues, e.g. the Hunger Marches, support for specific strikes or opposition to the Government's policies, which the leadership believed could escalate and intensify into serious class battles. However by 1938, general expectations first of imminent revolution and then the militant upsurge had been set aside. The Party leadership returned to its own roots and resuscitated the pre-war socialist revivals with their powerful spiritual balm of Utopianism. The Party revivals filled the space left by Labour activists' concentration on electioneering and their consequent neglect of active missionary work.[54]

In 1937 the Unity Campaign had launched its own revival campaign in which Pollitt's charismatic oratory and Party activists' organizational work played an important part. The Unity Campaign's disintegration left the CPGB alone in pursuing its goal of a popular manifestation for the 'real united front'. The subsequent two revival campaigns provided a public airing for the United People's Front for Peace and against Fascism. The National Council of Labour was determined to deny Communists any opportunity to speak on a Labour Movement platform. The revival campaigns became the only conduit through which Party politics might be *heard*. Public meetings of all kinds were still an important constituent of political culture and the Party needed exposure to maintain credibility and its own members' self-confidence.

The Party unveiled its Crusade for Unity in January 1938. The *Daily Worker* announced that there would be more than two hundred meetings in 'the Great Communist Party Crusade' and published a 'Campaign Who's Who' of the speakers including Willie Gallacher MP, Wally Hannington, Rose Smith, Palme Dutt, John Gollan, Arthur Horner, Dave Springhall, Ted Bramley, Idris Cox, Peter Kerrigan, Abe Moffat and Johnny Campbell as well as photographs of Party mining activists – Willie Allan from Northumberland, Jim Ancrum from Durham and Jack Davies from South Wales.[55] The inaugural meeting was held in the Manchester Free Trade Hall and there was an enthusiastic overflow audience to hear speeches by Pollitt and Gallacher. The *Daily Worker* proudly reported the *Manchester Guardian*'s comment that it had been some time since the hall had been so full for a political meeting.

> This is a sign of the times which all who are concerned with the political future in this country will do well to consider. There is not another political party in this country which at the present day could achieve these results or win this response . . . Yet not a single London daily newspaper outside the *Daily Worker* has reported these demonstrations.[56]

The party's revival meetings were the best of their kind: inspiring while also giving good entertainment value. Pollitt's prominence as a speaker at the meetings meant subjecting himself to a gruelling schedule. The frequency of his appearance was not merely due to his position as titular head of the Party. He now rediscovered his old pre-war form as an inspiring socialist missionary and evidently revelled in his ability to hold an audience with his vivid and pithy vision of socialism. Others speakers were seasoned veterans who had learned how to hold and inspire a discerning working-class audience. Pollitt remained the nonpareil. He was disarmingly open, to the point of flamboyance, about his passionate convictions. The wide appeal of his Lancashire Communism provides a fascinating counterpoint to the Lancashire populism of Gracie Fields and George Formby being developed and marketed at the same time.

The *Daily Worker* soon announced that the Crusade had gained 200 new members for the Party so far, but cautioned its readers that more than meetings were needed.

> The support for the Crusade should now be translated in the form of resolutions from all parts of the country demanding joint discussions between Labour and Communist leaders with a view to removing all barriers which stand in the way of a united campaign. This will open

the way for the greatest advance the Labour movement has ever known.[57]

Nevertheless, when the Crusade finished some weeks later, the daily round of Life Itself and mass work continued much as before. The new recruits who had signed up at the inspiring meetings were neither easily nor usually assimilated by the core of activists. Will Paynter retained vivid memories of the Party's revival meetings in South Wales and their attendant converts who mostly failed to materialize at subsequent branch meetings.[58] The *Daily Worker* and the newly relaunched *Party Organiser* both repeated injunctions to existing members to take recruiting seriously and to maximize the opportunities presented by the Crusade to broaden the Party's popular image and appeal. The exhortations became more insistent and even strident, reflecting King Street's frustration at its members' apparent refusal to change their ways.[59]

In January 1939 there was another Communist revival, the Crusade for the Defence of the British People. This time a manifesto was issued calling on 'every progressive man and woman to join in a campaign which will unite all the forces that are in opposition to the National Government'. Pollitt inaugurated the second crusade at Bethnal Green:

> The Communist Party had launched its crusade for the defence of the lives and livelihood of the British people because we have unshakeable faith in the common people and are confident that, whatever their views may be on the ultimate development of the present system, they will yet unite their forces and drive out Chamberlain and his Government, which has led Britain to the edge of disaster. Our Crusade is a challenge to every vested interest of monopoly capitalism. It is an urgent summons in the name of liberty to all lovers of justice to improve the conditions of the majority of the people . . . strengthen the Labour movement and curb the greed of the rich so that health and happiness will be within the reach of everyone while the mass movement towards Socialism is given a new impetus and force.[60]

The two crusades did not fulfil their organizers' expectations. The Party Centre had envisaged them as providing the spark to fuel the flames of the putative 'people's united front' and also to assist the growth of the CPGB into a mass organization. These socialist revivals nevertheless had a significant effect on Pollitt's and Campbell's unspoken priority, to prepare the working class for fighting Fascism. When in September 1939 Chamberlain decided at the last minute to declare war against Germany, he met no resistance and little opposition either from trade unions or the critical mass of shopfloor activists. It is difficult to avoid the conclusion that the way had been cleared for this surprisingly smooth passage over the previous two years by Party activists' unstinting energy and unremitting concentration on the European political arena.

Notes

1. Pimlott, B., 1986, *Labour and the Left in the 1930s*, Allen & Unwin: 96.
2. *Daily Worker*, 7 April 1937. For the Unity Campaign, see Pimlott, 1986, op. cit.: 94–106.
3. Ibid.: 105. For the attempt to involve the Unity Campaign in the London Bus Strike see p. 124.
4. See p. 87.
5. *It Can Be Done*, Report of the 14th Party Congress, p. 63. Pimlott attributes the Party Centre's indifference towards non-working class elements to the ILP (p. 94). While I can accept that the ILP took a more sectarian position than the CPGB in the discussions around the Unity Campaign, Pimlott presents no evidence for his assertion that the CPGB leadership had a preference for a broader all-class alliance in the period up to May 1937 which it diluted to assuage the ILP. Pimlott also ignores the Party's principled political commitment to radical populism in his assessment of its conduct around the Unity Campaign: 'The CP's aim was to further its own campaign to affiliate to the Labour Party' (p. 95). He evidently found it difficult to impute non-opportunist, non-ulterior motives to a communist party.
6. *Daily Worker*, 8 February 1938 (my emphasis). For the Crusade, see below pp. 245–6.
7. Noreen Branson's chapter, 'Professional Workers and Students, 1932–39' (Branson, 1985, op. cit.: 204–19) is useful about this aspect of Party activity.
8. Morgan, 1989, *Against Fascism and War*, op. cit: 41–2.
9. Interview with Willie Campbell by Nina Fishman. Willie Campbell was Johnny Campbell's stepson and he was working in Moscow at the time. He could recollect no occasion on which Johnny Campbell had spent long periods of time in Moscow.
10. Mahon, 1936, 'Our Work in the Trade Unions', op. cit.: 526. Morgan notes that Pollitt visited the British Battalion five times between February 1937 and August 1938. (Pollitt, 1940, *Serving My Time*, op.cit.: 96.)
11. Interviews with Les Ambrose, Jessica Ambrose and Sid Atkin by N. Fishman.
12. Interview with Sid Atkin by N. Fishman and Hwyel Francis, 1984, *Miners Against Fascism*, Lawrence & Wishart: 123–32. Kevin Morgan emphasizes the Communist Party's creative development of the 7th World Congress line against Fascism to include Chamberlain and the British Establishment. Morgan,1989, op. cit.: 73–8.
13. Interviews with Jim Forde, Ralph Fuller, Dick Etheridge and Benny Rothman by N. Fishman.
14. McKinlay, 1986, PhD, op. cit.: 194.
15. See Branson, 1985, op. cit.: 156–7. There has been insufficient research to enable an estimate to be made of the number of dual members. From the many surviving veterans who have recently revealed their dual membership, I think it is likely that the number was significant in some places when compared with the local memberships of both parties.
16. AEU National Committee Report, 1935.
17. VIAS was started in 1936 on the initiative of a gifted non-Party political maverick and intellectual, Geoffrey Pyke. Because of his passionate anti-Fascism, Pyke was in close contact with Party intellectuals like J. D. Bernal

and 'fellow travellers'. They introduced him to Party union activists in London, notably Joe Scott and Vic Wymans, who ensured that VIAS was taken up by trade union lay institutions. Joe Scott was its treasurer. See Lampe, D., 1959, *The Unknown Genius*, London: 64–8.

18. *Daily Worker*, 7 April 1938. It is likely that Tanner wrote the Circular in consultation with the leading London Party activists, the constitutional militants Joe Scott and Claude Berridge.

19. AEU National Committee Report 1938. See also *AEU Journal*, Editor's Notes for September 1936 and May and June 1938.

20. The TUC and the Labour Party had both proscribed LRD in 1933. In 1937 the AEU National Committee voted to affiliate to LRD, and Little subsequently agreed to join the LRD Executive. See *Labour Research*, August 1937: 193 and November 1937: 264. Little returned from his Soviet trip impressed by what he had seen and the trade unionists with whom he had spoken. He admitted that some of his prejudices had been dispelled. See AEU National Committee Report 1937. For Sammy Watson's activities in support of the Spanish Republican Government, see Arnot, op. cit., Vol. III: 265, 267 and 274.

21. *Manchester Guardian*, 5 June 1937.

22. *Daily Telegraph*, 3 June 1937. See also AEU National Committee Report, 1937.

23. For Jack Tanner's long association with Party AEU activists, see p. 22 and pp. 41–2. The four Lawther brothers, Cliff, Steve, Ernie and Will, were left-wing Labour activists from the 'Little Moscow' pit village of Chopwell in County Durham. They became friendly with Robin Page Arnot in Newcastle during the General Strike. Cliff fought in the International Brigade and was killed in February 1937. Steve became an NUGMW official. Ernie went to work at the Chislett colliery in the Kent coalfield and became financial secretary of the Kent Miners' Association. He supported Communist affiliation to the Labour Party in 1936. For Will Lawther's speech on the Black Circular see p. 85.

24. Paynter, W., 1972, *My Generation*, Allen and Unwin: 75–6.

25. *Daily Worker*, 12 September 1938. There were five Party delegates to Congress: Claude Berridge and Gilbert Hitchings for the AEU and Jack Davies, Horner and Paynter for the Fed.

26. Paynter, 1972, op. cit. The resolution upheld the right of the Spanish Republican Government to purchase arms and called for a coordinated policy in the Labour movement to pressurize the Chamberlain Government into lifting its ban on arms sales. It called on affiliated unions to raise a sum equal to 2s. 6d. per member to provide funds for the Republican Government to assist these purchases.

27. Crossman, R.H.S., 1950, *The God That Failed*, London 1950: 10. See also Morgan, 1989, op. cit.: 58–82.

28. Metal Bureau minutes, 23 September and 21 October 1938, loc. cit. This success is an interesting contrast with the failure of the latest projected rank-and-file wages campaign in the AEU simultaneously recorded by the Manchester minutes. See pp. 91–2 and Fishman MRC, loc.cit.: 249–52 and 318–21.

29. *Party Organiser*, Vol. I No. 2, August 1938. The firm was Mather & Platts and the author was 'Frank Allan' (*sic*). Frank Allaun was a young Party member who had been attending Metal Bureau meetings regularly though

he was an aspiring journalist. The Metal Bureau secretary had arranged for details of factory-gate meetings to be available to the local agitprop from January 1938 and for the chief agitprop speaker to be present at Metal Bureau meetings to discuss venues for possible future activities. (Manchester Metal Bureau minutes, 13 May 1938.) The agitprop organization was evidently a new initiative from the District Party leadership for Lancashire which was located in Manchester.

30. Buchanan, T., 1988, 'The politics of internationalism: the Amalgamated Engineering Union and the Spanish Civil War', *Journal of the British Society for the Study of Labour History*, Vol. 53 Part No. 3, Winter 1988: 50–4.
31. Manchester Metal Bureau minutes, loc. cit., 25 November 1937. The Gardner's proposal was typical of VIAS schemes under which management contributed the materials and the men contributed unpaid labour time.
32. *Daily Worker*, 27 January 1939 and 3 February 1939. The *Daily Worker* reports stated that workers came from de Havilland's Stag Lane, Handley Page at Cricklewood, the Chiswick Repair Depot of London Transport, Phoenix Telephone Co. in North London, Waygood Otis lift manufacturers in South London, Evershed and Vignoles engineers in Edmonton, Witton & James, ENV Engineering in Acton and Siemens. *New Propellor*, Vol. 3 No. 4. Ralph Fuller remembered attending the marches. (Interview with N. Fishman.)
33. Ibid.
34. Lampe, op. cit.: 65–6.
35. Buchanan, 1988, op. cit., footnote 48, p. 55.
36. *Daily Worker*, 14 and 22 February 1939. On 22 February the *Daily Worker* reported that the AEU London District Committee had officially requested shop stewards to bring members to the demonstration. Buchanan discusses the Executive Committee's decision to stop the District Committee's official participation, but does not explain the origin of their decision, which was presumably that the District Committee should have obtained prior permission from the Executive Council for their decision under rule. (Buchanan, 1988, op. cit.: 53.)
37. The only evidence of popular support for Franco which I have encountered comes from Eire. (*New Propellor*'s subscription lists for aircraft factory collections to help the Spanish Republican cause show that engineering workers in Belfast were notably more generous than their English colleagues.) Ernest Bevin had to travel to Eire to defend the TGWU's commitment to the Spanish Republican Government against a reaction from inside his own union, which was said to be motivated by the Catholic hierarchy. Similar problems were encountered by John McGovern, the ILP MP who had inherited John Wheatley's largely Catholic constituency in Glasgow.
38. Interviews with Bert Pankhurst and Johnnie Mansfield by N. Fishman. Pankhurst and Mansfield eventually joined the Party early in the war through their contact with the charismatic Frank Foster. Foster arrived at Fairey's at the beginning of the war and quickly became convenor. Though Communists had been active in the 'economic struggle' at Fairey's in Hayes since 1932–33, it was Foster who evidently made the first concerted attempts inside the factory to build up Party membership and establish a functioning factory group.
39. See Pimlott, op. cit.: 86 and 92–6.

40. Interviews with Charlie Wellard, John McArthur, Will Paynter, Ralph Fuller and Herbert Howarth by N. Fishman.

41. McArthur, J., 1981, *Militant Miners*, MacDougall, I (Eds.), Polygon Books, Edinburgh: 143.

42. Interview with Phil Abrahams, 14 January 1974, by H.Francis, transcript in SWML, p. 1.

43. Interview with Phil Abrahams, n d , Mervyn Jones, transcript in SWML, p. 46.

44. Interview with Len Jefferys, 11 October 1972, by H.Francis and D. Egan, transcript in SWML, pp. 25–6.

45. See pp. 100–1 and Appendix I.

46. See Francis, 1984, op. cit.: 156–224.

47. See N. Fishman, PhD, op. cit. Chapter 7.

48. N. Fishman, PhD, op. cit.: 310. Horner's manoeuvre was revealed almost half a century later by his young protégé Dai Dan Evans in an interview with Hywel Francis (transcript p. 12 and p. 14). Not even the Fed Secretary Oliver Harris knew about the pay-off.

49. Bullock, 1960, *Ernest Bevin*, op. cit.: 380–1 and 459–63.

50. *Daily Worker*, 14 April 1937. See also *Daily Worker*, 26 April 1937.

51. For the conciliation procedure and the unofficial strikes see Anthony-Jones, W.J., 1959, 'Labour Relations in the South Wales Coal Industry', University of Wales PhD: 27, 82 and 88. Anthony-Jones concludes that Horner's was the only one of the four 'Mondist' packages concluded in British coalfields between 1926 and 1939 which functioned effectively.

52. See interview with Frank Williams by H. Francis, 6 March 1973: 10 and 14–15.

53. For Lewis Jones, see Francis, 1984, op. cit.: 83, 168–9, and 102–3; and 1980, *The Fed*, op. cit.: 305, 307 and 354–5.

54. David Howell suggested to me that the successful Communist revivals of the late 1930s were facilitated by the II.P's advancing weakness and progressive introspection.

55. *Daily Worker*, 8 January 1938.

56. *Daily Worker*, 8 February 1938. The Unity Campaign had been kicked off at the Free Trade Hall in 1937 with a meeting at which Pollitt had spoken along with Maxton and Cripps. Pollitt's ability to draw a capacity crowd on his own must have been heartening for the Party.

57. *Daily Worker*, 12 February 1938.

58. Interviews with Will Paynter by N. Fishman.

59. For the Party Centre's emphasis on the recruiting side and resigned, frustrated injunctions to Party members about taking recruiting seriously see *Daily Worker*, 12 February 1938, 13 January 1939 and *Party Organiser*, Vol. I No. 6, January–February 1939: 3 and No. 8, April 1939: 2–3. The periodical had been relaunched to provide a forum to canvass internal Party issues; the publication reflected the Party's growth and the need to socialize new members into Party culture.

60. *Daily Worker*, 27 January 1939.

CHAPTER TEN

Fighting the War on Two Fronts

The CPGB's changes of line on the 1939–45 war are its most notorious vicissitude. The distorted train of events which has lodged in British collective memory is the Communist Party's enthusiastic support for Chamberlain's declaration of war on 1 September 1939, followed by its change to total opposition to the 'imperialist' war some six weeks later on the Comintern's orders, and its subsequent return to unqualified support for the war from the moment Hitler invaded the Soviet Union in June 1941.

British political historiography is also more aware of this aspect of CPGB policy before 1945 than of any other. Standard accounts of Britain in wartime are usally confined to a prominent mention of the CPGB's 'treachery' little different from the popular wisdom described above: both perceptions are clearly derived from the political capital realized by the Westminster political establishment at the time. The opportunity to discredit the CPGB in October 1939 was too good to be missed. The Cold War revived the need for anti-Communist demonology. The British Party's changes of line on the war may have been temporarily forgiven in the euphoria of the wartime Anglo–Soviet alliance. The CPGB's 'treachery' and susceptibility to Comintern diktat were revived and became one of the unquestioned assumptions of politically correct modern British history.

Despite the publication by Communist Party historians of the Central Committee minutes for the meeting at which the line was changed, there has been no serious revisionism about the CPGB's approach to the war from either Party or academic historians. They both accept the myth that still pervades with an intensity which is comparatively undiminished after half a century: the war was Britain's finest hour, and the Communists and Fascists who opposed it were a very small minority of pariahs tarred by Hitler's brush. Not surprisingly, a rather different and more complex picture can be constructed from the evidence.

As the situation had rapidly deteriorated in Europe after 1937, it became increasingly difficult to distinguish between Communist and left-wing Labour and trade union positions. Both were implacably hostile to the Chamberlain Government and mistrusted its foreign policy. Both continued to oppose the Government's rearmament programme on the grounds that the government could not be trusted to wage anything but a narrow class war for its own ends. Because rearmament was dominated by engineering, the AEU played a leading role in determining the TUC's attitude towards government overtures in 1938 for union cooperation in dilution. The response from Jack Little was as suspicious and political as that of Jack Tanner, Joe Scott and Claude Berridge. The CPGB's position that Britain should join with France in a defensive alliance with the Soviet Union also received strong support from the Labour left-wing.

The anti-Government positions of both the CPGB and the Labour left wing remained unchanged when it became clear that there would not be a Peace Alliance with the USSR. However, underneath this formal veneer was a slowly maturing commitment to providing qualified support if Chamberlain embarked on war against Germany both because it was preferable to leaving Hitler in sole possession of *Mitteleuropa* and also because it was generally believed that the course of war on the Continent was bound to precipitate an alliance against Germany between Britain, France and the USSR. On 19 July 1939, the *Daily Worker* reported a speech by Pollitt:

> 'The Communists believe that if the Fascists break out in war for the purpose of destroying the independence of a country, dissolving its parliamentary institutions, breaking up the Labour movement, murdering the Labour leaders and torturing the Jews, then it is in the interests of the working class movement and of Socialism that the Fascists should be defeated.' That position may be strange to some pathological pacifists of the Non-Conscription League. It was, nevertheless, the position approved of by the great majority of the militant workers of Britain during the Spanish struggle and it is the only possible position.[1]

The conclusion of the Non-Aggression Pact between Germany and the Soviet Union at the end of August did not produce any alteration in this position. On 30 August the *Daily Worker* printed a Central Committee statement:

> If as a result of fascist aggression, the world finds itself embroiled in war, the Communist Party will do all in its power to ensure speedy victory over fascism and the overthrow of the fascist regime. At the same time it will demand and work to achieve the immediate defeat of Chamberlain and a new government in Britain representing the interests of the common people and not the rich friends of fascism. Act, and act now, for Peace. Organise meetings and demonstrations for a new approach to the Soviet Union and the USA, for a new Government which will make this approach for the defeat of Chamberlain, which will be a deadly blow to Hitler! Organise emergency meetings of trade union branches, trades councils, local Labour Parties and Co-operative guilds and campaigns for this policy! . . . Let it be understood we will fight and defeat fascist aggression. But also let it be realised that the price of victory is the defeat of Chamberlain and a new Government for the British people.[2]

On 2 September the *Daily Worker*'s page one headline announced:

'Nazis Plunge World into War. Poland Invaded and Towns Bombed. The Mad Dogs of Europe – Hitler and His Nazi Government – have set out on their last bloody adventure.' Despite Chamberlain's refusal to issue an ultimatum to Hitler under the terms of the recently concluded Anglo-Polish Treaty, the CPGB Central Committee statement was bellicose:

> The essence of the present situation is that the people now have to wage a struggle on two fronts. First to secure the military victory over Fascism; and second in order to achieve this, the political victory over Chamberlain and the enemies of democracy in this country. These two aims are inseparable, and the harder the efforts to win one, the more sustained must be the activity to win the other.

Johnny Campbell spoke at a *Daily Worker* conference on the next day, when the British Government had finally been pressurized into declaring war.

> ... now that the struggle had started, he said, the working class could not be indifferent. For the victory of Germany over France would mean fascism in France and open the door to fascism in Britain. In spite of the peculiar nature of the alliance against Germany the working class must ensure that the war did not end until fascism in Germany was defeated and at the same time they must work equally hard to defeat the fascist-minded men of Munich in Great Britain itself.[3]

The Party Centre held consistently to the war-on-two-fronts position throughout September. Campbell's intellectual discipline ensured that the Party did not adopt an open-ended commitment to the war. Pollitt's profound anti-Fascist feelings were not allowed to swamp this 'people's united front' perspective which the two men had patiently and far-sightedly been constructing since 1937. Moreover, the war on two fronts position was actually popular. It coincided with the outlook of Party trade union activists who were hardly encountering mass enthusiasm for total war on the shopfloor. Memories of the last war acted as a strong preventive against any general rush of blood to the head about the glorious days which lay ahead. The British people were resigned to having to fight Germany; they were not sanguine about what lay ahead.[4] Within civil society there was a complicated ebb and flow of feelings towards events, both abroad and on the home front.

The CPGB's change of line over the war occurred at the beginning of October 1939. From the first there had been vociferous opposition on the Central Committee, led by Dutt and Rust, to the war-on-two-fronts position. Pollitt and Campbell had resisted pressure to declare this war imperialist and foment popular reaction against it in a bolshevik manner. The division inside the Central Committee more or less faithfully reproduced the split in the leadership in 1930 over the moderation of Class Against

Class. A few Young Turks like Johnny Mahon had switched allegiances since then, but most of the participants remained on the same side as in the earlier conflict between pristine revolutionary principles and revolutionary pragmatism.

Despite the mounting evidence that the Comintern favoured the Dutt–Rust position, Pollitt and Campbell held the majority on the Central Committee until Dave Springhall returned from Moscow. 'He informed the Central Committee that the Communist International believed the war to be an imperialist one to which the working-class movement should give no support.'[5] Over 2–3 October the Central Committee met to reconsider its stand. Pollitt, Campbell and Gallacher were the only ones who continued to speak for the war on two fronts. The Party's line was changed publicly on 4 October and further clarified in a new Central Committee manifesto on 7 October.[6]

There continues to be a lively controversy within Communist historiography about whether or not the Communist 'rank-and-file' agreed with the change of line on the war. Branson, for example, cites the membership's reaction against the war, recalling the Second International opposition to all capitalist wars and the senseless slaughter wreaked by the ruling class in 1914–18.[7] She has evidently chosen to emphasize these motives because they are acceptable to contemporary left-wing opinion. They are a plausible part of many Party activists' state of mind at this moment. However, on their own, they are not sufficient to account for the dramatic rejection of Pollitt and Campbell by Central Committee members who had been their reliable allies for ten years.

The published minutes of the Central Committee meeting on 2 October show that Pollitt and Campbell certainly believed that they could carry the majority with them against Dutt and Rust. These experienced and calculating politicians would hardly have been so optimistic if they had not believed that they could trim their own cloth to suit the Comintern's new requirements, as they had done in the past. The difference between the two sides on 2 October consisted of how to respond to the Comintern not whether to do so. Neither Pollitt nor Campbell had any wish or intention to leave the Comintern fold.

It is important to brush aside the prevailing assumption that Pollitt's and Campbell's position rested on the overriding importance of fighting Fascism. While anti-Fascism informed their logic, the practical consideration that the Party must remain in the bowels of the proletariat and safeguard its growing influence in the trade union movement was also crucial. They acknowledged the need for altering the balance in the war-on-two-fronts position to emphasize the political and class war against Chamberlain and British capitalism. But they believed that the change could be one of emphasis. The Comintern did not require the total change of position for which Dutt and Rust were arguing. Dimitrov had declared that Communist Parties involved in the war should revert to the united front from below, whilst exposing social democratic leadership. He had not instructed Parties to engage in revolutionary sabotage.[8]

There is undoubtedly much to be culled about the Comintern's position at this time from the freshly opened archives in Moscow. At this point, however, the available published evidence endorses Pollitt's and Campbell's expedient pragmatism. Unlike the early days of Class Against Class in 1928–29, the Comintern's own change of line was not motivated by revolutionary logic; it was determined instead by sheer expediency. If Hitler's invasion of Poland in early September had been repulsed, it is unlikely that the Comintern would have required any modification in its affiliates' positions.[9]

Pollitt and Campbell had before successfully persuaded the Comintern to make Britain an exception in its general line. Indeed, it is possible that the CPGB was unique in Europe in never being formally condemned by the Comintern and forced to change its policy. It is difficult to conclude that Pollitt and Campbell were being either Utopian or sentimental in their belief that they could again bend the Comintern line to suit their domestic British needs. Campbell had been in regular contact with the Comintern until the summer of 1938. His perception of what would pass muster in Moscow was arguably more accurate than most others around the Central Committee table.

Dutt and Rust succeeded against Pollitt's and Campbell's arguments by subjecting Central Committee veterans to the strong moral pressure of observing the Comintern line to the letter rather than bending it. They traded on the criticisms from Moscow which Springhall conveyed and arguably led the British Party to taking up a position in opposition to the war which was more extreme than the Comintern would have tolerated. The minutes show that Pollitt and Campbell reacted with frank disbelief as trusted allies like Ted Bramley, Johnny Mahon and Emile Burns deserted them to go over to Dutt and Rust's pristine revolutionary side.

Once Pollitt and Campbell had been bested by Dutt and Rust, the Central Committee was swift to impose democratic centralist discipline. Pollitt and Campbell duly acquiesced in the new line and performed the requisite *mea culpa*s. They were formally banished from the Central Committee for the duration of the war. The general secretary's post was assumed by Dutt. Pollitt took up a lowly post in the Party regional hierarchy in Manchester[10] and wrote his autobiography. Campbell was demoted from editor to lowly reporter of the *Daily Worker* and Rust resumed the editorial chair he had vacated in 1932 after Pollitt's and Campbell's defeat of the extreme Class Against Class line at the 12th British Party Congress.

Despite the attempts by the media and Westminster to capitalize on the CPGB's change in line, the Party's nominal anti-war position apparently roused serious hostility, mainly from people inside the political establishment who felt personally and/or intellectually betrayed. Victor Gollancz's well-publicized break with the Party and Pollitt is a notable example. Prominent supporters of the Popular Front had worked particularly closely with Pollitt in fighting Fascism. Their need not only to break with the CPGB but also to condemn its new position as beyond the pale stemmed from their desire to dissociate themselves from the opprobrium publicly heaped upon the Party by the establishment. Many had been compelled by personal considerations to occupy the moral high ground. They now condemned Pollitt for his expedient acquiescence because they found no political calculation tolerable except absolute opposition to Hitler.

The irony of the dramatic upheaval in the Party leadership was that Dutt and Rust quickly deemed it expedient to scuttle back to the war-on-two-fronts position without a murmur of disapproval emanating from Moscow. Their swift return to the pragmatic war-on-two-fronts position confirms the view that although the CPGB's change in line on the war was precipitated by the Comintern, the dramatic extent of its volte-face was due to the strong motivations of the remaining Young Turks and Dutt.

Dutt and Rust initially proclaimed a full Leninist position that the war was inter-imperialist. On Sunday, 29 October, Bill Rust spoke at a *Daily Worker* conference: ' "Let the workers arouse themselves and gain confidence in their own strength . . . we call on all trade unions to oppose the war and register the view that the workers must stop it." He urged the unions to develop their *independent* mass activity.'[11]

Rust's ally from Class Against Class, George Renshaw, had a letter in the *Daily Worker* on 3 November. He argued that Stop the War Committees should be formed 'to show the *Herald* and the National Government what we are ready for. In 1920, London dockers stopped the war on the Russian workers. Let us act to stop the war on the British people now.'

The *Daily Worker* had started to move backwards by 6 November. A leader about rationing failed to mention the imperialist war:

> Guns before Butter. The people want their butter and bacon. Learned articles about the delights and advantages of rationing will not put food into empty bellies. There is a growing feeling in the country that the present shortage is to be explained not by 'muddle' but by deliberate acts of policy. As the paper of the people we have given voice to that opinion.

At the end of December 1939 the *Daily Worker* published Rust's report to the Central Committee about the problems of developing a 'broad political movement of opposition to the war on a common platform'. He believed in this movement, but it needed 'to lie in the mass organisations of the working class, building on the growing opposition to the war; the trade unions, Labour Parties and Co-ops.'[12] Rust's prescription was, of course, disingenuous. He was well aware that there was no growing mass opposition to the war which would pressurize union leaders into stiffening their war-on-two-fronts position. Dave Springhall had earlier reported on the lack of mass support on the shopfloor for the Party line.[13] It is significant that Rust made no mention of the 'independent mass activity' he had invoked in October. He confined himself to intoning Pollitt's and Campbell's homilies about the need to work inside the official trade union movement.

Having extracted their pound of flesh, Dutt and Rust belatedly recognized that the line to which they had committed the CPGB was simply not practical politics. In order to rescue the Party from the precipice of sectarian isolation they were compelled to commence immediate and expeditious trimming. They had soon returned to the comparative safety of revolutionary pragmatism. They made no serious attempt to transform the habits of Party trade union activists. Johnny Mahon remained in residence as chief trade union propagandist dispensing his potent blend of trade union loyalism and rank-and-filism. The *Daily Worker* published no incitements to revolutionary defeatism either on the shopfloor or in the army. The expectations of Life Itself, officially revised to exclude imminent revolution after the 7th World Congress, were not altered back again to include it and an accompanying seizure of state power by the CPGB.

Dutt and Rust's notable reluctance to intervene in or alter daily shopfloor practice made it much easier for Party activists to accept the change of line on the war. Since Pollitt and Campbell remained conspicuously loyal to the new line, the Party 'rank-and-file' who agreed with them must have seen little point in resisting. Moreover, since the new line was almost immediately diluted, its full rigour was never really experienced or tested in trade union branches and the shopfloor.

It is hardly surprising that delegates at the London District Congress in January 1940 criticized the Party Centre's tendency to soft-pedal the Party's opposition to the war. The London District retained influential pockets of members who remained committed bolsheviks, like Peter Zinkin, and others for whom the echoes of the 1914–18 war reverberated. They expected a high-profile political presence dedicated to militant opposition and nostalgically distorted the actual role of the *ad hoc* organization of the 1914–18 shop stewards movement, like the West London Shop Stewards Committee and the Clyde Workers' Committee, to fit their contemporary expectations. Dutt parried the politically correct charges at the London District Congress with a strong dose of reductive logic: 'to fight for the needs of the people means at the same time to fight for the end of the war. The needs of the people are incompatible with the continuance of war. That is the heart of the matter'.[14]

Having confined the Party's political parameters to 'the needs of the people', Dutt and Rust placed participation in the 'economic struggle' back at the top of Party activists' priorities. The Comintern was predictably unconcerned at the British Party's early deviation from the Leninist anti-war line. Moscow remained genuinely indifferent to the spectacle of British Party members actually facilitating the war effort by conducting the 'economic struggle' in an orderly fashion. All the Comintern had actually required was a more forthright denunciation of the Chamberlain Government's imperialist motives in waging the war. Soviet foreign policy actually dictated that they should *not* seriously oppose the war effort. From the USSR's perspective, it was vital that Hitler should remain tied down in the West.

Evidence continues to accumulate that there was scant enthusiasm from the general public for fighting the war. Nevertheless, the weekly reports of Ministry of Labour's Regional Industrial Relations Officers (RIROs) record numerous incidents of fierce reaction by workers directed against conscientious objectors who had been directed into civilian work. It is notable that the Party's nominal anti-war line did not cause Party activists to be subjected to comparable abuse at work. The popular distinction between conchies and bolshies presumably stemmed from shopfloor observations that Party activists were neither shirking nor refusing to sacrifice themselves.

If there had been a reaction from below comparable with the conflicts which erupted in 1914–15 in mining and engineering, then the Party Centre might well have tried to build a serious rank-and-filist/bolshevik alternative. However, in the comparative calm which prevailed during the first year of phoney war, most Party activists went about their accustomed daily mass work along pre-war lines without hindrance from King Street. Dutt and Rust were faced with a dilemma. Having overturned the previous Party policy, they were now constrained to show that their new policy had indeed produced a change in Party members' practice.

Confronted with the need to argue that Party members' daily mass work had changed when in fact it had not, Dutt and Rust resurrected Pollitt's and Campbell's pre-7th World Congress rhetoric to provide much needed camouflage. They returned to the *modification* of independent leadership which Pollitt and Campbell had creatively developed in 1932. The 1935 permutation of the real united front was ostentatiously jettisoned. Instead of replacing it with the extreme independent leadership which they had championed in 1928–29, they substituted the 1933 transmutation which they had opposed at the time, the fighting united front of the rank-and-file. The definition which Pollitt and Campbell had constructed for this united front from below included the imperative that the Party must not become isolated from the organized working class. Deploying Pollitt's and Campbell's 1932 catechism, Dutt and Rust could argue that Party activists had to avoid committing the left-wing sectarian error.[15]

However, the rank-and-file movements which became an important part of the Party's approach to the wartime economic struggle did not even conform to the 1932 model. Dutt and Rust carefully adhered to the guidelines evolved by Pollitt and Campbell for unofficial union activity after the events of May 1937. They evidently had no wish to disturb the *modus vivendi* which had been established between full-time union officials and Party activists. The ASSNC had already been invested with fresh life and new tasks by the constitutional militants during the first weeks of the war.

The ASSNC National Committee had met on 17 September. It decided to expand its remit to include all armaments factories and to increase the circulation of *New Propellor* accordingly.[16] However, no provision was made for shop stewards committees in armaments factories to affiliate to the enlarged movement. The degree of rank-and-file organization which union activists judged to be required by wartime circumstances was evidently minimal. They did not envisage a parallel structure functioning alongside official union institutions.

Dutt and Rust accepted the framework for this 'rank-and-file movement' which had been laid down when the Party had been operating the war on two fronts line. In December 1939, *New Propellor* reported that the ASSNC National Committee had appointed Temporary Conveners to form area shop stewards committees. Though stewards committees were swiftly established in north-west London and Glasgow, we shall see that the Party Centre ensured they had only a minimal existence. There was evidently no practical will elsewhere to organize the local rank-and-file independently and Dutt and Rust made no attempt to engender it.

Nevertheless, the question of resurrecting the wartime 'shop stewards movement' had probably been debated at all levels of the union where veteran AEU members could remember 1914–18. Many non-Communist veterans agreed that union's rank-and-filist traditions should be revived in this testing time. Leading Party engineering activists organized a very successful 'national rank-and-file' conference in Birmingham in April 1940 to reflect the ubiquitous discussions taking place inside official union channels. The conference arrangements reflected constitutional militants' concern to safeguard themselves against charges of infringing AEU rules. It was not convened by the ASSNC and received hardly any advance publicity in the *Daily Worker* or *New Propellor*. News about it was carried along the extremely effective unofficial networks developed by Party militants.[17]

The conference resolution criticized union executives for putting support for the war before their duties to their members and concluded that this abdication made it necessary to 'co-ordinate the activity of all shop stewards through a national shop stewards movement'. But the ASSNC was not mentioned in the resolution at all. The constitutional militants clearly had even less intention of challenging existing union structures than they had done as young men in 1914–18. Nor did the text contain any trace of an overt anti-war position. The conference chairman anchored delegates conspicuously within the safe boundaries of trade union loyalism.

> it is now the duty of every shop steward to come forward and put new life into our powerful trade union movement . . . The struggle will be a grim one, which may entail such sacrifices as were the lot of the Tolpuddle Martyrs. We must carry on their glorious traditions, the traditions of the Clyde workers and the millions of Trade Unionists who have followed them in the fight for the best in trade unionism.[18]

The other aspect of Pollitt's and Campbell's 1932 perspective which Dutt and Rust revived was their optimistic anticipation of national wages movements. Memories of militant engineering and mining strikes in 1914–18 reinforced the belief that this new war would produce similar militant opportunities. Hopes were centred around engineering, where Party activists were numerous and influential and the AEU Executive Council were in the process of negotiating the national wage claim. In January 1940 the *Daily Worker* explained: 'The delay in meeting the men's claims has already led to widespread unrest in the [engineering] industry, particularly in the aircraft factories, where there have been threats of imposing an embargo on overtime until the wage claim is conceded.'[19]

There had not actually been unrest, let alone widespread unrest, in engineering. Party engineering activists evidently did not feel in a qualitatively different position on the shopfloor as a result of the phoney war economy. They offered only token and official resistance to national wage negotiations through union lay institutions. The Napier's factory fortress responded to the *Daily Worker*'s call for an industry-wide uprising to demonstrate that the rank-and-file meant to fight. But Napier's shop stewards could only manage a general downing of tools and walkout for one Saturday morning. The *Daily Worker*'s story was emblazoned with a page one headline, 'Engineers Take Biggest Wage Action of the War'.[20] The London RIRO reported with palpable relief on 17 February that there had been no response to the Party's campaign against the national wages settlement.[21] He too had been haunted by memories of the previous war which had now been laid to rest.

Pre-war practices in regard to political agitation also reasserted themselves. There was intense interest in the politics of the war among Communist and non-Communist union activists. As before the war, Dutt's 'Notes of the Month' in *Labour Monthly* were eagerly awaited and avidly read as a beacon shedding light on the tangled web of world events. His pronouncements were usually accepted, but only after much disputation when every point had been carefully rehearsed by activists whose self-image included making up their own minds.

But Party activists had not engaged in routine shopfloor proselytizing for these sophisticated and sophistical arguments before 3 September 1939. While they were deeply committed to the fight against Fascism, their daily mass work had never included serious politicking. They conducted political propaganda on the shopfloor only sparingly, after portentous developments like Munich had occurred, when their colleagues were actually interested in talking about national and European politics.

Most of the time, Communists reserved their political propaganda for non-Party activists who were conversant with political culture, isolated auto-didacts, and inquisitive youths. During the phoney war, Party stewards remained generally quiescent about politics inside the factory. They encountered scarcely any stirring of interest about the politics of the war from their colleagues. There was little enthusiasm either for fighting Fascism or not fighting Fascism. Party stewards had therefore continued to approach their daily mass work on the basis of fighting the 'economic struggle'. Their tactical abstention from politics was not viewed as suspect or sinister because workers had not been exposed previously to a daily diet of political propaganda from Party stewards. It was not until the summer of 1940 when the fall of France brought fears of a German invasion of Britain that the war finally became a deadly serious and therefore interesting matter for everyone.

*   *   *

British trade union leaders did not exploit the opportunity presented by the Party's anti-war position to instigate a general inquisition against Party activists. Not even Citrine, the Witch-finder General of the Labour Movement, tried to take advantage of the situation. This forbearance was similar to their initial ambivalence towards the 'Black Circulars' in 1934–35 and their subsequent reluctance to operate them. Their tolerance in 1939–40 was undoubtedly reinforced by the failure of the new Party Centre to produce or disseminate explicit anti-war propraganda.

The two unions where leaders took *pre-emptive* action to test the Party's intentions with regard to the new anti-war line were the AEU and the Fed. The Party's influence was strongest in these unions and they were consequently the most vulnerable to attempts to steer their policies away from the war-on-two-fronts position. The left-wing leadership of both unions was disinclined to accept on trust that Party activists would follow the Centre's lead in acquiescing in a diluted 'war-on-two fronts' position.

Jack Tanner was elected AEU President in 1939. His victory could not have been achieved without the Party's efficient election machine which marshalled votes outside his own patch in North London and the north-west Home Counties. He felt himself and was seen by his colleagues to be susceptible to left-wing pressure to oppose the war. Party engineering activists had been noticeably reticent about propagating the new anti-war line on the shopfloor or in the comparatively sympathetic atmosphere of shop stewards committees. However, they had proposed and carried anti-war motions at branches and district committees where they were more confident of finding a positive reception and also did not incur the risk of unleashing a serious backlash.

Regular attenders at meetings of these constitutional democratic union institutions where Party members were active understood the conventions by which trade unions and politics were intertwined. They were accustomed to listening to regular political debates and casting their votes as responsible trade unionists for or against the political line being argued by their Communist colleagues. The Southall and London AEU District Committees debated and carried motions from their branches in October and November 1939 which condemned the imperialist war. The successful conferences held by the Glasgow and Sheffield trades councils against the war in November and December 1939 were probably supported by their respective AEU district committees.[22]

Though all four committees had left-wing majorities, Party members were dominant only in London and Southall. In Sheffield and Glasgow the regular left-wing majority of non-Party committeemen either agreed with a full anti-war position or were willing to acquiesce in a resolution which opposed the war while stressing the importance of fighting the employers' profiteering. In Glasgow the ILP activists in the AEU would have been anti-war in September and already arguing that position *against* their Party colleagues. It is likely that left-wing Labour activists in Sheffield had opposed the war from the outset.

It is notable that the District Committees where Party activists were playing prominent roles – Manchester, Birmingham, Bristol and Coventry – did not register any opposition towards the war. The comparative isolation of Party activists who openly espoused an anti-war position was reflected at the 1940 AEU National Committee. There was no motion about the nature of the war; it was evidently deemed inadvisable to raise such a potentially divisive issue. This prudence was justified by the sizeable majority against the emergency war-on-two-fronts motion moved by Jim Clokey, a fellow-travelling delegate from Glasgow, and seconded by the delegate from Greenock, was roundly defeated by 30–9.

Votes on the other left-wing motions which dealt solely with the domestic engineering economic struggle continued to reflect the 'rank-and-filist' sentiments of the majority of delegates. Tommy Sillars, the Party veteran who was President of the Glasgow District Committee from Glasgow, and W. Somerville from Renfrew proposed to censure the Executive for settling with the engineering employers for less than the 10s. per week wage increase which the 1939 National Committee had approved and for instructing the Executive that the National Committee possessed the authority by rule to lay down policy for the union. It was lost by a narrow margin of only four votes. The Committee then proceeded to pass a motion instructing the Executive to seek a 3d per hour wage increase in the next round of negotiations with the engineering employers, to recall the National Committee if no settlement had been achieved by 30 September and to hold a ballot vote on any settlement.[23]

Tanner used his inaugural Presidential address to the National Committee to establish his credibility as a militant left-wing official. But he also issued a clear challenge to the Party and left-wing delegates to prove their trade union loyalism.

> This is an engineer's war. We are fully and personally aware of that fact. Every hour since I took office as President this has been impressed upon me.
>
> It is a machine war with a vengeance. Whether it is in the anti-aircraft defences, or the machines on land and sea, or in the sky, it is the engineer who stands behind them all . . . Such is the grave responsibility thrust upon the membership of our Union, and such is the collective responsibility that all of us present here to-day have to accept . . .
>
> There is need to think deeply and clearly, free from narrowness and prejudice, and to act decisively in the interests of the Union, its members and the whole working class . . .
>
> As engineering workers, we are in many respects better placed than we were in the last war. In 1914 and 1918 there were many unions in the industrial field we occupy, with their varying interests, constitutions, etc. To-day, the Amalgamated Engineering Union is decisive because of the size of its membership and the power of its organisation . . .
>
> In the last war we had no agreements recognising shop stewards. The needs of the situation during that time brought into being the Shop Stewards Movement. To-day we have shop stewards as an

integral part of the organisation able to perform their duties freely
and fully, backed by the strength of the Union . . . Shop stewards
are, I repeat, an integral part of the organisation, and they are performing one of the most vital functions of the Union in safeguarding
the conditions and rights of our members in the workshops. Without
their active work and loyal co-operation, the Union would be in a
sorry plight.

. . . Recently a conference of shop stewards of this and other
unions was held in Birmingham under conditions of secrecy – or
shall I say, intended obscurity. It was not called as a result of a
demand from below . . . because there is every opportunity and
facility for the interests of members to be adequately considered
within this Union. The holding of this conference, which I understand, decided to attempt to control the policy of the trade unions in
which the engineering industry, is a challenge to this National
Committee . . .

During the last war there were no agreements on dilution. To-day
we have such agreements, and providing we win this war, we will be
in a position to see that they are implemented after; if we do not win
this war, then no one present here will be concerned at all about
agreements, the restoration of custom and practice, many will not be
interested whether the sun rises or sets.[24]

Tanner had chosen a shrewd and politic gambit which simultaneously
pre-empted any serious challenge from his left flank and established his
authority with the minority of Executive Councillors to his right. Under
AEU rules the President was very much the *primus inter pares* inside the
Executive Council. He needed to convince the small centre-right caucus
on the Council that he would not surrender their authority to unofficial
'rank-and-file' elements. He also valued his special relationship with the
union's left-wing, but he wanted to retain it on his own terms.

The centre-right caucus seized on the Party's anti-war line to demand
punitive action against Communists in the union. Their motives were
dual. They responded from patriotism but scented the chance to reverse
the Party's growing influence inside the union. Tanner had no desire to
tilt the political balance towards the right and by bringing the conflict out
in the open he hoped to avoid any blood-letting. He anticipated that
Party activists' response would be in keeping with their previous constitutional militancy, well within the boundaries of union loyalism.

The Executive Council summonsed 14 Party activists, including Joe
Scott, George Crane, Edmund Frow and Charlie Wellard, to appear
before it to answer charges of attending the Birmingham conference. The
Council deemed their attendance sufficient grounds for exercising its
right under Rule 21 Clause 1 to expel members who 'injured or
attempted to injure the Union, or worked or acted contrary to the interests of the Union or its members . . . or otherwise brought the Union into
discredit'.[25]

This was the same rule under which Party activists had been called to account by the Executive in 1931 when they refused to appear and argue their case as a principled protest against the Executive Council's right to restrict rank-and-file activity. They were expelled and then reinstated by the Final Appeals Court.[26] In 1940 all the accused appeared before the Executive Council and Joe Scott conducted a vigorous defence on their behalf. Fourteen martyrs for trade union democracy would have been invaluable if engineering militants had been seriously building an 'independent shop stewards' movement'. Evidently, neither AEU Party activists nor the new Party Centre had any intention of fomenting such 'rank-and-file' activity and jeopardizing the Party's position inside the union.

Scott's defence did not treat the Executive as a kangaroo court. He presented a reasoned case which accepted the legitimacy of the AEU Rules. He pointed out that the Birmingham conference had taken no decisions which usurped the Executive's authority:

> He reminded Jack Tanner of his own activities during the 1914–20 period as leader of the Shop Stewards' Movement and editor of *Solidarity*. He cited Tanner's speech in Moscow in 1920 [at the Comintern Second Congress] and claimed that all the union's officials present had taken part in so-called unofficial activities at some stage in his (*sic*) career.[27]

As Tanner's putative successor on the Executive Council Scott had taken the additional precaution of arranging speaking engagements at AEU branch meetings for the whole day of the Birmingham conference. The respective branch secretaries verified Scott's presence to the Executive. In the light of this patently loyal defence, Jack Tanner had little difficulty in persuading the Executive to be content with issuing a Final Warning to the Birmingham Fourteen. Most Councillors were reluctant to depart from the wide latitude within which the union had traditionally allowed members to exercise the traditional 'liberty of the subject'. They were as susceptible to Scott's invocations of the union's loyal 'rank-and-file' traditions; they had a genuine respect for a British subject's unwritten constitutional freedom of association; they were also chary that the Registrar of Friendly Societies would de-register the AEU for punitive action against members who exercised these liberties.[28]

This encounter which ended in clemency cleared the air. Each side asserted their respective positions and then determinedly backed away from a confrontation. Party activists continued to abstain from serious unofficial activity. The Executive made no attempt to enforce its branch circular sent out after the Birmingham conference which instructed district committees and branch officials to inform all shop stewards that their stewards' credentials would be withdrawn if they attended any unofficial gathering in their official stewards' capacity. They were no doubt mindful of the sizeable minority who had voted for a motion at the 1940 National Committee condemning the branch circular despatched by the Executive in 1939 after the *Daily Worker* conferences which had been couched in similar terms.[29]

Moreover, the AEU Executive was dependent on the willing consent of district committees to enforce union policy in the branches and on the shopfloor. The structure of the union gave the district committees sovereign authority which the Executive felt it could only revoke under the most extreme duress. Party activists were influential on the district committees and union branches where most of the contentious unofficial activities took place. These were also the areas where the engineering industry and AEU membership were most concentrated. If the Executive Council had embarked on a punitive crusade against 'unofficial' activities according to a narrow interpretation of the rule book, they would have invited an energetically hostile response from these powerful institutions and a certain challenge to the Final Appeal Court.

It is hardly surprising that by the autumn of 1940 the AEU Executive and Party engineering activists had resumed the symbiotic relationship developed in the late 1930s. Neither the wartime emergency nor the Party's political anti-war line disturbed this *de facto* partnership from which each side gained vital objectives. By tolerating Party activism within the union, the AEU Executive gained a unique cadre force on the shopfloor which provided the basis for extending the union's membership and influence. By acting reliably within the union's rules and conventions, Communist engineers gained positive freedom of action inside a flexible and supportive institution on the shopfloor from which they could operate to enlarge and consolidate working-class power.

Party activists followed their acquittal by marked abstention from any activity which might arouse the Executive's ire. The National Committee was duly recalled on 28 November 1940 to consider the national wages claim which the employers had rejected. It decided, without prejudice to future claims or the union's freedom of action in the future, to instruct the Executive to apply immediately to the National Arbitration Court.[30] Despite the left-wing anti-war sentiments still prevalent among engineering activists in Scotland, Sheffield and London, there was no question of delegates proposing industrial action or defying Bevin's compulsory arbitration machinery.

Joe Scott attended the 1941 National Committee resuming his old role as leading Party delegate. He was chosen as Chairman of the Standing Orders Committee with the 'progressive elements' gaining a clear majority on it. The Committee met from 16 to 23 June; Germany invaded the Soviet Union on the 22nd. On 19 June the Committee passed a resolution calling for the ban on the *Daily Worker* to be lifted.[31] On 20 June delegates passed motions supporting the first three of the People's Convention's six demands, including friendship with the Soviet Union.[32] They also passed a motion by 27–25 whose content was a clear reference to the Birmingham Fourteen. It declared that 'more toleration should be shown to rank and file movements' and 'History demonstrates that progress and development in the trade union movement have directly benefited by the existence of such activity.'[33]

The *modus vivendi* survived further wartime stresses. There were warnings issued by the General Secretary, Fred Smith, about stewards' attendance in their official capacity to Party-sponsored conferences including the People's Convention. No expulsions were likely, however, because Party activists in the AEU were careful to observe the prescribed limits in undertaking unofficial extra-union activity in their 'individual capacity'.

The situation in the Fed was complicated by Arthur Horner's position as President and his own commitment to fighting the war against Germany for the same reasons as Pollitt, Campbell and Gallacher. Unlike these three, Horner could not bring himself to admit that he had been wrong to support the war and his high union office provided him with the cover to indulge his conscience. The *Daily Worker* reported on 13 October 1939 that the South Wales District Committee had supported the new line by 14–0 with one abstention, presumably Horner's, and then stated that reports of a split in South Wales were without foundation. This was the only Party district to which the story appended an explicit denial, despite the fact that the London district vote of 26–1 with one abstention presented more evidence of conflict.

As a loyal and committed Communist, Horner tried his best to condemn the war. His repeated attempts were minimalist, hypothetical and hedged with evasion. He began in apparent good faith but denunciations of war in the abstract were the most he could actually manage. He spoke in this sophistical vein at the Pontypridd *Daily Worker* conference at the beginning of December 1939.

> War only causes an aggravation of the class antagonisms ... Whatever our estimation of the character of the war, we cannot have a truce. The capitalist class, as a class, still exists, and the efforts of the working class must be to lessen and resist exploitation by the capitalist class.

Idris Cox defended Horner obliquely at the Cardiff *Daily Worker* conference, saying that although there might be differences about the war on an international scale there could be no differences about the war which the capitalist class was conducting here against workers. But Len Jeffries attacked those who supported this war as being enemies of the working class even though they might be official leaders.[34]

In South Wales substantial numbers of Party activists not only supported the anti-war line for principled bolshevik reasons, they also believed it to be practical politics. They were keenly anti-war for the best bolshevik reasons, but their political response was reinforced by the non-conformist pacificism in their own socialization which was still a strong part of the chapel culture in wartime Wales. Broomfield remarks on *Plaid Cymru*'s official pacifism at this time. He notes that there were more conscientious objectors in Wales than any other part of Britain.[35] We have also observed the numbers of coalfield activists habouring anti-Horner sentiments before September 1939 for rank-and-filist reasons. Horner's evident readiness to work with the state in the wartime emergency re-offended the rank-and-filist sensibilities which the pre-1914 Unofficial Reform Committee had imprinted so deeply into the coalfield's union culture.

However, Horner's continuing adherence to the war-on-two-fronts position was emulated by his close-knit group of Party supporters who provided a counterweight to the pressure against him building up inside the Party and the Fed. As Fed President, Horner discharged routine duties which involved cooperating with the Government's war effort and made the regular public patriotic professions which were expected of the trade union establishment. His refusal to toe the Party line was not challenged by the five Communists on the Fed Executive who were his protégés, but it rankled with the Labour MPs sponsored by the Fed who attended the Executive. Like Jack Tanner and the constitutional militants, the Labour left-wingers doubted Horner's 100 per cent commitment to the war-on-two-fronts position which they strongly espoused. They also resented the undoubted growth of his personal authority inside the union and saw the Party's anti-war line as an opportunity to take him down a peg and reassert their own influence.

It was the Party anti-war activists who opened the attack. They coalesced to ensure a rank-and-file challenge to the war on two fronts position from inside the Fed. The *Daily Worker* reported at the end of January 1940 that 38 lodges had passed resolutions calling for a special coalfield conference on the war. Most of them had taken anti-war positions.[36] Their determined challenge was mounted with the encouragement of Rust and Dutt, who must have agreed with Aneurin Bevan and Bill Mainwaring that Horner led an undeservedly charmed life. The Party Centre could point to Scotland where, because of the county unions' decrepit state, Communist miners had easily swayed delegate conferences against the war. Dutt and Rust chose to ignore the revitalized Fed's vigorous branch life and argued that the Scottish successes should be repeated in South Wales.[37]

The Fed's Labour MPs were delighted. They were furious that Horner had successfully outflanked them yet again with his support for the war on two fronts, and they relished the spectacle of his comrades trying to extract their pound of flesh at the coalfield conference scheduled for February. In the event, Dutt and Rust chose not to escalate the attack on Horner. The *Daily Worker* was punctiliously silent in the weeks preceding the conference and remained notably reticent during the fortnight after the conference was adjourned without voting in order for delegates to be mandated by their lodges on the two motions: the Labour left-wing's war on two fronts or the Party's anti-war.

As presiding officer, Horner could remain conspicuously aloof from the fierce arguments on the floor. Horner had spoken perfunctorily for the anti-war motion, and used his casting vote to ensure that both went forward to the reconvened conference. He was evidently determined to ensure that the decision was seen to be taken by the 'rank-and-file'. At the reconvened conference on 2 March a roll-call vote recorded 1940 votes for the war on two fronts and 607 for the anti-war.[38] The Party Centre and the South Wales district leadership speedily closed the whole episode with the minimum loss of face all round. The Fed's failure to adopt the anti-war motion was explained in the usual catechistic way: Party members had failed to do their daily mass work correctly. With the right mass work, the outcome next time would be different.[39]

Horner told the Fed's Annual Conference a few weeks later that he 'would operate majority decisions. When I cannot carry out the wishes of the majority of the members I will do the only honourable thing, that is, offer my resignation.'[40] He proceeded to perform his wartime duties as Fed President with renewed enthusiasm. The Fed's Labour MPs must have ruefully reflected that they might have been better off in not pursuing the matter so zealously.[41]

*　　*　　*

When the fall of France ended the phoney war, Dutt and Rust were well prepared for the popular change in mood. They had already discreetly eased Pollitt back on to the Politburo[42] and continued unobtrusively to trim. On the day Hitler and Petain signed the armistice, a Communist Party Manifesto was published in the *Daily Worker* which called for a new Government to come to power. Only then could the danger of 'Fascist invasion' and 'tyranny' be resisted.

> The real defence of the people requires a complete break with the interests of the ruling class. The interests of the people require the speediest ending of the war, not by surrender to Fascism at home and abroad, but by the strength of a free people organising their own

defence and leading the way to peace and unity with the working people of all countries.[43]

The Manifesto called on the organized working class 'to get together and develop such a mighty movement as can secure the formation of such a government (in which no representative of imperialism or friend of fascism served).[44]

The Coalition Government's determination to wage total war properly produced a fascinating series of interlocking and conflicting reactions inside the Party. Bevin's plans for the full utilization of labour in the war economy entailed a comprehensive planning apparatus. On the one hand, the Party Centre declared that they were 'Fascist' measures. The measures for directing labour which the Government believed were necessary to combat Hitler were compared to Nazi Germany. Dutt followed the logic of his pre-war arguments that capitalism had outgrown liberal democracy and required the corporate apparatus of a centralized State to survive. The Marxist–Leninist hypothesis that Fascism was the form most appropriate to advanced capitalism was proven because both sides in the imperialist war had now adopted it.[45]

This new phase of capitalism created new conditions for the class struggle. Marx and Engels had welcomed bourgeois capitalism's defeat of feudalism; Dutt now found reason to herald the defeat of bourgeois capitalism in the name of dialectical materialism. The liberal democratic values of bourgeois individualism would become redundant and fit only for the dustbin of history. This meant, of course, that many of the deeply rooted habits of British trade union culture would have to be discarded at the same time. Rank-and-filism, for example, drew substantially on 'bourgeois democratic' values for its resonance.

The practical conclusions for this line of argument were that Communists should accommodate themselves to the progressive new war machine in order to better exploit it for their own and the proletariat's ends. However, the opposite reaction occurred on the ground. Ted Bramley recalled that Party activists had responded to Bevin's 'Fascist' measures by preparing themselves to lead the organized working class in a mighty mass movement to 'restore the liberties of the people, to remove the dead hand of the police and to permit the free discussion of the mighty issues now at stake'.

Temperamentally, it seemed, most British Party members were incapable of welcoming the advent of a corporatist trade union movement which could do battle with a corporatist state. Bramley remembered the intensifying expectation that the Party must prepare itself for a protracted siege in defence of democracy in the working class's name. There would be conflict with the repressive State and its corporate union allies from which the Party would emerge as the sole leader of the democratic 'rank-and-file' working class.[46]

The actual political course followed by the Party between 11 May 1940 when the Coalition Government took over and 22 June 1941 when the Soviet Union was invaded by Germany followed the political course laid down by Pollitt and Campbell in September 1939 for the war on two fronts. Bevin's planned economy drew everyone into a collective working life where war production was paramount. Party trade union activists responded by *accepting* the corporate parameters of the total war machine and utilizing the opportunities presented by the planning mechanisms to strengthen shopfloor union organization. Because Bevin's corporatism was *not* Fascist, but relied instead on voluntarism for its effectiveness, Communists reaped rich rewards by operating as 'bourgeois democrats' within the planning apparatus, which Dutt no doubt dismissed as rather humorous Heath-Robinson specimens of the future advanced capitalism. The impressive advances made for the trade union movement and their own Party by leading skirmishes in the economic struggle, are described in the next chapter.

The effect of the Battle of Britain reinforced the new collective conviction, which endured until Hitler invaded Russia, that the country's fate hung in the balance. People developed an immense interest in the problems of the war economy. People worked enormous amounts of voluntary overtime to produce the weaponry to defend themselves and their families. There was real popular ferment. They were reflecting on the new collective institutions and thinking about what would happen after the war. Perhaps because so many parts of this war were familiar from 1914–18, people found time and space for ruminating about the peace despite their long and strenuous working hours.

The People's Convention Movement, launched in the Autumn of 1940 was the Party's attempt to exploit this quickening of the public pulse by creating the mighty mass movement which could be directed against the Coalition Government and towards unity with the working people of all countries. The left-wing Labour MP, D.N. Pritt, also sensed that the time to protest had come. Pritt had worked closely with the Party Centre on all its pre-war 'real united front' initiatives and it is probable that Pollitt convinced Pritt to begin his campaign at the end of June 1940 at one of the ASSNC's strongholds, Vickers aircraft factory at Weybridge. He spoke to workers there that 'in his view both the ruling class in general and the [Coalition] Government in particular were finished, and that the opportunity for the working class to come to power and establish a real workers' government was at hand'.[47]

The vehicle chosen to mount the campaign was the Vigilance Committee. Local vigilance committees had been formed during the 1914–18 war for the purpose of safeguarding trade union conditions. Both pro- and anti-war socialists and trade union activists had participated in them.[48] A National People's Vigilance Committee was established after a highly successful conference in July 1940 organized by Pritt and the Party. This committee began the campaign for Peace and a People's Government. Pollitt addressed a meeting organized by the Party at the end of July and attended by 15,000 people. Home Office reports described it as the largest meeting since the war had begun. Local and regional People's Conventions were held and there was a long and successful build-up to the National People's Convention in January 1941 with a great deal of support from local Labour parties and from inside the trade union machinery.[49]

The Convention's six immediate demands were rooted in populism and included 'the Defence of the people's democratic and trade union rights'. Dutt and Rust were hoping to put the Comintern's anti-war line into practice by nurturing the Convention as a peace movement; two other demands were for 'A People's Peace that got rid of the causes of war' and 'Friendship with the USSR'. They did not include any description of the war as being imperialist nor did the Convention label Bevin's war economy machine as Fascist.[50]

Party union activists were markedly successful in promoting the Convention. The Fed Executive supported the Convention Movement, despite strong pressure from the Labour Party and MFGB. Horner was one of its keenest proponents because it was not anti-war. His persuasive rhetoric must have swayed many non-Party Executive members. Party members were in a minority of three on the Executive and its original vote in favour of the Convention was 13–3. After Lodge resolutions had been received, there was a second vote of 10–8. The Fed annual conference upheld the Executive's decision in March 1941. (Four Fed delegates, including Horner, had attended the National Convention in January.)[51]

There was strong interest and support for the Convention inside the AEU. Local People's Convention Committees gained easy access to AEU branch secretaries' names and addresses, presumably through friendly AEU District Committee members. Many branch officers were puzzled about how to respond to the local committees' written requests that their branches send Convention delegates and wrote to the Executive for guidance. In December 1940, the Executive felt constrained to issue a circular pointing out that there could be no AEU branch delegates either 'branch or district officers, shop stewards or rank-and-file members'. Eighteen AEU lay officials had publicly supported the Convention in October 1940; however, the Executive was content to merely issue them a final warning.[52] At the AEU National Committee in 1941 a motion proposed by Jim Clokey, a 'fellow-travelling' left-winger from Glasgow, supported the Convention's six demands. It was passed and prompted a spirited exchange of views in the AEU Journal among non-Party activists.[53]

The People's Convention Movement was an inspired political initiative embarked on at a crucial political moment. It coincided with the extraordinary social flux produced by the gearing up of the total war economic machine and the upsurge in popular interest and involvement in the war.[54] The Convention's propaganda reached a far greater number of people than any of the Party's pre-war campaigns. As the Convention Movement kept gaining momentum, King Street was caught off balance. The Party leadership had no clear idea of where to steer this larger popular, enthusiastic response. There were 2234 delegates to the National Convention in London and Mass Observation reports noted '. . . the fact that these delegates had come from all over the country and from many sources untapped in ordinary conferences and leftwing meetings'.[55] The observers concluded that the majority of delegates came from the 'organised working class'.[56]

It transpired that delegates were not interested in discussing either the increased working-class suffering as a result of the war or the Government's conduct of it. The Mass Observation reports described 'the pre-eminent concern being the world to be created after the war, and social conditions to be aspired to at that time'. Clergymen and soldier delegates got much applause and the audience was more interested in their expressions of positive idealism than in listening to ARP problems and complaints about dependants' allowances. There was considerable criticism of the CPGB for criticizing British war conduct without also condemning German war atrocities.[57]

The Home Secretary, Herbert Morrison, received the Cabinet's consent to ban the *Daily Worker* under Defence Regulation 2D on 13 January 1941, the day after the National People's Convention. He told them that the newspaper's stories were 'calculated to have a bad effect on the morale of the people' . . . and [he] believed there was a risk in allowing Communist propaganda to continue into a period when circumstances might become more difficult'.[58] Morrison was unable to point to evidence that the *Daily Worker* encouraged outright opposition to the war. However, the *Daily Worker* had been the People's Convention's main source of publicity since Fleet Street's 'populist' papers loyally avoided mentioning this potentially 'subversive' campaign. It was the palpable success of the Convention Movement which prompted Morrison's move and ensured that the Cabinet finally accepted the proposal which he had first made on 23 December 1940.

If the Party Centre had been seriously interested in destabilizing the Government, they could have speedily abandoned their formal anti-war line and then pulled out all the stops to expand and escalate the Convention Movement. The *Daily Worker*'s content was virtually identical to the *Daily Mirror*'s except for its token and usually oblique anti-war references. Once the Party had expressed its intention of ceasing opposition to the war, the Cabinet's continuing suppression of the *Daily Worker* would have exposed its 'real and sinister' Fascist intent. Indeed, Morrison decided that he had no grounds for banning the monthly *New Propellor* because 'although edited and inspired by Communists, [it] has been careful not to associate itself with the Communist Party as such. It is devoted entirely to the exploitation of industrial grievances and contains no direct references to the war.'[59]

King Street could have issued a new daily newspaper along the lines of *New Propellor* at the same time as announcing a modification of its anti-war position back to the war on two fronts. Left-wing Labour MPs, like Bevan, would have found themselves in a genuine dilemma about whom to support – their party in government or the British people's unwritten constitutional right to freedom of the press. The ramifications of this democratic issue would have ensured that the popular ferment around the People's Convention continued and active consideration of political issues widened.

King Street was notably unwilling to let the People's Convention develop further as a genuinely popular movement. No plans were made to organize any more national events and the Party leadership did nothing to provide an alternative publicity and propaganda vehicle for the Convention Movement in the continuing absence of the *Daily Worker*. One of the principal reasons for the Party's quiescence was the widely held belief in Party circles that the Government would follow its ban on the *Daily Worker* by declaring the CPGB itself illegal. The general consensus was that the Party should keep quiet and remain legal in order to be better able to serve the working class in its hour of need. The Government evidently was not Fascist enough to justify underground resistance. Party union activists also feared retaliatory action from trade union executives and an adverse shopfloor reaction against Communism if the Party were banned. They were extremely reluctant to become martyrs and lose their strong positions on the shopfloor and union lay bodies.

James Hinton has shown that Palme Dutt was the only member of the Politburo who was keen to continue the momentum generated by the People's Convention Movement. Dutt was evidently willing to run the risk of incurring a government ban on the Party for the sake of facilitating the further popular development of the Convention Movement.[60] He could see that a quite unpredictable situation might develop if the Party leadership encouraged the Convention's popular appeal though he failed to acknowledge that the Party would have to abandon the Comintern line to do so.

Dutt understood the possibilities inherent in the People's Convention

Movement almost in spite of himself. His bolshevik nose had unerringly and involuntarily detected the smell of social flux and uncertainty alongside the collective commitment to fight the war. The rest of the old Young Turks were indifferent, if not actually uneasy, at the prospect of moving outside the known and predictable networks of left-wing trade union activism to the unknown terrain of real populism and genuine 'mighty mass movements'.

Within British political culture the successful mobilization of a 'popular' radical movement requires a sponsor connected to the political establishment. From John Wilkes to Lloyd George, these sponsors have organized and orchestrated the popular enthusiasms and 'people's will' so that the political establishment may notice it. Having launched a 'movement', they then interpret it to Westminster. Once the Party Centre had withdrawn Communist sponsorship, no other political group appeared to foster the People's Convention and it atrophied quietly and quickly, apparently without trace.

The popular radical impulses and inquisitiveness which fuelled the Convention can be seen behind the meteoric rise of the Common Wealth Party, formed in the summer of 1942 'by a merger of the 1941 Committee led by J.B. Priestley with Sir Richard Acland's Forward March movement'.[61] However, Common Wealth certainly had no serious intention to disable or dislodge the political establishment. Its wartime by-election successes remained isolated monuments to the genuine fluidity within in civil society at this unusual conjuncture.

The Party leadership concentrated all the Party's energies in an 'End the Ban' campaign for the *Daily Worker*. Party activists did not appear to mourn the Convention Movement's passing and conducted the campaign for the *Daily Worker* ban with zeal and righteous democratic indignation. An impressive crop of resolutions made their way through existing political and trade union institutions protesting at the Cabinet's infringement of British democratic liberties.[62]

* * *

The German invasion of the Soviet Union and the USSR's subsequent entry into the war produced another change in the Party's position on the war which proved to be more significant for its attitude to the 'economic struggle' than the previous policy shift. The British Party leadership abandoned not only its much-diluted anti-war line but also the war on two fronts perspective which had been the basis of most of the Party's practical politics. The Soviet Socialist Fatherland was at risk and there was now only one war for Communists.[63]

The veteran Young Turks who had called for Independent Leadership at the start of the war might have been expected to argue that the domestic class struggle must not be neglected. However, they became totally committed to directing all British proletarian efforts into increasing war production. They recognized that the British working class had the heroic revolutionary responsibility to defend the Soviet Union, the citadel of revolutionary socialism. This meant subordinating the 'economic struggle' to the over-riding need to make planes and tanks for the USSR. 'The main thing the trade unions require to concentrate upon is the development of the initiative of the workers at all stages in the production process. . . . [Communists'] first proposition [is] day-to-day co-operation on production questions at all levels within the enterprise.'[64]

Pollitt and Campbell resumed their official leadership positions and Pollitt threw himself immediately into a campaign to increase war production. He reminded the large working-class audiences of workers which he was addressing more or less continuously that they had to make sacrifices because it was they who were providing the vital ingredients essential for victory. Life Itself was finally justifying Pollitt's own faith: the working class had everyone's future in the palms of their hands and the sweat of their brow.

> The Tories must be made to realise that we are not living in 1935, when the last General Election took place, or in 1938 when Munich occurred, but in 1943, when the working class is the main force upon which both production and manpower for the army, navy and airforce depend, and upon whose fighting power, resilience and leadership the fate of Britain depends.[65]

The invasion of the Soviet Union also marked a watershed in the British people's collective attitude to the war and politics. It precipitated a keen popular interest in the Soviet Union's war effort and admiration for the Red Army's exploits, accompanied by an inquisitiveness about what Communists were doing and saying in Britain. This passionate partisanship continued for about 18 months.[66] Party activists also responded enthusiastically. Many of them had never doubted that Hitler would turn eastwards and they were profoundly relieved when he did so. Life Itself had finally justified their expectations; they could again fight Fascism with full force and in good faith. Many Party activists had been apparently repressing their own commitment to the general anti-Fascist politics being propagated by the Government machine and were glad to give voice to these feelings without recourse to Duttian sleight of hand.

Not surprisingly, there was a dramatic increase in the Party's membership in the 18 months after Soviet entry. Recruitment was facilitated by the higher public profile which Communists now felt able to adopt on the shopfloor. They were fortunate in being in the right place at the right time. The fight against Hitler was indeed an engineers' war and Pollitt's and Campbell's army of Communist shop stewards in war factories reaped the benefits. When the Sixteenth Party Congress was finally held in the spring of 1943 (it had been postponed from the autumn of 1939) Party membership stood at 60,000. At the Eighteenth Party Congress in September 1945, membership had declined by some 15,000 to 45,435. While this was nowhere near the figure of 100,000 which King Street had aimed for at the height of pro-Soviet euphoria in 1943, the Party finished the war with twice as many members as it had at the beginning.[67] In 1945, Peter Kerrigan observed that: 'membership still remains over-whelmingly weighted in favour of engineering and aircraft workers'.[68]

The period after Soviet entry into the war to VE Day is conventionally viewed as the Communist Party's finest hour. Historians point to the tre-bling of Party membership and its spectacularly increased public profile. Constant manœuvreing was indeed required at the Ministry of Information to contend with the Party's new-found flair for self-public-ity. Pollitt won more times than either Duff Cooper or the BBC cared to admit. Local Party officials, many of them newly appointed to cope with the increased membership, were ubiquitous. With the help of Party mem-bers with a flair for 'making an impact', they organized local activities to emphasize the Soviet Army's war effort; and they invented new and inge-nious links with the country's new ally. They also applied fertile imagina-tions to involving everyone in doing something for the war effort.[69]

The remains of the CPGB's public relations *coups* still survive as a sub-plot in the long-running mythology of the patriotic just war. However, the notable success in popularizing Uncle Joe's Army has been allowed to obscure the evidence that the Party's new pro-war production line was applied firmly within the established perspective of revolutionary prag-matism. Party union activists readily shouldered their responsibility for war production to help the Soviet Socialist Fatherland, but most were also reluctant to refrain from taking opportunities on the shopfloor. They interpreted Pollitt's declaration about the crucial importance of the working class to mean that it was incumbent on Party activists to heed their needs and requirements. When management were behaving in unfair, high-handed, or other unacceptable ways, it was a Communist duty to lead the opposition.

Moreover, King Street made no attempt to impose the new pro-war production line by laying down day-to-day priorities and tactics for Party activists. Consequently they continued to lead economic conflict when it occurred. Though pressure on factories to be seen to be supporting the Soviet Socialist Fatherland was intense, Pollitt and Campbell also pro-vided propaganda support for Party activists who were active in skir-mishes and even strikes. By operating within their tolerant guidelines, most militants were able to carry out the injunction that shopfloor activity should be subordinated to the war effort. Moreover, despite provocation from its left flank, the Party Centre continued to interpet the pro-war production line with shrewd forbearance. As a result the Communist Party held on to most of its union activists even during the sporadic outbreaks of 'war-weary' strikes which occurred in 1942–44, which ultimately led to Bevin taking punitive powers against strikers in Regulation 1AA.

In practice, Pollitt and Campbell distinguished between members who led strikes with the intention of minimizing the disruption caused and others who were keen to escalate the conflict without regard to lost production. Support from the Party Centre was forthcoming for the first and withdrawn from the second. In 1944 the four-day strike at Austin's Longbridge was condoned. In 1943 the prolonged strike at the Vickers shipyard in Barrow-in-Furness was implacably condemned and opposed.[70] We shall observe in the next chapter how most Party shopfloor activists reconciled the pursuit of proletarian self-sacrifice with their continuing encroachment on managerial prerogative and without inciting serious industrial action.

Notes

1. Kevin Morgan notes that Pollitt had argued initially that the Party should not condone preparations for conscription, not for pacifist reasons but in order to stand up for British voluntarist democratic tradition. Morgan, K., 1993, op. cit.: 104–6.
2. *Daily Worker*, 30 August 1939.
3. *Daily Worker*, 4 September 1939.
4. On 5 September, the headline over the *Daily Worker*'s leader reflected these memories and sought to focus them: 'August 1914, September 1939'. It continued 'The people hate war. It is they who – whether on the battlefield or in the crowded working class quarters during air raids – have to make the greatest sacrifices . . . But the people know that they are resolved that this is to be a *Different kind of War*. Whatever may be the aims, or the opinions, of a certain section of people in Britain, the common people, in the factories, on the land, everywhere, have one aim and one aim only: *the destruction of fascism and the repulsion of all attacks upon democracy* . . . Never again will they tolerate the presence in our country of people who are against the poor . . . They will not tolerate people who have been deaf to appeals to tackle the problems of poverty and unemployment'.
5. Branson, 1985, *History of the CPGB*, op. cit.: 267. She points out that there is some confusion as to whether Springhall returned on 24 September or the following week.
6. Ibid.: 267–8. The minutes of the meeting are published in King F. and Matthews, G., 1990, *About Turn*, Lawrence & Wishart. See also *Daily Worker*, 12 October 1939. The *Daily Worker* had published the Central Committee's resolution of 2 October on 4 October. However, the reso-

lution did not directly repudiate its Statement of 1 September and there had apparently been confusion about whether there was a new line. (See Mahon, op. cit.: 250–2)

7. See Branson, 1985, op. cit.: 270–73. Kevin Morgan also cites the pacifist, anti-ruling class war feelings of some members, but he is also keen to establish that there were many Party members who agreed with Pollitt and Campbell and kept faith with their views (Morgan, 1989, *Against Fascism and War*, op. cit.: 92–5).

8. *Communist International*, Vol. III, pp. 456–8. quoting Dimitrov in *World News and Views*, November 1939.

9. There is a useful discussion of the changes in the Comintern's position from the signing of the Ribbentrop Pact to its dissolution in 1943 in Urban, 1986, *Moscow and the Italian Communist Party* op. cit.: 152–61. She argues convincingly that the positions adopted by the Comintern were not motivated by the desire for world revolution. She shows that the main influences on the Comintern at this time were not its international affiliates but Stalin's foreign policy advisers. The Comintern's positions were formulated to further the Soviet Union's aims.

10. Morgan, K., 1993, op. cit.: 114. Pollitt returned to London in February 1940. Ted Bramley found a convenient pretext for suggesting Pollitt's return to London to facilitate his early resumption of a leading role in Party counsels.

11. *Daily Worker*, 30 October 1939 (my emphasis). *Daily Worker* conferences were held in all places where Party members were well-enough organized to convene them. Their stated aim was to influence trade unionists. The reports in the *Daily Worker* show that they were attended by the same networks of Labour and trade union activists who had been involved in previous anti-Fascist and pro-Spanish Republican activity. There is no evidence that most Party speakers adopted a Leninist anti-war position at them. Rust's use of the term 'independent' was a reference back to the call for Independent Leadership made during the Class Against Class period. See pp. 33–5.

12. *Daily Worker*, 20 December 1939.

13. Ibid.

14. *Daily Worker*, 29 January 1940.

15. See pp. 35–7 and pp. 54–5.

16. The aim was to increase *New Propellor*'s circulation from its current 30,000 to 35,000. *NP*, October 1939, Vol. 4 No. 9.

17. See *New Propellor*, Vol. 5 No. 5, April 1940.

18. Ibid. For the conference see pp. 285–6.

19. *Daily Worker*, 11 January 1940. See also 12 December 1939 and 18 January 1940.

20. *Daily Worker*, 22 January 1940.

21. LAB 10/356, 17 February 1940.

22. For the trades council conferences see *Daily Worker*, 17 November 1939 and 4 December 1939. The Southall District Committee motion was passed on 12 October 1939 (Southall District Committee minutes). George Crane had become a district committeeman in Southall by this time and another veteran Party activist, Ernie Athorn was chairman. For the London District Committee resolution see *Daily Worker,* 20 November 1939. The Sheffield AEU District Committee minutes for this period have not survived.

23. AEU National Committee Report 1940. The emergency war-on-two-fronts motion stated that trade union independence and opposition to the policy of the employing class was essential for unions to carry out their functions and defend their members' interests. It condemned Labour's policy of joining the Government which had sponsored the Trades Disputes Act and was the bitterest enemy of trade unionism. The motion of censure was defeated by 22–18. The motion tying the Executive to the 3d per hour increase was carried by 25–11 after an amendment diluting its constitutional militancy had been carried by 22–18.

24. Presidential Address to July 1940 AEU National Committee, Committee Report, pp. 212–13.

25. *AEU Rulebook*, 1935 ed.; and Frow and Frow, 1982, *Engineering Struggles*, op. cit.: 148. The Executive Council also cited Rule 22 Clause 8, lines 6–10 which stated that any member 'shall be excluded' who 'at any time works against the interests of this union or its members'.

26. Tanner had also been charged to appear before the Executive in 1931 for the same offence. He had just been elected ODD and stepped out of line with the Party activists to make his own peace with the Executive who did not enforce onerous terms. See pp. 41–2.

27. Frow and Frow, 1982, op. cit.: 148. See also *New Propellor*, Vol. 5 No. 8, August 1940. For Tanner's attendance at the Comintern Congress and close association with the infant CPGB, see Klugmann, Vol. I, op.cit.: 51, 64, 67–8.

28. For the Executive's fears about the Registrar's willingness to champion the liberty of the subject see AEU Executive Minutes, and 2 February 1937, pp. 186–190; and 2 March 1937, pp. 324–30. Scott had every expectation of succeeding to Tanner's Executive Council seat in 1939. However, his candidacy was declared invalid for a minor technical infringement of rule, a spoiling tactic which was probably masterminded by the General Secretary, Fred Smith. Scott had no compunction about taking his case to the High Court which upheld his right to stand. He was elected easily to the Executive in 1942.

29. The vote on the motion was 27–13. AEU National Committee Report 1940, *Daily Worker*, 1 June 1940, and *AEU Journal* May 1940. The 1939 circular asked district committees to merely instruct stewards that they must not attend unofficial and unauthorized meetings in their steward's capacity. It is notable that the AEU Executive had been similarly inactive in 1936 and 1937 after issuing circulars which threatened disciplinary action over participation in the ASSNC's unofficial ballots. See pp. 145–8 and 151–3.

30. *AEU Journal*, December 1940.

31. Branson, 1985, op. cit.: 327. Branson states that the resolution was passed by a large majority.

32. *The Times*, 21 June 1941. *The Times* did not publish any report of the resolution on lifting the *Daily Worker* ban. For the six People's Convention demands see note 50 below.

33 *New Propellor*, Vol. 6 No. 7, 18 July 1941. For the People's Convention see pp. 271–5.

34. The South Walian *Daily Worker* conferences are reported in the *Daily Worker* of 4 December 1939. On 13 February 1940 the *Daily Worker* published an article on the war by Horner which avoided describing it as

imperialist and omitted any reference to the fact that it was being fought against German Fascism and Hitler. See also Horner's article in *Labour Monthly*, November 1939: 664. There is evidence that the Scottish District Party was also seriously divided on the war, but that the pro-war elements were pressurized into silence. See *Daily Worker*, 9 and 13 October 1939.

35. Broomfield, S.R. 1979, 'South Wales in the Second World War: The Coal Industry and Its Community', University of Wales PhD: 582–3.

36. *Daily Worker*, 27 January 1940. There were anti-war resolutions from Area No.6, the Rhymney and East Glamorgan, Area No. 4, Pontypridd district of the Rhondda and Area No. 3, Maesteg, Ogmore, Garw and Gilfach valleys. Broomfield adds that Area No. 5, Aberdare and Merthyr, and the Tylorstown lodge had also passed resolutions. (Broomfield, 1979, op. cit.: 574.)

37. In May 1940, the last annual conference of the NUSMW passed a resolution disapproving of all war 'as a permanent method of solving social problems' calling upon the British labour movement 'to summon a National Conference of working class organisations to discuss steps to end the war' (*Daily Worker*, 4 May 1940). It had been moved by William Pearson on behalf of the Lanarkshire miners and seconded by James McKendrick from Lanarkshire.

   In April 1941 the newly unified Scottish National Union of Mineworkers conference passed a resolution approving the Soviet Union's policy and its ability to maintain peace within its borders for international socialist advancement. First approved by a show of hands by 50–21 and confirmed by a card vote of 38,700–12,500 (*Labour Research*, May 1941, p.78). Lanarkshire and Fife were the largest Scottish coalfields. After the UMS was disbanded in 1936, its members all joined the county union the Fife Kinross and Clackmannanshire Mineworkers' Association (FKCMA). Though Fife Communists were unable to penetrate the union hierarchy, they were able to efficiently mobilize the 'rank-and-file' inside the FKCMA.

38. See *Daily Worker*, 19 February 1940, Francis, 1980, op. cit.: 400 and Broomfield, 1979, op. cit.: 547 and 579. The *Western Mail*'s analysis of the vote stated that the Monmouth, Rhondda and Aberdare valleys voted for the pro-war resolution; all the unemployed lodges and some of the western valleys, notably Dulais, supported the anti-war resolution, while the rest of the Anthracite area and Garw valley were very evenly divided. The Communist councillor for Nantymoel, Fred Llewellyn proposed the anti-war resolution. Many of the Dulais lodges had been active in the campaign around the Spanish Civil War.

39. See Idris Cox's article 'South Wales Miners and the War' in *Party Organiser*, May 1940: 8–9.

40. Quoted in Francis, 1980, op. cit.: 400.

41. Broomfield, 1979, op. cit.: 575–7. The MPs attended Fed Executive meetings, and Horner regularly put them through their paces in order to illustrate what was happening in politics. His conduct of the Executive was much like Bevin's of the TGWU: everything of concern to the British working class was discussed. (See interview with Archie James, transcript in SWML: 20–1.)

42. Morgan, *Harry Pollitt*, op. cit.: 114.

43. *Daily Worker*, 22 June 1940. The Manifesto was also distributed as a leaflet. Its title was 'Learn the Lessons of France. New Government Must

Come to Power'. From the skilfully political prose it would seem that the author is Campbell.

44. Ibid.

45. See the *Daily Worker*, 24 May 1940 and Palme Dutt's articles in *Labour Monthly* of January and March 1941. Kevin Morgan discusses this aspect of Party policy in Morgan, 1989, op. cit.: 189–196. Dutt stated his arguments fully in *Crisis of the British People* which he was preparing for publication as the Soviet Union was invaded. He opposed the Party's decision not to publish the tract presumably because he believed its analysis of a new corporate era for advanced capitalism was still valid (Morgan, K., 1993, op. cit.: 116–7).

46. Interview with Ted Bramley by N. Fishman.

47. *Daily Worker*, 28 June 1940. The report stated that Pritt asked whether Vickers workers could run their factory better than management and was answered by loud cries of 'Yes!' There is a useful account of the People's Convention in Calder, A., 1971, *The People's War*, Panther, London: 281–4.

48. The *Daily Worker* announced that a Vigilance Committee had been established in Rochdale on 7 November 1939 by the Trades and Labour Council with CPGB representation on its executive. For further Second World War Vigilance Committees see N. Fishman, MRC, loc. cit: 99–101.

49. See Bowes, N., 1976, 'The People's Convention', University of Warwick MA: 27–87.

50. The Six Points of the People's Convention were 1) Defence of the people's living standards; 2) Defence of the people's democratic and (trade union rights; 3) Adequate Air Raid Precautions; 4) Friendship with the USSR; 5) A People's Government, truly representative of the whole people and able to inspire the confidence of the people of the world; 6) A People's Peace that got rid of the causes of the war (*New Propellor*, Vol. 5 No. 11, November 1940).

51. See Francis, 1980, op. cit.: 401 and Broomfield, 1979, op. cit.: 590–1 and 594. Horner enforced a consistent policy of maintaining only minority Party representation on the Fed Executive. He argued that the composition of the Executive should reflect the composition of the coalfield and that the Party should lead because it had gained support for its position inside the coalfield rather than because it enjoyed a numerical majority on the Executive. See N. Fishman, 1984, unpublished paper on the CPGB and coalmining.

52. Frow and Frow, 1982, op. cit.: 154. The Executive circular is reprinted in the *AEU Journal* for January 1941. For the AEU lay officials see Appendix II.

53. AEU National Committee Report 1941. The articles appear in the journals of August, September, October and November 1941.

54. Bowes, 1976, op. cit.: 281–2 and 300–1.

55. Ibid.: 99–100.

56. Ibid.: 107. Over 1000 came from London; 290 from Lancashire and Cheshire; 117 from Scotland and around 100 each from the North-east, Sheffield and the North Midlands, the Midlands and the eastern counties.

57. Ibid.: 10 and 99–101.

58. Branson, 1985, op. cit.: 310–11, quoting Morrison's memorandum to the Cabinet, 23 December 1940 in War Cabinet minutes 27 December 1940, CAB 65/10.

59. Ibid.: 320, quoting Memorandum from Herbert Morrison to Cabinet Committee set up to consider further action on the Communist Party, Cabinet Committee minutes, CAB 98/18 CA(41)4.

60. Hinton, J., 1979, 'Killing the People's Convention: a letter from Palme Dutt to Harry Pollitt', *Bulletin of the Society for the Study of Labour History*, No. 39.

61. Calder, op. cit.: 631. For his assessment of Common Wealth, see pp. 631–6 and p. 662.

62. See Branson, 1985, op. cit.: 325–8. The End the Ban Campaign continued to gain momentum after the Soviet Union's entry into the war, and was successfully integrated by Party shopfloor activists into their production propaganda. Les Ambrose remembered that the Austin Aero was festooned with End the Ban posters. (Interview with N. Fishman.)

63. Branson, 1985, op. cit.: 329–334.

64. Peter Kerrigan's speech to the 16th Party Congress, 'Congress Report,' CPGB pamphlet, 1943, p. 21.

65. Harry Pollitt's speech to the 16th Party Congress, ibid.: 9–10.

66. Calder, op.cit.: 300–304 and 401–5. Calder notes: 'Mass enthusiasm for Russia had waned significantly by 1944, though it was still enormous.' (p. 404). Memories of relief were frequently recalled to me in interviews and did not seem to be merely self-deluding hindsight.

67. For membership figures, see Appendix I.

68. *World News and Views*, Vol. 25 No. 3, 20 January 1945: 23.

69. See Chapter 11 pp. 293–6.

70. For the Austin's and Vicker's strikes see pp. 315–6.

CHAPTER ELEVEN

The Shopfloor War Economy 1939–45: Dual Power or Collaboration?

September 1939 – 'economic struggle' as usual

Communist engineers reacted to Britain's declaration of war on Germany from at least two perspectives: their political view of the war and their vantage-point as shopfloor activists engaged in conducting economic conflict on their own factory terrain. Most probably shared Pollitt's commitment to fighting Fascism. Nevertheless, the immediate implications of the anti-Fascist struggle were minimal for daily mass work in the factories. The *Daily Worker* did not include exhortations to shop stewards to move towards dual power and the formation of soviets to ensure that military operations were adequately supplied.

During September the *Daily Worker* warned activists to be prepared for the inevitable attempts by the Chamberlain government, war profiteers and bosses to shift the burdens and sacrifices of war on to the working class. It was assumed that the methods of self-defence adopted would be the same as in peacetime – the tried and tested conventions of economic struggle in each particular activists' patch. The circumstances of the phoney war pre-empted most people, including Party activists, from contributing significantly to the fight against Germany.

As serious dislocation and bottlenecks occurred in the *ad hoc* wartime economic machine, opportunities for building trade union organization increased. Consequently when the line on the war changed, Party activists were already fighting on the domestic front and exploiting the war's indigenous class applications. In practice most of them had ignored the anti-German, anti-Fascist aspects of Pollitt's declaration which implied negotiating and observing a truce in the economic struggle. We have observed that Dutt and Rust declined to enforce the full rigours of the anti-war line on shopfloor activists. The Secretariat's *de facto* return to a war-on-two-fronts position simply confirmed Party activists' own inclinations to continue the same course in the economic struggle which they had been pursuing before the change of line.

Nevertheless, the Lennist imperative for Communists whose country was fighting an imperialist war was to espouse revolutionary defeatism.

This true bolshevik logic involved inciting non-cooperation, strikes and even sabotage in factories and pits. It is notable that the Government could find no examples, either at home or abroad, where Communists were using the economic struggle for these revolutionary ends. George Orwell observed in his 'London Letter' to the *American Partisan Review* that 'it is doubtful whether the Communists have ever been able to do more than magnify legitimate grievances'. He added:

> In England the Communists whom it is possible to respect are factory workers, but they are not very numerous, and precisely because they are usually skilled workmen and loyal comrades they cannot always be rigidly faithful to the 'line'. Between September 1939 and June 1941 they do not seem to have attempted any definite sabotage of arms production, although the logic of Communist policy demanded this.[1]

We have observed that Party engineering activists carefully orchestrated the reappearance of the 1914–18 'shop stewards movement' in order to avoid giving the AEU Executive grounds to retaliate. The ASSNC had decided that the war, with its attendant risks of employers abusing workshop custom and practice, made it necessary to extend its remit to include all factories producing armaments and that its Acting Committee should 'work out areas for the setting up of area committees of shop stewards in these factories'. At its next meeting, the ASSNC National Committee agreed to sponsor local committees of shop stewards up and down the country. Nevertheless, the only committees which emerged were in Glasgow and north-west London, and these were pale imitations indeed of their 1914–18 predecessors.[2]

The ASSNC was duly re-named the Engineering and Allied Trades Shop Stewards National Council (EATSSNC) at the Birmingham national rank-and-file conference in April 1940 which, however, it had not formally convened because of the National Metal Bureau's foresight in spiking the AEU Executive Council's punitive response. The conference simply 'emerged' out of an earlier meeting which the *Daily Worker* reported somewhat disingenuously as appearing out of nowhere.[3] The size of the Birmingham conference attested to the Party's growing influence in engineering. There were 283 delegates from 107 factories employing 217,492 people, including five shop stewards committees and three Youth Factory Committees. The 'Provisional Committee' organizing the conference proposed a resolution which delegates adopted, a model blend of union loyalism and rank-and-filism.

> The unity of all sections of the engineering and allied trades, irrespective of the trade unions to which they belong, is more than ever necessary today . . . Established customs and practices, through the plans of the government and employers, stand in danger of being

swept away. These conditions can only be maintained by vigilant shop organisation . . .

It is . . . these men, women and youths in the shops, who must take up the struggles to preserve our trade unions, to greatly strengthen their trade union organisation, to elect shop stewards in every department and section of the works, so that we may get our trade unions serving the purpose for which they have been built, for which we pay our contributions, and to which end – the defence and advancement of the members' interests – policy must be directed.[4]

Forty-nine amendments were proposed to the resolution from the floor; most of them were probably more extreme in their militancy and reflected the increased interest being generated in trade union organization by the extraordinary circumstances of total war.[5] However, the Provisional Committee proved well able to contain this outpouring. Speakers for amendments vented their strong feelings and preached full-blooded rank-and-filism with rhetorical flourish but delegates returned home to work within established union structures.

Throughout the period when the Party opposed the war, there was only one time when the 'rank-and-file' asserted itself. In July 1940 the Communist President of the AEU London District Committee, Vic Wymans, led a delegation of 60 shop stewards from the London District Shop Stewards Quarterly to lobby the Executive Council at the AEU Head Office at Peckham Road.

They had three points to put forward: (1) The right to hold more frequent meetings of London shop stewards and full freedom of expression at these meetings. (2) Positive action by the union against the 'Men of Munich'. (3) That the Executive Council cease the persecution of active members of the union .[6]

The Executive called the police to eject the delegation and expelled Wymans from the union. Wymans's membership was restored unanimously by the Final Appeals Court in 1941 which decided that expulsion was too severe a penalty for the rule he had infringed.[7] After this incident, the 'rank-and-file' did not step forward again to claim its rights. The absence of serious unofficial activity reinforced the new AEU President Jack Tanner's point that the 1914–18 shop stewards movement had arisen out of necessity. Because this movement's demands and needs had been incorporated by the union and were now reflected in agreements and rule, there was no further need for an unofficial movement outside the union.[8]

Tanner did not peremptorily assert the central union's authority. Instead, he stressed the identity of interests between shop stewards and full-time union officials within a culture of active rank-and-filist trade unionism. If the engineering procedure which had evolved in the inter-war period in factories which retained their 1914–18 works committees had failed to cope with the stresses of war production in 1939–45, then rank-and-filism would certainly have assumed greater importance in Party militants' approach. However, the intricate conventions of workplace bargaining established in the mid 1930s stood up remarkably well to the strains imposed by wartime circumstances.

When hopeful activists sought assistance in extending union organization to their factories, they usually found solid support from both full-time union officials and Ministry of Labour people. Most of them had been on the receiving end of the mistakes made by their predecessors when they had been young shop stewards or subaltern civil servants during the 1914–18 war. The experience had been educational and caused them to be altogether more flexible in 1939–45 in their application of both law and procedure. They had also become profoundly committed to the virtues of 'proper' shopfloor collective bargaining.

Moreover, the avoidance of open-ended confrontation and set-piece battles which had been the basis of engineering activists' survival strategies in the late 1930s proved highly suitable for coping with wartime exigencies. Shop stewards had learned to exercise prudence in escalating parochial shop conflicts and to take care to leave themselves a convenient line of retreat. In fact, the shift in the shopfloor balance of power produced by the war allowed shop stewards in many factories greater latitude to develop trade union organization. They could follow up grievances more swiftly in the confident hope that management would feel constrained to make concessions and also nurture embryonic grievances without fear of retaliatory or pre-emptive action from foremen or supervisors.

In most firms where 1914–18 works committees had atrophied they were revived in 1939–40 by mutual consent. Where firms had never tolerated unions or shopfloor bargaining, trade union activists established *de facto* union recognition through skirmishing or insinuated it into the workplace in 1942–43 via Joint Production Committees. The often subtle intricacies of the bargaining conventions established inside 'factory fortresses' were transmitted with comparative ease to new stewards and stewards in hitherto ill-organized factories in London, Manchester and the Midlands. In Glasgow, however, the development of collective bargaining had been severely attenuated during the 1930s. There were only a few isolated enclaves like Beardmore's Parkhead Forge where militants could find successful models to emulate. It is hardly suprising that there were regular flare-ups of open-ended economic conflict here in the early part of the war.

Nevertheless, there were similarities to be found in the short, sharp skirmishes routinely recorded by the London and Glasgow Regional Industrial Relations Officers in non-unionized firms. The advice of both

RIROs was frequently sought by managements who had never encountered shop stewards before. Prejudice convinced them that essential prerogative was being threatened by newly elected stewards who presented formal demands. Employers were not only ignorant of the conventions of collective bargaining being practised in nearby firms but also dogmatically anti-union. The RIRO, J.B. Galbraith, observed in Glasgow:

> it is rather astonishing to find that inexperienced managements seem to have a dread of this kind of official [shop stewards]. They cannot rid themselves of preconceptions derived from the last war and from the activities of the shop steward movement at that time. It is not easy at times to convince them that there is a radical difference between unofficial and official shop stewards . . . During the last week or two officials of the Department have been successful in removing some misapprehensions on this point and in establishing a scheme of official shop stewards and their recognition.[9]

The shop stewards committees which appeared in north-west London and Glasgow after the ASSNC's rhetorical commitment to form them were not established in response to the exigencies of 'the economic struggle'. They were rather survivals of the strong rank-and-filist traditions of 1914–18 and reflected the continuity in British trade union culture. The engineering heartland which had grown up in north-west London in the 1930s had been assiduously cultivated both by the constitutional militants and Peter Zinkin. The West London shop stewards movement of the early 1920s must have lived on in reminiscences at most AEU branches. However, the erstwhile committee remained a hollow shell. Its failure to materialize in the flesh was probably due to strong pressure from Scott and Berridge to pre-empt 'unofficial activity' and a marked lack of interest from workers in the multitude of shopfloors in any extra-union link-up.

The Glasgow shop stewards committee was evidently founded in a rush of enthusiasm by YCL engineers and other young militants whose interest in their unions had been sparked off by the upsurge in the 'economic struggle' of 1937. They also had a rich vein of tradition on which to draw. Galbraith noted in December 1939:

> a committee not unlike the Clyde Workers' Committee of the previous war is in the process of being constituted. Of course there is a distinct difference in the circumstances as on this occasion the recognised trade union officials have not been placed in the position of being bound to detach themselves from all disputes and to be limited to suppression in regard to any strikes. Nevertheless, it is rather disquieting to find this tendency to a more extensive foundation for the propaganda in question.

Galbraith reported in January that the Committee had sent a circular to union branches soliciting funds for a campaign to safeguard working conditions, declaring that the TUC had surrendered and was co-operating with the Government in restricting the 'liberties which have obtained in the workshops'.[10] Though the Glasgow committee continued to function fitfully on a political level, we shall see that it had little practical effect on industrial conflict.

The Coalition Government outlawed strikes in July 1940 under Order 1305 which substituted compulsory arbitration as the final stage in disputes procedures. However, they were notably reluctant to enforce this law rigorously. Ernest Bevin and his veterans at the Ministry of Labour viewed Order 1305 as a reserve power, an ultimate deterrent which might easily backfire and overkill if actually used. As for the unions, the official wartime historian of munitions observed: 'No war-time strikes could thus be officially recognised by the trade unions, though a number of them were connived at, if not actually supported, by the unions, particularly at district and branch level.'[11] The official historian for manpower added: 'employers who pressed the Minister to take action were informed that they must first make full use of the joint negotiating machinery at their disposal and give the unions the maximum opportunity to maintain discipline.'[12]

The elastic interpretation of Order 1305 meant that full-time union officials continued to condone routine skirmishes taking place outside the letter of official procedure which management also tolerated as part of the cut and thrust of collective bargaining. Moreover, there were also occasions when full-scale strikes were mounted without the Ministry of Labour or the unions meting out retribution. An outstanding example is the successful collective 'holiday' by workers at Standard Shadow Factory No. 2 in Coventry in September 1940 to protest at the sacking of their AEU convener. The description of their strike as a holiday, a tactical euphemism to avoid prosecution, was maintained throughout by the strikers who were exceptionally well organized and disciplined. The shop stewards committee from Armstrong Whitworth at Baginton, Coventry's one factory fortress, functioned as the formal 'holiday committee', probably to protect the Standard stewards from possible legal repercussions. The holidaymakers were also helped by the TGWU's recently installed District Officer, Jack Jones, and the Party-dominated trades council.[13]

New Propellor reported coyly:

> A meeting of the shop stewards of all aircraft and engineering works in the city has been held, to hear the details of this holiday, and to consider how to build 100% trade unionism in all works. Large sums of money to enable the Standard men to have a good holiday were subscribed by the workers in the factories in this city and other parts of the country.[14]

There was initial apprehension from local employers and Ministry of Labour officials that the dispute might spread to other Coventry factories.[15] But since the stewards' committee were serious about winning the convener's reinstatement, they carefully refrained either from scoring political points or widening the dispute. After three weeks 'holiday', during which the official voices of both union authority and the State were mute, management reinstated the convener.

Of course, intractable disputes still occurred from which the stewards could salvage few concessions. Perhaps the earliest of these wartime 'no win' disputes was the British Auxiliaries' strike in Glasgow in September 1940. British Auxiliaries was a large comparatively well organized factory where management routinely negotiated with a functioning shop stewards committee. Like Standard's in Coventry, the strike at British Auxiliaries was for the reinstatement of the AEU convener. But the similarities ended there. The convener, Mr Cunningham, a Party member, was sacked for his alleged sexual harassment of (the contemporary terminology was 'making advances' to) a woman worker on the night shift. The strike was complicated by the fact that all parties, including management, refused to reveal the reason for Cunningham's dismissal. Rumour recited his offence inside the factory, but the official strike committee remained mum and demanded restitution for their 'victimised' convener.[16]

The strike lasted nine-and-a-half weeks during which support was forthcoming from engineering trade unionists throughout Scotland. The Glasgow AEU District Committee backed Cunningham's case unconditionally. There was strong pressure for a Glasgow general strike in solidarity and the high morale of local union activists made this possibility seem real enough to all concerned.[17] At this juncture the dispute was escalating aimlessly. The strike committee clearly had no notion of how to achieve a negotiated solution.

Eventually veteran Party activists and full-time Party officials closed ranks with AEU full-time officials and Galbraith to defuse the combustible situation. Galbraith concluded that 'the CP feared they would have their national position in the AEU damaged if they did not try to end the stoppage'.[18] The strike was ended without Order 1305 having been invoked or any management retribution being meted out to the returning workforce. The AEU District Committee continued to pursue Cunningham's sacking through official procedure, but he had found another job and informed them that he no longer required their assistance.[19]

Order 1305 continued to be notable for its absence from industrial conflict. Indeed, the one incident in which it was used in the early part of the war was notorious because the strike leader, the audacious young

Party toolmaker Reg Birch, virtually dared the State to proceed against the strikers. Birch was a protégé of Wally Hannington at Swift's Scales, a small engineering firm in Stonebridge, north-west London. Claude Berridge had used his influence to get Hannington started in the factory in 1939, after which union organization had begun to improve. Hannington soon became chairman of the shop stewards committee and led a successful one-week strike in the toolroom to win the District Committee's prescribed hourly wage rate. He was sacked due to Ministry of Supply pressure in late 1940. The ministry were presumably alarmed at Hannington's First World War record of leading militant action and feared disruption.[20] They did not realize that his presence was immaterial since he had already blooded Reg Birch in the best fighting rank-and-filist tradition.

Hannington's successor in the toolroom, Mr Leslie, became AEU convener. When Leslie was sacked for bad timekeeping in April 1941, Swift's workers had already notched up a series of combative and increasingly bitter encounters with management. In the immediate aftermath of this 'victimisation', some of the 180 workers and the full complement of youthful shop stewards went on strike to protest at management's refusal to let the stewards use the canteen for a mass meeting.[21] The strikers declined to return to work in order to facilitate a negotiated settlement. Under Birch's leadership they were in no mood to compromise. A week into the strike, the stewards went to see the RIRO. But they flatly refused to report the dispute under 1305 and to return to work to await the outcome of official procedure. Instead they handed the RIRO a communication for Ernest Bevin: 'Because of the chaotic state of production in other factories, together with the move against trade union organisation and democratic rights, we support and wholeheartedly endorse this action of resistance.'[22]

A strike against Leslie's sacking might have been won if the strikers had adopted the low-profile tactics of the Standard's holidaymakers. However, under Birch's leadership the dispute became a set-piece political battle aimed at discrediting the *bona fides* of the state and the whole employing class in the war effort. There was certainly ample evidence that Swift's management were incompetent.[23] But it was unthinkable that the Government should be forced to acknowledge this fact by strikers led by a Communist in the full glare of publicity. The Ministry of Labour had little option but to commence the legal battle in the face of such an explicit challenge.

In May 1941 seven shop stewards, aged between 21 and 34, including Birch aged 26, were arraigned in court.[24] The conflict can hardly have been welcomed by the constitutional militants. They could hardly repudiate the strike, and Birch apparently was not susceptible to moral pressure to give way. Support for the strikers was publicly elicited through *New Propellor*. One hundred and fifty workers representing shop stewards committees from 14 factories employing 26,000 workers attended the court hearing in solidarity with the Swift's stewards and they also held a meeting outside. The 14 committees also sponsored a conference during that week at which a Defence Council for the strikers was formed.[25]

However, the Defence Council took no action in defence of democratic and class principles. There were apparently no calls on the AEU District Committee for a strike in support of Swift's stewards. Nor did the many well-organized factory fortresses in London throw down the gauntlet in order to share the honour of the martyrs' crown. The palpable lack of serious solidarity compared with the British Auxiliaries' dispute is due to a combination of factors. There is the dominance of the constitutional militant tradition among AEU activists in London. They probably felt little sympathy with what was clearly and intentionally a political strike.

We have seen that at this time there was general apprehension among Communists that the Government was contemplating punitive action against the Communist Party. Many Party trade union activists were keen to keep their heads down over what they considered to be a gratuitous conflict and to save their energies for the economic struggle on their own shopfloors. They wanted to carry on waging the class war but on terms which did not lead either to their imprisonment or to their being forced underground.

The economic struggle in engineering firms in London was intensifying as Bevin's war economy machine gathered steam and built up its pressure on both workforce and management for maximum production. The conditions of economic warfare had actually been made more favourable for them by the wartime economic conditions and the Ministry of Labour's benevolent custodianship. Bevin's 'incipient Fascism' had made it easier for canny stewards to win concessions and advance trade union organization. In a factory with a functioning shop steward organization, well planned and executed skirmishes extracted better concessions from management.

The Party Centre apparently had neither energy nor will to fight the Swift's stewards political battle either as an issue of democratic principle or of a damning indictment of the Government's mismanagement of the war economy. In the continuing absence of the *Daily Worker*, it may have been comparatively easy for Dutt and Rust to plead that they lacked the means to escalate the struggle. In the event the Swift's stewards' case was finally heard in July 1941, just over a week after Germany had invaded the Soviet Union.

It is likely that the case was delayed for some weeks because the pro-secution was anxious to give tempers time to cool after the arraignment. The Government must have been keen to avoid sympathy strikes after the news of the Defence Council formation. The Recorder bound the defendants over to keep the peace for two years and gave them a stern warning.[26] His leniency was doubtless influenced by the Soviet entry to the war. The course of the war also made it unnecessary for the National Metal Bureau to impose a compromise retreat on Reg Birch who was probably looking forward to becoming its first political prisoner.

Fighting the Good Fight for the Soviet Socialist Fatherland

The Party Centre's exhortations about increasing war production to defend the Soviet Socialist Fatherland were taken extremely seriously by Party activists. They accepted wholeheartedly that their duty was to sup-port the Soviet people's fight against Fascism and to call upon the British working class to play its part in ensuring a Soviet victory against Hitler. However, the manner in which they responded varied greatly.

Many Party publicists and full-time workers were still inspired by the vivid images in Soviet propaganda of how the proletariat had risen to the challenge of socialist construction in fulfilling the first and second Five-Year Plans. They now tried to guide British workers towards equivalent deeds of socialist heroism. Erstwhile commissars bedecked their war fac-tories with the wall newspapers, posters and slogans which they had been taught were an essential part of the Soviet success story. Revolutionary agitprop and shock brigades might be unknown on most shopfloors but they were familiar weapons in the well-worn intellectual armoury of the YCL activists and *apparatchiks* who were back on the tools or inside a factory for the first time.

But despite British bolsheviks' best efforts, no British war factory became a hive of Stakhanovites. Most workers were tolerant and/or impressed by shock brigaders' zealotry but did not feel called to repeat their sacrifices. Management approved Norman Brown's and Arthur Exell's request to become a shock brigade of two at Oxford Radiators and gave them the dirtiest, most uncomfortable jobs to do on night-shift. The two men recalled sheepishly that no other workers came forward to join them but they felt compelled to carry on in stoic socialist silence.[27]

Keen Party members in Manchester looking for war work were guided by their engineering comrades into the Fairey aircraft shadow factory at Earnley Park. They organized the most conspicuous and exemplary polit-ical activity after Soviet entry into the war, zealously following the Party line to make proletarian sacrifices for the USSR. Party officials who had become neophyte shop stewards formed shock brigades and engaged in propaganda campaigns, marches and demonstrations in support of the production drive and the Second Front. At Fairey's in Hayes, similar activities were inspired by the dynamic Party convener Frank Foster who had come to Fairey's in 1939 just before the outbreak of war.[28]

Although Party engineers encouraged links between their aircraft factories and the RAF they looked forward most to the arrival and reactions of the Soviet trade union officials. They cherished their reactions to British production methods and felt renewed commitment to the war effort. For the rest of the factory, the arrival of a Soviet worker or RAF pilot was a welcome change from ordinary routine but the laying on of hands did not have a dramatic effect on their productivity. Most Party veterans knew that agitprop methods would not produce a transformation in British workers' approach to factory work and did not even try to imitate authentic bolshevik methods. They made serious efforts nevertheless to take the lead at what they believed to be their historic moment.

Shop stewards committees cooperated with management to organize production weeks to coincide with an impending visit of Soviet trade unionists or pilots or members of the Red Army. The Party Centre applauded shock brigades and wall posters when they appeared, but did not pressurize Party members in those factories where they did not. However, many local Party officials were less seasoned in their judgements of shopfloor situations than Pollitt and Campbell. They felt constrained to incite engineering activists to prove their bolshevik credentials through showing high-profile results from daily mass work.

At the very large EMI factory in Hayes, for example, the young Muriel Edwards, George Crane and other Party activists proved inspired self-publicists. The *Daily Mirror* came and photographed the young women workers alongside the Orliken gun which they were making to publicize their production drive. EMI women workers were drawn into production campaigns and became enthusiastic participants in the Party's special effort to involve women workers in the war effort. Their productivity probably benefited at least intermittently from the attention paid them by the *Mirror* and trade union and civic organs as a result. Edwards became an active participant in the Women's Parliament which the Party organized and was also involved in activity linking women trade unionists throughout West London.[29]

Soviet entry had a notable impact on pre-war factory fortresses. Their shopfloor advances under Party leadership had continued uninterrupted by the Party's anti-war line. But they were now extended and multiplied. Napier's in Acton Vale became a honeypot for Party activists in London towards the end of 1940 who were faced under Bevin's laws with finding engineering work. Peter Kerrigan came to Napier's to do his war work.

The young Walter Swanson arrived from Glasgow along with his formidable reputation as orator and militant.

Fred Arter, the Party activist who had developed Napier's as a union stronghold, made way for Swanson as convener and assumed the chairmanship of the shop stewards committee which management now formally recognized and accorded facilities. Swanson's convenorship gave him the lattitude to become the EATSSNC's charismatic leader. His rousing rhetoric was in constant demand to enthuse and arouse factories all over the south-east of England. Napier's management turned a blind eye to his frequent absences and concerted a cover-up with the union when his affair with a woman worker on site became problematic.[30]

In 1943 the loveable, but apparently unreliable, Walter Swanson was eased out of Napier's and the EATSSNC by the National Metal Bureau in an exercise of damage limitation. His place as Napier's convener was taken by the toolroom shop steward Fred Elms. Elms had been active in the Firestone strike and blacklisted afterwards. He had shipped to Spain as a ships' cook during the early days of the Civil War and then been active in Voluntary Industrial Action for Spain. He arrived at Napier's in the summer of 1939 and almost immediately became the toolroom's first shop steward. He shared Fred Arter's prudent approach and was an immensely popular convenor. The Napier's stewards relished his 'cockney' ways and were moved to reflect on his discursive disquisitions about how to move the shopfloor struggle forward.[31]

Napier's became affectionately and universally known to Party members and engineering activists as the Red Putilov.[32] (The Putilov armaments factory soviet in Petrograd had been a bolshevik stronghold in October 1917, and acquired a key role in the bolshevik mythology of the revolution.) By 1945, Party membership had increased to 200, including foremen who joined 'of their own free will'! There were six Party factory groups operating and Napier's became an important stop on the itinerary of Soviet metalworkers trade union officials. Ralph Fuller recalled their visits with awe and reverent affection. The Napier's shop stewards had taken the Soviet workers' reactions to production methods and suggestions for improvements very seriously indeed.

Nevertheless, Arter's pre-war practice of maintaining a low Party profile was vigilantly maintained. Arter and Elms had socialized a whole generation of able young stewards into the Party on their own terms. Ralph Fuller recalled, 'We never came out and said that we were Communist Party, though everyone knew very well that we were not in the Labour Party'. Elms counselled the Napier's Party stewards: 'If the men elect you in the shop then that's that. If they want to talk politics then do, but don't force it down their throats.' Thus, Napier's had not sent any official delegates to the People's Convention in 1941 because the shopfloor response to Party stewards' agitation had been indifferent. Only the red milling shop had sent its own delegate.[33]

At the Austin Aero, Les Ambrose merely added the imperative of producing planes for the liberation of the Soviet Union on to his already full agenda without according it any particular priority over domestic shopfloor aims. The total war economy reinforced the unions' already strong position on the shopfloor. By 1941 there was 100 per cent union membership and under Ambrose the AEU dominated the shop stewards committee. Although Ambrose had to recruit the women workers into the TGWU, that union's personnel were unable to compete effectively with him on the shopfloor. He recalled their full-time officials' ignorance of engineering procedure and their inexperience in the arcane and precise conventions of collective bargaining at the margins of official procedure. Ambrose and Teddy Ager provided regular advice to the TGWU officials and their stewards about how to deal with comparatively straightforward problems. It is hardly surprising that the semi-skilled male workers in the Aero elected to join the union which had the better bargaining record.

Ambrose took full advantage of the favourable wartime conditions to cement the connection between members and shop stewards and to develop the self-image of the shop stewards committee as a self-conscious centre of power. He instituted six-monthly factory-wide meetings for union members and monthly shop meetings when stewards reported to their members on the shop stewards committee's decisions. The extent of this union activity was unusual, even for war factories, and evidently fostered a strong loyalty felt by the new recruits for their factory organization.

The enhanced power and prestige of the shop stewards committee also had a potential value for the Communist Party which Les Ambrose took care to exploit. Because Party members were the most active element on the committee, the Party's shopfloor presence increased as the union became stronger. Keen and militant-minded workers wanted to join the Party to become part of this active core of Party stewards – most of whom Ambrose had recruited since 1938. Ambrose remembered that he ensured the factory group secretary was made shop steward so that he could deliver the *Daily Worker* throughout the factory unhindered.

At the height of the production effort the Aero employed 15,000 people. Ambrose recalled that there had been 400 Party members. Sectional Party meetings were held in the firm's time; and the Aero factory group committee, composed of leading Party members from each section, met in the air-raid shelter. (Full factory group meetings were held after working hours.) *New Propellor* sold 2–3000 copies while the *Daily Worker* sold 1000 copies which were paid for in advance and delivered to workers' benches or on the line.[34]

The Party Centre asserted that in order to win the war the British working class must take charge of the production drive, with breathtaking confidence in its activists' ability to mobilize the factories and pits. In the year after Soviet entry, the Party's energies were fully stretched in redeeming Pollitt's pledges. His proud speeches bore witness to the triumph of his faith. Life Itself was proving him right: *his* working class were the dominant force in the economy and society.

The National Metal Bureau swiftly encouraged the EATSSNC to take up the production drive. The AEU Executive was rendered markedly more tolerant of unofficial Communist activity by the Anglo–Soviet alliance and the EATSSNC was able to operate comparatively unhindered while remaining careful not to commit overt offences against the union rule-book. The EATSSNC organized two successful regional conferences on production in London and Merseyside in September 1941 and then mounted a national conference in October 1941 in London at the Stoll Theatre. 1237 delegates came from over 300 factories employing over half a million workers, easily the largest gathering of shop stewards assembled during the war. Walter Swanson of Napier's opened the conference on a note of proud proletarian self-sacrifice in a speech written for him by Dutt:

> We who meet here have as heavy a responsibility as the Government of our country. All the delegates here have been sent by the men and women in the war factories who so desperately want to play their full part in the common struggle.
>
> We desire it to be clearly understood that no one in this Conference claims in any way to speak officially for the respective Trade Unions of which we are members, and which all our endeavours are aimed at strengthening.
>
> We occupy our positions because the workers in the factories trust us and elect us to our positions as representatives, believing that we are the best custodians of their interests.
>
> ...we have now reached a stage in the war crisis where victory can only be won if we approach our problems, devoid of any sectional or craft interest, and only from the interests of our people as a whole.
>
> We need to end now all illusions that others have the duty of doing all the dying and fighting while we in Britain are not called upon to make such gigantic sacrifices. This war will not be won without it involving great sacrifices from all sections of the people. We can lessen the extent of these sacrifices to the degree that we here to-day fearlessly face up to the whole problem of production in a new way.
>
> ...we believe we will get the best results from our Conference, not merely by discussing the waste, mismanagement and inefficiency of present methods of control and direction of production, but what we can and will do to increase production from our side, and in doing so help to effect changes which will go right through industry even to the top.

Can we wait until the Government and employers are brought to their senses before we ourselves begin to set the example to show what we can do on our side to turn out munitions?

We cannot; and a glance at the map of Europe showing where Hitler has got to will prove we cannot – if we really mean to win . . .

We cannot over-emphasize that once the political conviction of the workers has been won, they will display an initiative, drive and energy to increase production never witnessed in this country before.[35]

The conference passed 29 resolutions underlining the extreme gravity of the war situation, the need for shop stewards to support the USSR, and ensure maximum production while insisting that earnings should not be affected by the production drive, that is, no cuts in piece-rates or bonus earnings. The conference agreed that: 'Immediate changes are required to help in ensuring sustained effort for maximum production: and in the first place Production Committees in every workshop.'[36]

There was strong Party pressure on the young EATSSNC secretary, Len Powell, to capitalize on the successful national conference by carrying the word to other platforms provided by Party activists. In the following months the EATSSNC organized conferences to promote the production drive in Cardiff, Manchester, Birmingham, Coventry, Glasgow, Tyneside, Barrow, Leatherhead, High Wycombe, Merseyside, Preston, Gloucester, Bristol, Hayes and Southall. After a lull there were further conferences in the Port of London, Kent, West Riding and Welwyn Garden City. EATSSNC committees were being formed in Ayrshire, South Devon, Merseyside, Birmingham, Coventry, South Wales, the West of England, Welwyn, Clydeside, Kent, Manchester, High Wycombe and the South Midlands.[37]

Pollitt returned to production when he spoke at the Stoll Theatre on 28 December. His speech was relayed to nine other full halls and heard by an audience of 12,000. 'The central theme of his speech and of the nation-wide campaign which followed, was that the successes of the Red Army marked a turning point in the war.' He called on the Government 'to plan production centrally . . . to eliminate private monopoly interests and exorbitant profit; and to give plenary powers to Production Committees'.[38]

The Communists and their rank-and-file vehicle the EATSSNC were not of course the only parties interested in production committees. The Joint Production Committees (JPCs) which were established in engineering firms over the autumn and winter of 1941 were the distillation of received wisdom and experience from the previous war. The JPCs were not dissimilar in composition or scope to the the joint works committees recommended by the Whitley Committee which reported on the causes of industrial unrest just as the 1914–18 war was ending. The committees' remit would not encroach on the territory already claimed by collective bargaining, for example wages and hours, but with the 'many questions closely affecting daily life and comfort in, and the success of, the business, and affecting in no small degree efficiency of working, which are peculiar to the individual workshop or factory'.[39]

It is notable that the trade union establishment had the same negative reaction to JPCs which it had voiced in 1918 to joint works committees. Most of the full-time hierarchy were concerned with the potential loss of power downwards to these new shopfloor institutions despite the specific restriction of their scope. One of the main reasons that joint works committees remained an isolated inter-war phenomena was the determination of union officials' to protect their own patch. In 1941 it required all Ernest Bevin's arm-twisting skills to force agreement from trade union officialdom to participation in JPCs.[40]

Some JPC enthusiasts were attuned to evolutionary socialism; others were committed to Whig paternalism; still others viewed them as a valuable adjunct to the new professional managerial ethos. The consensus was that some institution was needed to channel the shopfloor's energies into the war effort. Inman identifies three sources of inspiration: Bevin; the Ministry of Labour; and the Midlands Joint Regional Board on Production, part of the regional advisory network linked to the Ministry of Supply which was etablished at the beginning of the war. She concludes that the strong backing for JPCs from the employers' side on the Midlands Joint Regional Board in September 1941 was crucial in forcing the hand of the Engineering Employers' Federation (EEF).[41] We shall observe, however, that it was Communist shop stewards who became the practical midwives to JPCs. Without their continued commitment and energetic participation, JPCs would have amounted to little more than a well-intentioned exercise in social engineering designed to demonstrate that there really was a 'people's war' on the economic front.

Inman ignored the evidence that the Midlands employers had themselves been hard pressed by an enthusiastic lobby of shop stewards, among whom Communists were especially prominent. At the end of August 1941 the Midlands RIRO noted:

> According to a Press report of a recent meeting of workpeople . . . a representative of the men stated, 'We can see production problems from an angle the management cannot see. Given a voice in production we can go to the men and ask for greater output.' This attitude is indicate (sic) of contentions, expressed in many directions and becoming more insistent, designed to develop an element which, in pursuing criticism of works control, is exerting pressure for wider recognition of workpeople's representatives in managerial functions. Against this movement Trade Unions are exercising a restraining influence.[42]

At the end of September the RIRO observed that Harry Pollitt had been in Coventry addressing meetings about the need for the working class to take the leading role in production.[43] In October, the RIRO reported:

> In conjunction with widespread attacks on managerial standards the initiation of efforts to secure the representation of shop stewards in works control were brought to notice by the Director of a large Coventry undertaking, who asked for advice in dealing with two stewards alleged to have sponsored votes of censure against the firm's senior officials and to have organised collective request for removal of the Works Manager accompanied by a demand for representation of stewards on the Management Committee.[44]

The RIRO also quoted examples of 'subversive demands' from the Wolverhampton and Birmingham Trades Councils.

> At three meetings in succession, the Birmingham Trades Council has debated the question of the control of industry. The Executive Committee's views, it is understood, were towards representation for full public ownership with control by technicians and workers through trade unions and the Council resolved to support this policy. An amendment advocating collaboration with employers was rejected by a vote of 48 to 37.[45]

It is hardly surprising that the Midlands engineering employers swiftly matched their shop stewards' zeal by signing up for JPCs. They deemed it more prudent to cooperate with the engineering unions inside an official framework rather than allow stewards' demands to escalate 'outside procedure'. Nevertheless, the RIRO noted that the Midlands Joint Regional Production Board's recommendation for JPCs had not been welcomed by all employers, particularly in Coventry, where 'the repeated references to joint control are likely to confirm the fears in the minds of the employers, who look upon any division of managerial responsibility with extraordinary disfavour'.[46] But the operation of JPCs quickly settled into a mutually satisfactory routine. The RIRO's reports of subversive agitation surrounding the production question cease after the spring of 1942.[47]

By omitting the evidence of Communist influence, Inman smoothed out the signs that JPCs were instituted for other than patriotic and paternal motives. More recently Richard Croucher also declined to consider the agitation for JPCs by militant Midlands shop stewards though for somewhat different reasons. He apparently found it inconceivable that stewards' commitment to militant trade unionism could be translated into a campaign for such tame institutions of joint consultation as JPCs.[48]

A number of factors combined to produce the stewards' production agitation in the Midlands. The stewards were mostly young and had acquired little experience of fighting the 'economic struggle'. They lacked the benefits of advice from colleagues who were seasoned veterans and also did not feel their prudent restraining hand, a moderating influence which often affected London and Manchester neophytes. The Midlands war factories had undergone radical changes with the influx of labour from outside the region, the rapid expansion of aircraft shadow factories and the dislocation of the blitz.

If the Soviet Union had not been invaded, the increasingly volatile mood of the shopfloor, particularly in Coventry, would have ignited at some point, presenting a difficult choice for Communist activists. They would have had to choose between following the logic of their strongly professed rank-and-filism by leading militant unofficial action, or heeding the imperative of trade union loyalism to contain the conflict within manageable bounds and not impair the war effort. The high profile production campaign in the Midlands in the autumn of 1941 allowed militant shop stewards to divert their desire to encroach on managerial prerogative away from the economic struggle into the production drive. But the desire to tilt the balance of shopfloor forces away from management remained no less strong for being invested in Joint Production Committees!

Under pressure from Bevin and his civil servants, in February 1942 formal agreement was reached between the engineering unions and the Government to establish JPCs in Royal Ordnance Factories The engineering unions and the EEF signed a similar accord in March.[49] However, by this time there were already large numbers of JPCs which had been established largely in response to pressure from below. One hundred and eighty JPCs responded to an AEU inquiry in March 1942: of this total, 6.8 per cent had been set up before August 1941; 28.7 per cent before November/December 1941; and 35.6 per cent between January/March 1942.[50]

The practical operation of JPCs was eagerly scrutinized by contemporary 'labour relations' experts. They were optimistic that these fresh experiments in joint consultation could find a permanent place in peacetime engineering management methods, which they viewed as anachronistic and inefficient. In the midst of an anti-Fascist war the experts also pointed to JPCs as positive proof that a democratic society actually responded democratically to the extreme stress of a total war economy. The International Labour Organization, Nuffield College, Oxford and Political Economic Planning (PEP) all commissioned studies of how JPCs functioned to try to assess their long-term significance.[51]

Many activists, inside the Party and the non-Party leftwing, viewed JPCs as instruments for permanently tilting the balance of forces towards the working class. The *AEU Journal* carried a number of articles and lively correspondence about the significance for socialism of JPCs.[52] Jack

Tanner summed up the political ambitions of many socialist militants at the 1945 AEU National Committee:

> We have rich experience of the shop stewards movement of the last war. The work of the shop stewards in this war – the way in which they had had to become the Brains Trust and Information Bureaux on all the myriad wartime Orders and Regulations, and deal with the problems of the newcomers in industry – marks a big step forward.
>
> The Joint Production Committees which some of the more conservative brothers misinterpreted as a 'truce' with the employers and a piece of 'class collaboration' were in fact, and will be in future I hope, the most vigorous expression of working class initiative.
>
> There is no such thing in a democracy as power without responsibility. It was not until the organised workers in this country took on responsibility for war production, decided that their drive and their invention, their ideas and their skill, brains and leadership must be thrown wholeheartedly into the struggle that the decisive change occurred in our industrial war effort.
>
> The initiative – the impetus and driving force in industry – changed hands. That brothers and sisters is the first step towards the real control of industry, and it is by such experience that we learn to exercise power.[53]

The attitude of the Party Centre towards JPCs was less clear. Trevor Robinson, the gifted Lenin School graduate who was chairman of the EATSSNC, had recognized the potential of JPCs for becoming instruments of dual power from the outset. At this time he was AEU convener at the large Sheffield site of English Steel Company, part of the giant Vickers empire. He was deeply impressed both by the revolutionary possibilities of the war in general and JPCs in particular, and apparently envisioned the EATSSNC playing midwife to the birth of British soviets. He went to the Party Centre with his analysis, but found Pollitt and Campbell distinctly evasive.

They did not deny that JPCs might prove to be dress rehearsals for socialism, but they firmly staunched any discussion about whether the Party should take up a Leninist strategy to prepare JPCs as a Trojan horse for later use. They were anxious that Party members should be developing JPCs for one sole purpose: maximizing war production to save the Soviet Socialist Fatherland. The Party Centre sometimes found it expedient to hint broadly at JPCs' portentous socialist implications. But these were passing references made to reinforce a particular audience's proclivities.

Robinson's reaction was to withdraw from the EATSSNC and distance himself firmly from the Centre's equivocation. He concentrated instead on developing a Vickers' combine committee, an unofficial grouping bringing together the shop stewards committees from all Vickers' factories in order to discuss common problems and concert a common strategy in the economic struggle. The Vickers' combine was the first functional combine and attested Robinson's organizational abilities and bolshevik instincts for creating institutions from which to push the frontiers of working-class control further forward.[54]

King Street's principal concern was that JPCs should be an effective vehicle to harness working-class energies behind the production drive. The Party leadership was not disappointed when militant stewards failed to move JPCs on to the largely unexplored terrain of disputing managerial control over production. Moreover, except for Glasgow, most Party union activists apparently agreed with the centre. From their simultaneous vantage-point as Communists and union activists, Party stewards were content for JPCs to remain an extension/complement to engineering collective bargaining conventions. Thus, when Sir Walter Citrine took expeditious steps to deal with what he regarded as a threat from 'unofficial elements' to take over JPCs, neither the Party Centre nor engineering activists felt threatened. They continued to act confidently, and for the most part in good faith, inside the official union institutions.

In December 1941 Citrine told the General Council that unions would have to act quickly to bring JPCs and their machinery under official control, otherwise *ad hoc* unofficial machinery constructed by EATSSNC suporters would take over. He cooperated with the Ministry of Labour to construct a hierarchy of tripartite committees to deal with problems which individual JPCs had been unable to resolve satisfactorily. The Ministry of Supply's network of Regional Production Boards became the pinnacle of this due process.[55] The Party Centre enthusiastically welcomed this development as concrete evidence that the British war economy was moving further towards planned Soviet-style socialism. It vigorously promoted the use of this new multi-tiered machinery as a means of dealing with production bottlenecks and recalcitrant or incompetent managements who were unwilling or unable to efficiently utilize their resources to maximize production.

The Variety of Joint Production Committees

The agreement on JPCs between the EEF and engineering unions ruled items out of order which were inside official procedure, for example pay and conditions. In practice, such items were regularly tabled and considered by JPCs with the apparent complicity of employers. The Ministry of Aircraft Production (MAP) collected the minutes of two JPC meetings from 63 firms in January 1943. The MAP's analysis revealed that, out of a grand total of 1137 items, welfare, absenteeism, hours and wages accounted for 314. An EEF inquiry in the summer of 1942 confirmed this trend.[56]

The AEU undertook a second survey of JPCs in April–September 1942. Stewards reported on the subjects most frequently discussed: canteens (by 57 per cent of JPCs replying); absenteeism and bad time-keeping (by 41 per cent); and output bonus and guaranteed piece-work prices (by 21.5 per cent).[57] A third AEU survey of JPCs, completed in November 1942, found that 18 per cent had made no arrangements for reporting back to the workforce; 27.5 per cent posted JPC minutes on noticeboards, and 8.5 per cent circulated minutes (sometimes through a factory magazine). Shop meetings were held in only 12 per cent and factory meetings in only 11 per cent to report back on JPC deliberations. Interested individuals received reports in 11 per cent; and shop stewards committees heard report backs in 7.5 per cent which were then assumed to be passed downwards.[58]

The survey evidence revealed a surprisingly wide range of uses to which JPCs were being adapted by their trade union members. Not surprisingly, this variety was reflected in the lack of uniformity of Party members' response to JPCs. JPCs were established at factory fortresses, like Napier's and the Austin Aero, where they functioned more or less as Citrine and the EEF had decreed. At previously unorganized sites, ingenious Party shop stewards developed JPCs as a vehicle for gaining effective union recognition. JPCs enabled the trade union side to develop its negotiating skills and provided a vital venue from which management could be drawn into negotiations.

James Jefferys was secretary of the Dunlops' JPC in Coventry. He recalled using the Committee to fill the gaping hole where collective bargaining should have been. He was well aware that JPC members had to justify themselves to the workforce, who were sceptical not only about this new institution but also about the value of any collective negotiations. He wrote regular reports which publicized the achievements of the Committee. The JPCs success in gaining concessions on bread-and-butter issues from management encouraged the feeling that trade unionism had an important part to play on the factory floor.[59]

In Birmingham factories where collective bargaining was well established, older union loyalists treated JPCs with characteristic suspicion. Nevertheless, the veterans moved behind JPCs in order not to be seen to be lining up with management against them. Most Party members decided to give JPCs a fair try, and were pleased to find that they actually had their uses.[60] In Manchester and Sheffield, Joint Production Committees made comparatively little difference to the day-to-day functioning of Party activists on the shopfloor. Because negotiating machinery was not only intact but also functioning adequately for the most part, JPCs were gratuitous to the main task which Party activists set themselves – increasing trade union strength. Younger Party engineers often served on the JPC, like Herbert Howarth at ESC in Sheffield and Benny Rothman at Metro-Vic's, who had become shop stewards but were not figures of power in the factory. They found the business interesting and felt they made positive contributions to maximizing production. However, their contributions had not led to any significant advances in the production effort.[61]

We have observed that the unions' accumulated strength at West London aircraft sites and one or two engineering works had not been effectively transmitted to the rest of the expanding, prosperous engineering industry before the war.[62] At the outset of the war, some London employers had bowed to combined union and Ministry of Labour pressure to formally adhere to engineering negotiating procedure; many, however, had subsequently refused to yield any practical ground. In September 1939 a number of Party engineers in West London found jobs at sites with the intention of building union organization. The establishment of JPCs provided an opportunity for erstwhile shop stewards to prove their value to the people who had elected them. In 1942–43, Party union activists assumed a public profile on the shopfloor behind the protection afforded by Bevin's Essential Works Order and the acceptable face of the Soviet Army, with dramatic results.

The examples of the nearby factory fortresses continued to shine out as a beacon. Ralph Fuller remembered the erstwhile shop stewards from firms in Park Royal and along the Great West Road coming for advice and assistance about how to 'do what we had done in Napier's'. Like Pollitt and Campbell, Elms and Arter dispensed the general homilies of revolutionary pragmatism and counselled caution, commitment and patience. As observant constitutional militants, Elms and Arter were punctilious about not encroaching on the sovereign authority of either the London AEU District Committee or the ODD, Claude Berridge. They offered no glib formulae for success and made no attempt to encourage the increasingly volatile mood on the Great West Road shopfloors in 1942–43 to ignite and produce an militant, unofficial strike wave, as the West London aircraft factories had done in 1917–18.

The establishment in Park Royal of a second Napier's factory to make Sabre engines gave Napier's stewards an opportunity to physically transplant their strong union organization. They ensured that activists were among those going to the new site which was soon 'as well organized' as the one in Acton Vale. This quick flowering union growth must have been inspiring to the new stewards in other engineering factories on the estate. *New Propellor* reported in February 1941 that 36 shop stewards from 12 factories in Park Royal had formed an Area Committee. It recalled that the estate had formerly been a union black-spot, but that trade unionism had now been firmly established due to rank-and-file effort.[63]

While the Party's pro-war line discouraged the erstwhile stewards from precipitating industrial action, they nevertheless maintained active hostilities in good Communist faith. Moreover, the Party Centre's counsels actually strengthened the trade union forces in the West London theatre of the class war. When union organization is becoming embedded in a hitherto unorganized factory, management routinely win the first engagements. Workers are not yet habituated to the rituals of collective shopfloor conflict; shop stewards have no means of gauging how management will respond to their assertion of collective strength; management have the considerable advantage of the *status quo* in which their authority has been wielded without question from below. Because the West London stewards were disinclined to incite strikes in 1942–43, they had more time and more energy to develop their own organization and build collective confidence in the guise of pursuing the production drive before finally embarking on overt confrontations with management.

At the beginning of 1942 the RIRO noted that there had been real problems during the previous year in firms which were non-federated and had no experience of collective bargaining. Moreover, these problems were exacerbated because the new shop stewards were often 'certain workers who have established for themselves reputations as troublemakers'.[64] His reports during the year showed that workers were indeed pleased with the concessions which their new shop stewards were gaining for them and were forming a self-interested commitment to shopfloor trade unionism. 'Trade union officials have told us recently of the numerous requests which they receive for their services from factory employees, including new entrants and women, who desire to join Unions. As one official put it: "We do not have to look for members, they come to us nowadays." '[65]

> we must confess we are frequently being told that in a number of establishments the patriotism of workers depends upon the extent to which they are able to profit by the war. In this respect it is necessary to bear in mind that in these days we are getting into contact with some of the most difficult and stubborn employers who have for some years been waging war with trade unions and who now find that the powers and arguments which they were able to use are becoming less effective.[66]

> In a recent case where we came into contact with a number of shop stewards in company with Union officials, we noticed that the questions put by the Convener, which were of an intelligent nature, were brushed aside, and we were afterwards told that the man concerned was a troublemaker and did not merit attention . . . It seems doubtful whether it is wise to attempt suppression of such a man even though he may be a political agitator, considering that he is usually able to influence his fellow workers, and his failure to get a hearing

in government circles may result in a greater determination to get support from, and action taken by, the men with whom he comes in contact daily.[67]

After JPCs had been officially sanctioned the stewards in West London were quick to demand their establishment in their factories. Their agitation on the shopfloor concentrated on Pollitt's declaration that only the workers could ensure vital war production. Their arguments usually succeeded in wrong-footing management. In the autumn of 1942 Party stewards in West London began an offensive to build union organization. The 'Great West Road Shop Stewards Movement' sent deputations to local government to demand a Town Meeting in order to arraign management for their neglect of the production front. The RIRO observed with some trepidation: 'We have noticed that the stewards in most of the important factories in this part of London now have headed notepaper, and they send us typed letters with copies of correspondence, etc.' [68]

Despite its potential for offending the AEU and also for inciting industrial action, the National Metal Bureau acquiesced in the West London shop stewards unofficial movement. There was a clear need in the unorganized factories, which veteran activists understood very well, for stewards to come together. In addition, the Metal Bureau could rely absolutely upon trusted Party veterans in the nearby factory fortresses to keep an eye on the 'unofficial' body and ensure it remained within the confines of union loyalism. The physical proximity of West London to both the Party Centre, King Street and the AEU Executive at Peckham Road enabled Pollitt, Campbell, Scott and Jack Tanner to maintain a close watch on rank-and-file enthusiasms.

The RIRO's hopeful expectation that the Great West Road Shop Stewards would prove a short-lived hot air stunt were not realized.[69] At the beginning of 1943 he noted:

> The small number of employers of any size in the Great West Road area who are still refusing to recognise trade unions are receiving further attention by the shop stewards committee covering that district, and we understand action is to be decided upon at a meeting called for early next month. We have been able to assist in clearing up a number of recognition cases lately, but there are a few employers who have always successfully resisted the Unions and who have at the same time been careful to give no cause for complaint over wages and conditions.[70]

Two AEU convenors, Len Hine from the Ford's subsidiary Lincoln Cars and Mr Guelfgot from London Aeroplanes (most of whose management came from Ford's), procured a loudspeaking van in which they toured up and down the Great West Road dispensing pro-union, pro-production, anti-management propaganda. The loudspeaking van probably belonged to the London District Communist Party. The RIRO reported that the Secretary of the Brentford and Chiswick Trades Council had issued petrol for it to Hine and Guelfgot for defence purposes. The RIRO observed that Hine had 'spent some years in Russia', and '[as] with so many of his associates his self expression is very well developed.'[71] The message emanating from the van was a call to all workers to join the AEU. The recruiting pitch was laced with quotes from a recent government enquiry into London Aeroplanes and Alltools which had found both managements to be deficient. The peroration declared: 'full production would not be secured unless similar inquiries were forced [by the AEU] at other establishments'.[72]

In spite of the RIRO's best intentions, the atmosphere on engineering shopfloors in West London was becoming so charged that it could only be a matter of time before skirmishing broke out. Workers' current willingness to openly oppose what they considered to be arbitrary or unfair management actions was hardly a spontaneous whim. Over the following months the RIRO recorded some of the incidents in which workers had challenged managerial prerogative. For example, in June 1943, he noted that a shop steward had been suspended on the Great West Road for using bad language to a foreman. Three hundred workers had gone on strike in protest in spite of the steward's advice to them to stay at work.[73]

The emergence of shop stewards committees provided a collective leadership through which this populist reaction against authority was channelled into trade union activism. Listening to their stewards publicly and apparently fearlessly make charges of incompetence against management struck a chord with men and women for whom war weariness had finally set in. They were fed up with the unrelieved monotony and continual pressure of war work. Management, for their part, noted this sea change with some trepidation. In July 1943 the RIRO observed:

> at another [works] conference an employer objected to conceding some minor increases in wages on the ground that every concession in the past had been used as an argument in favour of concessions for other workers in the same establishment. He used a phrase which employers now use more and more frequently: 'We have to make a stand somewhere.'[74]

In August 1943 the RIRO reported that London Aeroplanes had sacked Mr Guelfgot. He had been pressing them hard on 'minor grievances' inside the Works Committee, and the RIRO implied that they had been made to feel uncomfortably insecure in their exercise of managerial prerogative.[75] The RIRO described the convenor:

[a] Polish Jew and admittedly an excellent aircraft fitter who attended punctually and regularly on his job . . . he was, however . . . never satisfied unless he was getting at the management about some complaint or other. One of the firm's complaints was that he was continually badgering non-unionists to join the union.[76]

In November 1943 Hine was sacked from Lincoln Cars for organizing without prior permission a meeting during working time to protest against Oswald Mosley's release. His sacking produced 'high feeling' along the Great West Road.[77] Mosley's release also prompted 'the well-known Mr Birch' to convene a meeting in the Landis & Gyr canteen on the borders of Park Royal during working hours, after management had refused permission. He asked permission to hold a further meeting to enable workers to hear the report of a deputation which had gone from Landis & Gyr to lobby MPs about Mosley. Management were on the point of sacking him when the RIRO intervened and 'advised them to act in a rather different way'.[78] The RIRO was understandably anxious to prevent Reg Birch, whose flamboyance and steely wit made him so eminently suited to becoming a popular hero, from gaining the martyr's crown.

Hine had probably met a similar fate many times before. This time his victimization for the trade union cause reverberated through war-weary West London engineering workshops. The tentative ties of loyalty which had been established between stewards and their members were greatly strengthened after workers had witnessed summary sackings meted out by a management evidently determined to maintain its authority. Workers who had not previously viewed themselves as trade unionists now became an angry rank-and-file. On 3 December the RIRO described an incident which had taken place at the Chiswick site of London Aeroplanes:

> there was a suggestion that five shop stewards might be discharged for holding a meeting without permission but the idea was over-thrown by higher authority. Any such discharge might have pro-duced a serious strike throughout the LAP organisation and perhaps even in establishments of the LPTB.[79]

The Party's ideological certainty that only the British working class could save the Soviet Socialist Fatherland acted to submerge the fate of the two men. Guelfgot and Hine probably dissuaded colleagues from striking to demand their reinstatement, because the socialist/Soviet/JPCs 'cause' was actually more important to them than their own personal fate. We have also observed the RIRO acting discreetly to curb management's worst intentions. His job was to facilitate war production and he evidently per-ceived workers as having greater potential than employers to 'cause problems'. His priorities therefore were to assuage shopfloor susceptibilities rather than management's pre-occupations as long as he scented no threat from below of 'anarchy'. He proved willing to pressurize managements along the Great West Road to deal 'fairly' and even leniently with shop stewards because the revolutionary pragmatism evolved by Party engineering veterans had thoroughly permeated West London trade union culture. The RIRO could see well enough that union loyalism from lay activists, was moderating any rank-and-filist tendencies on shop stewards committees.

The rank-and-file could clearly have been led into all-out battle by the Great West Road Shop Stewards Movement. However, Hine and Guelfgot remained sacked and Party militants made no attempt to precipitate a local revolt to avenge them. This apparent quiescence is in sharp contrast with the situation in July 1918 when the victimization of a woman shop steward and convener caused the West London Engineering Workers' Committee to organize a general strike of 15–20,000 workers. It lasted for four days until the Government intervened to force their reinstatement.[80] However, unlike the militants in 1918, Guelfgot and Hine left a lasting legacy behind them. The foundations of trade union organization in West London had been firmly laid. Rank-and-file union loyalism and union growth continued uninterrupted into the peace.

In Glasgow, JPCs' reception was complicated by the richness of the city's political culture. The local trade union establishment felt that JPCs obscured the all-important boundary between men and masters. Veteran ILP union activists and Trotskyist Workers International League (WIL) neophytes agreed that JPCs were fatally flawed instruments of class collaboration. This motley assortment of activists developed opposition to JPCs inside the AEU machinery and inside war factories. From the end of 1941 Galbraith recorded the growing division between Party members and fellow-travellers who were now 'undoubtedly . . . [using] their influence to prevent stoppage of work' and

> The other group [which] is heterogeneous in character and consists of individuals of the Communist persuasion who are opposed to Stalin's ideas of Communist policy and are in favour of using every opportunity to create disturbance with a view to world-wide dictatorship of the proletariat. Their attitude is, therefore, to make use of grievances or working conditions to bring about stoppages of work. Associated with them are a number of ILPers who share the view of the leaders of that Party with regard to the war and it is to be feared that the IRA is not without some representation. In addition to these elements which can be labelled, there are others of a rather nondescript character who find their motive in creeds which involve opposition to war in general. So far as the writer can estimate, it is this group which at present is the real danger, whatever may be the ultimate aims of the other lot.[81]

The political conflict reached its climax with votes on JPCs at the Glasgow AEU District Committee and Beardmore's Parkhead Forge. Both had been dominated by the Party since the 1920s, and Communist activists had to fight this issue much more seriously than they were accustomed to doing. In the summer of 1942 the Beardmore's shop stewards committee became irreparably divided over whether a JPC should be established in the factory. Party members forced a vote which supported JPCs, but the minority refused to accept the result and in their turn forced a works ballot, which showed 1300 for and 700 against a JPC. When the minority still refused to accept the result, the shop stewards committee disintegrated, making collective bargaining in this once-proud factory fortress impossible. Sectional industrial action became common and there was an exodus of militants from the Party including Jimmy Doherty, the veteran AEU convener and leader of the 1937 strike. The dissidents allied themselves with the WIL/ILP bloc in the city.[82]

Galbraith described the conflict in minute detail, fascinated by its complexity. He noted the considerable resistance from the 'more mature men brought up in the ASE tradition'.[83]

> their criticism is that in the absence of guarantees as to a new status for the workers after the war it will be wrong to place the knowledge of the workers at the disposal of the employers because this would enable the latter to intensify exploitation when peace comes ... a considerable proportion of the Clyde District Committee of the AEU hold this view. The younger men, most of them far to the Left, are considerably perplexed. It is quite clear that when Production Committees are set up the influence of the younger school is going to see that they are kept fully employed on questions which they will raise.[84]

Galbraith's prediction proved accurate enough. Many younger Party members had found work in the shipyards at the outset of the war. They seized the opportunity presented by Yard Committees, the title conferred on JPCs in the shipyards, to apply the serious-minded bolshevism which they had learned inside the Glasgow Party's education programme. They had declined to become union activists before the war because they regarded the local 'economic struggle' as too conservative. The young Party revolutionaries encountered little competition for places on the Yard Committees. Due to the ravages of the depression, there were few union veterans with craft conservative leavening left inside the shipyards. As Galbraith had already noted:

> There are signs of a revival of activity on the part of the shop stewards movement in the shipbuilding industry ... They [its leaders] are not so insistent in regard to a wage increase to plain-time workers as on the desirability of giving the shop stewards a recognised status in relation to methods of production and management in gen-

> eral . . . It cannot be doubted that the influential amongst them are
> extraordinarily keen on Production Committees without much con-
> tact with the trade union officials. In the writer's view the only way
> to deal with this problem is to set up Yard and Works Committees
> everywhere under trade union auspices . . . This will probably go
> against the grain in the the case of West of Scotland employers but
> the alternative is unilateral shop committees with all the troubles
> which these can engender.[85]

Like Trevor Robinson, the young Party stewards had recognized the
potential for JPCs as instruments of dual power. They eagerly tested this
new official machinery to discover how far they could extend their frontiers of control. Wilfully oblivious to the threat posed to union 'custom
and practice' by their 'radical' suggestions for increasing production,
they were also scornful of craft demarcation and union rivalries as illegit-
imate concerns of the 'economic struggle' because they divided the working class. They had only two Communist aims: helping the Soviet Union
to victory over Hitler and pushing back managerial prerogative. The
young Party stewards became regular suitors at Galbraith's office, enlist-
ing his support in clearing a production bottleneck or countermanding a
management instruction.[86] Inman commented that Galbraith 'was an
outstanding personality and his intervention was sought more frequently, and at an earlier stage of disputes, than in other areas where the
officers were sometimes less respected.'[87]

The conflict came to a head when the stewards on John Brown's Yard
Committee proposed to break down craft demarcation lines to allow
flexible working. Their proposal was then carried on the Clyde
Consultative Committee presided over by Galbraith. The veterans on the
district Confederation of Shipbuilding Unions adamantly rejected it,
indifferent to the fact that it had been put forward in order to avoid
potential redundancies. Nevertheless, John Brown's Yard Committee
were undeterred and carried their case forward outside the trade union
machinery, probably assisted by Galbraith who evidently retained a
youthful disposition towards radicalism.

> The question was discussed with the trade union executives by the
> Financial Secretary of the Admiralty in July [1942] and at a meeting
> between the Minister of Labour, the First Lord and the industry in
> September . . . the Boilermakers' Society made it quite clear that the
> only interchangeability it would accept was between the various
> crafts inside its own union. The employers . . . seem to have recon-
> ciled themselves to the unions' opposition, and reported at the
> Central Consultative Committee early in 1943 that the present posi-
> tion was regarded as reasonably satisfactory. There the matter rested
> for the remainder of the war.[88]

It is hardly surprising that when war-weariness produced an increased incidence of industrial conflict throughout Britain, political divisions intensified most on Clydeside. Not even in South Wales were the divisions inside the trade union movement reflected through the prism of socialist politics in the way they were there. Nevertheless, by the end of the war Glasgow Party members in engineering had gained the experience necessary to provide effective shopfloor leadership in the economic struggle. Having remained at one remove from day-to-day issues in the 1930s, young Party members had been blooded. They had not only acquired the ability to survive on the shopfloor but had also discovered the need to observe the limits of union custom and practice.

War-weariness and attempts to allay it

We have already observed the appearance of war-weariness in late 1942. The consequent increase in economic conflict was duly noted by RIROs up and down the country. However, the increase of friction on the shopfloor was not merely due to industrial fatigue. As the prospect of victory loomed larger, management became concerned to reassert their prerogative and orientate themselves towards the 'normal' peacetime cut- and-thrust of shopfloor life. War workers were also looking forward: they began to see disputes over wages as affecting their peacetime standard of living. Inman concluded that the engineering disputes in 1944 were related to the lack of potential for increasing piece-work and bonus earnings: radical alterations to production methods and products had ceased, while rate-fixers had become more experienced.[89]

Inman is probably conservative for patriotic motives in her estimate as to when the anticipation of the peacetime economic struggle began to affect both sides. As early as April 1943 the Midlands RIRO reported:

> Most people agree that there exists an underlying discontent which may be likened to the moroseness, the depression of a tired man, which engenders an unreasoning irritability. Victories like the recent ones in Tunisia act like stimulants on the Body Industrial and there can be no doubt about the potentially stimulating effect of the opening of a 'Second Front'. The Coventry area is said by some closely in touch with the workpeople, to be particularly agitated below the surface and there have certainly been many signs of touchiness in that quarter. The fundamental causes are probably no more tangible than those referred to above, but piecework prices, transfers of redundant workpeople, and possibly a tightening of disciplinary measures are the more likely sparks to cause a fire.[90]

Nevertheless, it is notable that despite this heightened tension, remarkably few engineering and shipbuilding disputes escalated into full-scale battles. The vast majority were neither prolonged nor protracted and the

Daily Worker treated them with studious forbearance. The 'rank-and-file' had legitimate grievances and no one was heeding them. War production could only be maximized when all the outstanding sources of conflict on the shopfloor had been resolved. After scrutinizing the Party's role in the war-weary engineering disputes, Croucher was unable to detect any general reaction against Communists either among activists or strikers. He found disagreements among the strikers, who included Party members and other militants, but no evidence of a popular rejection of Communists for being class collaborators. His conclusion reinforces the impression we have already received that most Party activists did not pursue the pro-production line at the expense of waging the 'economic struggle'.[91]

Having considered whether common factors underlay the serious outbreaks of industrial conflict, Inman observes, 'Many of these background causes of strikes, such as war strain or the slowness of procedure ... were common to all factories and shipyards. The fact remained that certain shops and yards were very much more prone to strikes than others'.[92] Her conclusion that compared with 1914–18 serious strikes in engineering were exceptional is upheld by the evidence. The strikes can only be satisfactorily analysed by reference to local circumstances and vicissitudes. The three protracted outbreaks of strikes which occurred in engineering and shipbuilding are examined below. Meanwhile it will be a useful corrective to look at two short industrial disputes led by Party activists which achieved satisfactory results by inflicting minimum damage on the war effort.

During the war the large multi-product engineering factory, Metro-Vic's, located in the industrial estate at Trafford Park, Manchester and owned by AEI Ltd, was finally transformed by the Party and left Labour stewards into a factory fortress. They refurbished and revitalized the functioning negotiating structure which had been maintained intact from the 1914–18 war.[93] Benny Rothman remembered that he had begun to hold regular shop meetings in the late 1930s in order to report back on the deliberations of the shop stewards committee and to discuss other issues on the horizon so that he could take his shop's attitude back to the shop stewards committee.

The increasing number of Party and left-wing Labour stewards ensured that the exemplary rank-and-file practice of establishing channels of direct democracy and control in the factory was extended to most other shops. Employment had nearly doubled from 16,000 in 1938 to 30,000 at the height of the war. Party membership increased from ten in 1936 to 150 in early 1942 and 250 by the end of that year.[94] The Frows described the variety of Party activities in 1942:

One leaflet, headed 'Second Front', was distributed in Trafford Park in fifteen thousand copies, many of them at Metros ... despite the long hours of work, the difficulties of travelling in the blackout and shift work, education classes were conducted. Discussions held in the lunch-hour started with thirty members and rapidly grew to over a hundred. A leading Communist opened on a subject, such as 'How a Communist Looks at Life' and then a syllabus on the 'History of Trade Unionism' was followed. The Metros group sold fifty pounds' worth of pamphlets and other literature during June [1942] and challenged any other factory group to beat it during August.[95]

In the spring of 1943 there was a strong shopfloor reaction to the National Arbitration Tribunal's Award No. 326, a complex compromise made in response to the engineering union's wage claim for an increase of $33\frac{1}{3}$ per cent in the basic rate of time workers.[96] Benny Rothman recalled that Party stewards at Metro-Vic's recognized that they must support 'the outcry over the Award'. Led by their stewards, all the workers in various shops exercised collectively their individual right to work on hourly wage rates, a right which had long been enshrined in the Manchester district's engineering bargaining convention. War production in the factory certainly suffered. The dispute was settled by negotiations carried out by the new chairman of the shop stewards committee, the young Party activist Hugh Scanlon. He succeeded in 'squeezing little bits here and there' from management.[97]

King Street's pro-war line did not inhibit the Austin Aero shop stewards from holding joint meetings with their few shop steward colleagues at Austin's Longbridge site to encourage them to take the offensive against management, citing the better wages and conditions in the shadow factory as an example to be emulated.[98] In September 1944 a revolt over piece-rate prices for non-war work precipitated strike action at Longbridge. The Aero stewards provided copious amounts of support and ensured that the strike was well organized and solid. The Midlands RIRO observed: 'Both sides regard the issue as one of "principle" and it was feared at one time that the firm's aeroplane works would be involved.'[99] Nevertheless, this strike was short, and strikers observed the normal engineering conventions by returning to work on the promise of an immediate official works conference with the understanding of concessions to follow. The small victory had profound effects. The Longbridge management recognized the shop stewards committee. From this beginning AEU activists embarked on the protracted mission of making the site into a factory fortress. Dick Etheridge recalled that there had been 70 to 80 Party members at Longbridge by 1945. He became AEU convener there at the end of the war.[100]

These examples would multiply in a more detailed examination of the war-weary skirmishes and near strikes. The success of Ford's shop stewards in gaining union recognition at Dagenham in 1944 was due in no small measure to the continued enthusiasm of Party shop stewards for fighting the economic struggle. It was their determination to attack management prerogative which provided the basis from which Citrine, Tanner and Joe Scott could apply national pressure on Ford's anti-union management who were caught in a pincer movement between the TUC and the Ministry of Labour on the one hand and the threat of unofficial shop stewards movement on the other.

The notable exceptions to the rule of small, tightly controlled conflicts were the shipyard strikes on the Tyne in September 1942 and at Vickers' in Barrow in September 1943; and there was a rash of strikes in the winter of 1942 in Clydeside engineering factories. On the Tyne and at Barrow union activists used their temporary wartime advantage to take umbrage at management violations of established custom and practice, the same violations which had offended but had to be endured in the inter-war slump. They were determined to redress long-standing grievances and insisted on their right to enforce union rules despite the wartime emergency. Neither Pollitt's exhortations nor the full panoply of the full-time officials' authority could deflect veterans from avenging accumulated defeats. (The young bolsheviks who had become shop stewards and convenors in the Clyde shipyards evidently kept the same craft/demarcation/overtime problems there well under control.)

The Barrow dispute was the more protracted and left deeper scars inside the union. Though Party members were involved on both sides, the conflict remained apolitical throughout. The Barrow AEU District Committee claimed its sovereign 'democratic right' under engineering rank-and-file traditions and AEU rule to conduct the strike. The AEU Executive, the Communist National Organizers, Wally Hannington and George Crane, and Jack Tanner were all agreed that there could be no compromise with the District Committee's refusal to follow the Executive Council's instructions. Despite their combined efforts, the lay officials would not give way. Hannington and Crane acted in Barrow on the Executive's behalf but were unable to move the Party militants on the District Committee.

The situation was resolved only when the Executive took the extreme action of dismissing the entire District Committee and then reinstating only those members who were willing to observe their instruction to call off the strike. On the Tyne, the sudden appearance of the WIL gave the strike a clear political overtone and the Party Centre assumed a higher political profile in exhorting the men to go back to work and win the war.[101] These two apparently intractable strikes played a significant part in convincing Bevin to enact Regulation 1AA which gave him the powers to summarily imprison strikers.

In Glasgow, the boilermakers at the Queens Park works of North British Locomotives went on strike over the transfer of skilled workers. They received solid support from AEU members at the works and the strike rumbled on relentlessly despite the best efforts of the Glasgow AEU District Committee. It was only settled after the Ministry of Labour had begun legal proceedings under Order 1305.[102] Galbraith observed that a 'kind of vendetta' had now developed between Party leaders and activists who had been expelled from the Party.

> The mere appearance of any of the Communist leaders in any dispute seems to stir up an almost waspish group intent on creating trouble. It is interesting to learn where workers of the Roman Catholic faith are receiving printed matter sponsored by their Church exhorting them to be careful to keep clear of any political complications in connection with their industrial difficulties . . . The big stoppage of work at the Queens Park establishment of the North British Locomotive Company Limited is an example of a Strike Committee composed of ex-associates of the Communist Party fighting bitterly against the control of the majority of the Communist Party members now on the District Committee of the AEU.[103]

The strike of women workers at Rolls Royce Hillington involving women workers and other 'temporary' engineering workers was more complex.[104] The underlying issue was management's refusal to yield ground to a newly established trade union organization, the same terrain from which the Midlands and the Great West Road shop stewards campaigns for JPCs had emerged. However, in Glasgow the local trade union culture was still attuned to set-piece battles of attrition. Only a few larger heavy engineering factories had maintained union organization and collective bargaining in Glasgow in the inter-war period. Unlike better-organized districts like Manchester, no mutually acceptable unofficial conventions had evolved for dealing with grievances flexibly and allowing conflict to be 'avoided' through limited skirmishing.

It is hardly surprising that the WIL found an ideal point of entry in the Glasgow economic struggle. The combination of war-weariness, escalating inner-Party conflict and the survival of the older reflexes which had marked economic conflict in Glasgow since the 1890s proved irresistible for the WIL political activists arriving from England.[105] They launched a 'Clyde Workers Committee' (CWC) in May 1943 based mainly on the factories where we have observed strikes in the winter of 1942. However, despite this spectacular beginning, Croucher concluded that the CWC's influence quickly waned after employers continued to make concessions to the fledgeling trade union organizations.[106] Harry McShane observed with hindsight that the Party had 'easily defeated' the Trotskyists. The Party had been better organized, and the Trotskyists' anti-war line had ultimately proved unpopular.[107]

By 1944, the Glasgow Party had more or less re-established its hege-mony in engineering. Its authority was tested in August 1944 by a strike at Albion Motors which lasted over six weeks. The AEU District Committee obeyed without enthusiasm the letter of the AEU Executive's instruction to order members back to work, but made no attempt to rebel.[108] The moribund CWC could unleash no mass solidarity action. Party engineers had finally learned not to over-react. They praised the District Committee for bowing to the Executive for the sake of 'trade union unity', and then waited for the strike to peter out. Harry McShane wrote in the *Daily Worker*: 'Unfortunately a section of them [Albion shop stewards] have been calling for strike action so persistently over a long period that they would prefer if someone else would take the responsibility for leading the workers back to work.'[109]

The WIL paper, *Socialist Appeal*, stated in April 1944 that the Party had lost its majority support on the AEU District Committee.[110] While the balance of power may have been more delicately poised than previ-ously, I think it likely that the Party was able to command a majority as long as Communists did not try to impose a political line which was at variance with local trade union culture. The Glasgow Party had actually managed to weather a round of expulsions and voluntary exits from absolute rank-and-filists who were unable to accept any limitation of the economic struggle even for the sake of the Socialist Fatherland. Despite this upheaval, the Party's standing had risen greatly. It was not merely one of the many left-wing groupings in the city, it was the most visible and energetic, and carried the greatest popular appeal.

Harry McShane remembered that as Glasgow Party secretary he had organized enormous meetings and demonstrations for the Second Front and that Harry Pollitt had been able to fill any hall in Glasgow.[111] The Party had also been crucial in extending union organization and the shop steward system on to the shopfloor in Glasgow and into the Clyde ship-yards. Without the discipline imposed by the Party leadership on its members and in turn on the workforce, it is doubtful whether the engi-neering unions would have been able to exploit the opportunities which the war had presented.[112]

Despite the comparative mildness of the war-weary strike outbreaks, King Street evidently decided that the British working class needed the Party's political direction. They reactivated the EATSSNC, which they had deliberately compelled to lie dormant following the six months of frenetic activity after the 1941 Stoll Conference through fear that its rank-and-filism should become uncontrollable.[113] In January 1944 a second 'great national conference' of the EATSSNC at the Stoll Theatre was announced which would discuss vital trade union and production issues.[114]

The second Stoll conference attracted 1422 delegates from 332 factories, representing 590,438 workers, about the same number as in 1941.[115] However, unlike the first time, the EATSSNC merely provided the platform. There was no suggestion that the unofficial movement would spearhead any future campaign. Since 1942, *New Propellor* had put forward 'rank-and-file' demands but had not mentioned the need for the EATSSNC to promote them. It was left to trade unions' 'coordinating' activity to achieve them.[116] The conference keynote speech by Finlay Hart, a full-time Party official who had gone back to the Clyde shipyards in 1942, underlined the EATSSNC's lack of ambition:

> The conference is not a challenge to the trade union leaders. It is meant to be of assistance to them. It would not be necessary to hold such conferences if the trade unions themselves provided opportunities for shop stewards of all sections of the engineering and shipbuilding industries being able to meet, exchange experiences and make their suggestions.[117]

The conference resolutions were rhetorical demands: legal guarantees were needed to prevent shopfloor victimization and legislation should ensure that JPCs survived in peacetime to ensure industrial reconstruction.[118] There was no provision made for delegates to monitor the progress of these demands through their respective official trade union organizations. No one in the National Metal Bureau believed that the EATSSNC would assume a leading role as a full-blooded rank-and-file movement to see that these demands were actually achieved.

The March 1944 conference acted as an efficient safety valve for the ventilation of grievances and the expression of 'rank-and-file' commitment to trade unionism. However, it did not address a number of strategic issues which were vital to the future of the trade union movement and the Communist Party's relation to it. The Party Centre and the leading constitutional militants were unaccustomed to addressing serious strategic questions affecting the union. Just as the implications for the union of the AEU National Committee's continuing refusal to admit women into membership had never been considered by the Party, so other crucial issues were allowed to fester without the Party's collective mind being applied to how they might be resolved.

As a result the destiny of Joint Production Committees was left hanging in the balance. To enforce the conference resolution favouring their continuance, the EATSSNC, that is the Party Centre, would have had to contemplate promoting determined industrial action. But there was no serious consideration of whether JPCs were worth fighting for and if workers could be mobilized in their support. Instead, their fate was decided by default. The rapid development of company-wide collective bargaining was another strategic issue which was bypassed.

The centralizing tendencies of the total war economy had drawn the separate sites of the increasingly concentrated heavy and aircraft engineering companies more closely together. But the logical extension of the goal of organizing factory fortresses to the level of company fortresses was not seriously pursued. Trevor Robinson used the more fluid environment of the wartime emergency to organize the Vickers Combine Committee. The Vickers Combine Committee was heralded by the Party Centre as an exciting innovation, but no thought was given as to how it might be incorporated inside official union institutions and engineering procedure.

A postscript on coal

The phoney war had even fewer repercussions for coalmining conditions than engineering. There were no immediate coal shortages, and evidently no government forethought that they might occur later on. Substantial numbers of miners volunteered for military service without any government hindrance. After the fall of France had wiped out one of the coalfield's main export markets, unemployment in the South Wales coalfield actually increased.[119] The legacy of the 1914–18 war for civil servants in the Department of Mines was either suppressed or ignored. This was in ominous contrast to the Ministry of Labour where civil servants remembered only too well their attempts to regulate production and industrial relations from above in engineering. As a result, they were as keen as Bevin to establish extensive joint and tripartite consultative machinery.[120]

The memory black-out at the Department of Mines may have been due to the very painful scars left by the vicissitudes of wartime state control and peacetime de-control of the coalfields. Nevertheless, the Department failed to anticipate and make provision for the problems which an expanding war economy with an apparently limitless demand for coal would present. The consequences proved fateful when the advent of total war produced severe and lasting coal shortages combined with a contracted, ageing and disaffected labour force.

It was clear that the war conditions would place the MFGB in a greatly improved position to win restored national collective bargaining machinery and in consequence to consolidate control over its affiliated unions. It was equally clear that the coal-owners had not forgotten 1914–18 and were intent on giving no hostages to fortune which the MFGB could exploit in any peacetime conflict over deregulation.[121] There was little evidence of patriotic self-sacrifice on either side, and no attempt made by the Department of Mines to massage it into existence. Conditions were consequently left to drift. In the summer of 1941 the problem of a short-fall in coal production reappeared after a gap of some 12 months caused by the effects of the loss of Britain's main export markets. This second time, however, the problem not only persisted but continued to intensify.[122]

The exodus of labour from the pits in the first 18 months of the war and the chronic under-investment by most coal-owners in capital throughout the inter-war years meant that the industry's chances of increasing production and productivity were slender at best.[123] And yet, as the total war culture took hold of British society from Government down to shopfloor worker, coal-owners and miners came under increasing pressure from the Government and 'public opinion' to deliver the goods. The 'economic struggle' in coalmining from the advent of the Coalition Government in May 1940 until the end of the war is at least a tripartite if not a quadripartite affair.

There were distinct roles for not only mining unions and coal-owners, but also the Department of Mines and the Ministry of Labour. Each had its own interests to further and defend; moreover, they were usually conflicting and also stretched into the peace. The continuing public and political interest in the progress of this drama – a legacy of the coalminers' place in British political culture – ensured that the Cabinet and Parliament paid an inordinate amount of attention to its course. It could not be said that any of the participants fully observed a wartime truce. As the war progressed, the peacetime implications of increasing coal production greatly preoccupied all the players.

After Joseph Jones left the MFGB in 1938 to join the Coal Commission, the MFGB had drifted. The remaining officers, Lawther and Edwards, lacked Jones's strategic sense and ability to mould current union policy to prepare for future problems. As Bevin's war machine began to generate an apparently limitless demand for coal, the MFGB was bereft of concrete suggestions and constructive plans to put to the Coalition Government for increasing output and productivity. The Minister of Labour hesitated long and hard before intervening in coalmining. Bevin had learned about the intractable problems of collective bargaining in the industry in 1926 and had no desire to get bogged down in that quagmire. Nevertheless, the continuing crisis of coal production meant that he increasingly intervened.

The Communist Party might have also played its part in this drama. Party activists were now dominant in the Scottish coalfield and highly influential in South Wales. The demise of the Spencer union in Nottinghamshire had opened the way for Party activists to win positions in the fused Nottinghamshire Miners Association (NMA). Party activists were even making headway in elections in the Derbyshire and Yorkshire unions, benefiting from the prestige accumulated by Mick Kane and the Harworth strike, and the fact that, as long-serving union officials retired, Party candidates for union office were often the most forceful and capable.[124] For the first time since 1925–26 the Party had the personnel inside the MFGB to substantially influence policy.

In Scotland, the war presented Party mining activists with their first opportunity to function openly and coherently inside the county unions after their long exile in the UMS. Party activists quickly established themselves on the ground in lodge and coalfield union positions. Once Party members had settled, they soon found that the coal-owners' conduct afforded them every chance to rebuild union organization. Galbraith described a strike at Gateside colliery, Cambuslang in 1940: 'Public opinion in this case cannot be said to be on the side of the coalowners who in Scotland seem to be impervious to current experience and are living in a world which has not had any real existence since the first half of the nineteenth century.'[125]

It would have been a comparatively straightforward matter to escalate the drama during the period when the Party opposed the war. The call for immediate nationalization of the coalfields was the obvious answer to the owners' unhelpfulness and parsimony. This move would have put great pressure on Labour MPs and the MFGB to follow suit. However, Dutt and Rust proved reluctant to disturb the hitherto cordial and close relations which had been so patiently developed by Pollitt and Campbell in the 1930s and of which the Party had become so inordinately proud. As in engineering, it became clear that the positions of influence and power which the Party had attained were not going to be abandoned for the sake of uncertain gains and an uncertain future.

There was no evidence, moreover, that any Party mining activists applied their minds to the complicated strategic questions involved. Horner became totally committed to increasing coal production and had no time or energy to fight the class struggle in the corridors of Whitehall for the MFGB. The Scottish mining activists were involved in merging the county unions in the early part of the war, and after the Soviet entry, they became the most formidable Stakhanovites in Britain. When Pollitt and Campbell returned to King Street they responded like Horner and threw themselves completely into the war effort.[126]

The coal-owners, however, unlike the engineering employers, had not laid their peacetime plans during the war.

> The Reid Committee whose members were the cream of the industry's professional management, appointed by the wartime Minister for Fuel and Power, had reported in 1944 that sweeping reorganisation and enormous capital investment were essential to secure the industry's future. The Reid Committee Report was as influential in

its own sphere as the Beveridge Report was for the Welfare State. During the lively discussion generated by the Report, it became clear that mining engineers, managers and 'progressive' coal-owners who were committed to the survival of the coal industry believed that nationalisation was the only feasible solution. The report put forward such a radically different vision of the industry from its existing status that only the Government had the authority, power and potential financial resources to effect the change.[127]

When the Labour Party won the General Election in July 1945 it was self-evident that one of their first enactments must be the nationalization of the coal industry. Horner's election as the first general secretary of the NUM placed Party activists in an even more advantageous position to influence the shape of the new National Coal Board. It was a position which Horner had no compunction in exploiting, not for the Party's narrow political ends, but in order to prove the superiority of socialized production.

Notes

1. *The Collected Essays Journalism and Letters of George Orwell, Volume 2, My Country Right or Left 1940–43*, Penguin, London, 1970, pp. 174–5. Ernest Bevin told the American Chamber of Commerce in July 1940 that 'There is no evidence in Norway, in Holland, in France, or in Belgium, that any part of the working class, whatever their political party might have been, operated as Fifth Columnists. The Fifth Columnists came from higher up.' *The Record*, August 1940. On the eve of the war, two Communists working at Woolwich Arsenal were arrested and detained without publicity. One of them was Percy Glading, a Young Turk who was also a veteran AEU activist and old intimate of Pollitt's. Charlie Wellard remembered this incident with a nod and a wink to indicate that there evidently had been espionage for the USSR going on. However, Branson does not mention this incident. See Branson, 1985, *History of the CPGB*, op. cit., ch. 23: 315–28, for her discussion of the Government's consideration of evidence of CPGB sabotage.
2. For the 1914–18 Committees, see Fishman MRC, loc.cit.: 428–30 and 502–4.
3. *Daily Worker*, 24 February 1940. The meeting was attended by 52 delegates from 27 of 'the most important engineering factories'.
4. *New Propellor*, Vol. 5 No. 3, April 1940. See pp. 259–60.
5. Ibid.
6. Frow and Frow, 1982, *Engineering Struggles*, op. cit.: 154–5. See also *New Propellor*, Vol. 5 No. 8, August 1940. The 'persecution of active members' probably referred to the Executive Council's summons to the Birmingham Fourteen, see pp. 264–6. I am aware of only one other 'persecution': Gilbert Hitchings, a leading Party engineer who as acting District Secretary in Bristol signed a manifesto supporting an 'unofficial' May Day demonstration. The Executive suspended him from office and banned him from holding any other union office for one year (ibid.). He apparently chose not to challenge their ruling at the Final Appeals Court.

7. *New Propellor*, Vol. 5 No. 10, October 1940; No. 12, 21 December 1940; *Engineering Struggles*, op. cit.: 154–5.

8. See pp. 263–4.

9. LAB 10/361, 29 June 1940. See also 8 and 22 June 1940 and 24 and 31 August 1940 and Charles Lamb's report on the increased recruitment and new shop stewards in Glasgow, *AEU Journal*, May 1940. For London see LAB 10/350, 3 January 1942; 11 and 25 April 1942; 16 and 23 May 1942. The RIRO noted that American employers were proving to be particularly anti-union.

10. LAB 10/360, 23 December 1939 and LAB 10/361, 6 January 1940. Inman noted that the Committee had offices in the same building as the Confed. District (Inman, P., 1957, *Labour in the Munitions Industries*, HMSO: 401). This co-existence shows a more tolerant attitude from the non-AEU skilled unions to the committee, and the abiding durability of a 'rank-and-filist' tradition in the Glasgow trade union culture.

11. Inman, 1957, op. cit.: 403. It became illegal to engage in a trades dispute without first reporting it to the Ministry of Labour from whence it proceeded through official procedure and compulsory arbitration if necessary.

12. Parker, H.M.D., 1957, *Manpower*, HMSO: 467.

13. Croucher, R., 1977, 'Communist Politics and Shop Stewards in Engineering, 1935–46', University of Warwick PhD: 199–202. The Coventry AEU official machinery was not involved until the final stages of the dispute. The persistent and punctillious craft conservatism of the local district committee probably inhibited their support for this irregular dispute which involved many semi-skilled workers. Jack Jones had become TGWU District Officer in 1939. He worked in close concert with Communist engineers in Coventry and Birmingham. Harold Marsh remembered attending meetings with Jones, probably of the Midlands Metal Bureau (interview with N. Fishman).

14. *New Propellor*, Vol. 5 No. 10, October 1940.

15. See *New Propellor*, Vol. 5 No. 10, October 1940 and RIRO LAB 10/350, 5 and 19 October 1940.

16. For a full background to the strike see Croucher, 1982, *Engineers at War*, Merlin: 100–107. There had been a history of conflict between management and the union at the factory, and previous conveners had also been sacked. Some strike committee publicity described workers as being 'on holiday'.

17. Galbraith's weekly reports, LAB 10/361, 5 October and 16 November 1940, and *Daily Worker*, 27 September; 11 and 21 October; 5, 13, 16, 18 November 1940.

18. LAB 10/361, 16 November 1940.

19. *AEU Journal*, April 1941.

20. *New Propellor*, Vol. 5 No. 2, January 1940, and Hannington, op. cit.: 333–35. Berridge was based in north-west London. His AEU branch was Willesden No. 2. He was also well known to union lay officials by virtue of being AEU District President. It is likely that he found out about vacancies in the Swift's toolroom and arranged for an AEU member to speak for Hannington with the relevant foreman who may well also have been a union man. Hannington needed an entrée back into engineering after his many years away from the tools as an unemployed agitator.

21. Information obtained from Mr Rayment, who worked at Swift's in this period, during interview with Muriel Rayment by N. Fishman. Mr Rayment remembered that 60 workers who had been directed to the factory from Birmingham had never come out on strike.

22. London RIRO's court evidence reported in *The Times*, 3 July 1941.

23. Swift's management had been found deficient and even bungling by the Ministry of Supply. See *Daily Worker*, 5 and 10 December 1940 and RIRO report LAB 10/356, 7 December 1940.

24. *The Times*, 2 July 1941. Six men stewards were in the AEU and there was one woman steward in the TGWU. Birch was apparently the only Party member.

25. *New Propellor*, Vol.V No. 5, 16 May 1941 and No. 6, 18 June 1941.

26. *The Times*, 4 July 1941.

27. Interview with Norman Brown and Arthur Exell by N. Fishman. On shock brigades, see 'Shock Brigades – A Guide. How to Start Them. How They Work'. YCL, n.d., *c*. 1942 and WNV, 12 September and 13 October 1942.

28. Interviews with Mick Jenkins, Johnnie Mansfield and Bert Pankhurst by N. Fishman.

29. Interview with Muriel Rayment (née Edwards) by N. Fishman.

30. Interview with Ralph Fuller by N. Fishman. For Fred Arter's impact on Napier's see pp. 212–5.

31. Ibid. Napier's workers viewed themselves as West Londoners and not 'cockneys'. Fuller described Elms's accession to convener as 'a natural process', because he had already proved an excellent shopfloor leader.

32. Eric Hobsbawm remembered the sobriquet immediately when I invoked it. It was fondly recalled by Ralph Fuller, who had seen the gates of the Petrograd factory being torn down by the workers in one of 'those films'.

33. Interview with Ralph Fuller by N. Fishman.

34. Interview with Les Ambrose by N. Fishman.

35. 'Arms and the Men', Full Report of the Conference of the EATSSNC and *New Propellor*, EATSSNC, n.d.: 4–5. The conference was described in EATSSNC publications as 'the Stoll Conference' and 'the historic Stoll Conference'. Information on Swanson's speech from Douglas Hyde. Hyde remembered that Swanson had not been pleased to be given a prepared text.

36. Ibid.: 21.

37. Paper by Len Powell for Party Secretariat, ca. late summer 1942 lent by Len Powell to N.Fishman.

38. Mahon, 1936, 'Our Work in the Trade Unions', op. cit.: 275.

39. Whitley Committee Report, quoted in Cole, G.D.H., 1973, *Workshop Organization*, Hutchinson Educational, Appendix E: 153.

40. See Hinton, J., *Shop Floor Citizens, Planning and Democracy in the British Engineering Industry, 1941–47*, Edward Elgar, 1994. These boards were established as a result of strong pressure from Citrine for tripartite corporate bodies which could engage in joint consultation and support the war effort. The Board's initial title was the Midlands Joint Consultative Committee on Production. The official version of the genesis of JPC s is found in Inman, 1957, op. cit.: 377–9.

41. Ibid.: 378–9 and 392–4.

42. LAB 10/351, 30 August 1941.

43. LAB 10/351, 27 September 1941.
44. LAB 10/351, 25 October 1941.
45. LAB 10/352, 17 January 1942.
46. LAB 10/351, 8 November 1941; see also the report for 11 October 1941 and LAB 10/352, 21 February 1942.
47. See *Birmingham Post*, 27 October 1941 and *New Propellor* Vol. 7 No. 2, 12 February 1942 and No. 3, 7 March 1942 for reports of agitation around production.
48. Croucher, R., 1982, op. cit.: 149–60.
49. Inman, 1957, op. cit.: 379.
50. Results quoted in International Labour Organisation, 1943, 'Joint Production Committees in Great Britain', Series A (Industrial Relations) No. 42, Montreal. Eight out of the 15 large factories surveyed, employing more than 10,000 workers, had JPCs by this time. Nearly one-third of the next largest factories (employing between 2500 and 10,000 workers) had JPCs. Out of the total 740 factories surveyed, 21 per cent had JPCs. Some had been formed by upgrading the pre-existing Joint Works Committees which had been functioning before the war, but most had been formed in early 1942.
51. International Labour Organisation, 1943, 'Joint Production Committees in Great Britain', Series A (Industrial Relations) No. 42, Montreal, and Riegelman, C., 1944, 'British Joint Production Machinery', ILO Series A, No. 43, Montreal; Nuffield College, 1943, 'Social Reconstruction Survey', Mem. 45, Revised Memo on Joint Production Committees, (Margaret Stewart), May; *Political and Economic Planning*, No.189, 26 May 1942, on JPCs. Stewart was a journalist who worked for *The Economist*. (Information on Margaret Stewart from James Hinton.)
52. See *AEU Journal*, December 1941 and January 1942.
53. AEU National Committee Report 1945, Presidential Address. It is likely that Yvonne Kapp wrote this speech, since she had been writing Tanner's speeches regularly for some time. Kapp had worked for the Labour Research Department before the war, and had been appointed by Tanner to become the AEU's research officer soon before the German invasion of the USSR. Tanner would probably have had a shrewd idea that she was in the Party because of her LRD job. (Information from James Hinton.)
54. Interview with Trevor Robinson by N. Fishman. Robinson was a vicar's son who had grown up in Sheffield. After his return from the Lenin School he had a spell as a full-time Party official in Manchester and then returned to Sheffield where he applied his mind to becoming an engineering shopfloor leader in various smaller factories before the war.
55. See letter from TUC General Council to Executives of Engineering Trade Unions, quoted in AEU National Committee Report, 1942, and Citrine Committee Report on Regional Boards, Cmnd 6360, May 1942. See also Hinton, n.d. , *Shop Floor Citizens*, op. cit.
56. Inman, P., 1957 op. cit.: 383. Inman discusses JPCs' tendency to deal with collective bargaining issues rather elliptically on p. 385. She describes the growth of JPCs on pp. 380–2.
57. Results quoted in 'Joint Production Committees in Great Britain', 1943, ILO Series A (Industrial Relations), No.42, Montreal, and Riegelman, C., 1944, 'British Joint Production Machinery', ILO Series A, No.43, Montreal: 119. The surveys were commissioned by Yvonne Kapp. The

returns have been 'lost' by Peckham Road in the process of weeding out redundant files. Kapp remembered that Ian Mikardo had devised a primitive method of coding them using knitting needles. (Interview with N. Fishman.) The incidence of bonus and piece-work items being discussed may well have been underreported since the AEU was officially against their appearing on JPC agendas.

58. ILO Series A, No. 42 and No. 43, op. cit.
59. Interview with James Jefferys by N. Fishman.
60. Interviews with Harold Marsh and Les Ambrose by N. Fishman.
61. Interviews with Benny Rothman and Herbert Howarth by N.Fishman. Herbert Howarth remembered that an older trade unionist had warned him sternly about the dangers of collaborating with the gaffers on these new institutions.
62. Beside the aircraft factories, there were two engineering sites in West London which had maintained a strong trade union presence in the inter-war period, the LPTB maintenance and repair works at Chiswick and the AEI coach works at Hendon. There had been a chequered history of union organization at AEI, with a protracted and difficult dispute being fought to a stalemate in 1937. Party engineers had been a continuous influence there.
63. Vol. 6 No. 2, 15 January 1941. Park Royal was a large industrial estate built during the 1914–18 war. In the inter-war period, the estate had prospered as innumerable small and medium-sized engineering firms had been established, as well as a very large Guinness brewery. The Great West Road engineering factories were an extension of the Great Western Trading Estate which had also been built during the 1914–18 war. (Smith, D.H., 1933, *The Industries of London*: 81.)
64. LAB 10/358, report for 3 January 1942; see also 11 April 1942.
65. LAB 10/358, 25 April 1942.
66. LAB 10/358, 16 May 1942.
67. LAB 10/358, 23 May 1942.
68. LAB 10/358, 3 October 1942.
69. LAB 10/358, 17 October and 7 and 28 November 1942.
70. LAB 10/359, 30 January 1943.
71. LAB 10/249, Report to Permanent Secretary, Ministry of Labour, Mr Bevan from London RIRO on London Aeroplanes. Hine was active in the Willesden NUWM in the early 1930s, along with Wally Hannington, and is likely to have been a veteran Communist.
72. LAB 10/249, loc.cit. The inquiry had been held after pressure from the AEU and the AEU was subsequently recognized at both sites.
73. LAB 10/359, 25 June 1943.
74. LAB 10/359, 16 July 1943.
75. Ibid.
76. Ibid.
77. LAB 10/359, RIRO report for 26 November 1943.
78. Ibid. Landis & Gyr was a Swiss engineering firm making electricity and gas meters. Birch was eventually dismissed in late May 1944 for allegedly playing darts in the toolroom after repeated management warnings. There was indeed the popular reaction against his sacking which the RIRO had earlier anticipated. (I am indebted to James Hinton and Terry Monaghan for this information.)

79. LAB 10/359, 3 December 1943. We have observed that the London Passenger Transport Board repair works in Chiswick had long been a factory fortress for the unions and the CPGB.

80. Hinton, J, 1969, op. cit.: 385 and 390–4 and Claydon, 1981, op. cit.: 142 and 154–5. The ASE London District Committee had strongly supported the West London Engineering Workers Commitee in 1918.

81. LAB 10/362, 22 November 1941. See also LAB 10/363, 8 August 1942.

82. N. Fishman, MRC, loc. cit.: 523–5 and 529–31; Croucher, PhD, 1977, op.cit.: 342. Croucher concluded that in 1941 the Party was influential at Beardmore's; Rolls-Royce Hillington; North British Locomotives, Queen's Park; Albion Motors; and British Auxiliaries. Its presence was strongest at Beardmore's. Ibid.: 319.

83. LAB 10/363, 11 July 1942, see also report for 1 August 1942.

84. LAB 10/363, 28 March 1942, see also 2 May 1942.

85. LAB 10/363, 10 January 1942.

86. Interview with Arnold Henderson by N. Fishman. Henderson was AEU convener at John Brown's and vividly recalled his dealings with Galbraith. Galbraith was a graduate of Glasgow University whose first job was as Poor Law Commission Investigator into the effect of outdoor relief on wages. During 1914–18 he served in the wages regulation department of the Ministry of Labour, becoming the head of that department for the Midlands and South Wales by 1923. He then moved back to Glasgow to become Ministry of Labour conciliation officer.

87. Inman, 1957, op. cit.: 405. She noted: 'In 1943 the Clyde Shipbuilders' Association reported that there was a wide-spread tendency on the part of the workmen to ignore their official delegate and report disputes through the shop stewards to the Ministry of Labour. Local trade union officials received their first notice of a strike not from the shop stewards but from the Ministry of Labour Conciliation Officer or the Employers' Association (pp. 401–2).

88. Ibid.: 151–3. Inman's account is sanitized to exclude the lively young Party stewards without whom the incident would not have taken place.

89. Inman, 1957, op. cit.: 327.

90. LAB 10/353, 3 April 1943. References to disputes in the Midlands occur in reports for 13 and 20 March; 18 September and 23 October 1943. LAB 10/354, 28 January; 18 February; 19 and 26 May; 7 July; 6 October; 3 and 10 November 1944. However, there were no major strikes.

91. Inman, 1957, op. cit.: 197–250.

92. Ibid.: 402.

93. For a fuller description of Metro-Vic's before the war, see N.Fishman, PhD, op. cit.: Chapter 5.

94. Interview with Benny Rothman by N. Fishman.

95. Frow and Frow, R., 1983, 'Manchester's Big House', Working Class Movement Library: 5, 7 and 13. Ibid.: 13. The Frows record that there was a meeting held in Trafford Park in August where 12,000 people heard Harry Pollitt, Arthur Horner and Pat Devine, a local Party leader.

96. For Award No. 326, see Inman, op. cit.: 348–9.

97. Interview with Benny Rothman by N. Fishman. Hugh Scanlon was an instrument-maker and accordingly knew very little about the intricacies of piece-work. Benny Rothman provided this vital information. Probably because of the accession of the well-organized United Machine Workers'

Association (UMWA), Manchester District AEU had come to terms with piece-work payments systems much earlier than other engineering districts. Piece-rate bargaining conventions were therefore better and earlier developed in the district to enable union members to reassert workshop control. (Interview with Edmund Frow by N. Fishman.) For the difference between Manchester and Coventry piece-work bargaining conventions, see N. Fishman, MRC, loc. cit.: 342–6. Croucher refers to the Metro- Vic dispute in passing (see Croucher, 1977, PhD, op. cit: 346, note 1).

98. Interview with Les Ambrose by N. Fishman.
99. LAB 10/354, 22 September 1944. For reports of the strike which are evidently truncated by wartime censorship, see *Birmingham Post*, 19, 20 and 21 September 1944.
100. Interview with Dick Etheridge by N. Fishman.
101. See N. Fishman, MRC, loc. cit.: 537–8. There is an account of the strike in Croucher, R., 1982: *Engineers at War, 1939–45*, Merlin: 218–26. The history of the AEU at Vickers in Barrow awaits full investigation. Croucher does not take into account the District Committee's previous conflicts with the AEU Executive, notably in 1937. For the Tyneside strike, see Croucher, Ibid.: 181–6.
102. See LAB 10/363, 14 November 1942 and Croucher, 1977, PhD, op. cit.: 330–4, 344, 363–5; Croucher, 1982, op. cit.: 188.
103. LAB 10/363, 7 November 1942. Croucher gives an incorrect date and file reference for this observation by Galbraith, op. cit.: 187.
104. For the Rolls-Royce strike and another strike at Barr & Stroud, see Croucher, 1977, PhD, op. cit.: 360–5.
105. For the WIL in Glasgow see ibid.: 351, and Croucher, 1982, op. cit.: 175–7 and 187–9.
106. Croucher, 1977, PhD, op. cit.: 351; 363–5. Because of the protracted conflict about JPCs at Beardmore's, the WIL appears to have won recruits to the CWC here, including Jimmy Doherty.
107. McShane, H., 1978, *No Mean Fighter*, Pluto Press: 236.
108. See Croucher, 1977, PhD, op. cit.: 371–2.
109. *Daily Worker*, 11 October 1944. See also the conciliatory report of the return to work, *Daily Worker*, 20 October 1944.
110. Croucher, R., PhD, op. cit: 369.
111. McShane, 1978, op. cit.: 235. He recalled frequent aggregate meetings of 400–500 party members in the city.
112. For an overview of the economic struggle in Glasgow in the inter-war and wartime period, see N. Fishman, MRC, loc. cit.: 502–38.
113. See N. Fishman, MRC, loc. cit.: 291–3.
114. *Daily Worker*, 27 January 1944.
115. *Daily Worker*, 13 March 1944. The *Daily Worker* had previously predicted a much higher attendance. (*Daily Worker*, 24 February and 11 March 1944.)
116. See *New Propellor*, Vol. 8 No. 1 January 1943. For the EATSSNC's earlier assertions about the need for its local organizations of shop stewards to co-ordinate trade union activities for themselves, see pp. 285–6 and 297–8, and Fishman MRC, loc.cit.: 270–1, 278–80, 287, 292.
117. *Daily Worker*, 13 March 1944.
118. See *New Propellor*, Vol. 10 No. 10, October 1945.
119. See Court, W.H.B., 1941, *Coal*, HMSO: 53–61, 68–85 and 115–6;

Francis, 1980, op. cit.: 397–9 and Supple, B., 1987, *The History of the British Coal Industry*, Vol. 4, 1913–46, *The Political Economy of Decline*, Clarendon Press, Oxford: chapters 11 and 12.

120.   For the Department of Mines' war plans see Court, 1941, op. cit.: 46–9. In 1939 the Department of Mines was part of the Board of Trade. Its responsibilities were transferred to the Coal Division of the Ministry of Fuel and Power which was created in the Summer of 1942.

121.   See Page Arnot, Vol. III, op. cit.,: 287–97. In 1938, after the Spencer union had disappeared, Joseph Jones led the MFGB Executive in an attempt to finally unite affiliated coalfield unions. This initiative had been backed by the CPGB in principle; but Party activists in the Yorkshire and Lancashire coalfields had declined to argue seriously against the parochial sentiments being expressed by 'rank-and-file' activists. The question of unity had 'lain on the table' after Joseph Jones' retirement until 1943.

122.   Court, 1941, op. cit.: 102–3 and 107–14.

123.   For the inter-war coal industry see Supple, 1987, op. cit.; Court, W.H.B., 'Problems of the British Coal Industry Between the Wars', in *Scarcity and Choice*, Edward Arnold, and Buxton, N.K., 1970, 'Entrepreneurial Efficiency in the British Coal Industry between the Wars', *Economic History Review*, Vol. 23: 483–94.

124.   Griffin, 1962, op. cit., and Williams, 1962, op. cit.: 866–7; and interview with Betty Kane by N. Fishman.

125.   LAB 10/361, 2 November 1940.

126.   For Scottish Party activists' attempts at revolutionary Stakhanovism see Moffat, A., 1942, 'Miners' Plan for Victory', CPGB, 22 April 1942. King Street responded belatedly with very general and largely rhetorical proposals for nationalization. See Pollitt, H., 1944, 'Take Over the Mines. The Case for Nationalisation', CPGB, 12 April 1944. Pollitt's pamphlet was prompted by the strikes precipitated by the Porter Committee's wage award in the Spring of 1944, and argued that nationalization would increase miners' will to produce coal.

127.   Fishman, N., 1993, 'Coal: Owned and Managed on Behalf of the People', Fyrth, J. (Ed.), *Labour's High Noon*, Lawrence & Wishart: 64.

CHAPTER TWELVE

Conclusion

It is difficult to avoid the conclusion that by 1945 Pollitt and Campbell had achieved their ambition, conceived in 1929–30, to make the Communist Party an important force inside the official trade union movement. The Party's membership had grown most in the unions where it had already been strongest in 1939. Abe Moffat had become the General Secretary of the united National Union of Scottish Mineworkers. Other Party veterans occupied important full-time positions in this new union which became one of the regional affiliates of the National Union of Mineworkers (NUM) when it finally emerged from the MFGB in 1946. Arthur Horner remained the dominant figure in the Fed and won an easy victory to become Secretary of the NUM. He joined the Party's long-time sympathizer, Will Lawther, who became President.

There had long been a practical coincidence of views and outlook between Party and non-Party mining activists. The conspicuous productionism of Horner and Moffat during the war enhanced the sense of fellow-feeling within the new union. The Labour Party's stunning victory in the July 1945 General Election made nationalization a certainty. The prospect of cooperating with the government to build socialism loomed ahead with its intoxicating promise of proving wrong the Jeremiahs who thundered that ordinary working men were simply incapable of assuming the responsibility of running industry.

The Party emerged from the engineers' war with its influence in the AEU significantly strengthened. The location of Party activists in the large and medium-sized firms in the main engineering centres throughout Britain had enabled the National Metal Bureau to assemble a formidable election machine. It began with the large AEU branches whose numbers were swelled to include the wartime recruits and extended up through the District Committees where Party activists were dominant to those where they were simply a force to be reckoned with.

By 1945 two out of three AEU National Organizers were Party members. Two out of seven Executive seats were held by Party members. Three out of the seven new Regional Officers for the Executive Division were Party members – including the recently expelled and reinstated Vic Wymans.[1] Communist representation in these full-time positions was reinforced by the innumerable and important lay positions held by Party activists in the districts and branches. Finally, there was the cohort of shop stewards and convenors. As Jack Tanner remarked to the Labour Party Conference in 1946, Communists 'were a very large proportion of the leading shop stewards in the engineering industry'.[2]

The Party's political standing inside the AEU rose in proportion to its shopfloor and organizational influence. *New Propellor* reported that 76 AEU District Committees and 557 AEU branches had supported CP affiliation to the Labour party. The second highest number of branches was the TGWU with 273.[3] The 1944 AEU National Committee passed a resolution calling on the Labour Party to 'rally all progressive bodies against the forces of reaction', and endorsed the Executive's stand on unity as a step in this direction. It further welcomed and supported the CPGB's fresh application for affiliation to the Labour Party.[4] In 1945 the National Committee voted 31–19 to instruct the Executive to press for Labour/CPGB discussions on an electoral truce.[5]

The strong Communist presence inside lay bodies influenced the Executive's attitude towards Party-sponsored 'unofficial movements'. When delegates from the Midlands division put a motion to the AEU National Committee attacking the EATSSNC, the Executive made no attempt to support their complaints.[6] The EATSSNC for its part had become equally conciliatory, if not wholly trustful, towards full-time officialdom. In 1942 a Party-inspired motion in favour of the Second Front was passed at the AEU National Committee from whence it was proposed at the TUC by President Jack Tanner. When Congress carried the AEU motion by a substantial majority, *New Propellor* observed: 'Bro. Tanner did a good job. The general workers' unions, TGWU and NUGMW, voted against. If the members of those unions were to insist on their branches meeting and attending when they do, resolutions could be adopted which would not only influence their unions but also the Government.'[7]

In fact, the Party had also significantly increased its presence inside the TGWU. The TGWU's success in gaining women members in engineering in the early part of the war had finally established the union as a serious force in the industry, fulfilling Bevin's long-cherished ambition to challenge the AEU for hegemony. It had been AEU shop stewards, many of them Party activists, who had done the initial recruiting on behalf of their rival union. It was ironic but fitting that one of the bright young women now on the TGWU GEC from engineering should be Muriel Edwards, a youthful Communist from EMI, one of the party's new factory fortresses in its heartland of West Middlesex.

Edwards refused to be intimidated or patronized by the stuffy male hierarchy she encountered on the Executive and insisted on speaking out of turn before the 'elders' around the table uttered their words of wisdom.[8] She was flanked on the GEC by two other Party activists, Bert Papworth from the London buses and Sam Henderson from the Glasgow trams. Papworth had been re-elected on to the GEC in 1943 where he had proved as charismatic as ever. The following year the GEC had elected this same rank-and-file renegade whom in 1937 the present General Secretary, Arthur Deakin, had attempted to consign to total oblivion, on to the TUC General Council.

TGWU full-time officials were not elected, as in the AEU, but appointed by the GEC. Because the political balance on the GEC had not turned leftwards until during the war, the Party's representation in the union's full-time hierarchy was lower than it was in the AEU. Nevertheless, despite Deakin's evident disapproval, Party activists were also beginning to make inroads here. Until July 1949, when they were banned from holding full-time and lay offices the GEC found it difficult to turn down Party aspirants when they were the most able candidates for the job.[9] It seemed counter-intuitive to reject men and women who were patently committed union loyalists and also excellent at recruiting new members when their only 'crime' was belonging to a Party connected to the USSR, Britain's wartime ally. Moreover, they had usually proved themselves by conspicuous activism within the TGWU's elected lay machinery of district, regional and national trade groups and the parallel geographic committees.

*   *   *

I have tried to show that Communists' success inside trade unions was due to a complex, interconnected and even conflicting number of elements. The most conspicuous conflict was between trade union loyalism and rank-and-filism. It has been clearly visible in the episodes in the economic struggle which we have observed, standing out like a golden thread in an already rich and detailed tapestry. Pollitt's and Campbell's achievement was to weld these two conflicting elements tightly together, with the ideological bonding agents, the united front and Life Itself, into the perspective which I have described as revolutionary pragmatism.

Revolutionary pragmatism was a guide to action in the real world of British trade union and workplace culture, both arenas which positively bristled with subtle, often parochial, traditions and an intriguing variety of interlocking vested interests. In contrast to the Young Turks, Pollitt and Campbell wisely refrained from imposing uniformity on the Party activists waging the economic struggle. Their model of democratic centralism was highly derivative of working class non-conformism. It relied on individual consciences to interpret the real world according to their own lights and assumed that their commitment to the faith of Life Itself would sustain them through the difficult trials which always lay ahead.

Nevertheless, when the real world produced trials which Party activists were unable to surmount without difficulty, Pollitt and Campbell intervened. The difficult dilemmas which Party activists faced usually revolved around choices between union loyalism and rank-and-filism. Pollitt's and Campbell's advice was invariably to place union loyalism first. They stressed that Life Itself would ultimately tip the balance towards the rank-and-file within the trade union movement. Their advice was usually accepted by militants though sometimes too late to avoid damage being done to activists' and the Party's authority.

The trade union establishment were firm anti-Communists. In the 1930s the elders assembled at the General Council never tired of reminding activists that the British trade union movement was already a 'real united front'. While they publicly denounced the 'unofficial elements' who sought to 'disrupt' the movement, privately they acknowledged that these activists usually behaved with conspicuous loyalty towards their union.

A discussion on the AEU Executive Council in February 1937 yields up these candid revelations in a lapidary fashion. One of the more 'right-wing' councillors, J. Kaylor, had been given a copy of a circular letter addressed to members of the 'Communist Metal Workers Group' advertising an emergency Metal Conference at which Joe Scott, who had been AEU ODD for North London since 1935, 'would make an important Report on the policy and the role of the Party and the Trade Unions'. Kaylor submitted a resolution which demanded that Scott either resign from the Communist Party or be expelled from the union.

> In the course of general discussion Bro. Kaylor said that the Circular Letter clearly indicated that the Communist Party . . . are functioning not as a political party but as a Trade Union, the whole of the Agenda [for the Metal Conference], except one item, consisting of purely matters of Trade Union interest . . .
>
> Bro. Clark said it was no new role of the Communist Party, as suggested by Bro. Kaylor, but had been their openly proclaimed policy since 1924. Since that time, they had had groups in every [trade union] Organisation and had organised National Meetings of such Groups. For a time, this type of activity had been suspended during the period when they had adopted a hostile attitude to Trade Unionism, but the old policy had been resuscitated and their present endeavour is to honourably work within the Trade Unions and to use every endeavour to influence Trade Union policy with a view to bringing it into line with the Party's political policy.
>
> It was possible that Meetings of the kind to be held on Sunday [Conference to be held on 7 February 1937 about rearmament] may hit this Union hard, but he had never known that any political party had been prohibited from having consultations with the Industrial Side of the Workers' Movement . . . he could foresee that our D.C.s [District Committees] would be asked to adopt the findings of Meetings such as Sunday's Conference, in which event E.C. [Executive Council] would require to meet and deal with that aspect of the situation when it arose.[10]

[Bro. Hutchinson] thought Bro. Clark had put the position very clearly, and it had to be acknowledged that it was impossible to control the Liberal and Conservative types of mind any more than the Communist. We had had the same sort of experience during the War . . . For his part, he could only wish that the E.C. were as determined in damning Capitalism as they seemed in their attitude to Communism.

Bro. Tanner . . . said that the Communist Party had been active and had done this sort of thing for years past . . . Other Authorities had followed a similar policy, as, for example, the old S.D.P. [Social Democratic Party – forerunner of the BSP], the I.L.P. and the Socialist League. There was nothing new in the Movement at all, and it was simply a case where those of one opinion or a certain political outlook have decided to get together either inside or outside of the Trade Unions with a view to influencing Trade Union policy.[11]

. . . the President [Jack Little] said that E.C. would have to consider some means of controlling such Meetings, without, at the same time, interfering with the liberty of the subject, his view, however, being that when a member becomes a Full-Time Official, he to some extent loses that liberty.'

[Bro. Kaylor] wanted to be fair to Bro. Scott – just as fair, in fact, as on a former occasion he had been to Bro. Tanner when he had said that he could not be married to both the Communist Party and the A.E.U. We were not polygamists, and the A.E.U. is a jealous mistress.[12]

As a result of the discussion, Kaylor withdrew his motion. The Executive Council instead agreed to instruct Scott not to attend this Conference or any other similar meetings which dealt with the internal affairs and policy of the AEU.[13] Scott duly did not attend the Conference. The episode concluded a month later, when Scott had attended the Executive Council to give his reply in person to their instruction. The Council, for its part, duly accepted his contention that membership of the Communist Party was compatible with holding full-time office in the union. But they continued to insist that he should attend no Party meetings at which the AEU's 'internal affairs' were discussed.[14] Joe Scott undoubtedly continued to attend Party meetings which discussed AEU business. Executive councillors undoubtedly 'knew' that Scott did so. It was simply not in either's interest to press the issue further.

*   *   *

We have seen that revolutionary pragmatism was not imposed on Party activists. In this period Pollitt and Campbell had neither the means nor the will to operate a tightly disciplined democratic centralist structure with regard to their members' conduct of trade union and industrial 'daily mass work'. Party members voluntarily adhered to the flexible guidelines emanating from the Party Centre and combined them with large amounts of their own acumen and judgement. The variety of ways in which Party members approached the 'economic struggle' was due to the widely differing local, regional and corporate trade union cultures; different collective bargaining conventions; and the vicissitudes of economic forces and shopfloor morale. Because revolutionary pragmatism was not prescriptive and most Party activists were supreme pragmatists, they learned from experience and discovered not only how to lead economic conflict successfully but also how to survive on the shopfloor.

The contrast between their practical, common-sense approach and profound Communist faith in Life Itself presents a rich irony often remarked on by 'unbelievers'. There is no doubt that the two qualities coexisted of necessity. Ralph Fuller pondered seriously with his mates in the Napier's milling shop about what Lenin would have done in their place. Trevor Robinson, Lenin School graduate, was determined to encroach on managerial prerogative on the factory floor because he knew that the revolution would not arrive before dual power was generally in place. John McArthur sold tickets to Saturday night UMS dances and connived with Liberal shopkeepers on the Fife County Council against the Scottish squirearchy for the sake of the revolution in which he had believed since hearing John McLean and reading *The Miners' Next Step* during the 1914–18 war.[15]

The proof that the two extremes of practicality and Utopian faith were functional lies in the evidence. Activists operated effectively within their polarity. Communists' belief in Life Itself enabled them to deal with these situations in a more balanced, determined way and, as we have seen, often with greater objectivity than their non-observant colleagues. I spoke in 1989 to a Party member of some half-century's standing in 1989 about the vital role 'Life Itself' had played in the CPGB's collective make-up. He smiled and recalled how often he had heard the refrain in the Party's common parlance.

The conviction that mundane, practical and compromising activity would ultimately lead to a socialist revolution is millenarian. 'Having faith' was fundamental to working-class nonconformism; it was transmitted to British socialism and thence to the CPGB. We observed how many of the founding cohort of Communists had been lay-preachers or lay-socialist preachers. They adapted their non-conformist faith into the revolutionary 'bolshevik zeal' in Life Itself, the faith which also marked Soviet Communists in the 1930s.

Armed with Life Itself, Communists were often endowed with more stamina than other activists. They approached the usually boring and thankless tasks involved in being a shop steward, union branch officer and full-time official in good heart. Performing these jobs was fulfilling the Party's injunction to 'daily mass work'. They were keeping their part of the bargain with Life Itself and had little doubt that the proletarian revolution would eventually be delivered. It was, in part, the failure of non-Communist trade union leaders to attend to the 'faith' element in trade union culture which made Party members so indispensable in the inter-war period. Revolutionary pragmatism had become the dominant culture of British trade union activism by 1945. Ernest Bevin observed in the late 1930s that militants were in increasingly short supply and expressed considerable concern for the future of the movement which he felt could not survive without them.[16]

Heroes, heroines, martyrs and willing performers of thankless routine tasks were indeed in scarce supply and became scarcer as the 1930s proceeded. It was Communist Party activists who provided a source of inspiration for the rising younger generation when the 1939–45 war produced conditions in which militancy could again thrive. The new recruits to the Party valued their identity as Communist trade union activists. By 1945 the contours of this identity with its attendant perspective of revolutionary pragmatism were familiar and easily recognizable on the shopfloor and in the pits. It proved highly accessible for the youthful shopfloor activists in search of a world-view.

*   *   *

Party activists' participation in unions and economic conflict made a major contribution to the revival and wartime expansion of British unions between 1933 and 1945. Pollitt's and Campbell's achievement in orientating Party activists towards the trade union movement and the 'economic struggle' was as significant as Togliatti's leadership of the Italian Communist Party in the gestation of Italy's post-war democracy or Thorez's commitment of the French Communist Party to the Popular Front in 1934–36. Nevertheless, the British Communist achievement has been largely ignored by academic historians. It has been distorted by the mythology of Party biographies, official history and oral tradition and by the demonology of the Party's ideological enemies of the post-war period. Fighting the Communist Party still plays a large part in the self-justifying recollections of trade union leaders and books about them.

The omission of Communists' contribution to rebuilding the inter-war trade union movement faithfully reflects the image which its non-Party leadership began to project in the early post-war period. The Cold War gave non-Party union leaders a compelling reason to distance themselves and their institutions from anything Communist. Bevin and Citrine had rigidly enforced the appearance of this difference in the 1930s. It had been clear at that time to anyone who cared to look that Party members were playing important and constructive parts. For a brief period during the war the camouflage of anti-Communism was allowed to drop for reasons of expedience. However, from the late 1940s British trade union leaders reconstructed the careful façade which systematically denied the presence and contribution of Party activists.

Labour leaders pointed to the Communist Party's small numbers in relation to the size of the Labour vote and manual workforce to prove their point about the Communist Party's unimportance. Historians have tended to accept this evidence without question. For example, Tolliday observes that Party activists at Ford's Dagenham and Briggs 'had been prominent in the shop floor struggles leading up to [Soviet entry into the war]'; he declines to examine what significance their efforts had for the achievement of union recognition at the two factories, nor is he prepared to examine the detail of Party activists' actual conduct *after* Soviet entry when he assumes that Party activists were vigilant in maintaining the industrial peace. The implicit justification for these omissions was the correct observation that only a minority of trade union members at Ford's, Briggs were Party members.[17] When dealing with trade union organization at Austin's, Tolliday makes the same omissions, again presumably because it is demonstrably true that only a minority of trade union members were in the Party.[18]

We have observed that this minority consistently produced major changes on the shopfloor and down the pit. The conclusion which stands out from the evidence is that a significant, and in some cases decisive, number of trade union activists at economically strategic workplaces were Communist Party members. We have seen, moreover, that the Party activists were usually, though by no means invariably, the most effective leaders in the 'economic struggle'. They always claimed to speak for the 'rank-and-file'. The evidence shows that in crucial incidents of economic conflict, the Party activists who led their workplace colleagues had every reason to feel confident in speaking on their behalf, in the name of the 'rank-and-file'.

Nevertheless it is important to avoid the trap of Party/Labour history mythology and insist that this coincidence of activists and 'the masses' was a constant feature of the daily life of any factory or pit. We have seen very clearly that pragmatic Party activists were well aware of the ebb and flow of shopfloor mood, and recognized that any grievance needed to be nurtured patiently before workmates might feel strongly enough to fight for redress. We have observed only a few examples of Party activists overreaching themselves in attempts to encroach on managerial prerogative. In the post-war period, such incidents occurred more regularly and with more adverse consequences. The failure of revolutionary pragmatism to openly acknowledge the constant conflict between trade union loyalty and rank-and-filism became a far more serious liability. In the post-war period, Party activists multiplied the number of factory fortresses by dint of inspired hard work. After their successes, the temptation to move beyond conventional boundaries of collective bargaining was strong, and victimization the ultimate result.

Nevertheless, revolutionary pragmatism cannot be said to have failed Party activists in their daily encounters with management on behalf of their workmates. Its conflicting imperatives provided a reasonable guide to action as long as the Party activists also brought their own pragmatic inclinations and the reflexes of their local union's culture to bear. It is clear that Party activists were incapable of becoming serious 'reformists' in the post-war world, even when they had left the Party. But their inability to pursue partial, reformist goals is rather a tribute to the durability of revolutionary pragmatism with all its shortcomings and limitations.

*   *   *

The Party's increased power and influence inside trade unions brought the unaccustomed problems of success in its train. Pollitt and Campbell did not deal with them as creatively or with the same independence of mind with which they had faced the problems of adversity in 1929–30. Then they had confronted the Young Turks' schemes for revolutionary unions and seizing state power within the twelvemonth with great determination and an overriding commitment to make the Communist Party both the heart and brains of the British proletariat. It seems that after 1945 the two men were increasingly constrained by new and conflicting priorities, including the imperative to publicly defend and uphold the superiority of the socialism being practised in the USSR and Eastern Europe.

One of the notable problems of success that the Party faced was how the satisfactory integration of its large numbers of new members into a Party culture which assumed that its members had a mission, were 'called' to their vocation as Communists. We have seen that King Street had aspired to become a mass party before the war, but that popular status had continued to elude it. In 1945 the leadership believed that the Party's extraordinary wartime growth could continue and that mass membership was finally within grasp. The Party Centre accordingly made strenuous efforts to forge a more accessible catholic identity which would enable 'ordinary people' to integrate into this hitherto closed and distinctively Calvinist institution.

The Party leadership was clear that increased shopfloor membership and the responsibilities of becoming a popular party meant fundamental changes in how factory groups were functioning. We have observed that most factory groups were previously kitchen cabinets for shop stewards committees.[19] During the war, where Party membership had expanded, the increased size of factory groups had precluded their fulfilling this important function.[20] Consequently, Party activists lost an important aid to fighting the economic struggle. The sense of Communists acting as a Leninist vanguard to organize the shopfloor was also diluted.

King Street continued to press Party union activists to widen the Party's appeal and seek recruits. Nevertheless, the Party Centre also expected its activists to occupy strategic positions inside factory fortresses of union power. Examination of the subsequent vicissitudes of party organization with regard to factory groups and mass membership in the post-war period belongs to another book. It is sufficient here to note that the conflict between the Party Centre's aim of being a party of mass, popular appeal and the importance Party activists attached to having unofficial institutions from which to exercise shopfloor leadership, was never satisfactorily resolved.

We have seen that the perspective of revolutionary pragmatism did not include any strategic calculation of where the Communist Party was steering the organized working class. Pollitt and Campbell did not seriously address the questions of achieving the Party's programme of immediate demands either in the inter-war period or during the war. At the end of the war, circumstances were particularly auspicious for achieving both immediate demands as well as substantial structural reforms. There was the first majority Labour Government, the favourable balance of class forces brought about by the war economy and the ideological advantage enjoyed by the working class as the embodiment of 'the democracy' when the war had been fought against fascism and for democracy. However, neither King Street nor Party trade union activists had given much thought to how the opportunity which these circumstances presented might be utilized.

The result was that the chance was missed to achieve substantial changes both inside the trade union movement and in the institutional arrangements for collective bargaining. The Party Centre and Communist union activists put forward immediate demands, e.g. for trade union mergers along industrial union lines and for the legal protection of shop stewards from victimization. However, the 'campaigns' to achieve these demands were stillborn, like the initiatives taken in 1937–8 to fight for the Party's immediate programme.[21]

The campaigns' results were derisory because insufficient attention, determination and energy were applied to them by the Party leadership and members. It would seem, to paraphrase the aphorism of the first revisionist of Marxism Eduard Bernstein, that 'the movement' was everything and the goals aimed at were actually unimportant. Perhaps Party activists' fundamental orientation towards 'the revolution' precluded their thinking seriously about reform and immediate demands.

Party activists continued to beaver away at their daily mass work throughout the Cold War. They occupied important lay positions in factories and union branches. The triumphalist post-war British trade union establishment simply could not afford to expel or outlaw Communists. The effect of the TGWU's prohibition on Communists holding lay office merely resulted in Party activists who were stewards or elected to regional committees and trade groups nominally ceasing to hold a Party card.

The AEU President Jack Tanner and the NUM President Will Lawther underwent a violent reaction against their own fellow-travelling past in 1948–9. However, their offensives against Communism had counterproductive effects. The Communist Party held on to its influence in both unions. As Party activists busily extended trade union membership and eroded managerial prerogative in Birmingham and Coventry engineering factories and South Yorkshire and Scottish pits, the Party itself gained young enthusiastic recruits keen to emulate their achievements.

The Party turned the apparent disaster of the Cold War to good account by developing the sub-culture of 'fellow traveller' within revolutionary pragmatism. 'Fellow travelling' activists and office-holders were conspicuous in most unions by the mid-1950s. They were self-confident, numerous and publicly committed to supporting Party causes. The serious blow dealt to the Party's prestige by the USSR's suppression of the Hungarian revolution in 1956 proved a temporary setback. By the mid-1960s, the strategy of a 'broad left' alliance in which the Party played an important role had become conventional wisdom for all union activists committed to rank-and-filist aims.

*   *   *

Citrine, Bevin, Deakin, Morrison – the list is endless – were overweeningly proud of the British Labour Movement's immunity from the Red scourge. They condescended to the French and Italians about their susceptibility to this terrible contagion and, of course, preached to the German unions about the weighty responsibility for Hitler's rise to power borne by German Communists. However, the British trade union movement was just as infected by the Communist incubus as its continental counterparts. In 1932 Pollitt and Campbell vacated the political arena voluntarily for the sake of the real united front in which they passionately believed. Until *The British Road to Socialism* appeared in 1951, the CPGB made no serious attempt to become a force in its own right in parliamentary politics. In trade unions, the Party's chosen sphere of operation, Pollitt and Campbell had made the Communist Party a force to be reckoned with.

It could be said that Pollitt and Campbell had the last word. With significant exceptions, the official union leadership had consistently refused to deal with the substance of revolutionary pragmatism in its many manifestations. They froze out Party members at the national level while continuing to depend on them for the daily round of trade union business on the shopfloor and in union branches. But they failed to take up political cudgels and argue the case against revolutionary pragmatism on its merits. The British trade union establishment felt that Communism should not be 'legitimated' by dignifying its convictions with counter-arguments. Consequently they lost the battle for the hearts and minds of activists by default. It was not until the AEU Executive Councillor from Tyneside, Bill Carron, constructed an election machine around the counter-ideology of Catholic anti-Communism that the 'reformist' officials found an approach which could muster votes against Party candidates for full-time office, though it notably failed to displace them on the shopfloor.

Because the 'reformist' Labour leadership denied that the Party was more than a flea on the mammoth hulk of the British proletarian carthorse, they never engaged in the serious political conflict which characterized the rest of post-war Europe. Significant working class political forces in France, Italy, Germany, Belgium and even Spain had effectively distanced themselves from the legacy of Stalin's Marxism–Leninism by the late 1950s. Not so, the British. The British maintained that they had no need to do so. Because they declined to enter this political battle, revolutionary pragmatism flourished unaltered, unadapted and conservatively fixated on the inter-war balance of class forces. The fact remains that the CPGB failed to become an agent for structural reform in the post-war world despite its adoption of a serious reformist programme, 'The British Road to Socialism' in 1951.

The failure of the post-war generation of trade union leaders to adjust to the changed circumstances of the post-war economy and to consolidate increased trade union power in appropriate reforms has been observed and often lamented. That failure, however, is a fault in the social democratic side of the movement. The CPGB, after all, made no secret of its indifference to partial political reforms and its devotion to socialist revolution. Pollitt and Campbell cannot be blamed for the fact that Citrine and Bevin failed to generate an accessible and coherent ideological perspective.

Notes

1. See Appendix II.
2. Quoted in Hinton, 1994, *Shop Floor Citizens*, op. cit.: 9.
3. *New Propellor*, Vol. 8 No. 5, May 1943.
4. AEU National Committee Report, 1944.
5. *New Propellor*, Vol. 10 No. 7, July 1945.
6. AEU National Committee Report, 1943.
7. *New Propellor* Vol. 7 No. 10, October 1942.
8. Interview with Muriel Rayment by N. Fishman. For the AEU's failure to admit women see pp. 205–6.
9. See Allen, V.L., 1957, *Trade Union Leadership*, London: 272–3. Allen records that in 1946–48, there were nine publicly acknowledged CPGB members out of the TGWU's 34-member Executive Committee and three Party members serving on the nine-strong Finance and General Purposes Committee, the TGWU's 'lay cabinet'. When Deakin pushed through his prohibition on Communists holding office, nine full-time officials resigned their union posts rather than leave the Party. See also Hyman, R., 1993, 'Praetorians and Proletarians', Fyrth, J. (Ed.), *Labour's High Noon*, Lawrence & Wishart: 179–86.
10. AEU Executive Council minutes, 2 February 1937: 186 7.
11. Ibid.: 187.
12. Ibid.: 188. We have already encountered the 'former occasion' in 1931 when the Executive had threatened Tanner with expulsion for signing an appeal to District Committees to take action against an Executive Council settlement with the employers (see pp. 41–2).
13. Ibid.: 189–90.
14. See pp. 152–3.
15. John McArthur described his experiences as a councillor to me with some relish. He had clearly enjoyed embarrassing the squirearchy. (Interview with John McArthur by N. Fishman.) For Ralph Fuller see pp. 213–6. For Trevor Robinson see pp. 302–3.
16. The *Daily Worker* reported a speech which Bevin made to the Glasgow TGWU: '. . . he warned the members that we were in this country gradually evolving to a system of state capitalism . . . he often felt he was sorry to say, that there was not the same fighting instinct in the younger men as there was in the older generation . . . He finished with a passionate plea for unity and the will to win, stating that although he had occasions at times to battle with the left-wingers, well, he did admit that many of them were good trade unionists' (21 May 1934).
17. Tolliday, S., 1985, 'Government, employers and shop floor organisation in the British motor industry, 1939–69', *Shopfloor bargaining and the state*, Tolliday, S. and Zeitlin, J. (eds.), Cambridge University Press: 114–5.
18. Ibid.: 109–110. Tolliday notes that at the end of the war trade union organization at Austin's Longbridge was 50 per cent. He lumps this figure in with Vauxhall's 25 per cent and Morris 30 per cent, and describes them all as 'still . . . fairly weak'. This judgement is no doubt correct when compared with the position in the 1960s. However, if a different standard of comparison is adopted the conclusion is different. Austin's 50 per cent union density in 1945 is a very substantial improvement on the situation in 1935. Tolliday makes no mention of the increase in trade union activity at Austin's during the war, or the 1944 strike. (See p. 315.)

The increases in union organization at Morris and Vauxhall's, though less dramatic than at Austin's, occurred from a lower and less favourable base. Party activists at these two sites were also crucial in providing the personnel and inspiration for union recruiting. Tolliday observes the increases without enquiring into their source. (I am indebted to Len Holden for information on Vauxhall's. His talk to the LSE Seminar Carworkers' on 24 April 1981 provided additional information. (Information on Morris from interview with Arthur Exell and Norman Brown by N. Fishman.)

19. See pp. 215–6.
20. See pp. 295–6.
21. See pp. 202–7.

CPGB Membership 1931–45

Total Party membership, June 1931–August 1945

1931	June	2,576
	September	6,263
1932	November	5,400
1935	February	6,500
1936	October	11,500
1937	May	12,250
1938	September	15,750
1939	September	18,000
1940	March	20,000
1942	January	27,000
	March	46,751
	June	59,319
1943	July	47,000[a]
1944	August	45,000 (ca)
1945	August	45,435

[a] The figure of 47,000 is given in the Executive's Report to the 17th Party Congress in October 1944 for the period July 1943 to August 1944. At the 16th Party Congress, held in July 1943, Pollitt reported a membership of 60,000. This figure was also given in *Organising for Offensive Action*, CPGB pamphlet, February 1943.

Sources: CPGB Congress Reports, 1932, 1935, 1937, 1938, 1943, 1944, 1945; Central Committee Report to 1939 Congress (postponed); *Discussion*, November 1936, p. 12; *The Communist Party in Wartime*, CPGB pamphlet, March 1940; *Mobilising the Party for the Second Front*, CPGB pamphlet, October 1942.

Total Party membership by district, 1926–1946

London

Note: Between 1937 and 1938 London District had seven branches transferred to the Kent District. During 1944 there would also have been branches transferred to the new Party Districts of West Middlesex and south east Essex.

1926	(after General Strike)	1,560
1937	March	2,450[a]
	April	4,900[b]
1938	March	3,700[a]
	April	6,400[b]
1940	March	8,000
1942	January[c]	9,000
	March	15,500
	September[c]	23,000
1943	December[c]	16,693
1944	December	18,360[d]
1946	June	13,588[e]

Scotland

1926	(after General Strike)	1,507[f]
1937	June[g]	2,000
1940	March	over 3,000 for the first time
1942	January[c]	3,243
	March	6,120
	June	7,572
1943	December[c]	9,088
1944	August[c]	8,407
	December[c]	8,738

Lancashire

1926	(after General Strike)	680[h]
1937	May[i]	1,235
1940	March	2,000 (ca)
1942	January[c]	1,600
	March	5,000
	June	5,500
	September[c]	5,748
1943	December[c]	6,830
1944	August[c]	5,441
	December[c]	5,819
1946	September	just over 3,000[a] (4,100[b])

The Midlands

Note: The Midlands District included Birmingham, Coventry and the Black Country.

1926	(after General Strike)	326[j]	
1938	March	489	
1939	March	844	
	July	928	
1940	March	1,000	
1942	January[c]	1,200	
	March	4,000	
	June	6,018	
	September[c]	5,891	
1943	October	2,420[a]	(3,703[b])
	December	3,678	
1944	August[c]	3,237	
	September	2,442[a]	(3,162[b])
	December[c]	3,381	

South Wales

1926	(after General Strike)	slightly over 1,500
1937	May[k]	membership less than in 1935
1940	March	growth not up to expectations
1942	January[c,l]	1,214
	March	2,064
	June	2,546
	September[c,l]	2,881
1943	December[c,l]	2,825
1944	August[c,l]	2,724
	December[c,l]	2,729

Yorkshire

Note: Party district boundaries in Yorkshire were not stable and figures are therefore given for different areas.

1926	Sheffield (after General Strike)	1,200
1935	Sheffield (January)[n]	once had 800 members but not now
1940	North Midlands (March)[o]	1,000

1942	South Yorkshire (March)	1,596
	(June)	2,596
	West Riding (March)	1,150
	(June)	1,400
	Yorkshire (January)[c,p]	1,471
	(September)[c,p]	4,283
1943	Yorkshire (December)[c,p]	3,581
1944	Yorkshire (August)[c,p]	3,092
	(December)	2,729
1945	Yorkshire (March)	2,725

[a] Subscription paying

[b] On the books

[c] These figures were supplied by James Hinton in a letter to N.Fishman of 13 May 1979, based on *World News and Views articles*.

[d] This figure is taken from the 1945 *London District Congress Report* covering the period September 1943 to December 1944.

[e] The figure given for subscription-paying membership to the 1946 District Congress was 13,284.

[f] This figure is arrived at by adding membership for the Glasgow area (including surrounding coalfields, mainly in Lanarkshire) and Fife.

[g] From an article in the *Daily Worker*, 1 June 1937.

[h] This figure is for Manchester only.

[i] From the *Daily Worker*, 22 May 1937. The article observed that membership had been around 500 at the time of the May 1935 Party Congress.

[j] This figure is for Birmingham only.

[k] From the *Daily Worker*, 1 June 1937. The article reported that membership in the Rhondda was now only 231.

[m] These figures are for the whole of Wales. North Wales membership remained very small. *Labour Monthly* reported that in January 1942, South Wales membership was 1094, while Hinton's figure for the whole of Wales is 1214 (*Labour Monthly*, May 1942). In March 1942, North Wales membership was 160; in June 1942 it was 200.

[n] From the *Daily Worker*, 30 January 1935

[o] The North Midlands district included Sheffield, Nottingham and North Derbyshire. It was later contracted to become the East Midlands district, with Sheffield then being included in the South Yorkshire district.

[p] It is likely that the Yorkshire district included South Yorkshire, the West Riding and Teesside. In March 1942 Teesside had 200 members; in June 1942 it had 600 members.

Sources: Brief summary of District Organisation Reports, CPGB, 1926; London District Congress Reports, 1938, 1945, 1946; The CP in Wartime, op. cit.; Mobilising the Party, op. cit.; Lancashire and Cheshire District Congress Report for October 1945–September 1946; Party Organiser, March and July 1939; Report to Second District Congress by Yorkshire District Committee, 1945.

**Percentage increase in membership for CPGB districts:
January 1942 to December 1944**

London	121
Scotland	169
Lancashire	263
Midlands	181
Wales	125
Yorkshire	112

Trade Union Status of Delegates to CPGB Congresses, 1935–45

13th Party Congress, 1935

Of 294 delegates, 234 were in trade unions.

AEU	25
TGWU	41
NUGMW	19
NUR	15
ASLEF	6
NUVB	4
AUBTW	2
ETU	4
Boilermakers	2
ASW	2
NUTGW	6
UMS	8
SWMF	8
YMA	1
Durham MA	1

14th Party Congress, 1937

Of 501 delegates, 397 were in trade unions, 203 held official positions (including shop stewards and branch offices).

15th Party Congress, 1938

Of 539 delegates, 367 were in trade unions; 138 held official positions.

National Conference, 1942

1196 delegates gave details.

AEU	260
TGWU	142
NUGMW	41
NUR	28
ASLEF	41
mining unions	72
building unions	53

16th Party Congress, 1943

Of 406 delegates, 399 were in trade unions.

AEU	92
TGWU	70
railway unions	33
mining unions	19
electrical unions	21
building unions	6
agricultural unions	9
CAWU	27
others	122

(full-time union officials: 7)

17th Party Congress, 1944

Of 754 delegates, 699 were in trade unions.

AEU	193
TGWU	81
NUGMW	29
NUR	32
ETU	33
mining unions	52
AUBTW and others	11
ASW	14
CAWU	41
AScW	13
teachers' unions	29
miscellaneous	160

(full-time union officials: 10)

18th Party Congress, 1945

Of 789 delegates, 679 were in trade unions.

AEU, ETU and others	188
TGWU	78
NUGMW	34
NUR, ASLEF and others	40
AUBTW, ASW and others	39
NUT, AScW and other professional unions	74
CAWU, and other clerical unions	84
NUM	58

Sources: Congress Reports for 1935, 1937, 1938, 1943, 1944, 1945; Report of National Conference, May 1942.

Comunist Party Members Elected to AEU Office, 1933–45

Note on the structure of the AEU

The primary unit of the AEU was the District Committee. It was an elected lay body, which met frequently, probably at least once a fortnight in the engineering centres. The District Committee was serviced by an elected District Secretary, a post which was full time in the important engineering districts. Members were elected on to the District Committee from branches and also from the shop stewards quarterly meetings ('quarterlies'), which all stewards in the district were supposed to attend to report on conditions in their workplaces. The quarterly had the right to elect one delegate to the District Committee for every 5000 members. The District President, and the District Secretary when it was a lay office, were elected yearly by branch ballot.

District Committees were grouped into 20 Divisions which were serviced by an Organising Divisional Delegate (the ODD). (The number of Organising Divisions was increased to twenty six in 1939.) District Committees elected two delegates to the Divisional Committees which met at least twice yearly. The Divisional Committees proposed motions and elected two delegates to the AEU National Committee, the policy-making body of the union which met yearly.

The Executive Council of the AEU consisted of seven members, elected by geographic division. The principal officer was the President, elected nationally. The EC was serviced by the General Secretary and two Assistant General Secretaries, also elected nationally.

All full-time officers were elected for three-year terms by secret ballots held at branch meetings. Elections for the new posts of Regional Officers were first held in 1944. TUC delegates were lay members of the union, with one TUC delegate elected for each two Organizing Divisions.

1933   National Committee delegates: Joe Scott
1934   National Committee delegates: Joe Scott, Billy Stokes
1935   National Committee delegates: Billy Stokes, Claude Berridge, Tommy Sillars
       TUC delegates: George Crane, Bill Ward
       ODD for Division 20: Joe Scott

1936   National Committee delegates: Billy Stokes, Claude Berridge, Len Tomkins
     TUC delegates: George Crane, Bill Ward
1937   National Committee delegates: Len Tomkins, Tommy Sillars, Jack Longworth, Gilbert Hitchings, Edgar Riley
     TUC delegates: George Crane, Bill Ward
     ODD for Division 14: Billy Stokes[a]
1938   National Committee delegates: Len Tomkins, Claude Berridge[b], Ernie Athorn
     TUC delegates: Bill Ward, Claude Berridge, Ernie Athorn, Gilbert Hitchings
     ODD for Division 20: Joe Scott
1939   National Committee delegates: Claude Berridge, Ernie Athorn, Gilbert Hitchings
     TUC delegates: Claude Berridge, Gilbert Hitchings
     ODD for Division 11: Bill Ward
     ODD for Division 20: Claude Berridge[c]
1940   National Committee delegates: Gilbert Hitchings, Edgar Riley, Tommy Sillars, Steve Nuttall, Jim Malcolm, Vic Wymans
     TUC delegates: Ernie Athorn
1941   National Committee delegates: Joe Scott, Bill Heppell, Harold Ingle, Fred Arter
     TUC delegates: George Crane, Johnnie Brown
     ODD for Division 13: Bill Ward
     ODD for Division 25: Claude Berridge
     ODD for Division 26: Ted Taylor
1942   National Committee delegates: Bill Heppell, Tommy Sillars, George Crane, Charlie Hoyle, Jim Crump, Edmund Frow
     TUC delegates: George Crane, Les Ambrose
     Executive Councillor for Executive Division 7: Joe Scott
     National Organiser: Wally Hannington, George Crane[d]
1943   National Committee delegates: Bill Heppell, Jim Crump, Charlie Hoyle, Joe Oliver, Bill McQuilkin, Reg Birch, Harold Marsh
     TUC delegates: Les Ambrose, Joe Oliver
1944   National Committee delegates: Bill McQuilkin, Reg Birch, Edmund Frow, Les Ambrose, Fred Elms, T. McLaren
     TUC delegates: Les Ambrose
     Regional Officer for Executive Division 1: Tommy Sillars[e]
     Regional Officer for Executive Division 3: Bill Heppell[e]
     Regional Officer for Executive Division 7: Vic Wymans[e]
1945   National Committee delegates: Bill McQuilkin, Reg Birch, Fred Elms, Harold Marsh
     TUC delegates: Edgar Riley, Fred Elms, Herbert Howarth

Executive Councillor for Executive Division 6: Gilbert Hitchings
Executive Councillor for Executive Division 7: Joe Scott
National Organizers: Wally Hannington, George Crane, Les
   Ambrose
Regional Officer for Executive Division 4: Jim Crump

Source: AEU National Committee reports, 1933–45 and *AEU Journal*, 1933–45.

District Officers

Because elections to lay district offices were not reported in the *AEU Journal* it is not possible to give a comprehensive list of Party members elected to office.

London	Tommy Knibbs	District Secretary 1933–42
	Claude Berridge	District President 1937–39[f]
	Vic Wymans	District President 1940–44[f]
Sheffield	Bill Ward	District President 1934–39
	Harold Ullyat	District Secretary 1942–45[g]
Glasgow	Tommy Sillars	District President 1934–39
Coventry	Billy Stokes	District President 1934–37
Birmingham	George Crane	District President 1938–39
Liverpool	H.S. Rule	District President 1940; District President 1945

*   *   *

Supporters of the People's Convention

Joe Scott, chairman, shop stewards committee, Betts, London[h]

Les Ambrose, convener, Austin Aero; Birmingham AEU District Committee[h]

F.H. Poole, convener, Rover No.1 shadow factory; Birmingham AEU District Committee

Edmund Frow, shop steward, Salford Electric; Manchester AEU District Committee[h]

H. Ullyatt, convener, English Steel Corporation

Joe Goss, chairman, shop stewards committee, Elliotts, Battersea[h]

Fred Arter, chairman, shop stewards committee, Napier's; London AEU District Committee[h]

Walter Swanson, secretary, shop stewards committee; convener, Napier's[h]

F.J. Dickinson, shop steward, Short's; secretary, Chatham Trades Council

Thomas Nimmo, convener, Kryn and Lahy

Peter Spetinckx, convener, Kryn and Lahy Aircraft

Jim Crump, convener, Rover No. 2 shadow factory; Birmingham AEU District Committee[h]

Bill Warman, shop steward, Armstrong Whitworth; chairman, Coventry Trades Council (Sheet Metal Workers)[h]

T. McLaren, convener, James Howden Ltd, Glasgow[h]

Tommy Sillars, Glasgow AEU District Committee[h]

Jim Clokey, Glasgow AEU District Committee

H.S. Rule, president, Birkenhead No. 1 Branch AEU, president, Liverpool AEU District Committee[h]

W. Ross, Kettering Labour Party

Councillor Jack Owen[h]

Herbert Howarth, Sheffield AEU District Committee[h]

Harold Cosslett, Swansea AEU District Committee

Arthur Immison, secretary, Hove Branch AEU

W. Rogers, Letchworth AEU District Committee

Hugh Scanlon, Manchester District Committee[h]

A. Roach, delegate to Trades Council from AEU Birkenhead No. 1 Branch

George Craig, chairman, AEU Branch Jarrow No. 2

Source: New Propellor, Vol.5 No.10, October 1940.

[a] Billy Stokes left the CPGB soon after being elected.

[b] Claude Berridge was disqualified from attending the National Committee on an election technicality.

[c] In 1939 the number of ODD divisions was increased from 20 to 26. Claude Berridge stood for the ODD division which Joe Scott had vacated in order to stand for Executive Councillor.

[d] In 1942 the number of National Organisers was increased from one to three.

[e] Elections for the new posts of Regional Officer were first held in 1944.

[f] Both Claude Berridge and Vic Wymans were expelled from the AEU during their tenure of office but were later reinstated by the Final Appeals Court.

[g] Harold Ullyat was not in the CPGB at the time of his election in 1942 but joined soon afterwards.

[h] People's Convention delegates known by N. Fishman to be in CPGB.

Trade Union Membership, 1921–45

	1921	1925	1929	1933	1934	1935	1936	1937	1938
TGWU	–	376,251	422,836	378,869	433,816	493,266	561,908	654,510	679,360
AEU	410,988	234,323	221,529	191,539	205,585	228,539	275,444	331,953	368,508
B&MM	38,914	17,198	18,351	12,869	13,029	14,444	18,107	22,630	24,767
NUGMW	356,403	313,981	290,877	241,447	269,357	300,145	366,467	439,287	452,367
Boilermakers	100,934	74,287	64,568	50,395	49,865	49,719	50,750	53,320	55,926
SWMF	117,610	129,155	74,466	63,337	76,949	110,494	112,743	120,280	121,062
DMA	151,253	155,773	132,081	122,824	124,445	124,613	124,647	127,157	124,783
YMA	156,722	164,196	102,557	95,416	103,194	113,465	133,677	136,455	137,165

	1939	1940	1941	1942	1943	1944	1945
TGWU	694,474	743,349	948,079	1,133,165	1,122,480	1,070,470	1,019,069
AEU	413,094	494,454	605,542	714,467	778,584	898,508	789,954
B&MM	27,986	31,707	34,033	35,248	35,845	33,610	30,902
NUGMW	467,060	479,318	597,890	720,666	726,487	660,604	604,753
Boilermakers	60,058	67,714	75,404	83,293	88,938	89,486	85,006
SWMF	123,677	120,575	103,341	107,465	106,493	104,589	102,034
DMA	122,031	115,097	110,958	111,569	111,010	112,325	110,194
YMA	136,083	138,633	142,470	144,406	141,394	139,769	133,768

Source: Report of the Registrar of Friendly Societies, Part 4, 1921–45

Bibliography

I. Primary sources

A. Archive material

AEU Executive Council Minutes, 1933–45, Modern Records Centre, University of Warwick.

AEU Southall District Committee Minutes, 1931–45, Modern Records Centre, University of Warwick.

The Dunlop Rim and Wheel Co.Ltd, Joint Production Consultative and Advisory Committee, 'Report on Minutes of Year's Work, 1942–1943', lent by James Jefferys to N. Fishman.

Bob Lovell Papers, Marx Memorial Library.

Minutes of the Manchester Metal Bureau and other papers, Working Class Movement Library, Salford.

Miners' Federation of Great Britain, Executive Council minutes and Conference minutes, 1936–7, National Union of Mineworkers headquarters, Sheffield.

Paper written by Len Powell on the EATSSNC for the Party Secretariat, ca 1942, lent by the author to N. Fishman.

Letter from Billy Stokes to Party Secretariat, 16 October 1936, in possession of Richard Croucher.

Rank-and-file pit papers, 1927–31, University of Warwick, Modern Records Centre, including *The Harworth Spark* and *The Harworth Rebel.*

TGWU General Executive Council Minutes and Finance and General Purposes Committee Minutes, 1933–45, University of Warwick, Modern Records Centre.

TGWU Region 5 Committee Minutes, 1933–45, Transport House, West Bromwich.

TUC Organization Committee, files on Ford's, University of Warwick, Modern Records Centre.

B. Public Records Office material

Ministry of Labour, Weekly Reports of Regional Industrial Relations Officers for Scotland, the North West, the Midlands and London, 1939-45. (The reports are denominated by the prefix, LAB followed by numbers denoting region and date.)

Reports of the Registrar of Friendly Societies, Part 4, 1921–45.

C. Published material

AEU National Committee Reports, 1920–45.

AEU Final Appeals Court Report, 1932, in Working Class Movement Library.

AEU Financial Reports, 1933–45.

AEU Rulebook, 1935 and 1945 editions.

CPGB Congress Reports, 1932–45 in Marx Memorial Library.

CPGB Central Committee Report, 1936, in Marx Memorial Library.

CPGB Executive Committee Reports, 1932–45, in Marx Memorial Library.

CPGB District Congress Reports, for London District, 1935–45; for the Midlands and Lancashire and Cheshire, 1945–6, Marx Memorial Library.

TUC Reports, 1935–6, Congress House.

J.S. Williams Papers, South Wales Miners' Library, Swansea.

D. Pamphlets published by CPGB

'Communist Industrial Policy: New Tasks for New Times', 1923.

'Communist Work in the Factories. The Work of a Factory Group', 1925.

'Communism is Commonsense, A Statement of Aims and Policy', July 1926.

Brief Summary of District Organisation Reports, 1926.

John Mahon, 'Communism and Building Workers', n.d., ca 1936.

John Mahon, 'Trade Unionism and Communism, An Open Letter by John Mahon', n.d., ca 1936.

'Men and Motors', Foreword by Jack Tanner, 1935.

Abe Moffat, 'Miners' Plan for Victory', April 1942.

Harry Pollitt, 'Friday Night till Monday Morning', September 1937.

Harry Pollitt, 'Workers of Britain, Unite!', April 1943.

Harry Pollitt, 'Take Over the Mines. The Case for Nationalisation', April 1944.

Harry Pollitt, 'Answers to Questions', May 1945.

Harry Pollitt, 'Plan for Coal', July 1947.

Harry Pollitt, 'The Miners' Next Step', September 1948.

'Harry Pollitt's Report to the Central Committee, 4–5 January 1936', CPGB, 1936.

London District Communist Party, 'The London Bus Strike. What Next', 1937.

London District Communist Party, Four Session Syllabus, 'Communist Party Leadership in the Factories', n.d., ca 1946–7.

W. Wainwright, 'Why you should be a Communist', January 1942.

'The Communist Party in Wartime', mid-March 1940.

'Shock Brigades – A Guide. How to Start Them. How They Work'. YCL, n.d., ca 1942.

'Our First 50,000', March 1942.

Sam Blackwell, 'Birmingham Against Hitler', 1943.

Sam Blackwell, 'Some Guiding Points for Strengthening Party Organisation', n.d., ca 1943–4.

The Communist Party: Its Theory and Practice, No.1, 'Problems of Factory Group Organisation', revised edition, January 1943.

'Britain for the People, Proposals for post-war policy', Executive Committee of CPGB, May 1944.

Jack Owen, 'Spotlight on the Tyne', 1944.

'Engineering Prospects and Wages', 12 March 1945.

'Engineers On the Move Again, Communist Special', n.d., ca 1946.

Party Organiser series:

'Communist Organisation for Victory', August 1942.

'Mobilising the Party for the Second Front', October 1942.

'Organising to Win the Offensive', December 1942.

'Organise to Mobilise Millions', March 1943.

'Strengthen Our Organisation', February 1944.

E. Pamphlets published by the ASSNC and the EATSSNC

'The Aircraft Workers' Case', ASSNC, n.d., ca 1935–6.

'The Shop Stewards' National Council Movement', EATSSNC, n.d., ca December1940.

'Arms and the Men, Full Report of the Conference of the EATSSNC and *New Propellor*', EATSSNC, n.d., ca 1941.

'JPCs – How to Get the Best Results', EATSSNC, n.d., ca 1942.

'Shop Stewards, Every Workers' Guide to Workshop and Shipyard Trade Union Organisation', EATSSNC, August 1943.

'Millions Like Us, Report of the Engineering and Shipbuilding Workers Conference called by the Shop Stewards National Council', EATSSNC, n.d., ca 1944.

F. Other pamphlets and reports

Metalworkers Minority Movement, 'The AEU. A Review and Policy', January 1928.

The Labour Party, 'The Communist Solar System', 1933.

National Unity Campaign, 'The Unity Campaign', Speeches of Cripps, James Maxton and Harry Pollitt at the Free Trade Hall, Manchester, n.d., ca February 1937.

Report of a Court of Inquiry, (Doughty Report), HMSO, Cmnd 6284, 1941.
Report of Citrine Committee on Regional Boards, HMSO, Cmnd 6360, May 1942.

(All CPGB pamphlets are in the Marx Memorial Library MMM, ASSNC, and EATSSNC pamphlets can also be seen there.)

II. Oral evidence

A. *Interviews by N. Fishman*
(The principal place of activity covered by the interview is given in brackets, and where necessary the subjects covered.)

Les and Jessica Ambrose, 28 March 1979 (Birmingham)
Jack Askins, 31 January 1979 (Manchester)
Sid Atkin, 6 December 1977 (Birmingham)
Ted Bramley, 9 February 1978 (London)
Norman Brown, 4 March 1981 (Oxford)
Willie Campbell, May, June and September 1992 (Johnny Campbell)
Jack Cohen, 27 September 1977 (Coventry)
Idris Cox, 21 December 1978 (South Wales)
Max Egglenick, 9 May 1983 (West London)
Dick Etheridge, 6 December 1977 (Birmingham)
Arthur Exell, 4 March 1981 (Oxford)
Jim Forde, 7 March 1979 and 19 October 1983 (West London)
Mrs J. Forde, 7 March 1979 (West London)
John Foster, 31 July 1979 (South London)
Edmund Frow, 31 January 1979 and 10 April 1979 (Manchester)
Ralph Fuller, 5 and 14 July 1978; 13 August 1979 (West London)
Charlie Hall, March 1980 (Dagenham)
Sid Harraway, March 1980 (Dagenham)
Finlay Hart, 16 June 1978 (Scotland)
Margot Heinemann, 12 March 1978 (Birmingham and coalmining)
Arnold Henderson, 16 May 1978 (Glasgow)
Marion and Joe Henry, 15 May 1978 (Scotland and Letchworth)
Herbert Howarth, 12 April 1979 and 8 March 1981 (Sheffield)
Charlie Hoyle, 5 March 1979 (London)
James Jeffreys, 4 April 1978 (Coventry)
Mick Jenkins, 9 April 1978 (Manchester)
Betty Kane, 8 April 1981 (Yorkshire)
Bridget Kane, September 1991 (Nottinghamshire)
Yvonne Kapp, 2 August 1977 (London)

Harry Lyall, 25 September 1978 (Dagenham)
John McArthur, 18 May 1978 (Scotland)
Bill McQuilkin, 15 May 1978 (Paisley)
Johnnie Mansfield, 7 March 1979 (West London)
Harold Marsh, 13 March 1979 (Birmingham)
Jack Mitchell, 25 June 1979 (Dagenham)
Reg Moors, 10 February 1981 (West London)
Con O'Keefe, March 1980 (Dagenham)
Bert Pankhurst, 7 March 1979 (West London)
Bert Papworth, 7 February 1978 (London)
Will Paynter, 9 May 1977, 29 November 1977 and 8 May 1978 (South
    Wales and coalmining)
Len Powell, 11 July 1979 (London and the EATSSNC)
Mrs Muriel Rayment (née Edwards), 13 August 1979 (West London)
Mrs Winifred Renshaw, 2 March 1979 (London)
Ernie Roberts, 22 August 1981 (Coventry)
Trevor Robinson, 11 April 1979 (Sheffield, Manchester and the
    EATSSNC)
Benny Rothman, 31 January 1979 (Manchester)
Bob Saunders, 15 May 1978 (Glasgow)
Guy Stobbs, 19 April 1978 (Ayrshire)
Fred Tinsley, October 1979 (Dagenham)
Jon Vickers, 13 February 1978 (London and ETU)
Bill Warman, 5 December 1977 (Coventry)
Charlie Wellard, 2 and 29 August 1978; 13 October 1978 (South
    London)
Peter Zinkin, 28 February and 19 October 1978 (ASSNC)

B. Other interviews

Transcripts in South Wales Miners Library
Interviews with Jock Gibson in possession of Peter Caldwell (Lanchester
    Tapes, CT65 and interview by Peter Caldwell).
Interview with Jock Kane by Charles Parker, in Charles Parker
    Collection.
Interview with Harry McKendrick by Steve Tolliday (transcript in pos-
    session of Steve Tolliday).
Interview with Harold Horne by Len Holden (notes in possession of Len
    Holden).

III. Newspapers

Birmingham Post
Daily Herald

Daily Telegraph
Daily Worker
Ilford Guardian
Ilford Recorder
Manchester Guardian
Midland Daily Telegraph
Nottinghamshire Journal
Reynolds News
The Times
Western Mail

IV. Periodicals

AEU Journal
Busman's Punch
The Communist
Communist Review
The Conveyor (published by the Oxford Communist Party, 1933–4)
The Conveyor ('rank-and-file' engineering paper, published 1936–8)
Discussion (published by the CPGB)
Engineers' Bulletin ('rank-and-file' paper, published 1934–5)
The Ford Worker (published by the Dagenham Communist Party, 1933–5)
International Press Correspondence
Labour Monthly
Labour Research
New Propellor
Party Organiser (published by the CPGB, 1932, and 1938–45)
The Record (journal of the TGWU)
Siemens Shop Stewards Journal (published by the Siemens Shop Stewards Committee, 1933–9)
South Wales Miner (published by the South Wales Miners Rank and File Movement, 1933–5)
The Worker (published by the National Minority Movement)
Workers' Life (published by the CPGB)
World News and Views

V. Secondary sources

Adereth, M., *The French Communist Party a critical history (1920–1984)*, Manchester University Press, 1984.
Allen, V. L., *Trade Union Leadership*, London, 1957.

Arnot, R. Page, *The Miners, A History of the Miners' Federation of Great Britain*, Allen and Unwin, vol. II, *Years of Struggle*, 1953; vol. III, *In Crisis and War*, 1961.

Ash, Timothy Garton, 'Germany Unbound', *New York Review of Books*, 22 November 1990.

Bell, Tom, *The British Communist Party*, Lawrence and Wishart, 1937.

Branson, Noreen, *History of the Communist Party of Great Britain, 1927–41*, Lawrence and Wishart, 1985.

Brinkley, Alan, 'The Best Years of Their Lives', *The New York Review of Books*, 28 June 1990.

Buchanan, Tom, 'The politics of internationalism: the Amalgamated Engineering Union and the Spanish Civil War', *Journal of the British Society for the Study of Labour History*, Vol. 53, No. 3, Winter 1988.

Bullock, Alan, *The Life and Times of Ernest Bevin*, Heinemann, vol. I, *1881–1940*, 1960; vol. II, *1940–45*, 1967.

Buxton, Neil K., 'Entrepreneurial Efficiency in the British Coal Industry between the Wars', *Economic History Review*, Vol. 23, 1970, pp. 483–494.

Calder, Angus, *The People's War*, Granada, 1971.

Carr, E. H., *The Twilight of the Comintern, 1930–1935*, Macmillan, 1982.

Clegg, H.A., *Labour Relations in London Transport*, Blackwell, 1950.

Clegg, H.A., *General Union in a Changing Society, a short history of the National Union of General and Municipal Workers 1889–1964*, Blackwell, 1964.

Clegg, H.A., Fox, Alan, and Thompson, A.F., *A History of British Trade Unions since 1889*, vol. I, *1889–1910*, Oxford, 1977.

Clegg, H.A., *A History of British Trade Unions since 1889*, vol. II, 1911–1933, Oxford, 1985.

Cole, G.D.H., *British Trade Unionism Today*, Gollancz, 1939.

Cole, G.D.H., *Workshop Organization*, Hutchinson Educational, 1973.

Copeman, Fred, *Reason in Revolt*, Blandford, 1948.

Corfield, Tony, 'The Busmen's Rank and File Movement', *The Record*, June, July, August, October, November 1963; January, February, March, April, May 1964.

Court, W.H.B., *Coal*, HMSO, 1951.

Court, W.H.B., 'Problems of the British Coal Industry Between the Wars', in *Scarcity and Choice*, Edward Arnold, 1970.

Crossman, Richard, 'Introduction', *The God That Failed*, London 1950.

Croucher, Richard, Engineers at War 1939–45, Merlin, 1982.

Degras, Jane, ed., *The Communist International*, Oxford, vol. I, 1956, 1919–1922; vol. II, 1960, 1923–1928; vol. III, 1965, 1929–1943.

Fainsod, Merle, *How Russia is Ruled*, 1963.

Fearon, Peter, 'The British Airframe Industry and the State, 1918–35',

Economic History Review, 1974, Series 2, Vol. 27, pp. 243–8.

Fearon, Peter, 'A Reply', *Economic History Review,* 1975, Series 2, No. 28, pp. 660–1.

Fishman, Nina, 'Coal: Owned and Managed on Behalf of the People', in Jim Fyrth, ed., *Labour's High Noon, the Government and the Economy, 1945–51,* Lawrence and Wishart, London, 1993.

Fitzpatrick, Sheila, ed., *Cultural Revolution in Russia, 1928–1931,* Bloomington, Ind., 1978.

Fitzpatrick, Sheila, *The Russian Revolution, 1917–1932,* Oxford University Press, 1984.

Francis, Hywel, *Miners Against Fascism,* Lawrence and Wishart, 1984.

Francis, Hywel and Smith, David, *The Fed, a History of the South Wales Miners in the Twentieth Century,* Lawrence & Wishart, 1980.

Frow, Edmund and Frow, Ruth, 'Bob and Sarah Lovell, Crusaders for a Better Society', Working Class Movement Library, Manchester, 1983.

Frow, Edmund and Frow, Ruth, 'Clem Beckett and the Oldham Men Who Fought in Spain', Working Class Movement Library, Manchester, n.d., ca 1980.

Frow, Edmund and Frow, Ruth, 'The Communist Party in Manchester, 1920–1926', Working Class Movement Library, 1982.

Frow, Edmund and Frow, Ruth, *Engineering Struggles,* Working Class Movement Library, Manchester, 1982.

Frow, Edmund and Frow, Ruth, 'Manchester's Big House in Trafford Park', Working Class Movement Library, 1983.

Gallacher, William, *Revolt on the Clyde,* Lawrence and Wishart, 1942.

Griffin, Alan R., *The Miners of Nottinghamshire, 1914–1944,* London, 1962.

Groves, Reg, *The Balham Group,* Pluto Press, 1974.

Hannington, Wal, *Never on Our Knees,* Lawrence and Wishart, 1967.

Hilton, J., ed., *Are Trade Unions Obstructive?,* Gollancz, 1935.

Hinton, James, *The First Shop Stewards Movement,* Allen and Unwin, 1972.

Hinton, James, 'Killing the People's Convention: a letter from Palme Dutt to Harry Pollitt', *Bulletin of the Society for the Study of Labour History,* No. 39, 1979.

Hinton, James, 'Coventry Communism: A Study of Factory Politics in the Second World War', *History Workshop Journal,* No. 10, Autumn 1980.

Hinton, James, *Shopfloor Citizens, Planning and Democracy in the British Engineering Industry, 1941–47,* Edward Elgar, 1994.

History of the CPSU(B), International Publishers, New York, 1939.

Holton, Bob, *British Syndicalism 1900–1914,* Pluto Press, 1976.

Horner, Arthur, *Incorrigible Rebel,* Macgibbon and Kee, 1960.

Hough, Jerry, with Merle Fainsod, *How the Soviet Union is Governed*, Cambridge Mass., 1979.

Hyman, Richard, *The Workers' Union*, Clarendon Press, Oxford, 1971.

Hyman, Richard, Report of Society Conference, 'Officialdom and Opposition: Leadership and Rank and File in Trade Unions', *Bulletin of the Society for the Study of Labour History*, No. 46, Spring 1983.

Hyman, Richard, 'Rank and File Movements and Workplace Organisation 1914–1939', in C.J. Wrigley, ed., *A History of British Industrial Relations*, vol. II, 1914–1939, Harvester, 1987.

Hyman, Richard, 'The Sound of One Hand Clapping: A Comment on the "rank and filism" debate', *International Review of Social History*, Vol. XXXIV, 1989-2.

Hyman, Richard, 'Praetorians and Proletarians', in Jim Fyrth, ed., *Labour's High Noon, the Government and the Economy, 1945–51*, Lawrence and Wishart, London, 1993.

Inman, P., *Labour in the Munitions Industries*, HMSO, 1957.

Jackson, Julian, *The Popular Front in France*, Cambridge University Press, 1988.

Jefferys, James B., *The Story of the Engineers*, Lawrence and Wishart, 1945.

'Joint Production Committees in Great Britain', ILO Series A (Industrial Relations), No. 42, Montreal 1943.

Jones, Jack, *Union Man an Autobiography*, Collins, 1986.

King, Francis and Matthews, George, eds, *About Turn*, Lawrence and Wishart, London, 1990.

Klugmann, James, *History of the Communist Party of Great Britain*, vol. I, 1919–1924, Lawrence and Wishart, 1968; vol. II, 1925–6, Lawrence and Wishart, 1969.

Lampe, David, *Pyke, the Unknown Genius*, London, 1959.

Lawson, Jack, *Man in the Cap*, London, 1941.

Lenin, V.I., ' "Left-Wing" Communism – An Infantile Disorder', first published June 1920. *Selected Works*, vol. III, Progress Publishers, Moscow, 1971, pp. 345–429.

McArthur, John, *Militant Miners*, Ian MacDougall, ed., Polygon Books, Edinburgh, 1981.

McKinlay, Alan, 'From Industrial Serf to Wage-Labourer: The 1937 Apprentice Revolt in Britain', *International Review of Social History*, Vol. XXXI, 1986, Part I.

McShane, Harry, *No Mean Fighter*, Pluto Press, 1978.

Macfarlane, L.J., *The British Communist Party, Its Origin and Development until 1929*, Macgibbon and Kee, 1966.

Mahon, John, *Trade Unionism*, New People's Library, Gollancz, 1938.

Mahon, John, *Harry Pollitt*, a biography, Lawrence and Wishart, 1976.

Martin, Roderick, *Communism and the British Trade Unions, 1924–1933, a Study of the National Minority Movement*, Oxford, 1969.

Mass Observation, *Enquiry into British War Production* (between October 1941 and March 1942), London, 1942.

Mass Observation, *War Factory*, London, 1943.

Matthews, George, 'The Quest for Unity', *Comment* 3, 7 February 1981.

Matthews, George, 'Affiliation: the arguments', *Comment* 4, 21 February 1981.

Matthews, George, 'Affiliation – for a united working class movement', *Comment* 5, 7 March 1981.

Milne-Bailey, W., *Trade Unions and the State*, Allen and Unwin, 1934.

Morgan, Kenneth O., *Labour People*, Oxford University Press, 1987.

Morgan, Kevin, *Against Fascism and War: Ruptures and continuities in British Communist politics, 1935–41*, Manchester University Press, 1989.

Morgan, Kevin, *Harry Pollitt*, Manchester University Press, 1993.

Nuffield College, 'Social Reconstruction Survey', Mem. 45, Revised Memo on Joint Production Committees, (M. Stewart), May 1943.

Parker, H.M.D., *Manpower*, HMSO, 1957.

Parker, R.A.C., 'British rearmament 1936–9: Treasury, trade unions and skilled labour', *Economic History Review*, No. 379, April 1981.

Paynter, Will, *My Generation*, Allen and Unwin, 1972.

Pelling, Henry, *The British Communist Party, A Historical Profile*, Adam and Charles Black, 1958.

Pimlott, Ben, *Labour and the Left in the 1930s*, Allen and Unwin, 1986.

Plummer, Alfred, *New British Industries in the 20th Century*, London, 1937.

Political and Economic Planning, No. 140, 7 February 1939, 'Labour Relations in Engineering'.

Political and Economic Planning, No. 189, 26 May 1942, on Joint Production Committees.

Pollitt, Harry, *Serving My Time*, Lawrence and Wishart, London, 1940.

Ree, Jonathan, *Proletarian Philosophers*, Clarendon Press Oxford, 1984.

Richardson, J.H., 'Industrial Relations in Great Britain', ILO Series A, No. 36, 1933.

Riegelman, Carol, 'British Joint Production Machinery', ILO Series A, No. 43, Montreal, 1944.

Robertson A.J., 'The British Airframe Industry and the State in the Interwar Period: A Comment', *Economic History Review*, 1975, Series 2, No. 28, pp.649–52.

Rowe, J.W.F., *Wages in Practice and Theory*, Routledge and Kegan Paul, London, 1928.

Smith, D.H., *The Industries of London*, London, 1933.

Stavall, Tyler, 'French Communism and Suburban Development: The Rise of the Paris Red Belt', *Journal of Contemporary History*, Vol. 24, 1989, pp. 437–60.

Stavall, Tyler, *The Rise of the Paris Red Belt*, California University Press, 1990.

Supple, Barry, *The History of the British Coal Industry: Vol. 4, 1913–1946, The Political Economy of Decline*, Clarendon Press, Oxford, 1987.

Lord Taylor of Mansfield, *Uphill All the Way*, Sidgwick and Jackson, 1972.

Thomas, Brinley, *Economica*, 1937, New Series 4, 'The Influx of Labour into London and the Southeast 1920–36' and 'The Influx of Labour into the Midlands 1920–1937', *Economica*, 1938, New Series 5.

Tolliday, Steven, 'Militancy and Organisation: Women Workers and Trade Unions in the Motor Trades in the 1930s', *Oral History* II, 2, Spring 1983.

Tolliday, Steven, 'Government, employers and shop floor organisation in the British motor industry, 1939–69', in *Shopfloor bargaining and the state*, Steven Tolliday and Jonathan Zeitlin, eds, Cambridge University Press, 1985.

Tolliday, Steven, 'Management and Labour in Britain 1896–1939', in Steven Tolliday and Jonathan Zeitlin, eds, *The Automobile Industry and Its Workers*, Polity Press, 1986.

Tolliday, Steven, 'The failure of mass production unionism in the motor industry, 1914–1939', in *A History of British Industrial Relations*, vol. II, 1914–1939, C.J. Wrigley, ed., Harvester, 1987.

Torr, Dona, *Tom Mann*, Lawrence and Wishart 1944.

Tsuzuki, Chushichi, *Tom Mann, 1856–1941: The Challenges of Labour*, Clarendon Press, Oxford, 1991.

Urban, Joan Barth, *Moscow and the Italian Communist Party*, Tauris and Co., London, 1986.

Waller, R.J., 'Sweethearts and Scabs: irregular trade unions in Britain in the 20th Century', in P.J. Waller, ed., *Politics and Social Change in Modern Britain*, Harvester, 1987.

Watmough, P.A., 'The Membership of the SDF, 1885–1902', *Bulletin of the Society for the Study of Labour History*, Spring 1977, No. 34.

Watson, W.F., *Machines and Men*, London, 1935.

White, Joseph, *Tom Mann*, Manchester University Press, 1991.

Wigham, Eric, *The Power to Manage: a History of the Engineering Employers' Federation*, London, 1973.

Williams, J.E., *The Derbyshire Miners*, Allen and Unwin, 1962.

Wrigley, Chris, 'The Trade Unions Between the Wars', in C.J. Wrigley, ed., *A History of British Industrial Relations*, vol. II, 1914–1939, Harvester, 1987.

Yates, M.L., *Wages and Labour Conditions in British Engineering*, London, 1937.

Zeitlin, Jonathan, 'The Labour Strategies of British Engineering Employers, 1890–1922', in H.F. Gospel and C.R. Littler, eds, *Managerial Strategies and Industrial Relations*, Heinemann, 1983.

Zeitlin, Jonathan, 'From Labour History to the History of Industrial Relations, *Economic History Review*, Second Series, XL, 2, 1987, p. 120.

Zeitlin, Jonathan, ' "Rank and Filism" in British Labour History', *International Review of Social History*, Vol. XXXIV, 1989–91.

Zinkin, Peter, *A Man To Be Watched Carefully*, People's Publications, 1985.

VI. Unpublished secondary sources

Anthony-Jones, W.J., 'Labour Relations in the South Wales Coal Industry', University of Wales PhD, 1959.

Barrett, James, '*Busman's Punch*, Rank and File Organisation and Unofficial Industrial Action among London Busmen 1913–37', University of Warwick MA, 1974.

Bowes, Nita, 'The People's Convention', University of Warwick MA, 1976.

Broomfield, S.R., 'South Wales in the Second World War: The Coal Industry and Its Community', University of Wales PhD, 1979.

Burdick, Eugene, 'Syndicalism and Industrial Unionism in England until 1918', Oxford University D Phil, 1950.

Carr, Frank, 'Engineering Workers and the Rise of Labour in Coventry, 1914–39', University of Warwick PhD, 1979.

Claydon, T.J., 'The Development of Trade Unionism among British Automobile and Aircraft Workers, c.1914–1946', University of Kent at Canterbury PhD, 1981.

Clinton, Alan, 'Trades Councils from the beginning of the Twentieth Century to the Second World War', University of London PhD, 1973.

Croucher, Richard, 'Communist Politics and Shop Stewards in Engineering, 1935–46', University of Warwick PhD, 1977.

Davis, P., 'Syndicalism and the Yorkshire Miners, 1910–1914', MSc, University of Leeds, 1977.

Fishman, Nina, unpublished paper, 'Trade Union Organisation at Ford's Dagenham, 1933–45', 1982.

Fishman Nina, 'The British Communist Party and the Trade Unions, 1933–1945', unpublished typescript, 1987, University of Warwick, Modern Records Centre.

Fishman, Nina, 'The British Communist Party and the Trade Unions,

1933–1945: the Dilemmas of Revolutionary Pragmatism', University of London PhD, 1991.

Garside, W.R., 'The Durham Miners Association, 1919–1947', University of Leeds PhD, 1969.

Hastings, R.P., 'The Labour Movement in Birmingham 1927–45', University of Birmingham MA, 1959.

Hinton, James, 'Rank and File Militancy in the British Engineering Industry, 1914–1918', University of London PhD, 1969.

Holden, Len, talk on Vauxhall Motors to Carworkers Seminar, LSE, 24 April 1981.

Hyman, Richard, 'The Workers' Union, 1898–1929', Oxford University DPhil, 1968.

Kibblewhite, E., 'The Impact of Unemployment on the Development of Trade Unions in Scotland, 1918–39: Some Aspects', University of Aberdeen PhD, 1979.

McEvoy, Denis, 'From Firm Foundations, A Study of the Trade Union Recognition Strike at Cowley, July 13 to July 28th 1934', Paper for Westminster College of Education, Oxford, 1972.

Mason, Anthony 'The Miners' Unions of Northumberland and Durham, 1918–31, with special reference to the General Strike of 1926', University of Hull PhD, 1967.

Ravden, Colin, 'Parliamentary Elections and the British Communist Party, a historical analysis, 1920–1978', unpublished paper.

Tolliday, Steven, 'Managerial Strategies and Shopfloor Bargaining: Standard and Austin, 1929–60', unpublished paper, March 1982.

Tolliday, Steven, unpublished paper on trade union organization of women workers in the Midlands, April 1983.

Weekes, B.M., 'The ASE, 1880–1914', University of Warwick PhD, 1970.

Whiting, Richard, 'The Working Class in the "New Industry" Towns Between the Wars: The Case of Oxford', Oxford University D Phil, 1977.

Index